CYRUS CLAY CARPENTER

and Iowa Politics, 1854-1898

by Mildred Throne

State Historical Society of Iowa

Iowa City 1974

Library of Congress Catalogue Card 74–7532

ISBN 0–89033–000–X

Preface

For twelve years Mildred Throne, author of this noteworthy biography of a colorful and vigorous Iowa governor, served as associate editor of the *Iowa Journal of History and Politics,* a scholarly journal formerly published by the State Historical Society of Iowa.

She came to the post well qualified. An Iowa native, born in Ottumwa and educated in the public schools there, Miss Throne earned an undergraduate degree from the University of Chicago and a master's degree in history from the University of Iowa. For three years she assisted Professor Louis Pelzer in editing the *Mississippi Valley Historical Review.* Under Dr. Pelzer's direction she completed requirements for her doctorate and was granted the degree in 1946. For the following two years, she taught history at Washburn College, Kansas.

When she assumed the associate editorship of the *Iowa Journal of History and Politics* in 1948, Dr. Throne was recognized by colleagues throughout the nation as knowledgeable, able, and possessed of integrity. Papers read at sessions of national historical associations were well received. Passionately devoted to research and writing, Dr. Throne found time both to perform editing chores and to write more than a dozen articles on the Grange and allied agricultural topics pertaining to Iowa. She edited and published some fifteen diaries and journals. Her book reviews were judicious, penetrating, and, as was their author, kindly. Indeed, Mildred Throne's gracious, helpful advice and co-operation earned for her the deep gratitude and loyal affection of those who relied upon her for assistance. All this was underscored in a tribute published in the *Mississippi Valley Historical Review:* "She gave generously of her time and her knowledge of Iowa history to research historians and was especially helpful as adviser of graduate students working on topics in her fields of interest."

When Dr. Throne died on July 7, 1960, at age fifty-eight, she left a manuscript upon which she had labored for years. This was her life of Cyrus Clay Carpenter, elected governor in 1871 and again in 1873. The biography exemplifies Mildred Throne's historical talents—the scholarship is sound, Carpenter's career and contributions are balanced, the writing is deft. It is a notable addition to previously published volumes in the Iowa Biographical Series. The book was prepared for publication under the supervision of Dr. Peter T. Harstad, Director of the State Historical Society of Iowa, and L. Edward Purcell, Editor of *The Palimpsest.*

Philip D. Jordan

Contents

Illustrations

Introduction

———•·•·•———

IT IS APPROPRIATE that this book should appear on the eve of the Bicentennial of the American Revolution. Cyrus Clay Carpenter was Governor of Iowa midway between the Revolution and the present. Not only is this a biography of an Iowa politician, but it provides perspective for the political development of the state and nation. The perceptive reader can look backward from Carpenter's era to the formative years of the United States. How had the two party system, the revolution in science and technology, the settlement of a continent, the flood of immigration, and the fighting of a bloody Civil War affected Revolutionary concepts of self government? Were the basic principles and political institutions of Jefferson's era still applicable to a Midwestern state in the 1870s?

The reader can also project forward from an era when Governor Carpenter—while the legislature was in session—read the essays of Thomas Macaulay and milked his own cow! Such habits may indicate as much about a self-educated, unassuming man as they do about Iowa during the 1870s. The years before the popular election of Senators may seem quaint and distant to those acquainted with the complexities of the twentieth century. Yet, many issues of Carpenter's day have a striking currency: party loyalty, the third house, political corruption, impeachment, the railroads, the rights of labor, the distribution of wealth. The frontiersman from Fort Dodge provided perspective on the latter subject when he asserted in an 1874 speech, "the silk dress has got into the farmer's house," and then went on to advocate the manufacture of consumer goods "near the farmer's door." Thus Carpenter nudged forward a basic economic principle of Henry Clay (after whom he was named). To what extent is the present equilibrium between farming and manufacturing in Iowa rooted in such thought? In a different context, it is interesting to ponder a seemingly contradictory term which Carpenter used more than once in his speeches: "thinking masses." The term exudes a refreshing optimism to the 1970s. Thomas Jefferson's faith in human potential was still burning in Iowa in Carpenter's day.

Carpenter also held the orthodox Jeffersonian view that education is the key to the betterment of mankind. Throughout his public life he supported education at all levels. He read widely, was by no means an ignorant man, but was self-conscious about his lack of formal education. On one occasion, Governor Carpenter stumbled woefully in his speech in the presence of the President of the University of Iowa and confided in his diary, "I never hated any thing worse." He urged Iowans to make the Iowa City institution "what Ann Arbor is to Michigan, or Harvard to Massachusetts." Simultaneously, he backed the normal school concept for the training of teachers. He was stricken with double consternation when it became apparent that the State Treasurer under his administration had mishandled the funds of the State Agricultural College at Ames—an institution he helped found as a fledgling legislator. No Jefferson in his grasp of intellectual matters, Carpenter was a hard-working, practical politician who rarely transcended the issues of the day.

More important than providing perspective forward and aft, this book presents details about a successful, vote-getting politician as well as the electorate, party machinery, and times that called him forth. One can envision Carpenter in his prime, stumping the hamlets and towns of Iowa. His face becomes expressive, his voice rises, and the farmers listen attentively as he explains the excessive costs of "exchanging commodities over long lines of communication, by expensive agencies, and at exorbitant charges for transportation. *This is the skeleton in every Western farmer's corn-crib.*" Practical Iowan that he was, Carpenter not only diagnosed the situation but did something about it.

Mildred Throne has used the life of C. C. Carpenter as a framework for analyzing Iowa politics, particularly the intricacies of the Republican Party, during a complicated period. While reading the sixteen chapters that follow, readers may gauge for themselves how effectively Carpenter and the author handled their respective challenges.

———•◆•———

With this biography, the State Historical Society resumes its long-standing tradition of publishing the results of research into the Iowa past. This manuscript was ostensibly complete at the time of Mildred Throne's death fourteen years ago. It was not the privilege of any of the current staff of the Society to have known Mildred Throne. However, we are keenly aware of the standards she maintained while editing the *Iowa Journal of History and Politics*.

Early in the process of preparing this book for the press, we laid down the principles that we would strive to maintain Mildred Throne's standards and that this would remain her book. Therefore, we checked references and quotations, read for typographical errors and slips, made those corrections which we felt she would have made had she been present to see the book through the press, but in no way did we revise the volume in the light of more recent scholarship, or in any other way. The book is Mildred Throne's.

Two books published within the last decade are closely related to aspects of Iowa history treated in the following pages. These are: Stanley P. Hirshson, *Grenville M. Dodge: Soldier, Politician, Railroad Pioneer* (Bloomington, 1967) and Morton M. Rosenberg, *Iowa on the Eve of the Civil War: A Decade of Frontier Politics* (Norman, 1972). Readers who desire a recent bibliography of items on the period of Iowa history treated in this volume are invited to consult the notes for chapters eight through twelve of Leland L. Sage's *A History of Iowa* (Ames, 1974). Those who do so may conclude that few historians have been productive in the field of late nineteenth-century Iowa history. Since the early 1960s, there have been several emphatic shifts in the historiography of the Reconstruction period of United States history. Undoubtedly, this volume would have emerged differently had it been written more recently; however, no recent scholarship supersedes or invalidates Miss Throne's contribution.

Almost all members of the Society's staff worked in some capacity to transform this nearly forgotten manuscript into print. Claudia Majetich checked the notes and in so doing kept the Library staff busy. Henrietta Zagel read proof as did Timothy N. Hyde who also prepared the index. Lynn Gezon typed a good share of the manuscript. Editor L. Edward Purcell participated in and coordinated all phases of the project from book design to mailing the last galley sheet to the printer. Others helped in ways too numerous to mention.

Peter T. Harstad
Director

CYRUS CLAY CARPENTER

Cyrus C. Carpenter and Iowa Politics, 1854-1898

ONE

A Young Man Goes West

ON A JUNE DAY IN 1854 a young man trudged wearily across the prairie of central Iowa. He had left Homer, then the county seat of Webster County, early that morning, after a night spent in a two-room log "hotel." This was truly frontier country; in twenty miles he had passed but two rude log cabins. At last, about five o'clock in the afternoon, he came to a ridge and saw below him a "most enchanting sight." He was on a plateau that sloped gently down to the Des Moines River. Between him and the river lay perhaps a dozen large barracks, neat and whitewashed, arranged in orderly rows. On the prairie in front of these buildings cattle grazed lazily. Cyrus Clay Carpenter had reached the end of his journey.

He was not a big man, except in heart and mind. He stood but five feet eight inches tall, his thick brown hair was unruly, and his chin sported a curly brown beard. His wide-set, brown eyes glowed on that June day when he first saw Fort Dodge, for he had found a home. Here his life would be centered for the rest of his days. He would leave Fort Dodge often—for Pike's Peak in search of gold, for the South during the Civil War, for Des Moines as Governor of the state, and for Washington as a Congressman —but he would always return. Here his roots would sink deep and sure.

Fort Dodge in June of 1854 had been, until recently, just that—a fort on the frontier, manned by a company of United States Infantry under command of Captain Samuel Woods. Their military task completed, the soldiers had moved on to a farther frontier in Minnesota, leaving their deserted barracks to Major William Williams, the sutler of the post. Williams remained and set about building a town that was still little more than a dream when young Cyrus Carpenter arrived.[1]

Many young men all over America were "going west" in the 1850s. In fact, young men—and women, too—had been moving westward ever since the days of Jamestown and Plymouth, two centuries before. Carpenter was merely following the pattern set by his forebears in the seventeenth century.

The first of his line to take up the westward trek was a William Carpenter, who at the age of sixty came to America with his son, also named William. They, with the younger William's wife, Abigail, five small children, and a servant, Thomas Banshott, had set sail from Southampton, England, in the ship *Bevis,* a tiny craft of 150 tons burden, in May of 1638. There were only eight families on the *Bevis,* but, with children and servants, the passenger list came to sixty. Coming mostly from the English counties of Hants and Wilts, these pioneers were laborers of one kind and another. The group included only one "gentleman"—a Richard Dummer. The rest were wheelwrights, tailors, carpenters (the two Williams followed this trade), tanners, and one "husbandman." Arriving in Massachusetts, the company scattered, the Carpenters going first to Weymouth.[2]

The elder William returned to England on the *Bevis,* but the son William remained to found one branch of the Carpenter family in America. The English ancestry of these Carpenters has been traced back to the fourteenth century, to a John Carpenter who was a Member of Parliament in 1323. There was also a fifteenth century John who was town clerk of London from 1417 to 1438, a Member of Parliament in 1436 and 1439, and who "bequeathed to the corporation of this city certain lands and tenements for the purpose of maintaining and educating four boys and sending them to the Universities," a bequest from which grew the City of London School, established in 1834. On the pedestal of a statue of this John Carpenter, placed in a niche on the principal staircase of the school, the story of his beneficences was carved, concluding with praise for one "who . . . desired 'To do justly, love mercy, and walk humbly with his God.' "[3] Whether by coincidence or heredity, many of the qualities praised in the fifteenth century John Carpenter of London can be found in his nineteenth century descendant, Cyrus Clay Carpenter of Iowa.

The William Carpenter who stayed in Weymouth with his wife and children became a freeman of that settlement in 1640, a constable in 1641, and several times a member of the General Court of Plymouth, where Governor William Bradford, whose second wife was William Carpenter's cousin, "favored him in all his measures." Another cousin, known to genealogists as "William of Providence," pointed out to "William of Weymouth" the attractions of an inland settlement known as the "Seekonk plain," and William Carpenter took up the trail westward again. In 1643, Reverend Samuel Newman of Weymouth led a group of the members of his church into the interior of Massachusetts to Seekonk, near the present-day Rhode Island border. This Indian name—spelled variously in sixty-four different ways, from Sea Cauque to Sinkhunch—was soon changed to Rehoboth ("The Lord has made room for us") by Reverend Newman. A "town" in the New England sense of a settlement and surrounding fields, Rehoboth, "not above 40 Miles from Boston," soon came to be "a Towne not dispicable." Here, and in nearby Attleboro, the descendants of William Carpenter lived for over 150 years.[4]

In 1789, the young men of Rehoboth and Attleboro were restless; the reason: "The difficulty of obtaining near home, and from their own resources, an adequate supply of land, urged them to seek ampler room in some new region and on cheaper soil." [5] Among these restless young men was John Carpenter, the fifth in descent from the William who had moved to the Massachusetts frontier of Rehoboth in 1645. With him was a brother, Daniel, and another Carpenter (possibly a cousin)—Josiah. These three Carpenters, together with six other young men, set out in 1790 for the frontier of Pennsylvania.

John, the grandfather of Cyrus, was twenty-three years old at the time, one year younger than the grandson would be when he resumed the westward march sixty-four years later. The journey of the "Nine Partners," as they came to be known, is a familiar one, repeated by thousands of other young men during the following century. They traveled through New York State, distrustful of the promises of the Mohawk Valley because of reports of much sickness, and were temporarily attracted to Cherry Valley, until they heard there had not been a month in the past five years when there had been no frost. In Cherry Valley they met William Cooper, the inevitable frontier land agent, who offered them a trip free of charge in his boat, "to view lands of which he had the agency." Thus the Partners came to Susquehanna County in Pennsylvania, a wilderness where no white man lived. Liking what they found, in spite of the "heavy forests and rugged hills," they contracted to buy a piece of land four miles long by one mile wide, for £1,198.[6] "The writings were drawn and signed, on a hemlock stump, May 22, 1790." [7] John's grandson said of the Partners, many years later: "They came to North-Eastern Pennsylvania because here they could buy more acres with a short purse then in Eastern Massachusetts. . . . So with an axe, and a rude saw, and a yoke of oxen for each householder—hauling sleds hewn from the native timber, upon which were packed their scanty wearing apparel and household furniture—they invaded the wilderness." [8]

From the nucleus of the "Nine Partners Settlement" came the town of Harford. Here Cyrus Clay Carpenter was born on November 24, 1829. His father, Asahel, the son of Partner John, had married Amanda Thayer in 1822. Amanda was the daughter of Aaron Thayer of Medway, Massachusetts, who, although not one of the original "Nine," had followed them to Harford in the early years of the colony.[9] Eight children were born of this marriage: six boys and two girls. Two of the boys, John and Asahel, and the two girls died in infancy. The remaining four brothers were Gideon Judd, Frederick D., Cyrus Clay, and Robert Emmett.[10] The father, Asahel, died of consumption in 1842; his wife, a year or so later.[11] Thus, when Cyrus was only thirteen or fourteen years old, he and his orphaned brothers were parceled out to the numerous Carpenters and their relatives—Tylers, Thayers,

Thachers—in and around Harford, and here they grew to young manhood surrounded by the transplanted culture of their New England forebears.

Harford, in Susquehanna County, Pennsylvania, was a tiny center of New England culture, as were many other small communities across the land from Massachusetts to the Middle West. The pioneers of America carried more than axes and household furniture with them; they brought their church, their schools, and their politics. While felling the forests or breaking the prairies of Middle America, they did not forget the larger interests, both spiritual and material. "They believed then, as they believed afterwards, that every patriot had political opinions and every honest man had a religious creed," said Cyrus Carpenter when, as a man of political affairs, he returned to his birthplace in later life.

In Harford, of the three essentials of a wider life—church, school, politics —the school came first. Barely four years from the time the "writings" were signed on the hemlock stump, a school had been organized, and daily sessions were held at Deacon John Tyler's house. But even a common school, even the "three R's," did not satisfy the ambitious pioneers of the Pennsylvania wilderness. In 1817, only twenty-seven years after the founding of the settlement, Reverend Lyman Richardson opened a private school to prepare young men for college. Out of this grew the Harford or Franklin Academy, with classes held sometimes at Richardson's home, sometimes in the "Center School House." Here Cyrus Carpenter came in 1849, and here he received a few months of advanced schooling, all he had in addition to his common school education to prepare him for the larger world.

Only four years were needed to start a school at Harford; the church was slower in coming. Reverend Samuel Newman had led his congregation from Weymouth to Rehoboth in the early seventeenth century; by the late eighteenth century the congregations led the way. Ten years after the Nine Partners established their town, "missionaries searching the wilderness" found Harford and an eager audience. During these years the settlers had kept their New England Congregationalism alive by their own efforts, just as they had established their own organized government. On the one hand, they held church services on Sunday, often "under the back roof of each others cabins;" on the other, they governed themselves by the traditional township system of New England. When at last they organized their church —"congregational in form"—it was by a vote of the people.[12]

Politically, the Carpenters and others at Harford were probably New England Whigs, or National Republicans as they were known in the 1820s. Cyrus' middle name—Clay—would indicate a family reverence for the great Whig, Henry Clay, who dominated American politics in 1829 when the third Carpenter son was born. But forces were already at work that would submerge the Whig party. New England reform movements, growing strong in the decade of the 1820s, reached to the remote corner of Pennsylvania, where the sons and daughters of Massachusetts still looked eastward for spiritual guidance. Revivalism, accompanied by temperance and abolitionism, swept over Harford in these years. By 1829, a Temperance Society, with John Carpenter one of the charter members, was organized, and the three local distilleries were closed down by their owners, one of them being Deacon John Tyler. Convinced of the evil of their business ways, the distillers "scarcely stopped to think twice before they put out the fires of their distilleries forever, and wiped out the capital they had invested in the business along with it forever," wrote Cyrus Carpenter. Whether this romantic explanation of a somewhat unbusinesslike destruction of property is true, or whether the force of public opinion, stirred by revivalism and reformism, might have had some influence on their action, is a question not answered by this son of Harford.

But temperance was not the only reform measure agitating the North in the 1820s. Antislavery sentiment rose on the crest of the wave of reform. In New England, William Lloyd Garrison founded his *Liberator* in 1831; in the South, slaveholders defended their "peculiar institution;" and the seeds of civil conflict were sown. Harford, remote but aware of the reform movements stemming from the East, organized an Anti-Slavery Society which had two hundred members by the close of 1836. And from this movement the Free-Soil party grew. Years later, when Cyrus Carpenter met George W. Julian in the halls of Congress, he remembered that his first vote had been cast for the old Free-Soiler in the presidential election of 1852, when Julian was a candidate for Vice President on the Free-Soil ticket.[13]

Thus, the New England-Harford influence left a deep impress on young Cyrus. By tradition, by environment, by education he would be a temperance man, a Republican, and a church-goer. Although in later life he strayed from the folds of Congregationalism to those of Methodism, he never failed to practice his religious beliefs on all the days of the week. He grew up to be a sober young man; no doubt early hardship, coupled with the generally serious outlook of his generation, contributed to this solemnity.

His early years followed a familiar pattern for young boys on the frontier of the 1840s—summer work on the farm, a few months schooling in the winter, a few years of teaching in country schools, and then attendance at the local academy. In Carpenter's case, certainly, this was the course of his education. In his later years, the fact that many of his contemporaries had eastern university or college training and degrees caused him much regret, but his own education, scanty though it was, gave him a sound foundation. Habits of study and serious reading that never left him can probably be traced back to the fifteen months he spent at Harford Academy.[14]

As the year 1849 opened, the Carpenter brothers were scattered. The eldest, Judd, had set out for the gold fields of California; the youngest, Emmett, was with relatives in Harford; while the second, Fred, had married early and for a number of years dropped out of the lives of his brothers. Cyrus, who had been teaching school at Herrick in Susquehanna County, returned to Harford with his small savings in his pocket, his few possessions carried in his hand, and with his heart set on attending the Academy.[15]

On a spring day Cyrus walked across the campus and with "awe and trepidation" sought out the president, Reverend Lyman Richardson. The school, begun so modestly by Richardson in 1817, was now a full-fledged academy with a campus, a half-dozen small buildings, and four teachers. In 1849, it was known as Franklin Academy; the following year the name would be changed to Harford Academy; still later, it took the more ambitious title of Harford University, which it kept until its close in 1865. When Cyrus Carpenter entered Harford, Richardson taught the classes in "Mathematics and Natural Sciences;" Willard Richardson, a nephew, taught "Ancient Languages and Belles-Lettres;" while Mrs. Harriet Richardson and Miss N. Maria Richardson between them taught courses in "French, Botany, Drawing, Painting, Embroidery, Wax-Flowers, and Gilding"—these latter frivolities for the "young ladies" who attended the school. In 1849, there were "104 males, 48 females" at Harford.[16]

President Richardson took an interest in young Cyrus Carpenter and helped him find lodgings. The rent at Harford was $2.00 for a term of thirteen weeks. Board came to $1.38 per week, but for many boys, including Cyrus, this was too large a sum: ". . . as I must needs board myself, and cook my own rations," said Cyrus, "I did not find a convenient place for one in my circumstances." But Richardson solved his problem by giving him a room in his own quarters.[17]

At Harford, Carpenter took courses in Greek and Latin, the foundation stones of higher education in the nineteenth century, and he studied mathematics under President Richardson, including a course in surveying that proved useful on the Iowa frontier a few years later. Elocution was a standard part of the curriculum: training in public speaking and oratory was an essential for young men interested in politics—and what young man was not a budding politician in the 1840s? Years later, Cyrus acknowledged his debt to Willard Richardson, "a natural teacher and a born leader of the young." Under his tutelage Cyrus learned composition, rhetoric, and declamation, and on one afternoon a week joined in the exercises of the Literary Society, where Willard Richardson "gave large latitude" to the enthusiasms of his students. But it was for Lyman Richardson that Carpenter reserved his highest praise: "He was the best man I have ever known." A scientist, a preacher, a teacher, Richardson left a strong impress on his young student's mind. Many of the attributes of Richardson, as Carpenter described them—

honesty, devotion to duty, love of fellowmen—would be found later in Carpenter, the Iowa statesman.

At the end of the summer term of 1849, when the other students left for home, President Richardson sought out Cyrus and asked him where he was going. Young Carpenter, who had no home to visit, replied that he was going to look for haying and harvesting work. "Well," said Richardson, "I have considerable hay to cut—why not work for me?" So for six weeks Cyrus and the president cut and stacked hay together, "in the fields about the Academy." Then, following a fall term of another thirteen weeks of schooling, Cyrus left and taught school at Hollisterville in Wayne County, to replenish his dwindling purse. Another spring term in 1850, when he lived with a farmer and milked ten cows morning and evening for his board, another term of teaching country school, this time in Clifford Township, and another spring term at Harford in 1851 ended his schooling. "The fifteen months I spent at the Academy were the most profitable and happy months of my life." [18]

Pennsylvania had little to offer a young man with no funds in 1851. So Cyrus set his face westward, in the tradition of his ancestors. His first stop was at Johnstown, Ohio, where Uncle Henry Tullar welcomed him. Again he taught country schools and joined in the social life of the young people. Literary and singing societies were popular, and Cyrus was active in them. As befit the schoolteacher, Fourth of July orations were a part of his activities, and here he began his long career of patriotic and political speaking.[19] Such was his life from 1851 to the spring of 1854. Many from Ohio were emigrating to Iowa in these years; Cyrus joined them.

"Left Johnstown for the far west biding adieu to friends and home," wrote Carpenter on Monday, May 15, 1854. He had about $100 in his pocket as he set out to seek his fortune. On foot, by stage, and by river packet he journeyed across Ohio and Indiana and thence to Chicago.[20] From Chicago he traveled to Rock Island, possibly by the newly completed Rock Island Railroad. Crossing the Mississippi River on the ferry, Carpenter entered Iowa at Davenport. A steamboat at the wharf took him down to Muscatine, where he boarded a stagecoach for Iowa City. Traveling had proved expensive; he now had but $5.00 left of his original hoard. He found Iowa City, the capital of the state, "assuming a good many airs" because of its booming railroad prospects, so he set out after two days for Fort Des Moines in the interior.[21]

Fort Des Moines was then a "new and unfinished" village of some 1,000 population. During the few days that Carpenter remained there, he explored the surrounding country, returning at night to the Everett House. His funds were still shrinking, and there seemed no prospect even of a schoolteaching job. Around the hotel at night he heard talk of a "Fort Dodge" eighty-five miles away, and decided to try his luck there. Having a "good deal more confidence left than cash," he shouldered his "carpet-sack" and started on foot for Iowa's farthest frontier.[22]

The way to Fort Dodge was more trail than road. Keeping close to the Des Moines River, Carpenter made his way through woods and across prairies, stopping at night at some convenient cabin where, in true frontier fashion, the latchstring was out at all times. He reached Boonesboro on a Saturday. The next day being Sunday, he did not travel. On Monday, he started early and reached Homer, then the county seat of Webster County, which consisted of about a dozen log cabins and a two-room hotel. On Tuesday morning, June 27, with just seventy-five cents left of his $100, Carpenter set out on the last twenty miles of his journey. He passed but two cabins that day, one at Brushey Creek and the other at Holliday's Creek. At five o'clock he came in sight of the barracks that constituted Fort Dodge.[23] His journey westward was over.

TWO

From Surveyor to Politician

———•◆•———

FORT DODGE, on that June day in 1854, was neither a fort nor a town; only four or five families lived in the few houses and barracks that comprised the settlement. Established in 1850, first as Fort Clarke, then as Fort Dodge, the frontier post had been intended as a protection against possible Indian marauders. Some dozen or so buildings had been completed by the spring of 1853, when the troops were ordered northward into Minnesota. By July, the fort was abandoned. The sutler for the fort was "Major" William Williams, whose military title had been earned during militia duty in his native Pennsylvania. The Major liked Fort Dodge and thought he saw in it a great future as a city on the path of the westward movement. Therefore, when the troops left the fort, the sutler remained.[1]

Many supposed that the site of the fort still belonged to the United States government as a "reservation." Individuals and groups were already eyeing the location and making plans to buy it from the government, which usually sold such reservations to the highest bidders. Major Williams, shrewd and foresighted, knew that, by virtue of an 1846 land grant to the state of Iowa for improvement of the Des Moines River, the fort site and the land surrounding it (being on an odd-numbered section) actually belonged to the state and not to the federal government. Therefore, while others were looking over the land, he hurried off to Ottumwa and bought all of section 19 on which the fort was located. Returning via Des Moines, he bought several hundred acres on the adjoining even-numbered sections from the government land office there.[2] Thus he stole a march on the slower-witted land seekers and returned to his domain to lay out a town.

All this had taken place in the early months of 1854. By March, the Major began to survey the original plat of Fort Dodge. The population at that time consisted of Williams and his son, James; William R. Miller and his family, who had sought refuge in the fort when their lands, some nine miles north, had been threatened by the Indians; and John Hefley, a former sergeant at the fort, and his wife. The following month, John Scott and his brother, Robert, and family left their claims to the south and moved for safety to Fort Dodge. Williams had given Miller one of the fort buildings, on the condition that he open a "public house."[3] To this frontier hotel Cyrus Carpenter found his way upon reaching Fort Dodge. Entering the tiny settlement, Carpenter met Major Williams, who took him by the hand and told him that "the west was full of opportunities for young men who had force and a will to stick."[4] That the young man had both these qualities in abundance was soon apparent.

Cyrus was indeed "at the jumping-off place." North to the Minnesota line and west to the Missouri River there was hardly a "human habitation." Here was the very edge of the Iowa frontier. That a young man with seventy-five cents in his pocket and all his worldly goods in a carpetsack should choose this spot for his future home, should say to himself "Here I remain," indicated his optimism and hardihood.[5] He had passed up the bustling Iowa City and the strategically located Fort Des Moines, where he found no promises or prospects, and had chosen an almost unpeopled fort site as the place to put down his roots.

Landlord Miller was a true frontiersman. He had been born and "partially raised," as Carpenter phrased it, in Sangamon County, Illinois. He could neither read nor write, but he had a good store of native wit, and his life had been spent in keeping ahead of settlement. "He had traded with the Indians," Carpenter recalled, "run a hotel, manufactured whiskey, and drank considerable of his own manufacture." During the Lincoln-Douglas debates in 1858, Miller recalled that he had once hired Abe Lincoln to "run a law suit for him" and that he was "a right smart man."

When Carpenter had deposited his carpetbag at Miller's hotel and arranged for his supper and a night's lodging, he next asked about finding work. Miller was then farming the vegetable garden which the soldiers had laid out at the fort during their stay; Carpenter could hoe his potato patch, he said. The young man agreed and sat down to his supper, deciding that "it was better to be born lucky than rich." Luck was still on his side, it seemed, for during the evening another visitor sought shelter at the hotel. He had the contract for a survey of several townships a few miles west of Fort Dodge, he told Miller, and was now going to Fort Des Moines to look for a surveyor to take over his work. Since it was hard not to eavesdrop in the small confines of a frontier hotel, Carpenter listened to all this with growing interest. Approaching the stranger, he asked how much experience a surveyor would need to do this work. "O, more or less, according to the man," was the answer. Carpenter explained that although he had studied "the science of surveying" he had never had occasion to practice it but was willing to try. The surveyor, George Berry, talked to Cyrus for a while, decided he "would do," gave him instructions on how to reach the surveyor's camp, and left at once to return to his crew of five "hands" who were awaiting him. So, on Carpenter's first day in Fort Dodge he had made friends and had found work.[6]

The next morning, he set off for the surveyor's camp, which he reached about noon, finding only the cook in attendance. When Berry and his men came in after dark that night, Carpenter watched in amazement at the gusto with which they attacked the standard surveyor's fare—boiled beans, boiled pickled pork, bread, and coffee. Not until his first full day as a surveyor did Carpenter come to appreciate this menu.

His first night in a tent was far from pleasant. A storm, which had been threatening all day, broke at last with more violence than he had ever before experienced. In the morning Lizard Creek on which they were camped was out of its banks, and when the party started on its four-mile march to the surveying site, the high wet grass soon soaked the men to their knees. As they approached a crossing of the Lizard in single file, Carpenter wondered how they would ford it. He soon found out. The leader of the file, without breaking step, "waded right in without removing any of his clothes." Each followed suit, and all eyed the newcomer to see how he would react. But their "new hand," not to be outdone, "marched right on to the other shore" with the best of them. This was only the first of many crossings of the meandering creek that they made during the day, in addition to wading through innumerable sloughs, and soon they were all thoroughly soaked.

After they had "run" their lines for two miles, Berry sat down at the last corner and told Carpenter to take the compass and try his hand at running a random line east. This done, with "a tolerably close connection," Berry decided that his new hand was all right.[7] This was on a Thursday. Saturday night's sunset "never gave me so much pleasure," said Carpenter. He was completely exhausted from three days of as hard work as he had ever done in his life, but the thing that troubled him most was that the clothes with which he had begun work were in tatters. He had worn a pair of "kip boots" and black woolen trousers. By Saturday night there was nothing left of his boots except the soles, which he had tied onto his feet with strings cut from the boot legs. The wool of his trousers had been torn to shreds below the knees. Had it not been for the lining of the "pantaloons," which was evidently of more sturdy material than the wool, he would have been in an even sorrier state.

Sunday morning Carpenter announced his intention to go to Fort Dodge to get something to wear. "A kind of incredulous smile" appeared on the faces of the other men, but they all gave him errands to do for them. One wanted tobacco, another bedticking with which to patch his trousers, another wanted thread, while all wanted mail and newspapers. Carpenter was rather surprised that none of them gave him any money to make these purchases, but he started at once on the twelve-mile walk to Fort Dodge. Upon reaching the settlement he looked up Major Williams and told him what he needed but that he had no money. Williams took him to the store recently opened by son James and fitted him out with army pants, some hickory shirts, and a pair of stout boots. He also gave him all the tobacco, thread, bedticking, and other sundries that the boys had asked for and, in addition, loaded him down with the extra newspapers and magazines left over at the newly opened post office. When Carpenter reached camp, just as the sun was going down, the warmth of his reception surprised him. He was greeted with cheers, and his purchases and newspapers received with excited shouts. He was now "fairly installed as one of the boys."

Their attitude somewhat puzzled Carpenter, however, and not until thirteen years later, when he was Governor of Iowa, did he learn that they had never expected to see him again. At that time an old man came to his office to see some original field notes of a survey of Lee County. The man was George Berry, his first employer, who was surprised to find that the Governor was his former "hand." Berry then asked Carpenter if he remembered his first Sunday in camp and his trip to Fort Dodge for supplies. When the Governor assured him that he certainly did, Berry said, "Well, when you left we all said that would be the last we would ever see of you. And when you came back that night, we were surprised, and I thought I had a good hand." [8]

Carpenter's first job lasted for eight weeks. When the work was done, the party returned to Fort Dodge, where they camped together for the last time and "made a night of it." The rest of the men then went on to their homes in southeastern Iowa, while Carpenter remained at Fort Dodge. Several more families had now settled in the town and on claims close by, so it was easy for the young man to find a job. He began work at once, haying and harvesting, and doing some private surveying for individuals. Surveyors were much in demand on a new frontier, and Carpenter's services were often needed. He spent the closing months of 1854 in Kossuth and Palo Alto counties as compassman for a Mr. Bell who had the government contract for that area. During this job he earned a salary of $3.00 a day. [9]

Back in Fort Dodge again in early January of 1855, Carpenter at first found no demands for his talents either as surveyor or farmer. But with frontier versatility, he soon stumbled into another type of work—schoolteaching. Families were now coming into Fort Dodge with increasing frequency and with the usual quota of small children. Landlord Miller himself had "a large family of children" who spent their evenings trying to teach themselves spelling and arithmetic. No teacher could resist this need; almost before he knew it, Carpenter was helping them with their lessons. News travels fast in a small community, and the need for a school was great. Quickly a school district was organized, one of the log houses repaired, and the first school in Fort Dodge opened to some twenty-four pupils of "all ages and sizes, from twenty years old down to five." Carpenter taught this assorted group for two months, using any and every kind of textbook that came to hand. The "readers" ranged from Fox's *Book of Martyrs* to the *Columbian Orator,* and the spellers, arithmetics, grammars, and geographies offered as wide a range. "I was not much richer than when I began," reported Carpenter, "and my scholars were very little wiser." [10]

One of the newcomers to Fort Dodge early in 1855 was Cyrus' young brother, Emmett. Cyrus had been able to restrain the younger man's enthusiasm for California and had persuaded him to come to Iowa. Their brother Judd in California would have liked to have them with him and had sent them money in 1854, but Cyrus had chosen Fort Dodge for his home and had convinced Emmett to join him.[11] In May of 1855, the two brothers were part of a surveying team to subdivide eight townships in Emmet and Kossuth counties. There they worked throughout the spring, wading sloughs, fighting mosquitoes, dodging prairie fires, and running their lines.

One Sunday they were visited by a band of Indians who first asked for tobacco and then proceeded to inspect the camp. One brave filched a piece of pickled pork from a barrel and hid it under his blanket. Knowing that he must protect the food supply, Carpenter "put on a bold front," walked up to the Indian, took the pork from him, and returned it to the barrel. Another picked up a tin cup; Carpenter took it away and tossed it into a nearby tent. When a third stole a bell, tied it to his ankle, and strutted about to the high amusement of his fellows, Carpenter seized a section stake and confronted the show-off, motioning him to take off the bell. With some hesitation, and in surly fashion, the Indian complied. After demanding and receiving more tobacco, the Indians at last retired in good order. Carpenter, who had only been interested in protecting the foodstuff from the marauders, did not think of his danger at the time, but two years later, when he heard of the Spirit Lake Massacre, he "thought of that Sunday on the prairie and was thoroughly scared." [12]

In retrospect, "those were rough but royal days" for Cyrus Carpenter.[13] In between surveying trips he returned to Fort Dodge, where the population was growing so rapidly as almost to burst the seams of the original fort buildings. Since the frontier populations always raced ahead of the government, none of the land around Fort Dodge was actually on the market and would not be until the government established a land office. Following the usual tradition, the settlers formed a "Claim Club" to protect their pre-emptions until such time as the government should be ready to sell the land. The club at Fort Dodge had organized as early as July 22, 1854, and as new settlers came in they joined the organization. According to the bylaws, each member was allowed a claim or claims totaling 320 acres; he must live on the claim and erect a "cabin 16 × 16 feet shingled and enclosed so as to live in it valued at $30;" he must put in at least $10 worth of improvements monthly; and "any person going on anothers claim that is valid, shall be visited by a Com[mittee] of 3 from our club and informed of the facts & if such persons persist in their pursuits regardless of the Com or claimant they shall be put off the claim by this Club." Landlord Miller was chosen the first chairman, and William A. Young was elected secretary. On January 9, 1855, Miller resigned, and E. H. Albee was elected chairman in his place. Cyrus Carpenter, who had just returned from a surveying trip, was nominated for secretary to succeed Young, but he "respectfully declined," and another was chosen in his place. On the same day Carpenter entered his claim, as a member of the club, to the "East half of section nineteen (19) Township ninety (90), North Range thirty (30) West." [14]

On March 3, 1855, President Franklin Pierce signed a bill establishing three new land office districts in Iowa, one of them at Fort Dodge. [15] Land excitement there immediately doubled and trebled. Nothing could enhance the prospects of a town more than the location of a land office. It meant the opening of another segment of the vast public domain to purchase, and land seekers and "land sharks" arrived from the older regions, armed with money and warrants. Land was the great commodity of the frontier. While some sought homes, others sought fortunes by buying and selling the land. Cyrus Carpenter was of this latter type; although he had been reared a farmer and although he had a small farm near Fort Dodge all his life, his real interest lay in the land as a source of revenue. Yet he never made his fortune. Land dealing, like horse trading, called for a flexible code of ethics; Carpenter, already known in Fort Dodge as "Honest Cy," did not have this necessary flexibility. [16] He would make many warm friends in his life, and a few enemies, but he would never make much money.

The summer of 1855 was a feverish one in Fort Dodge. In preparation for the opening of the land office in November, thousands poured into the district that comprised the present-day counties of Webster, Hamilton, Hardin, Humboldt, Wright, Franklin, Kossuth, Hancock, Winnebago, Worth, and Cerro Gordo. Since Carpenter had traveled much of this area on his surveying trips, his knowledge of the terrain stood him in good stead, and he opened an office in Fort Dodge "as a Land Agent, surveyor, and tax-paying agent." [17] Easterners interested in speculating in western lands usually dealt through such agents, sending them funds and land warrants to invest, and charging them with the obligation of keeping up the taxes. Two of Carpenter's clients were David McMullen and Hans Rees, both of New York City. They each signed contracts covering 2,000 acres of land, allowing the land agent one-half of the profits above ten per cent of the original capital invested. Former friends in Ohio also sent Carpenter land warrants to invest. [18] The scarcity of this type of correspondence in the Carpenter Papers,

Cyrus Carpenter

Kate Carpenter

Ft. Dodge in 1869

however, indicates that Cyrus was doing less than the traditional "land office business."

As the date set for the opening of the federal land office at Fort Dodge approached, the little town was flooded with land speculators and immigrants, all eager to buy claims. "Before the day arrived for opening the Land Office," wrote Carpenter, "it became apparent that unless there were some concessions all around in respect to the manner of entering land, there would be trouble." [19] Ver Planck Van Antwerp had been appointed receiver and William H. Merritt register of the land office, but their instructions were to sell the land on a first-come-first-served basis. When the law did not conform to frontier practices, the settlers themselves took things into their own hands. At Fort Dodge they agreed to draw numbers for turns at the land office. Cyrus was not fortunate—his number was "away up near two hundred," but his brother drew number forty five. Consequently, Cyrus left his land warrants with Emmett to invest, while he himself went to Sioux City, where another land office was opening, with warrants for "about ten thousand acres." [20]

The winter of 1855–1856 was long remembered in northwestern Iowa as "the *cold winter*." "The snow averaged two feet on the prairies, with a crust on it so thick and strong at times that horses and loaded teams traveled on the crust as on ice," according to the memory of one resident.[21] Carpenter left Fort Dodge on December 1, 1855, during a comparatively mild, wet spell, but he soon was overtaken by blizzards and did not reach the Sioux City area for eight days.[22] Back in Fort Dodge, where the storm also raged, a young man died within sight of the town, and Emmett waited anxiously for word from his brother. Finally a letter arrived from Cyrus, written from "Sergeant Bluff City" and dated December 15, 1855. He wrote that he had arrived "two or three days since and have been shut up for the last two days with the cold and snow." He considered Sioux City a "humbug" because of its location, but supposed that the company that owned the site would make a "nice speculation out of the thing." Because of the heavy snow, he did not know just what type of land he had entered—whether good prairie or slough—but he was "going to chalk on to some of it however haphazard hit or miss." [23] Early in March, a party of men arrived from Fort Dodge, accompanied by brother Emmett, and together the two Carpenters returned home.[24]

Other interests beside land selling occupied Carpenter's time during 1856. All his life, in spite of resolutions often repeated, he never could stay far from the political scene. Every young man on the frontier, with some gift for public speaking, was sure to be in great demand either as speaker or as candidate. This was the era of the breakup of the old Whig party, and feeling ran high as splinter groups tried to take over its somewhat threadbare mantle. As early as the fall of 1854 one of these splinters—the Know-Nothing or American party—moved upon Fort Dodge in the guise of an Englishman from Dubuque, a doctor from Hardin County, and several Fort Dodgers. Major Williams, a Democrat, made short work of this invasion, but he could do little against the rising tide of Republicanism, of which Cyrus Carpenter was an enthusiastic advocate.[25]

Carpenter's first political office in Fort Dodge was that of county surveyor, a post to which he was elected in August 1855.[26] He held the position until 1857, when he resigned to campaign for the state legislature. Politics was not new to Carpenter; letters from his old friends in Ohio indicate that they already had recognized in him the qualities of a politician. J. M. Davies wrote, after hearing of Carpenter's candidacy, that he was sure he would be elected, adding that "if the election was to be decided in Johnstown I have no doubts but what you would be elected by an overwhelming majority, for dont you remember how you run for *constable,* as soon as it was known that you was a candidate the opposition scarsly [*sic*] got a vote." Davies added that he fully expected Carpenter to be sent to "the Legislature of your state." Another friend had written in 1854, advising Carpenter to "quit wandering about on those desolate plains. . . . Surveying is not your calling and you know it. You was made for a greater man than you ever hope to be if you follow that business. Why Cyrus I expect to vote for C. C. Carpenter for Congress yet, and no joke, or flattery." [27] These prophecies may have been induced by the bias of friendship, yet they both came true.

It took little campaigning or political wisdom to win an election to a minor office in sparsely populated Webster County in 1855. Carpenter was obviously fitted for the work of county surveyor, so that his election to that post had been only a minor triumph. Yet every bit of experience gained in a small political way would help him in the future.

During 1856, in addition to his work as land agent and as county surveyor, Carpenter was active in the rapidly developing Republican party. Iowa Republicanism was formally organized on February 22, 1856, at Iowa City, under the guidance of Governor James W. Grimes.[28] Although delegates from Webster County did not attend the Iowa City convention, Republicanism soon reached Fort Dodge. Opportunities for political organization and activity were plentiful in 1856; there were three nominating conventions and elections during that year. The first election, in April, aside from choosing certain minor officers, turned on the hotly fought issue of the location of the county seat for Webster County. The winner was Fort Dodge, the loser, Homer, by a vote of 409 to 264.[29] Next, in preparation for the August election for members of the General Assembly, three Republicans of Homer sent out a call on May 27 to "Mr C C Carpenter & others of Ft Dodge" for a "county convention." [30] Equally important in the August election would be the choosing of delegates for a constitutional convention to rewrite Iowa's constitution. This called for a district convention, which was held at Eldora in Hardin County.

Carpenter was a delegate from Webster County to this Eldora meeting. These conventions were the training schools for the state's politicians; here they learned the tricks of their trade. The district covered thirteen counties: Fayette, Bremer, Butler, Franklin, Grundy, Hardin, Hamilton, Wright, Webster, Boone, Story, Greene, and Humboldt. Since all the appointed delegates were not able to attend the convention, some had given their proxies to those of the other counties who would be in attendance. Only Hardin County was fully represented. Carpenter held proxies from Humboldt and Greene. On the way to Eldora he was joined by Morgan Everts, Hamilton County's delegate, who held the proxy from Wright County.

Once in Eldora, they found that although there were no avowed candidates for delegate to the constitutional convention, the general trend seemed to be toward Sheldon G. Winchester of Eldora. Deciding that they could "at least enliven the proceedings a little," Carpenter and Everts went into a caucus of their own with the Fayette County delegate, a Mr. Seeley. These three decided to throw their strength to Coker F. Clarkson, the delegate from Grundy County, who had recently moved to Iowa from Indiana. Carpenter had met Clarkson at the land office in Fort Dodge and had struck up an acquaintance that soon ripened into a lifelong friendship. (When Clarkson and his sons later became owners and publishers of the influential Des Moines *Register*, their paper was always ready to back Carpenter in any political activity he might enter.) The Hardin County delegates, learning what was going on, tried to weaken the Clarkson forces by the clever expedient of electing Carpenter chairman of the convention and Clarkson secretary. Their stratagem did not work, however. Clarkson, innocent of the plan, was the most surprised man in the convention when his name was read by the tellers as the ballots were counted. Carpenter, Everts, and Seeley had worked well, and votes for their candidate were delivered on schedule. By the time Fayette County was reached in the roll call, Clarkson had been nominated. But the schemers had counted without their candidate: Clarkson rose and withdrew his name, saying that he had so recently moved to Iowa and was so busy opening his farm that he could not serve. The Hardin County man, Winchester, was then nominated to the satisfaction of all and was later elected.[31]

The third election of the year was not of a political nature, but dealt with a matter that caused as much, if not more, interest than politics. The dream of every community, the hope of every farmer and businessman, was for a railroad. Iowans had been importuning Congress for years for a land grant, such as the Illinois Central grant of 1850, so that the state could bring the magic iron rails within its borders. At last, on May 15, 1856, President Franklin Pierce signed the act granting lands in Iowa for four east-west lines. Governor Grimes immediately called a special session of the General Assembly, and the grant was allocated to the Burlington & Missouri River Railroad, the Mississippi & Missouri Railroad, the Iowa Central Air Line, and the Dubuque & Pacific. Every town in Iowa now began bidding for a place on the rails. Fort Dodge, a logical point on the northernmost line of the grant—the Dubuque & Pacific—called an election for September 22. On that date Webster County voted a $200,000 bond issue to aid in building the road, with 331 in favor, 201 opposed.[32] This was not a sudden decision on the part of the residents of Fort Dodge and Webster County. As early as October 1855, a railroad meeting had been held at Fort Dodge in the interests of the proposed Dubuque & Pacific Railroad. Representatives of the road from Dubuque addressed the meeting, and speeches were also made by "Messrs. Carpenter, Garaghty, Duncombe and Lucas." [33] This was probably Carpenter's first contact with the railroads, a contact which would be continued through most of his political life.

Land, politics, railroads. Fort Dodge was riding high in 1856, with dollars and population mounting dizzily. Land seekers and speculators kept the land office busy; the slavery issue kept politics at white heat; and railroad builders brought promises of future greatness. Then in March of 1857 came a reminder that the raw frontier had not yet been conquered. Word reached Fort Dodge of a brutal massacre by the Indians at Spirit Lake in Dickinson County to the north. The notorious Ink-pa-do-tah and his band of Sioux Indians, angered by the murder of Sidom-i-na-dotah and his family by a settler, Henry Lott, sought revenge by murder and pillage in the small isolated settlements around Spirit Lake.[34]

Major Williams had feared just such an outbreak for some time. Enough of a frontiersman to realize the dangers and horrors of Indians on the warpath, he promptly gathered a company of volunteers to go to the rescue of whatever survivors there might be. He soon had enough men for three companies, two groups from Fort Dodge and one from Webster City, totaling over 100 men, and on March 25 they started for Spirit Lake.[35] The winter had been bitterly cold, and snow still lay deep on the prairies.

Carpenter at the time was traveling in Kossuth and Palo Alto counties with Angus McBane, trying to look over some lands that McBane owned there. Finding the snow too deep for any kind of exploration or survey, they were on their way back to Fort Dodge when, a few miles south of a straggling settlement known as the "Irish Colony" in Palo Alto County, they met the expedition heading for Spirit Lake.[36] The two men at once "enlisted" in Company A of this small army, becoming privates under the command of Captain Charles B. Richards. Carpenter, with two years of experience on the prairies in all sorts of weather, was a welcome addition to this "army," since most of its members, unaccustomed to the rigors of winter travel, were fast losing their enthusiasm. The hardships that this group of men underwent called for the last ounce of stamina, and had it not been for a good core of tough frontiersmen, who kept the men together, many of them would never have survived the experience. When the command reached Mud Lake in the southeast corner of Clay County, after toiling through ever deeper snowdrifts all day, most of the men were so exhausted that they threw themselves on their blankets and went to sleep without a bite to eat. Captain Richards, Lieutenant F. A. Stratton, and several of the hardier men stayed up until after midnight, cutting wood, building fires, and baking pancakes. As they finished a batch of the cakes they would awaken "some tired and hungry man and give him his supper."

The following day, volunteers went forward as an advance guard, Carpenter among them. About noon they met an oxcart coming toward them with a handful of men and women who had escaped from the Indians. A runner was sent back to the main body to bring up food to save the starving and a doctor to treat the wounded. The next day, the advance guard received word that troops from Fort Ridgely had been at Spirit Lake and found no Indians. Returning to the main command, they reported their findings and, after a consultation, decided to send a small detachment north to the lakes to give decent burial to the victims, while the rest of the expedition, with supplies running dangerously low, returned to Fort Dodge. J. C. Johnson of Webster City, captain of Company C, and Captain Richards of Company A led some twenty volunteers north, while the rest of the men turned southward toward home.

A spring thaw had set in so that by the time the main body reached the Irish Colony the men were drenched. That night a spring blizzard overtook them, and soon their wet clothes were frozen stiff. Huddled under what shelter they could find, they awaited the returning burial party from Spirit Lake. At last all had returned except two. Captain Johnson and William Burkholder were caught in the storm. Frantic search the next day revealed no trace of the lost men, and the expedition had to go on without them. Burkholder was the son of Henry Burkholder who had moved to Fort Dodge with his family from Ohio just a month before the expedition set out.[37] Young William and Carpenter had become friends, and it now fell to Cyrus to carry back the tragic news of the loss of their son to Mr. and Mrs. Burkholder, and to his sister, Kate, who would one day become Mrs. Cyrus C. Carpenter.[38]

The hardships endured on this rescue mission were frightful. At one time the men were marooned for thirty-six hours in the midst of a blizzard, with no shelter except a wagon cover and two tents stretched across the wagon bodies to provide some protection from the storm. When the snow at last abated, and they could set out again, they broke into small parties and made their way as best they could toward Fort Dodge. Many became crazed with the cold and the lack of food; feet and hands were frozen; clothes became tattered rags. The stronger kept the weaker moving, and by some miracle all returned in safety except Johnson and Burkholder, whose loss darkened the joy of those who at last found the warmth and friendship of their own firesides.

Carpenter had now been in Fort Dodge for two years. He was a part of the bustling life of the little village; in fact, he was one of the "old settlers" by this time. Land speculation was at its peak in 1857, prospects were bright, and politics were boiling. This was the year in which Carpenter's political interests pushed all other activities into the background.

THREE

A Legislator in Des Moines

———•—•—•———

THE FRONTIER AT MID-CENTURY offered a wide variety of careers to young men. Tradition has pictured the pioneer as a man with a hoe and an axe, hacking a farm out of the wilderness. Equally important to the opening of new lands, however, were the townsmen—merchants, lawyers, doctors, preachers, mill-owners, blacksmiths, newspaper editors—who brought the commercial products, the law, and the culture of the East to the new West. And most of them had one overriding interest—politics. National issues were argued on the frontier with no less enthusiasm than in the East, and in any new community a man with a flair for oratory—be he lawyer or blacksmith—might soon find himself campaigning for public office. Such a man was "Honest Cy" Carpenter of Fort Dodge.

In 1857, the political scene in Iowa was changing rapidly. Iowa's Republican party had been launched in February of 1856; in 1857, the state capital had been moved inland from Iowa City to Des Moines, in recognition of the westward trend of the population, and a new constitution had been written. The legislature that would meet in 1858 would be the first to gather at the new capital of Des Moines, in the new statehouse on Iowa's "Capitol Hill," under a new constitution. Economically, a financial panic gripped the nation, and by 1858 even the bustling Iowa frontier began to feel its influence.

Before the "crash," however, the land business of northwestern Iowa had "kept everything in confusion, and brought about a great deal of dissipation and reckless speculation." [1] The Fort Dodge land office opened again in the spring of 1857, and in two months 403,660.58 acres were sold either for cash or for land warrants. [2]

Meanwhile, Cyrus Carpenter had again gone west to Sioux City to enter lands for his clients and for himself. There is evidence that he and a group of Fort Dodge friends even considered speculating in a townsite in that locality, but nothing came of it. [3] By July, Carpenter returned to Fort Dodge and, putting aside his land speculation, threw himself into the political turmoil.

From mid-July until the year's final election on October 13, Carpenter worked hard for the success of Iowa's burgeoning Republican party. In 1856, Iowa Republicans had fought the presidential campaign with vigor, enthusiasm, and success. A majority of the 92,000 Iowans who voted that year had preferred Republican Frémont to Democrat Buchanan. Now, with 1857, came the contest for the governorship and for a legislature that would elect a new United States Senator from Iowa. James W. Grimes, who had entered the statehouse as a Whig and was now leaving it as a Republican, had his eye on the United States Senate. It was up to the "Grimes men" of the party to choose a legislature that would send him to Washington.

First came the state convention, meeting at Iowa City on August 19, to name candidates for Governor and Lieutenant Governor. Webster County's delegation included young Cyrus Carpenter.[4] There were only 158 delegates present to cast the 338 votes of the convention. Bad roads and long distances had kept many of them at home, but those present held the proxies of the missing members, so that the business of the meeting went forward as planned. Carpenter, aside from representing Webster County, had been designated as the alternate for the Hamilton County delegate at that county's convention on August 13.[5] Among the members present were many Carpenter would know better in the coming years. Henry O'Connor of Muscatine was a rising young Republican who would try for the gubernatorial nomination in 1871 with Carpenter as his successful opponent. Another man, of even more importance to Carpenter's political career, was Grenville M. Dodge of Council Bluffs, then a comparatively unknown railroad surveyor, who would later rise to fame as a Civil War general, a power in Iowa and national politics, and a great railroad builder.

The convention met, organized, nominated, and resolved in the manner of all political gatherings. Ralph P. Lowe, a lawyer from Lee County, won the nomination for Governor, while Oran Faville from Mitchell County, a former teacher turned farmer, received the Lieutenant Governor's place on the ticket. After adopting a platform that endorsed freedom, deplored slavery, and congratulated Iowans on their new constitution and their retiring Governor, the convention adjourned, and the members scattered to their homes.[6]

Hardly had Carpenter reached Fort Dodge before he sent out a call, as chairman of the Webster County Republicans, for a district convention to nominate a candidate for the 1858 state legislature. The Thirteenth District consisted of the seventeen counties of Cerro Gordo, Worth, Franklin, Hancock, Wright, Winnebago, Kossuth, Webster, Hamilton, Calhoun, Pocahontas, Palo Alto, Sac, Buena Vista, Clay, Dickinson, and Emmet.[7] The convention met at Webster City in Hamilton County on September 9, with Charles Aldrich, Carpenter's close friend, as chairman. Thirty votes, divided among seven men, were cast on the informal ballot for representative, with Carpenter getting the largest number—fourteen. After several of the candidates had made "some very appropriate remarks," the first formal ballot was taken: Carpenter now received sixteen votes, while the remaining fourteen were divided among three other contenders. On motion, the nomination was made unanimous for Carpenter, and his political career was launched. The convention then endorsed the state platform and the administration of Governor Grimes and closed with "three hearty cheers" for the candidate.[8]

In spite of the fact that Carpenter had been in Iowa only three years, he was already well known in his district. On surveying trips throughout northwestern Iowa, and in the land business that took him into most of the counties of the district, he had made many friends in this still sparsely settled area. He had also, according to the Webster City editor, "labored with his pen, and upon the stump, in awaking the people to a vigorous effort against the Black Democracy," [9] so that he already had the qualities of a popular candidate—many warm friends and the ability to make a good "stump speech."

Carpenter wasted no time in opening his campaign. Even before the Democrats of the district had chosen a candidate, he had spoken at Algona, where a "large audience" exhibited the "utmost enthusiasm." When the Democrats nominated another Fort Dodge man—John F. Duncombe—people looked forward to some rousing joint debates between the opposing candidates. But, defying accepted practice and tradition, Duncombe evaded Carpenter's efforts to lure him into a face-to-face meeting. Rather, he relied on attacks upon Carpenter in his newspaper, the Fort Dodge Sentinel. Since Fort Dodge had no Republican paper at that time, Carpenter's editorial support came from the Webster City Hamilton Freeman, edited by Charles Aldrich, who was always ready to meet the personal attacks made by the Sentinel and to return them with good measure. In this year of rising bitterness over the whole troubling issue of slavery, local considerations received little attention. Although Carpenter and Duncombe were running for a seat in a state legislature, where their job would be to legislate on local issues, the Republicans branded attempts to bring up state or district problems during the campaign as mere "bogus" Democratic tricks. The Democrats naturally discussed every local issue they could, probably to avoid defending the proslavery cause, a most unpopular subject in Iowa. Carpenter's campaign, commented his defender in Webster City, was conducted on a high level of statesmanship, in "shocking contrast to the cuddling, sneaking operations of the Democracy, who go around 'seeking who they can take in' with local clap-trap." [10]

John F. Duncombe in many respects was a worthy and popular opponent. He, like Carpenter, was a native of Pennsylvania. Both men were of almost the same age, Carpenter being two years the elder. Duncombe had had many of the opportunities denied to Cyrus; he had grown up on his father's farm, had been sent to Allegheny College, and had studied law. After being admitted to the bar in 1855, he had migrated to the West, settling in Fort Dodge in April of that year. There he began the practice of law and in 1856 widened his activities by establishing the town's first newspaper, the *Sentinel,* in company with A. S. White. Webster County was, and would remain for many years, a strong island of Democracy in the swelling tide of Republicanism, and some credit for this should go to Duncombe and his newspaper. Democrat Duncombe and Republican Carpenter, who became the leaders of their respective parties in northwestern Iowa, were opposites in many ways—Duncombe, tall, cold, and formal; Carpenter, short, warm, and friendly; Duncombe, a financial success in everything he tried, from newspaper editing to railroading; Carpenter, a poor hand at money making. In only one field was Carpenter almost always the victor. Politically, he was on the right side at the right time, while Duncombe had the misfortune to back a party rapidly losing power in Iowa. Benjamin F. Gue years later wrote of Duncombe: "Had he been a Republican he might have attained the highest official positions in the State." Duncombe's formality earned for him the sobriquet "Ridiculous Pomposity," while his self-assurance led one of his enemies to call him the "Great 'I.' " [11]

The campaign between these two men ran on through September, with charges and countercharges. Although the voters were divided on the slavery question, no one disagreed on the need for railroads. Therefore that was one of the "local issues" on which the Democrats attacked Carpenter, claiming that he did not support the proposed Dubuque & Pacific Railroad with sufficient enthusiasm. Governor Grimes wrote to Carpenter after the election: "Jones [the incumbent Senator, Democrat George Wallace Jones] & his friends had their hearts set upon electing Duncombe as he is a warm friend of Jones and an agent of his Rail Road. The whole influence of the Rail Road was brought to bear against you." So great was the pressure on this one issue that Carpenter felt called upon to state his position unequivocally at a Republican rally in Webster City on October 8, when he was under direct attack. The Webster City *Hamilton Freeman,* in reporting the meeting, italicized Carpenter's statement of his position: *"He believes the state by all constitutional means should foster the D. & P. R. R. and hasten the day of its completion. Any such law which might be introduced would receive his hearty support if he was elected."* [12]

As the time of the election drew near, the *Sentinel* increased its criticism of Carpenter, accusing him of "abusing Duncombe personally," a charge which the *Freeman* indignantly denied. On October 6, C. B. Richards of Fort Dodge wrote to Carpenter, out on canvass, that "the Dem are working like hell," getting up "bogus tickets with your name spelled wrong." Since each party printed its own ballots, this was an ever-present danger and a popular practice in frontier elections. Richards advised Carpenter to "blow on this like the Devil." Two days later the *Freeman* reported this trick to its readers, urging them to "Beware of Split Tickets," and claiming that "the Democracy have circulated about four cart-loads of split tickets throughout this District."[13] In a whirl of accusations and denials, the campaign came to an end, and on October 13 the voters went to the polls.

"Glory Enough for One Day!" Thus the *Freeman* announced Carpenter's election.[14] In spite of headlines and enthusiasm, however, it had been a narrow victory. Because of the distances and difficulty of communication in northwestern Iowa, the *Freeman* could not print its triumphant headline until October 29. Up in Dickinson County on the Minnesota border, for instance, after the canvass of the ballots showed an almost unanimous vote for Carpenter, the question arose as to how the returns were to reach Fort Dodge. One man finally volunteered to make the long trip, but when only part way to Webster County he met Emmett Carpenter, who was on his way north to collect the returns from the isolated counties around the lakes. Since the election was close, every vote counted, and Dickinson County voters liked to believe that their returns swung the balance to their favorite.[15] Some voters in northern counties were not sure of their district, and in Worth County some even cast their votes for the candidate of the Twelfth District, while others voted for Carpenter of the Thirteenth.[16]

So close was the vote, in fact, that there was some talk that Duncombe might contest it. But it was soon evident, as the returns from the rest of the state came in, that the election had been a Republican victory and that one more Democrat in the House would not change the vote for United States Senator—the paramount issue in the campaign. The Republicans had elected the state officers and had gained control of the General Assembly by a margin of twenty-two to fourteen in the Senate and forty-one to thirty-one in the House.[17]

In spite of their victory, however, the Republicans had cause for concern. In the presidential election of 1856, Frémont had carried Iowa by a majority of 8,000; in 1857 Lowe was elected Governor by a margin of only about 2,500 votes. The Dubuque *Times* scolded the party for this lack of interest, accused the Democrats of producing a "feeling of indifference," and warned Republicans that they "must become better organized, and turn out more fully, or they will lose the State."[18]

But such worries were far from the thoughts of Carpenter and his supporters. Webster City held a "Carpenter Supper" on November 4, with feasting, dancing, and the drinking of toasts. The local paper was at pains to point out that "no wines or liquors" were drunk during these toasts—a fact that would "astonish the 'rank and file' of Democracy, and probably the leaders." [19]

Carpenter's speech on the occasion, although in many respects typical of the times, contained sections that indicate that the young man was a thoughtful observer of life about him. He had been on the Iowa frontier for only a few years, but he had watched and been a part of the rapidly developing society. As he saw it, in the "rise and progress" of the western states, "there have been three distinct and separate eras." First came the pioneers, "with no apparent object in view but to keep in advance of civilization." They broke the sod, built cabins, planted fields of corn, and made "a butcher's shop of the boundless forests." But "fast upon the track" of the pioneer came the land speculator, the second era of the frontier opened, and "the whole country becomes a scene of wild and giddy speculation." But now, said Carpenter, we have passed this second era, and have reached the third —that of "genuine laborious effort, for solid wealth, and permanent improvement." With a combination of standard cliches and occasional flashes of colorful and original phraseology, Carpenter then launched into the usual panegyric of good times ahead, with the people opening farms, erecting homes, establishing factories, and building railroads—all under the protection of "a discriminating protective Tariff." He concluded by thanking them in properly glowing terms for the honor they had shown him, and by promising that he would look back upon the occasion as "the most cheering 'Oasis' in the Desert of my life." [20]

During the two months before the convening of the Seventh General Assembly, Carpenter, like all members of that legislature, was besieged with advice, suggestions, and requests for support. The first big issue that attracted attention, as soon as the makeup of the legislature had been determined, was of course the election of a United States Senator. Iowa's first two Senators had been Democrats. Augustus Caesar Dodge had been replaced by Whig (later Republican) James Harlan in 1855; now a Republican legislature in Iowa had a chance to remove the other Democratic Senator, George Wallace Jones. Retiring Governor Grimes was spoken of most often and seemed to have the largest support not only among the legislators but throughout the state.

An impartial observer would have expected Grimes to be the unanimous choice of his party. He had been a popular Governor; during his administration and under his guidance the Republican party had been organized and had now conducted two successful campaigns. Most of the minor Republican officials of the state—Carpenter among them—looked upon Grimes as the only possible choice to represent Iowa in Washington. However, as in all political parties, even new ones, strains and tensions had developed.

Certain elements in the state were jealous of the position and influence of Grimes and his wing of the party. These dissidents offered various excuses for their opposition.

The ever-popular "locality" issue was agitated: most of Iowa's chief officials were from the southern half of the state—surely the next Senator should come from the north, in justice to the claims of geography. Another argument advanced was that all Republicans elected had been former Whigs; the other groups that made up the new party—Anti-Nebraska Democrats or Free-Soilers—felt that one of their number should now have the senatorship.[21] There is also evidence that some of the Republicans were restive under what they considered dictatorial elements in the party. John Teesdale, editor of the Republican Des Moines *Iowa Citizen,* was a supporter of Grimes and himself a candidate for state printer, but in his columns he consistently and sanctimoniously refused to discuss the senatorial question or to publish articles written by others on the subject. Two Republicans, writing under the pseudonym "Iowa," submitted their rejected comments to the Democratic editor of the Des Moines *Iowa State Journal* who, always ready to contribute to Republican disaffection, published them. The *Journal's* editor, William Porter, strongly opposed any "gagging" of the press, while "Iowa" compared Teesdale's action to the dictatorship of Louis Napoleon. Everybody knew, Editor Porter chimed in, that Teesdale was "owned, body, soul and breeches, by one of the candidates for U. S. Senator," that he was "under the pay and committed to the fortunes of one of the candidates."[22] Granting the political animus of the Democratic paper, there would still seem to be some evidence of a certain lack of harmony within the Republican ranks. For many years the existence of what came to be known as the "Des Moines Ring" or the "Des Moines Regency" caused many intraparty fights. The struggle for the senatorship in 1858 was one of the first of these squabbles.

Carpenter, as a freshman legislator, was only on the outskirts of this fight. On November 17, 1857, Elijah Sells, Republican secretary of state, wrote Carpenter what was patently a form letter to all Republican members of the General Assembly, congratulating him on his election, pointing out certain important issues that would come before the legislature, and suggesting the priority of the claims of Grimes on the senatorship. On November 1, Carpenter had written to Governor Grimes, asking for a report on the Des Moines River Improvement Lands. Grimes sent the report with a letter in which he discussed the various problems facing the state, assured Carpenter that "we shall not allow you to be ejected from your seat" should Duncombe try to contest the election, and closed with the statement—hardly a surprise to Carpenter—that "Perhaps you are aware that I am a candidate for the Senate in lieu of Gen Jones." He would be pleased if Carpenter should support him, Grimes said. Carpenter, who admired the Governor tremendously, undoubtedly answered with the proper assurances.[23]

The second issue that claimed Carpenter's attention in the months before the legislature met was the question of the disposal of the lands along the Des Moines River, originally granted to the state by Congress in 1846 for improvements in the navigability of the river. The state had at first appointed a board to administer the lands, but in 1853 the grant had been transferred to the Des Moines Navigation and Railroad Company. Very little had been accomplished by way of "improving" the river, either by the state board or by the new company, with the exception of a few dams. By 1857, with the railroads pushing into Iowa, interest in river navigation waned, and the various railroads began to clamor for a transfer of the remaining lands of the grant to them. In addition to this contest, there was considerable doubt as to the exact extent of the grant, owing to the faulty wording of the original act. Some claimed the lands extended only from the mouth of the Des Moines to the Racoon Fork at Des Moines, while others, particularly in the counties north of Des Moines, insisted that the grant extended northward to the Minnesota border.[24] Whatever the extent of the grant, several railroads wanted it, in particular the Dubuque & Pacific, the road in which Senator Jones and John F. Duncombe were most interested, and the road which, according to Grimes, had worked against Carpenter's election because of his declared position in favor of granting the lands to a proposed north-south line along the river—the Keokuk, Fort Des Moines & Minnesota Railroad.[25]

Carpenter's district favored the transfer of the lands to the north-south railroad rather than to any of the east-west lines that had already been allotted their share of the 1856 railroad land grant. On December 19, 1857, citizens of Fort Dodge held a meeting "for the purpose of memorializing the Legislature of the state upon the subject of the Des Moines River grant." Resolutions were adopted asking that the lands be granted "for the construction of a Railroad from the city of Keokuk on the Mississippi river through the Des Moines valley, said Railroad to be co-extensive in length with said land grant." The committee that drew up the resolutions consisted of Carpenter, Charles B. Richards, Samuel Rees, John M. Stockdale, and Robert K. Wilson.[26] On the day of the meeting Carpenter wrote to Iowa's representatives in Washington, asking their support for the transfer of the congressional land grant to this projected road. Senator Harlan answered cordially, promising his support; Timothy Davis of Dubuque, Representative from the Second District, promised "any service in my power to divert the grant to a more useful and patriotic purpose."[27] There is no record of Representative Samuel R. Curtis' reply, but he probably sided with his Republican colleagues. Naturally, help was neither solicited nor expected from Senator Jones.

With the ball rolling on the Des Moines River grant project, and with his position as a Grimes man fully established, Carpenter departed early in January of 1858 for Des Moines, "a little shabby frontier town of less than 3,000 inhabitants."[28] The journey by stagecoach from Fort Dodge to the new capital city took two days. Hoyt Sherman, a Des Moines banker whose brother, William Tecumseh Sherman, would soon win fame in the Civil War, had suggested rooms for Carpenter at the home of Willson Alexander Scott on the east side of the river near the new statehouse, "at $8 per week." Most of the hotels on the west side of town charged as much as $2.00 per day, Sherman explained, and, although they would furnish "Omnibuses or Carriages to the Capitol," they would probably charge extra for such service. The quarters at Scott's would be "first rate," he assured Carpenter.[29]

The space between the river and the capitol was a muddy swamp, although it had been marked out in streets, lots, and alleys in the optimistic days before the crash of 1857 had called a halt to real estate booms. But the people of Des Moines tried to make up for the shortcomings of their little town by a lavish hospitality—at least as lavish as the frontier could afford. On the west side of the Des Moines River, at the "only hotel of much pretentions"—the Demoine House—stagecoaches daily "deposited the members, strangers, and gentlemen of the 'Third House' [lobbyists], as they came to the new capital on their various missions." There Governor Grimes had rooms, and there Ralph P. Lowe awaited his inauguration. The "soft coal stoves glowed with a red heat" to welcome the shivering passengers who had ridden for long hours "through the great snow drifts that filled the sloughs and ravines" along the primitive roads surrounding the capital.[30]

Among the thirty-six Senators and seventy-two Representatives who made up the Seventh General Assembly were many who would later make their mark in state and nation. There were two future Governors: Samuel J. Kirkwood and Cyrus C. Carpenter; two Lieutenant Governors: Benjamin F. Gue and Nicholas J. Rusch; and a Senator, James F. Wilson of Fairfield. Many future Congressmen were also starting their political careers in 1858. The clerk of the House was twenty-two-year-old William Peters Hepburn, whose long career in Congress made him one of the best-known of Iowans. There were, in addition, two future Cabinet members: William W. Belknap, Grant's Secretary of War, who would resign in disgrace; and George W. McCrary, Secretary of War under Rutherford B. Hayes. Kirkwood would also serve as a Senator and as Secretary of the Interior under Garfield and Arthur. There was J. B. Grinnell, who had founded the town and college of that name, and who later joined forces with the Liberal Republicans. Samuel E. Rankin was also serving in the House; his "defalcation" when state treasurer during Carpenter's first administration would cause "Honest Cy" considerable embarrassment.[31] In the Senate there was Alvin Saunders of Henry County, later to become Territorial Governor of Nebraska and a United States Senator from that state.

The leader of the Democrats in the House, Dennis A. Mahony, former editor of the Dubuque *Herald,* was only thirty-seven in 1858, but because of a palsy that caused his head to shake, he appeared much older. "When he rose to speak," Carpenter wrote years later, "he stood with the tips of the fingers of both hands touching the desk before him. He never made a gesture, but just talked with an accuracy of diction and a force of logic which always gave him the undivided attention of the House." [32]

The statehouse, where the legislature assembled on January 11, 1858, was a new three-story brick building, erected at a cost of about $30,000 by a group of East Des Moines businessmen known as the Capitol Building Association. It stood south of the present Capitol Square on the site now occupied by the Soldiers and Sailors Monument. This was then known as "Scott's Addition," a real estate development of Carpenter's landlord, W. A. Scott. The first and second floors of the capitol were divided into offices for the state officials, the supreme court, and the state library, while the third floor contained the House and Senate chambers.[33] Here, in this modest structure, Iowa's government was carried on for twenty-six years.

Carpenter's first contact with "practical politics" was something of a shock. He wrote to Kate Burkholder in Fort Dodge:

> Well for one week I have been in the legislature and I find that it is no such great thing after all. There is something about every thing done in this place cold formal and designing. After all I had rather spend an hour with good warm hearted friends than to meet with business committees and prepare the cold formalities of legislation. You will perceive by the newspapers that I keep doing something tho' I believe my ambitious ardor will begin to cool down a little after I have seen a little more of the sad selfishness of legislation. The usual excitement and turmoil incident to the election of the U S Senator now agitates the Gen Assembly and I almost fear that Gov Grimes is going to be sacrificed on the altar of some other mans selfishness. While I am writing to you, in the adjoining room I hear half a dozen men concurring and attempting to concoct a plan whereby they can secure the defeat of Grimes. And when I think of the base schemes they are willing to resort to in order to defeat the man who has done more for the Republican party and our state than any other man living; my heart sickens at the name of politics.[34]

Traditionally, the party caucuses to name candidates for the senatorship were held almost as soon as the legislature had organized. But Grimes' opponents waged a delaying action in order to marshal their forces against him, and repeated caucuses were held before an agreement on a date for the vote was reached. True to its campaign of silence—the Democrats called it censorship—the Republican *Iowa Citizen* of Des Moines made no mention of these political maneuverings. The Democratic papers, however, lost no opportunity to jibe at the Republican factions that were holding up the vote. In his letter to Kate Burkholder on January 15, Carpenter mentioned that he had just returned from "an exciting caucus of the Republican members of the Legislature." The *Journal* described this caucus in more detail:

> The Republican members of the Legislature, together with the candidates, and the members of the "Third House," have a good time of it in caucusing together. The members have had a number of meetings, but brotherly love will not prevail, and the meetings so far have not answered the question as to "who shall be U. S. Senator?" On Friday evening [January 15] a caucus was held, and as we learn from our special messenger, some nice sparring in a quiet way was the result. A motion to proceed to balloting as soon as possible for a candidate for Senator was promptly negatived, and afterwards it was agreed to hold a caucus this evening for the purpose of deciding *when* the nomination should be made.
> . . . . Grimes and his friends want to go into a nominating caucus immediately, but his opponents are determined to delay it as much as possible. While every day Grimes is losing strength, the opposition are gaining, and organizing and harmonizing their forces. The Ex-Governor's chances are growing beautifully less and smaller by degrees, and the arrogant tone adopted by himself and friends now begins to quaver with the fear of approaching defeat.[35]

A reporter of the Dubuque *Herald* held the opposite view. He commented on January 13 that: "The opponents of Gov. Grimes for the Senatorship are doing their utmost to put off the day of election with the hope of defeating him," but he was sure they would not succeed.[36] At last, when the rebel faction was unable to delay longer or to develop a winning combination against the ex-Governor, the Republicans caucused on Monday, January 25, fourteen days after the legislature had met, and nominated James W. Grimes for the Senate to succeed George W. Jones. Grimes received thirty-eight of the sixty-two votes cast on the first formal ballot, and his election was at once declared unanimous.[37] His unsuccessful opponents were James Thorington of Davenport, Judge William Smyth of Linn County, and Timothy Davis of Dubuque. Other serious contenders, especially Fitz Henry Warren of Burlington, William Penn Clarke of Iowa City, and F. E. Bissell of Dubuque (whom Grimes had earlier expected to show the greatest strength against him), had dropped out of the contest.[38] Grimes reported his success to his wife:

> I have just been nominated by the Republican caucus for United States Senator, for six years from March 4, 1859. I received the nomination on the first ballot, by five majority. My vote would have been much larger,

and nearly unanimous, on the second ballot—as many voted for persons in their own counties on the first ballot, by way of compliment, who would have voted for me on the second ballot, and for me on the first had their votes been necessary.[39]

The closing words, "had their votes been necessary," indicate that the Grimes forces had things well in hand, and that all plots against him had failed.

The Democrats, who had been watching the Republican fight from the sidelines, met and named Benjamin M. Samuels of Dubuque—a purely honorary nomination, since the majority of Republicans in the legislature made the election of Grimes by that body a mere formality, once the Republican caucus had reached agreement.[40]

Meanwhile, the work of the legislature progressed, interspersed with the festivities incident to a new government. The citizens of Des Moines had entertained the members of the legislature in what Carpenter called "a whole-souled western 'blow-out.'" The inauguration ball was "a *great* '*scrouge*,'" but the inauguration itself was, to the idealistic young man, "a solemn and impressive ceremony."[41] On the evening of January 25, complying with tradition, Senator-elect Grimes entertained at the Demoine House, with a dinner "got up . . . on temperance principles" for 178 guests.[42]

All was not feasting and parties, however. In the brick capitol, the formalities of legislation and the informalities of party strife went forward as usual. The opening days of the legislature were taken up not only with the senatorial contest, but with the discussion of a resolution dealing with the government of Kansas. The Iowa legislature, of course, had nothing to do with the admission of another state into the Union, but the whole nation had been stirred by antislavery, "Bleeding Kansas," the Dred Scott Decision, and now by the efforts to make Kansas a slave state under the Lecompton Constitution. Such was the widespread agitation over these issues that mere "localisms" were forced into the background in most northern states. Certainly this was the case in Iowa, where most of the candidates for the General Assembly had campaigned on national issues—as had Carpenter—almost to the exclusion of mere state problems.

On January 19, John W. Rankin of Lee County introduced into the Iowa Senate a "Preamble and Joint Resolution" condemning the admission of Kansas under the Lecompton Constitution. Iowa's two United States Senators were "instructed" and the two Congressmen were "requested" to oppose the admission of Kansas; furthermore, the Senators were "requested" to resign "unless they can support the foregoing resolves." This latter was, of course, directed against Senator George W. Jones. In addition, the resolution was an effort to force the Democratic members of both houses of the state legislature to defend an unpopular measure.

In the Iowa Senate, however, the Democrats refused to debate the issue at all. Senator Rankin delivered a long speech favoring his resolution. At its close, a deep silence fell upon the chamber. Republicans stirred restlessly, waiting for some Democrat to rise in rebuttal. "The Democratic Senators," reported an editor, "sat behind their desks smiling complacently upon the uneasiness of their Republican friends, and displaying no intention of replying to the lengthy speech just delivered." Taunted by the Republicans in an effort to anger them into debate, the Democrats still refused to answer. The Republicans, frustrated in their efforts to start a fight, surrendered and allowed the resolution to come to a vote, when it passed on a strict party basis. In the House, on the next day, the Democratic members were not so reticent. Mahony offered a substitute that was voted down by the majority. When the minutes appeared the following day in the newspapers there was no mention of Mahony's proposal; in fact, the only space given to the whole debate was the following: "At four o'clock and 30 minutes the committee [of the whole] rose, and by its Chairman, reported the resolutions back without amendment and recommended their passage." When Mahony protested the omission, the Speaker replied that it was "in accordance with parliamentary rule and the usage of this House," and his decision was sustained. Needless to say, Democratic editor William Porter made the most of this "Tyranny of the Majority" in the columns of his paper.

The resolutions thus passed both houses, by a party vote in each case, without setting off the fireworks the Republicans had expected and intended.[43] A note of warning was sounded, however, when Lincoln Clark of Dubuque announced, immediately after the vote, that he would "on tomorrow or some future day, present a protest against the passage" of the resolution.[44] Several weeks passed, and nothing further was heard from Mr. Clark.

The subject was not closed, however. On February 17, catching the Republican majority unawares, twenty-two Democrats, headed by Lincoln Clark, introduced a "Protest" and moved that it be "spread upon the Journals of this House." [45] The ensuing debate resulted in such a parliamentary tangle, with motion following motion, with demands for the previous question, with points of order raised, that finally even the Speaker had lost all hold over the proceedings. "Several appeals were made to the good sense of the House to put an end to these disgraceful proceedings," reported Editor Porter. "The House at the time, had no 'good sense,' or if it had it had forgotten its possession of that enviable qualification; so no one would withdraw his motion or call." When at last a vote was reached, as to whether the protest could be entered in the Journal, only eight voted against its inclusion. Dennis Mahony promptly gave notice that he would "at some future day" present a protest against both the original resolution and the protest of his fellow-Democrats. With that, the House adjourned.[46]

An anticlimax came the next morning. Overnight Clark had studied his law and had found that the whole controversy was unnecessary, since any member could enter a protest in the Journal without a vote of the House.[47] Of more significance, since it indicated the trend within the Democratic party, was the "Protest" by Dennis Mahony and four other Democrats that was entered in the Journal without comment.[48]

These two Democratic pronouncements illustrated the growing split in the party—a split which would eventually lead to the defeat of 1860. The Republican resolution had, aside from opposing the admission of Kansas under the Lecompton Constitution, condemned President Buchanan and all others in the government who had consented to that constitution. Clark and his Democratic group objected to this condemnation, claiming that the General Assembly of Iowa "has no jurisdiction in Law over the President of the United States," and no power or right to condemn Senators of other states for their actions. Then followed the statement to which Mahony and his four associates took exception: Clark had, in effect, agreed with the Republicans that there was something very wrong with the adoption of the Lecompton Constitution in Kansas, that the people did not have a chance to "pass their judgment" upon it, and therefore Congress had the right to "go behind the constitution" as presented and inquire into its legality. Mahony, on the other hand, took the extreme position that the people of Kansas had the right to delegate their powers to the state legislature, and that Congress had no right to "go behind the constitution" as presented to them by the duly constituted power of the people of Kansas.[49] Thus were the lines drawn, not only between Republican and Democrat, but between Democrat and Democrat.

This conflict within the Democratic party of Iowa was a reflection of the battle being waged in Washington between the followers of Stephen A. Douglas, who opposed the admission of Kansas under the Lecompton Constitution, and those who stood behind President Buchanan in his insistence that the provisions for voting on the Kansas document should stand. The "Little Giant" from Illinois waged a valiant fight to wrest control of his party from the President and the Southern Democrats. "By God, Sir, I made Mr. James Buchanan!" Douglas said, "and by God, Sir, I will unmake him." [50] The result was the ill-fated geographical split among the Democrats, with Northerners following Douglas and Southerners supporting Buchanan. In Iowa, every Democratic paper except the Dubuque *Northwest* rallied behind the Illinois Senator. Lincoln Clark and his supporters were of this wing of the Democratic party, while Mahony and his four colleagues stood behind the President. The Dubuque *Express and Herald,* formerly edited by Mahony, was a Douglas paper; its attacks on the rival *Northwest* were quite as virulent as those traditional between Democrats and Republicans. The *Northwest* editor, in the opinion of the *Express and Herald,* was "base hearted and unprincipled," "an imported scavenger of political filth," "a poor nincompoop." [51] In the face of this violent language, it is not surprising to discover that the *Express and Herald* found no room in its columns for a report of the Mahony protest, which supported the administration's position. Mahony was taking a stand different from that of his one-time associates; therefore, rather than attack him personally, they chose to ignore him.

National issues occupied only a small part of the time of the General Assembly, in spite of this early preoccupation with the affairs of the nation. Probably the most important legislation before the Seventh General Assembly was the enacting of Iowa's first banking laws. The 1846 constitutional convention, dominated by anti-bank Democrats, had succeeded in prohibiting any banks of issue in the new state. The constitutional convention of 1857, with changing times and changing party emphasis, had provided for the legalizing of banks in the state, although not until after a considerable struggle with the Democratic members. [52] Even then, Governor Grimes in his farewell message warned the legislators of the General Assembly "that banks are to be established to secure the *public welfare* and not to promote the purposes of the stockholders and capitalists, and that it is far better that banks should realize small profits, than that the public should be liable to injury by their suspension or failure." [53]

The result was a "Free Banking Bill" so complicated and involved that no bank was ever established under it; in 1870 the law was repealed. The legislature of 1858 seemed satisfied with its work, however, since the bill passed the House by a vote of 40 to 25, the Senate by a vote of 23 to 5. Those in opposition were largely Democrats, but there were a few Republicans among them. Philip B. Bradley, Democrat of Jackson County, had the last word in the House; immediately after the bill's passage, he proposed an amendment to the title of the bill, substituting the word "swindling" for "banking." Needless to say, his motion lost. [54]

A bill to establish a State Bank and branches was introduced into the Senate, where it was debated off and on for about four weeks before passage by a vote of 28 to 4; the House concurred, with a slight amendment, 45 to 18. Carpenter, as a loyal Republican, voted with the majority in the House. Both bills were accepted by an overwhelming majority of the voters at an election on June 28. [55]

Banks and railroads were exciting topics of conversation and legislation during 1858. But while the tangled financial arguments for and against banks may have confused many, there was no mystery about a railroad. It was something that every town wanted; every county was willing to vote aid to a prospective railroad; every legislature besieged Congress with petitions for larger land grants. By 1858, the four east-west lines that had benefited by the 1856 federal grant were building as fast as local aid and Eastern financiers made it possible. The southernmost—the Burlington & Missouri River—had reached Mount Pleasant from its starting point at Burlington, and was now nearing Fairfield. The Mississippi & Missouri had completed its main line from Davenport to Iowa City, had pushed branches southwest to Muscatine and Washington, and was trying to get construction under way west of Iowa City. The Iowa Central Air line, starting from Clinton, was pushing toward Clarence, some forty miles away. To the north the Dubuque & Pacific had reached only across Dubuque County to Dyersville in its race for the far Pacific. With east-west roads assured, Iowans turned their attention to north-south lines, and the one that attracted the most attention in the spring of 1858 was the Keokuk, Fort Des Moines & Minnesota, which planned to build along the Des Moines Valley and wanted the unused land grant of the Des Moines Improvement Company to help them do so. By 1858, the road had reached only as far as Bentonsport in Van Buren County, from its starting point at Keokuk.[56]

By this time it had become obvious to all that the Des Moines Navigation and Railroad Company, which had taken over the task—and the land grant —of the Des Moines Valley Improvement project, was a complete failure. There was no doubt that the Seventh General Assembly would cancel its agreement with the Navigation Company and would transfer the land grant to a railroad. Webster County had already voted its preference for the Keokuk, Fort Des Moines & Minnesota road. The House appointed a committee of five on the "Improvement of the Des Moines" with Carpenter of Webster County as chairman. His Republican colleagues were Thomas Mitchell of Polk County and C. E. Millard of Warren; the Democrats were Squire Ayers of Van Buren County and Cornelius Beal of Boone.[57]

In response to a request from this committee, Governor Lowe on February 16 sent the House a message on the status of the Des Moines River grant, with the suggestion that a joint committee be appointed to settle with the Navigation Company. Carpenter and Belknap from the House and William Loughridge from the Senate were chosen.[58] That the committee was "stacked" in favor of transferring the grant to the Keokuk, Fort Des Moines & Minnesota was obvious, since the three members came from counties along the Des Moines valley—Carpenter from Webster, Belknap from Lee, and Loughridge from Mahaska. Mahony at once protested the Senate's choice of Loughridge, and the House agreed with him. Certain Senators also doubted the advisability of placing Loughridge on the committee, but a compromise finally was reached by adding a fourth member, J. W. Jenkins from Jackson County.[59]

The real struggle within the legislature on the whole question of the lands originally granted for the improvement of the Des Moines River was a geographical rather than a political contest, although party strife could seldom be quelled for long. Cornelius Beal, Democrat of Boone, a county through which both the east-west Iowa Central Air Line and the north-south Keokuk, Fort Des Moines & Minnesota would run, combined political hostility with a partiality for the Air Line road into an attack on the River Lands settlement in general and C. C. Carpenter in particular. This hostility finally resulted in a fight—certainly verbal and possibly physical—over a debate on quite another issue, resulting in the publication of a letter by Beal in the Des Moines *Journal,* in which he accused Carpenter of lying. There were rumors in Fort Dodge that the two had come to blows, and Kate Burkholder chided Cyrus: "La! Carpenter how indiscreet in you indeed. To conduct [yourself] so in the Hall of Representatives. Talk about command of self after this will you." [60] In the debate over members of the special committee for the Des Moines River settlement, Beal had tried to have W. W. Belknap, then a fellow Democrat, replaced by Horace Anthony, a Republican but a resident of Clinton County, where, it must be inferred, the interests of the Air Line road would have received more support. Beal's efforts in this failed, undoubtedly increasing his animosity toward the whole scheme.[61]

A great deal of mystery surrounds the final settlement between the state and the Navigation Company. That there were behind-the-scenes deals is fairly certain, but just what these deals were and who participated are matters of conjecture. Although two writers later stated that the Navigation Company and the Railroad Company were actually one and the same, not a hint of this appeared at the time.[62] Had such been the case, surely some of the opponents of the settlement would have brought it out during the lengthy debates in both the House and the Senate. Since they did not, either the allegation is false or it was a wonderfully well kept secret in 1858.

The final agreement provided that the Navigation Company should pay the state the sum of $20,000 and should receive the part of the land grant that had so far been certified to the state, in return for canceling their contract. According to Governor Lowe's message to the General Assembly, the original size of the 1846 grant from Congress was 853,430 acres, of which 593,430.89 acres had been certified to the state. Of these, the state had sold 327,314.53 acres, while some 205,489.23 had been transferred to the Navigation Company since it had taken over the work, leaving some 37,000 acres yet to be sold.[63] This is only one set of figures, however. Many variations of the totals appeared during the long struggle over the lands.

The location of the grant was another point at issue, since nobody, either in the state or federal governments, could agree as to just where the grant should be located. No less than four or five different decisions had come from Washington over the years, each contradicting the preceding. Did the grant extend only to the Raccoon Fork of the Des Moines River, or did it extend to the source of that river? Several clear-cut answers had been given, only to be reversed within a year or so by a different official or a new administration. Meanwhile, squatters had moved into the area above Des Moines, locating on odd-numbered or even-numbered sections as they made their choices. Herein lay the seeds of a tragedy of errors in which the innocent victims of the shifting governmental decisions lost the lands they had improved and paid for in good faith.[64]

When the Navigation Company began to lay claim to certain of these lands above Des Moines, the people protested violently. As early as January 20, 1858, Carpenter received an agitated letter from a constituent in Dakota City in Humboldt County, north of Fort Dodge:

> Our Neighbourhood has been the scene of Considerable excitement for a few days past. A Mr Warner from Fort Demoin Purporting himself to be agent of the Demoin River Co has been up here and appointed old Billy Miller Sub agent or Rather a (Spy) and we are having quite a time over it. We have all made up our minds that we will pay no attention to the *damed* [sic] old Skunk he has skined all the odd Sections about here of all the Best of the Timber and now he is turning traitor against us. We will give him *Hell* under the shirt before he gets through with it. Now Friend C. I want you to see the Gov or Sec of State . . . and ask what Decisions have been made if any. Whether the River Company has any Title or are they like to have any to the lands up here Can they do any thing with us as the thing stands Is the legislature doing any thing about the Matter.[65]

This letter was more profane than most of the correspondence received by Carpenter on the River Land question, but all carried the same tone—do something about the titles and about having the lands transferred to a railroad to be built up the Des Moines valley. Whereas the Navigation Company was completely discredited, and the giving of any lands to that company was violently opposed, yet a grant of the same lands to a railroad—as yet an unknown evil—was heartily supported. Letters and petitions "praying for a diversion" of the land grant were numerous.[66]

Although his constituents seemed to be of one mind as to the disposal of the land grant, Carpenter's colleagues in the House were not nearly so unanimous. The joint committee, the officers of the Navigation Company, and the state commissioner for the lands, Edwin Manning of Keosauqua, finally reached agreement, and the result was reported to the Senate on March 10, to the House on March 15. In addition to providing for the financial and land settlement with the Navigation Company, the resolution stipulated that some 25,000 acres above the Raccoon Fork should not go to the Company and that the balance of the congressional grant should go to the Keokuk, Fort Des Moines & Minnesota to aid in building that road. Of these lands, one-fourth were to be applied to building the road above the city of Des Moines.[67] To the majority of the legislators, and to a majority of the people of the state, this was a logical disposition of the grant. Lands for railroad purposes were to lie along the line of the track—such had been the case with the 1856 grant. A minority of the members, however, sought to change this admittedly short-lived tradition and divide the lands among certain other roads in which the legislators may or may not have had financial interests.

The issue was debated in the Senate for several hours on March 10. J. B. Grinnell of Poweshiek County, on the projected line of the Mississippi & Missouri Railroad, objected to the diversion of the lands to the "Des Moines Valley Railroad" as the Keokuk, Fort Des Moines & Minnesota was popularly called, and argued in favor of dividing the grant among other roads. Samuel J. Kirkwood of Iowa City—also on the line of the Mississippi & Missouri—likewise opposed, as did several others in the final vote in which a stubborn nine stood out against the diversion.[68]

Grinnell's argument was repeated when the resolution came up for consideration in the House on March 15. There the opponents were more vocal, they forced debate on the measure through four days of bitter controversy, voting of amendments, recommitting to the committee, and all the usual parliamentary delays. Ellsworth N. Bates of Linn County argued strenuously for a diversion of the lands to railroads throughout the state. The rights of all the people had been "outraged" by the Navigation Company, he said, therefore all should benefit in the settlement. George W. McCrary replied that such a suggestion was "contrary to all the customs of the State heretofore. Lands had been granted to the roads through which they run." The officials of the Navigation Company, argued W. H. Seevers of Mahaska County, were "a set of scoundrels and swindlers," but "we are in their clutches" and must accept the agreement. T. W. Jackson, representing Tama and Marshall counties, said that diversion of the lands to any road but the one in the valley would be "the grossest injustice ever done in Christendom." Finally tempers cooled, Mahony proposed several minor amendments which were accepted, and the resolution passed with only one vote in opposition.[69]

One of Mahony's amendments had stipulated that the Navigation Company be given sixty days to accept the agreement. The alacrity with which the company agreed to the terms would seem to indicate that they had made a good bargain and wished to take advantage of it before the legislators changed their minds. The measure was signed by Governor Lowe on March

22; on April 15, the officers of the Navigation Company met in New York and accepted the terms.[70] Meanwhile, a bill had been introduced into Congress to permit the transfer of the lands originally granted for river improvement. Moving ponderously, Congress as last agreed to the transfer to the railroad company on July 12, 1862.[71]

Carpenter, while serving on the joint committee for the settlement, had taken little part in the debate, except to speak out for the interests of his section and incidentally of the north-south railroad, when he strongly opposed giving part of the lands to any road except that to be built up the Des Moines valley.[72] The attitude of people "above the Raccoon Fork" was mixed as to the whole transaction. At Boone, the editor of the *News* lashed out "in the most approved billingsgate" at Carpenter and others for their stand, according to Carpenter's friend Aldrich. In reply, Aldrich advised the Boone County people to "cork up their wrath and keep their shirts on. It will be cooler by-and bye." [73] "One of the People," writing in a Des Moines paper, claimed that much of this discontent could be traced to the Mississippi & Missouri Railroad, which wanted some of the land grant. He warned the managers of the road to be careful or they would "raise an excitement" in Polk County that would "sweep away" the $300,000 county loan that they were asking for.[74] The rumblings and grumblings continued, and Carpenter received his share of the barbs.

Although the part Carpenter played in the River Land settlement would rise to plague him for many years, another action of the legislature in 1858 had more bearing on his immediate political future. This was a squabble over four townships—Ranges 27, 28, 29, and 30 West of Township 90 North. These townships along the northern border of Webster County had been separated from Webster and given to Humboldt when that county had been created by the Sixth General Assembly in 1857. That, at least, was the memory of the legislators and the evidence of the newspapers. However, the act establishing Humboldt County failed to list Township 90. A further complication arose from the fact that between the meetings of the Sixth and Seventh General Assemblies a new constitution had been written and adopted, providing that no county boundaries could be changed without a vote of the counties involved. When, therefore, a bill was introduced into the Senate to correct the act of 1857 by adding the four townships known collectively as "Township 90" to Humboldt, the citizens of Webster County bombarded Carpenter with letters, pleas, threats, and petitions.

Satan and his abode seemed to have played a large part in the excitement, judging from the letters received. A. M. Dawley, in a communication considered by J. J. Barclay as "impertinent & uncalled for," warned Carpenter that if he did not work against the bill "all hell wont save you from the [charge] of being bought." Barclay suggested that all those who were "finding fault" with Carpenter should "go to *Hell* with their opinions," but J. D. Burkholder (Carpenter's future father-in-law) assured him that he had been right in his course of action, and therefore he "need not fear the combined powers of men & Devils." [75]

When the bill in dispute, which had passed the Senate without any dissent, came up in the House, Carpenter presented an amendment calling for an election to decide the issue. His motion lost, and the bill passed the House by a vote of 40 to 21. That Carpenter was right in his amendment was confirmed by the State Supreme Court in 1860, when it declared the act of 1858 void and the act of 1857, as printed, correct.[76] But this vindication was two years in the future; in 1858, Carpenter bore the brunt of the attack at home. Aside from the usual Democratic carping, a split among Webster County Republicans resulted in numerous accusing letters that left Carpenter in the middle of a family fight. Dark and unsubstantiated hints of bribes and of shady dealings among land speculators as a background to "Town 90" were bandied about. Small wonder, then, that Carpenter returned to Fort Dodge somewhat embittered with politics.

Before that return, however, Carpenter had played his role as a legislator conscientiously if quietly. Aside from the hot arguments over Lecompton and the River Lands, the Seventh General Assembly had accomplished worthwhile and lasting, if not spectacular, work. Sparked by the enthusiasm of three young legislators—Benjamin F. Gue of Scott, Robert A. Richardson of Fayette, and Ed Wright of Cedar Counties—a reluctant legislature was induced to provide for the establishment of an Agricultural College and Farm.[77] This was the genesis of Iowa's famous agricultural college at Ames. Of equal importance was the long awaited general education bill, upon which previous legislatures had received the advice of Horace Mann.[78] A Commission was also appointed to codify the laws of Iowa to conform to the new constitution of the state. An asylum for the blind was established at Vinton; the boundaries of the state's judicial districts were revised; and all the other matters, large and small, which come before a state legislature were handled with a greater or lesser degree of "politics," depending on the importance of the issue.

In all this, Carpenter took an unspectacular part. He voted with the Republicans on party issues, with the majority on nonpolitical ones. His first term as a state legislator, like his later two terms as a Congressman, indicated that as a lawmaker he did not have the necessary fire and force to play an outstanding role. In his quiet way he made many friends; his lack of aggressiveness made few enemies. That some of his constituents were not entirely happy with his record is evident from attacks on him in the press, but since most of the anti-Carpenter papers were Democratic, this was an expected hazard of political life.

That Carpenter had not been able to secure one of the state institutions for his district left many disgruntled. Although he had tried to push through a bill for the establishment of a deaf and dumb asylum "at or near Fort Dodge," an economy-minded legislature, faced with a mounting business depression, refused to consider it. During the 1857 campaign one of the local issues had been a demand by Hamilton County that their representative do something about getting an insane asylum located there, and Carpenter, in a letter to the Webster City paper in October, had promised to do what he could.[79] That he made no effort to fulfil this pledge, and instead worked for a state institution at Fort Dodge in Webster County, did not add to his popularity in Hamilton. This, coupled with the suspicions aroused by the River Land settlement and the discontent over "Town 90," left a cloud upon Carpenter's first venture into public office. He could get some comfort from a letter by Elijah Sells, Secretary of State: "I hope you may not find it a difficult task to induce your constituents to forget your 'short comings' I apprehend that they will not be able to find any man that will serve them more faithfully." [80] But Carpenter needed more than Sells's endorsement to win again in a still strongly Democratic district.

No one could have predicted in 1858 that Carpenter would go on to the governorship and to Congress. But this first term as a lawmaker was an indication that he would not be successful as a Congressman. Throughout his career, he was more at home as an executive than as a legislator.

When the Seventh General Assembly adjourned on March 23, 1858, the members scattered to their homes, some to mend political fences, some to return to their neglected occupations. Carpenter, who had entered his first term of state service with enthusiasm, returned to Fort Dodge wiser in the ways of politics and eager to improve his finances which were in their usual precarious state. He at once resumed his land business at Fort Dodge, but other interests soon distracted him. For the next year his attention vacillated between politics, the Pike's Peak gold rush—then at full tide—and the attractions of young Kate Burkholder.

FOUR

Politics and Pike's Peak

———•••———

THE YEARS 1858 and 1859 were bad ones for Cyrus Carpenter. Everywhere he faced failure. He had returned to Fort Dodge in March of 1858, wiser politically but poorer financially. Having fallen victim to the "wild and giddy speculation" of 1856–1857, he had borrowed over $3,000 at ten per cent interest and had invested it in lands with "inchoate and incumbered [*sic*] titles" in northwestern Iowa. A novice at speculation, he had held his lands too long and was submerged in the Panic of 1857. Two years of "close financeering" were required to dispose of his holdings and pay his debts.[1] Faced with this task in the spring of 1858, he had to forego personal political ambitions.

But because of his term in the legislature, Carpenter was an important man in Webster County Republicanism. During the preliminary skirmishing for the 1858 campaign for minor state offices, Thomas F. Withrow, Governor Lowe's secretary, wrote that Carpenter would be "held responsible for Fort Dodge and the regions round-a-bout."[2] And Carpenter did his best. In spite of preoccupation with his financial troubles, he found time to take part in the judicial campaign, attending the district convention as a delegate from Webster County and later verbally routing two "Black Democrats" who were trying to disrupt a Republican mass meeting at Fort Dodge. His efforts there were reported by a witness as a "castigation [that] was the nicest thing that I have heard in a long time."[3]

This was merely a happy interlude, however. The election of lesser state officials might stir up temporary excitement, but all eyes were turned toward 1859 and the gubernatorial contest, which promised an unusual amount of political animus. The Democrats, fighting a losing battle, seized every opportunity to point out the sins of the Republicans; the Republicans, still not sure of themselves, sought zealously for a winning combination of candidates; and the railroad promoters, with the financial sources of the East drying up, brought pressure on both parties for further local aid.[4]

As early as June of 1858, in the midst of the political campaign of that year, articles began to appear in the newspapers on the possibility of state aid for the building of the railroads bogged down by the panic. Iowa's constitution expressly forbade the loaning of state credit to "any individual, association, or corporation," but the railroads thought they saw a way around this prohibition. Another section of the constitution provided that any state debt over a certain amount must be submitted to the vote of the people.[5] The editors of newspapers throughout the state and the people who were always writing letters to those editors engaged in a short-lived if heated constitutional discussion throughout the summer and fall of 1858. Those in favor of granting state aid to railroads proposed that a special session of the General Assembly be called for the purpose of voting such aid, subject to the approval of the electorate. To bring pressure to bear, a "railroad convention" met at Iowa City early in December and passed resolutions "in favor of a judicious system of State aid to such railroads as are of State importance to an amount not exceeding eight millions of dollars." This resolution was not unanimous, however. Only thirteen counties were represented, whereas the backers of the convention had hoped for ten representatives from each county in the state. The Johnson, Muscatine, Benton, Marshall, and parts of the Scott and Clinton delegations were strongly opposed to the "whole aid scheme." Leading those in opposition was Samuel J. Kirkwood of Iowa City, soon to be the Republican Governor of the state, and Le Grand Byington, also of Iowa City, a leading Democrat.[6] Supporters of the resolution also came from both parties, an indication that the railroad influence did not control either the Democrats or the Republicans, but rather sought support wherever it could be found.

The railroad men had been busy throughout the year, pressing their ideas upon the politicians of the state. Platt Smith of Dubuque, active in the Dubuque & Pacific Railroad, had written to Carpenter in November, enclosing a clipping of a long article he had contributed to one of the newspapers. Both the letter and the article took the position that although the constitution forbade the state from creating a debt, this was a "restriction upon legislative authority and not upon the people." The people, who wanted railroads, would be glad to dispense the state's credit, Smith argued.[7]

The railroaders contended that without state aid to build more lines immigration would go elsewhere—to the states that were aiding the railroads directly, such as Minnesota and Missouri. Lands without railroads would not sell, they claimed. This argument ignored another reason at that time for lack of immigration and purchase of lands—the continuing financial depression. The Iowa population, which had increased 169.4 per cent between 1850 and 1856, increased only 30.3 per cent between 1856 and 1860.[8] This decline in new settlers, obvious by 1858, was seized upon by the railroad interests as an argument for state aid. Build more railroads, they urged, and new settlers will come, in ever increasing numbers, bringing wealth to a state now in the doldrums of a depression. Many citizens of

Dubuque and Davenport led in the movement, but they were more vocal than effective, for they discounted or ignored the realities of politics.

Of more importance to the Republicans in 1858 than the influence or needs of railroads was the problem of the next election. They had won in 1857 by a slight margin; therefore, all their energies were bent upon continuing their control in 1859. The Democratic "line" for 1859 was clearly seen in 1858: Republican extravagance and Republican corruption were to be the touchstones that, it was hoped, would return the Democrats to power. An extra session of the legislature, called to vote anywhere from three to ten millions of dollars to railroads, would give the Democrats another item to add to their "story of reckless expenditure." Carpenter had intimated in a letter to Withrow that he opposed the calling of a special session, and Withrow had replied:

> A tremendous effort will be made to induce the Governor to make the call. I have written him a long letter, begging of him not to take a step that must result in the defeat of the Republican party. Sells, Edwards, Kirkwood, Grimes, Hoxie, Seeley and other reliable Republicans, in and out of the Legislature are very much opposed to the movement. It may be well for you to address the Governor upon the Subject. I am satisfied that he is disposed to listen [to] the voice of his friends. A letter from you indicating your own views and those of your friends will have an influence. . . . We must keep our skirts clear of this thing.
>
> Again, the moment you commence railroad legislation that moment corruption will take possession of the government. The state must not tamper with corporations if she would keep her legislation pure.[9]

Governor Lowe, urged on by the majority of his party, stood firm against the pressure from railroad men and their supporters and refused to call the extra session, although there is a suggestion, in a letter from Grimes to Kirkwood, that Lowe personally favored the idea of state aid.[10] The Governor's action, then, is an indication that the state had not yet come under complete control of the railroad interests. In 1858, the power of the corporations was realized and resisted. Withrow, soon to become a leader in the Republican party, wrote Carpenter that "a few desperate men . . . aided by Railroad Speculators" had failed in this attempt to coerce the state administration, but he foresaw the influence the roads would wield. "The railroad power is today the strongest power in the State," he continued, "The whole scheme is a monster of most awful mien." [11] But, in spite of Withrow's fears, the Governor and his party withstood this influence and decided against it.

Governor Lowe's other troubles could not be solved so easily. Aside from the Democratic cries of extravagance, the Republicans had to face down reminders that their superintendent of public instruction, James D. Eads, had been unable to account for some $46,000 of the funds entrusted to his care. These arguments, plus a continuing financial stringency coupled with a bad crop year, made it inevitable that someone must be sacrificed in the interests of party victory. The logical choice for the sacrifice was, of course, the Governor. Lowe, after only one term, had to go.[12]

Although the press maintained the usual fiction that the contest was wide open, behind-the-scenes political manipulators had decided upon Samuel J. Kirkwood of Iowa City for the next Governor. He had the powerful support of Senator Grimes and—somewhat tardily—that of John A. Kasson, chairman of the state central committee. Kasson, a newcomer to Iowa and to Iowa politics, had risen fast under the patronage of Governor Lowe. Sensing the trend away from Lowe, Kasson worked to soothe all feelings by suggesting that Lowe, as a reward for withdrawing, be given a seat on the state supreme court.[13] The nominating convention was scheduled for June 22 in Des Moines, but not until April was the name of Kirkwood mentioned as a possible candidate by the influential Des Moines *Citizen*. On May 4, that paper definitely announced Kirkwood as a reluctant candidate, whose "disinclination . . . to take an active part in political matters" had been overcome by the urgings of his friends.[14]

That the traditional "disinclination" had been overcome many months before this announcement and that Kirkwood had been actively though quietly campaigning in his own behalf for some time was politely ignored in the press. A hard core of Kirkwood men, led by Senator Grimes, had been working busily since early in the year, lining up delegates for their man. On February 26, John W. Thompson of Davenport had written Carpenter that "Kirkwood has things in his breeches pocket."[15] Therefore, when the state convention met in Des Moines on June 22, it went through the usual motions, but the result was never in doubt. Lowe withdrew gracefully if not happily at the proper moment—just before the balloting began —and Samuel J. Kirkwood was nominated by acclamation to the relief of everyone except, perhaps, Lowe. To placate the strong German element in the state, somewhat suspicious of taints of Know-Nothingism among the Republicans, the convention then named Iowa's best-known German, Nicholas J. Rusch, for Lieutenant Governor. Lowe, as a consolation prize, was awarded one of the three supreme court nominations.[16]

Carpenter, in spite of urgings from friends, was not a delegate to the convention. His financial status did not allow him much leeway for political activity. By March, he had withdrawn his name from any consideration either for representative or senator from his district, although many had urged him to run for the state Senate.[17] However, he gave hearty support to Luther Pease, county judge of Webster County, for the Senate, and he wrote letters to Republicans throughout the district in Pease's behalf. The response was not enthusiastic. A former Fort Dodger warned Carpenter to "cast loose from such d—d old grannies as Pease & Richards or you will be ruined by your friends." [18] Others agreed to go along with Pease because of their friendship for Carpenter, whose personal popularity was still high, and a certain amount of questionable political maneuvering resulted in the nomination of Pease at the district senatorial convention at Sac City on August 10. The Democrats, on August 2, nominated their strong man, John F. Duncombe, and the fight was on. [19]

Carpenter did a good deal of traveling and speaking for Pease during the months of the canvass, even though he could afford neither the time nor the money. Political campaigners always paid their own way in this period, and, as a popular stump speaker, Carpenter was in great demand.

Most important to candidates was the support of local editors, many of whom wielded considerable political influence. In Fort Dodge, Duncombe's *Sentinel* was a mighty force for the Democrats in northwestern Iowa. Carpenter's friend Aldrich upheld the Republican cause in Webster City, but since Hamilton County and Webster City were outside the Thirty-second senatorial district, his pen could help Pease but little. Out in Sioux City, the *Eagle* claimed political independence but leaned toward Duncombe. E. H. Edwards of Sioux City wrote Carpenter that the *Eagle's* editor, Seth W. Swiggett, might be persuaded to change his allegiance "provided satisfactory arrangements can be made to compensate him for the Sacrifices he will necessarily have to make." A postscript to the letter made this suggestion more concrete: "Knowing the character of Mr. S. I would suggest that a very paltry Sum would be no inducement to him." [20] No sum, paltry or otherwise, was forthcoming, however, and as a result, the Sioux City *Eagle* not only supported Duncombe but neglected even to mention the name of the Republican contender for the office.

Another Sioux City suggestion, this time from John W. Charles, was that the Republicans start their own paper. If, wrote Charles, "your Republicans at 'head quarters' will assist me to the amount of $250 or $300.00 I will start the Concern." But sober second thought, plus the refusal of the state central committee to help out, discouraged Charles, who was a land and insurance agent by profession. Admitting that he knew nothing about the newspaper business, he then suggested that if a man could be found with a capital of $1,000, and the proper political beliefs, a paper could be started with an assured subscription list of 500. [21] Nothing came of these ideas, however, and Pease had to struggle along with what weak Republican editorial help already existed.

Since newspaper buying in Sioux City had not proved feasible, Carpenter himself journeyed there to speak in behalf of Pease and the Republican cause. The handbills advertising this event urged "Democrates and all" to come out and "hear the other side." This invitation gave Sioux City's other

Democratic paper, the *Register,* its chance. Political tradition required that you either ignore your opponent or attack him with all the sarcasm at your command. The uncorrupted editor of the Sioux City *Eagle* continued his policy of silence by even failing to mention Carpenter's presence in the city, but Editor F. M. Ziebach of the *Register* chose to report Carpenter's efforts in behalf of the Republicans:

> His *speech,* occupying nearly two hours, was the dullest, dryest, stupidest, most disjointed and silly jumbling together of ignorance, inconsistency and falsehood we ever had the misfortune of listening to. His "charges" were like those of a bob-tailed animal in fly time—wild and ineffectual. His diction was bungling—his delivery prosy, sleep inspiring—his bearing awkward and "bold as a sheep." Long before he had "passed from the consideration" of his "second point," nearly all the Republicans had left the room, and, seated on the steps leading to the hall, were "cursing their luck" for inviting the Democrats to hear "the other side." They were badly sold, and freely and frankly acknowledged, that another such speech would leave to the Democracy a clear field in Woodbury county.[22]

Ziebach concluded with the statement that since it was well known that Pease himself could not make a good speech, the fact that he had chosen Carpenter to speak for him was an evidence of poor judgment and should convince the voters that he was not the man to represent them in the state Senate. Since Carpenter, throughout his political career, was considered one of the best "stumpers" in the Republican party, Ziebach's report of the Sioux City speech can be considered as motivated more by partisanship than by truth.

Two weeks later, Ziebach published in horrified capital letters the fact that Pease had voted "TO STRIKE THE WORD 'WHITE' OUT OF THE CONSTITUTION OF IOWA, thereby proclaiming his fealty to the odious doctrine of *Negro Equality*." This accusation harked back to the vote on the 1857 constitution and on the special amendment to remove the word "white" from the article on suffrage. While the new constitution had been accepted, the amendment had failed by an overwhelming vote. That Pease's vote did hurt him in the 1859 campaign was confirmed by a letter to Carpenter from J. W. Denison, successful candidate for state representative from Crawford County. "Am sorry Pease was not elected. His vote on the word 'white' worked against him and was the means I think of giving a Democratic majority in our County. It was made an argument against the Republicans as being Abolitionists." [23] On the very eve of the Civil War, a taint of abolitionist leanings meant political death in Iowa.

The Republicans won the 1859 election, with a working majority in both the House and Senate, while Kirkwood defeated the Democratic candidate, ex-Senator Augustus Caesar Dodge, by a margin of about 3,000 votes, only 500 better than Lowe's victory in 1857.[24] But Carpenter's efforts in his district had been without success; Duncombe went to the Senate, while Democrat Samuel Rees of Fort Dodge won the seat in the House held by Carpenter in the 1858 Assembly.

This minor disaster, coupled with his financial woes, plunged Carpenter into a black depression. Eager to get out of Fort Dodge, with the Democrats "crowing over their recently achieved victory," he went on a surveying trip up to the Minnesota border in company with Kate Burkholder's brother, Barton. It was a "dull and dreary country," he wrote. "I am sick of this whole state and all its associations and I have a great notion to go to some warmer climate where there is more money to be made than there is in this country. . . . I wish I was at Pikes Peak and was making some money." [25]

There was a good reason for Carpenter's interest in "making some money." Late in 1858, he and Susan Catherine Burkholder—known to her friends and family as Kate or Sis—after uncertain advances by the shy Cyrus and gentle encouragement from the lady, had become engaged. The Burkholder family had come to Fort Dodge from Ohio in 1857. Since unattached young girls were scarce on the frontier, Kate soon had plenty of suitors and enjoyed to the full the lively social life of the small town. In the fall of 1858, she had gone to Dakota City in Humboldt County to teach school. She was lonely and isolated there, and her letters to Carpenter, full of homesickness, finally drew from him a tentative declaration of his feelings for her. He had never "declared himself," he wrote, because he knew "there were others here who were more agreeable to you than myself," and because of his "biting stinging poverty" which prevented him from offering her the "comforts, conveniences, and luxuries" she should have. Kate's reply swept aside all his arguments; she went down the list of her suitors, demolishing their prospects one by one, and chiding Cyrus for thinking she wanted to make a "rich match." His answer, long and gloomy, told her of his family troubles, his financial woes, his fears for the future, his reluctance to stand in her way to a better marriage.[26] That such an unhappy proposal should have won Kate's heart seemed unlikely, but such was the case. It was to be a long and rather turbulent engagement; not until 1864, when Carpenter had changed his title from "Honorable" to "Captain," did the marriage take place. Kate remained faithful to him through many trying times: his deep depression of 1859; his two-year stay in Colorado; and his service in the Union army during the Civil War. He proved a difficult and exasperating suitor, often moody and sometimes jealous, but Kate's patience, understanding, and good sense saw him through and brought him to a settled, peaceful, and happy marriage.

During the spring and summer months of 1859, while Carpenter campaigned for his friend Pease, he likewise debated with himself his future prospects. He had always wanted to study law, but his poverty and his need to earn even a meager living had prevented him from doing so. To become a lawyer now, he would need to spend at least a year in study, he told Kate. Would she wait that long? [27] But Kate was to wait longer than that. The dream of studying law was pushed into the background for a time by a new urge—that of trying his luck in the gold fields of Colorado, or Kansas as the area was then known. The Pike's Peak gold rush was in full swing, with conflicting reports in almost every issue of every paper. Brother Judd in California tried his best to discourage Cyrus; Judd had gone west during the 1849 California gold rush, and he knew the hazards and disappointments of dreams of Eldorado. Instead, Judd urged Cyrus to come to California.[28] But Cyrus had a stubborn streak; in March of 1860, he set out for Pike's Peak, where he hoped to recoup his many losses and find the capital with which to start his married life. He left Fort Dodge on March 22, in company with three other Fort Dodgers—A. F. Watkins, J. L. Lewis, and J. N. Darling. Traveling with wagons drawn by mules, they made good time to Council Bluffs, where they arrived eight days later. On the way they had fallen in with some men from Webster City, also heading for the gold fields, and the two groups made up a substantial wagon train.[29]

Many men who took the long trip over the plains to Colorado or California contracted with their home papers to send back letters telling of their experiences. Just before leaving Fort Dodge, Carpenter had received a letter from Frank W. Palmer, then editor of the Dubuque *Times,* asking him to send "an occasional letter for publication," for which he would "make some satisfactory recompense." Carpenter's first letter to Palmer's paper, written at Omaha on April 6, gave a sketchy description of the trip across Iowa. "I thought I would write you frequently," the traveler concluded, "but I find after walking 20 to 25 miles each day, over dusty roads, assisting to get wood, water and hay, at night, and then devoting a long hour to currying and taking care of my mules—our sole reliance upon this trip—I feel in but poor mood to write." [30]

The gold seekers' journey followed a trail by now well marked by thousands of travelers. They left Council Bluffs on April 2 and crossed over to Omaha, where they remained several days, "fitting out" for the trip across the plains. They bought corn at 25 cents a bushel; oats at 30 cents; sugar, 10 cents a pound; coffee, 14 cents; rice, 7 cents; dried apples, 12½ cents, "and other things in proportion." On April 6, they set out for the Platte River, which they followed to Fort Kearny, reaching there a week later.

By that time they had settled into the routine of plains travel, and the inevitable frictions had developed. One of their party, Carpenter wrote to Kate, was "kind of an old woman," complaining of everything. "When the dust blows it hurts his eyes and he whines about that. When the sun shines it makes his head ache. When he walks two or three miles his feet get sore." Somewhat smugly, Carpenter added, "I walk more than any of them frequently never get into the wagon from morning till night. still I find nothing to complain of." He had no patience, he concluded, "with a man or woman that is forever whiney." When he reached his destination, he added, he would "dissolve all partnerships and act alone." [31] Such was the strain of westward travel that many a friendship could not stand up under weariness, heat, dust, and monotony.

Upon reaching Denver on April 28, Carpenter sold the foodstuffs he had left, keeping only a two-months supply and his mules and wagon, and made a profit of $100. "I am satisfied that a man can make money in this country if he hits the right lead," Carpenter wrote to Judd hopefully. Remembering his experiences with land speculation in Iowa, Cyrus assured his brother that he would "try and keep out of any speculation," especially if it would mean the loss of his mules. He promptly shouldered a pick and shovel and set forth to look for "the right lead." [32]

For eighteen months, with only slowly diminishing enthusiasm, Carpenter sought this "lead." Gone were the low spirits of 1859. "I *will conquer fate,*" he wrote to Kate in September, even though by that time he had spent $400 and "not made one cent." [33] Doggedly he searched. Over snow-packed passes, down precipitous mountain sides, he trudged from gulch to gulch—from the Blue River Diggings to Iowa Gulch, to Georgia and Humbug Gulches—with no success. The bank of a pit caved in on him at Blue River Diggings, and he hobbled around on crutches for several weeks. A forest fire swept down the mountain side and destroyed his shanty at Georgia Gulch. He was lost in a blizzard in the mountains for one bitter night, while wolves howled around him. "I am not discouraged," he wrote to Kate, "nor do I intend to become so. . . . I will make something turn up by the most determined efforts." [34]

Judd urged him to come on to California, and for a time he seriously considered doing so. He assured Kate that if he decided to try his luck on the Pacific Coast, he would first come back to Fort Dodge, where they could be married and then make the journey to California "by water and the Isthmus of Panama." [35] Kate did not like the idea of going so far away from home and family, however; in each letter she urged him to come back to Fort Dodge. And in each reply he put her off, promising to return soon but pleading for the chance to make a successful strike. During the winter of 1860–1861 he practiced law in Denver—an indication of the laxity of legal requirements on the frontier. Judd had sent him some law books from California, and with the barest modicum of study, Cyrus began pleading the claim and mining laws of the territory.[36]

In the rough courts of Colorado he gained experience in the practice of law, even if on a somewhat informal level. "Less than a week ago," he wrote to Kate in April 1861, "a man was shot down in the Court room where I was speaking and I have become so habituated to such ruffianism that when he was picked up and carried out I went right on with my speech, not stopping five minutes." The Territory of Colorado had been organized in February of 1861, and Carpenter hoped that now "something like law and order will prevail." [37]

In Colorado, as in Iowa, Carpenter took part in politics. Colorado's first territorial nominating convention for a Delegate to Congress and for members of the territorial legislature came in July 1861. Carpenter, then at Georgia Gulch, was one of a large field of Republicans mentioned for the position, but the nomination went to Hiram P. Bennet, who easily defeated his Democratic opponent in the August election. Some of Carpenter's new friends urged him to apply for some position under the territorial government, but he refused.[38]

More and more, as civil war threatened, Carpenter wanted to get back to Iowa. After the Republican triumph in the presidential election of 1860, he had written to Kate: "I suppose . . . I could get an appointment under [Lincoln's] administration but I despise the idea of just depending upon office for a living." Nevertheless, Kate urged him to make a try for such an appointment, but again he refused. "I want to get in the habit of living independent of Politics, independent of appointments, independent of popular clamor, and then I will be all right." [39] Carpenter never achieved this goal of independence from politics, and in spite of all he said from time to time, he was never really happy outside the political field.

As the spring and summer of 1861 wore on, and the news from the battle fronts came in, Carpenter wavered back and forth as to what he should do. If war came, he had written Kate on May 5 (the news of Sumter not having reached him yet) and he were in Fort Dodge, he would want to respond to the call for volunteers. When his fears of war became a reality, he longed to be in Iowa so that he could enlist. He wrote to Governor Kirkwood, offering his services in any capacity and set about making plans to return home in the fall. Kirkwood's reply dampened his hopes; the Governor wrote that there were more men offering their services than the government could use. By September, recruiting was going on in Colorado, but Carpenter suspected that the new troops would be left on the frontier posts, while the seasoned soldiers there would be sent east. He had no desire to "lie around one of these frontier Forts for $200 per month." Instead, he would "pursue the civil avocations of life" until the government needed him. "But I think the powers that be ought to appreciate me sufficiently to give me an office if I should go into the service," he wrote, displaying a self-confidence that he had almost lost during the years of depression and failure.[40]

The months of searching for wealth in Colorado had proved fruitless. Despite repeated warnings from his brother Judd, he had made the long, hard journey to the gold fields; he had worked with pick and shovel; he had practiced law, or what passed for law, in the mining camps; he had staked out claims, only to find his property valueless; he had even considered for a time joining a group of Iowans who were laying out a townsite. In the fall of 1860, with hopes still high, he had written Judd that he planned to make $2,500 before he left Colorado; later he wrote Kate that when he had made $1,000 or $1,500, he would come home; by the spring of 1861 he decided that if he could amass $300 he would return to Fort Dodge; by September his goal was reduced to "enough to get home with." [41]

But in spite of his lack of success, Carpenter was not discouraged. Perhaps the war overshadowed his personal misfortunes. In the melting pot of the gold fields he had met many Southerners—possibly the first he had known—and the "violence and blustering bragadocio of the chivalry" gave him a low opinion of them.[42] More and more his letters to Kate breathed vengeance on the South. "I want to go into the army if this war continues and in my opinion it will. If the country is going to ruin what man is there with the soul of a *man* who wants to survive his country, and if we succeed as I think we will in the end, I want some share in the glory of the achievement." [43]

At last, Carpenter could stay no longer on the fringes of events, far from news of the war. He set out for Fort Dodge in the fall, arriving there late in November 1861.[44] He was as poor, if not poorer, than when he started westward, but the war had so far distracted him from his personal desires, even that of an early marriage, that the gloom and despondency of 1859 had given way to confidence and hope for the future—even a future darkened by civil strife.

-FIVE-

Feeding the Union Soldiers

————◦—•—•—◦————

CARPENTER, thirty-two years old and with some prominence in his part of the state through having held political office, was in no hurry to join the army, once he had returned to home and friends. The usual procedure for a man of his age and standing was either to raise a company of his own and be elected an officer, or to apply for a commission through the good offices of friends in positions of political influence. Carpenter chose the latter course. Iowa's delegation in Washington in late 1861 consisted of Senators James Harlan and James W. Grimes and Representative James F. Wilson, who had succeeded to a seat in the House when Samuel R. Curtis resigned to accept a commission. Iowa's other Representative, William Vandever, had also entered the army but had not yet been replaced.[1] Thus, Carpenter depended on Harlan, Grimes, and Wilson to further his cause with the War Department.

Wilson wrote early in January 1862, that the Iowa delegation had recommended Carpenter as assistant quartermaster on Brigadier General Thomas A. McKean's staff, but that a shake-up in the War Department was holding up the appointment.[2] Simon Cameron, Lincoln's first Secretary of War, had proved corrupt and inefficient; in order to remove him with the least unfavorable reaction, Lincoln appointed him ambassador to Russia and filled his place with Edwin M. Stanton.[3] All this took place in January, while Carpenter's friends in Congress tried to push through a commission for him.

Arrangements with Stanton took several weeks more, but at last, on February 25, 1862, Carpenter received word from Grimes and Wilson that an appointment as "Commissary of Subsistence" had been confirmed. On March 3, he received his commission as captain, with orders to report at once to the Commissary General in Washington, D. C. "I do not know what my pay will be," Cyrus wrote to Judd, "But I am told that it is a paying position."[4] His orders were later changed, and he was sent to St. Louis to report to Major General Henry W. Halleck. In mid-April, Carpenter left Fort Dodge for Dubuque, there to board a steamboat for the trip down to St. Louis, a busy military center.[5]

The war in the west, at first overshadowed by events along the eastern seaboard, was just coming into prominence. The unwieldly Western Department, originally commanded by the ineffectual General John C. Frémont, had been divided into the departments of Kansas and Missouri. The Department of Missouri, consisting of the states of Missouri, Iowa, Minnesota, Wisconsin, Arkansas, Illinois, and that portion of Kentucky west of the Cumberland River, was placed under the command of Major General Halleck in November 1861.[6] In the spring of 1862, Halleck's command consisted of three armies: the Army of the Mississippi, commanded by Major General John Pope; the Army of the Ohio, commanded by Major General Don Carlos Buell; and the Army of the Tennessee, commanded by Major General U. S. Grant.[7] Grant's brilliant victories at Forts Henry and Donelson in February, and his bloody triumph at Shiloh on April 6–7, had but recently brought him national fame.

When Carpenter arrived at St. Louis on April 22, Halleck had gone to Pittsburg Landing to supervise the advance on Corinth. After the usual amount of "red-tapism," the new commissary was finally ordered to Pittsburg Landing, the site of the recent battle of Shiloh. To help him in his work, about which he knew less than nothing, he was advised to hire a civilian clerk "who knew something about the business."[8] Upon his arrival at Pittsburg Landing on the Tennessee River on May 1, Carpenter was sent down the river several miles to Hamburg, where he was placed in charge of subsistence for the Army of the Mississippi under Pope. Carpenter soon found that he was going to be "immersed all over in business," but he was not worried. He did not expect the war to last more than another thirty days.[9]

At Hamburg, Carpenter and his civilian clerk—who received $75 per month—were charged with the feeding of some 32,000 troops, very soon increased to 40,000. Amidst "confusion confounded," the new commissary set to work. The advance on Corinth was under way, and in two days Carpenter had sent 100,000 rations, weighing about 300,000 pounds, out on the roads toward that doomed city. Steamboats brought his supplies to the landing; he had to supervise the unloading and storing of beans, peas, rice, ham, "mess beef," coffee, sugar, potatoes, hard bread, and desiccated mixed vegetables. By the middle of June, he had four clerks but was still "perfectly overrun with business."[10]

All this activity, in the midst of the confusion and turmoil of a citizen army still not adjusted to the ways of war, filled Carpenter's days and nights with a seemingly endless round of duties. Once at Hamburg, when he thought he had at last completed his tasks for the day, 600 wagons arrived from General William T. Sherman with an order for supplies. Sherman was under Grant in the Army of the Tennessee, and Carpenter had all he could do to feed Pope's Army of the Mississippi. In despair, Carpenter rode to

Halleck's headquarters in search of advice. There the General Superintendent of the Commissaries, a Captain Hawkins, laughed at Carpenter's tale of woe and told him that he had had to send Sherman's men "some where," and urged him to keep up his spirits. So, back to Hamburg Carpenter went, to fill those 600 wagons with food. Next came the 21st Illinois, landing from boats without anything to eat; again Carpenter's stock of rations was drawn on. Late at night he sat down to write to his brother, commenting wryly, "It is singular how *fortune has favored me.* I already do the largest business of any commissary along the River." [11]

While Carpenter wrestled with the problems of supply at Hamburg, the Army of the Mississippi pushed toward Corinth. On May 30, that stronghold was evacuated, and Pope's men took part in the dilatory pursuit of the Confederates. Pope, "pugnacious and confident and conceited," was not admired by his commissary. [12] "I do not think much of Gen Pope as a man yet I consider him a good General," Cyrus wrote to Kate. He was a "wicked profane and overbearing old scallawag," who treated Carpenter with scant courtesy. [13] Therefore, when Pope was called east to take command of the Army of Virginia, Carpenter was happy.

The Army of the Mississippi was then turned over to General William S. Rosecrans, whom Carpenter admired. Halleck also had been shifted; he was ordered to Washington on July 11 to assume command of all the Union forces. Six days later, Grant took over the Armies of the Tennessee and the Mississippi. [14] This constant shifting of officers, as Lincoln sought desperately for a winning combination, only added to the confusion.

By the end of June, even before the many changes in command, Carpenter began preparations for a move. The railroad from Memphis to Corinth had been opened, so the troops no longer needed to depend on water transport for goods and supplies. Still sanguine about the outcome of the war, Carpenter expected that within weeks or at the most a few months "the Back-bone of this giant Rebellion" would be broken. But a month later, still at Hamburg in spite of rumors of removal, he had lost some of his confidence in an early end to hostilities. He still thought, though, that "a year from this fall" he would be at home and taking part in the politics and business of Webster County. [15] On July 24, Rosecrans ordered Carpenter to Iuka, Mississippi, a few miles southwest of Hamburg on the line of the Memphis & Charleston Railroad and seven miles from the river at Eastport, his new base of supplies. [16]

A lull seemed to have settled over the armies of the West; Carpenter was busy but not harassed as he had been at Hamburg. His hopes for an early end to the war were growing dimmer, however. He found no Union sentiment in the South, he wrote to Kate. Assuming the role of an armchair general, he displayed a vindictiveness surprising in so mild a person.

He would raise an immense army and sweep through the South with "The Broom of destruction." Furthermore, he "would march through the state of Alabama leaving such a desert waste in the rear of my army that it would be necessary for any man attempting to cross the country thro' which we passed to take sufficient Rations in his Haversack to last him across."

The indifferent attitude of his fellow officers shocked Carpenter: "Nine tenths of the officers in the army do not care any more for the principle at stake than a savage cares about the Bible and such a laxity of all moral restraint in money matters among officials makes me sometimes doubt the existence of all good." [17] A month later the corruption within the ranks still shocked him:

> I would resign and come home to-day if I could do so with credit. I am disgusted with the whole institution one would think that in the present perilous position of our country all a soldier would care for, would be to help save the Government. But every man from highest to lowest, with few and those *very few,* exceptions, seems to think this was a great money-making institution. Stealing and the most heinous rascality is so common and so pattent [sic] that I shudder for my country. I thank God that I have no desire to make a cent more than belongs to me tho' I am frequently asked why dont you do so and so others are stealing and you being a Com Sub will place you in the category of Scoundrels whether you take the benefits or not. . . .[18]

Carpenter was to remember these words when, as a candidate for Governor of Iowa, he was attacked by the opposition on these very grounds—he had been a commissary of subsistence, therefore he must have enriched himself.

At Iuka, Carpenter set to work supervising the building of a large storehouse for his supplies. He was given a force of "contrabands"—escaped slaves—but found them of little use to him. They worked about three days and then came to him, begging for passes to go home and visit their families. Naively expecting the slaves to greet the Union soldiers as liberators, Carpenter was disgusted to find that many of them did not want liberty. They preferred to stay with their wives and children, even as slaves.[19] This perfectly natural attitude astonished Carpenter, whose sentimental concept of the mission of the North sometimes clouded his deeper understanding of people, whatever the color of their skins. He became bitter about the contrabands and displayed no sympathy with their plight, swept up as they were in the tide of war, dislodged from the moorings of home and family, and given a freedom they did not know how to deal with. Carpenter's attitude reflected that of many Northern soldiers whose first personal contact with the slaves was disillusioning. Abolitionism received a rude jolt when confronted at first hand with the reality of the South's "peculiar institution."

The Northern agitation for emancipation during the summer of 1862 worried Carpenter, whose judgment of the larger issues of the war, politics, and diplomacy was clouded by his immediate contact with the victims of slavery. On September 24, Carpenter wrote to Emmett that "a proclamation of Emancipation . . . would be the most terrible thing [that] could befal [*sic*] our army and the country and the President knows it." What Carpenter and the troops in the field could not have then known, was that two days before Lincoln had issued his "preliminary proclamation," to take final effect on January 1, 1863.[20] The political necessities in Washington were not seen by the soldier in the field, confronted as he was with personal knowledge of the helplessness of the contrabands. Perhaps Carpenter glimpsed the terrible problems which would beset the nation once millions of black men were freed, but he could have no conception of the equally terrifying problems facing the harassed President in Washington.

By the time the news of the Emancipation Proclamation reached the western troops, Carpenter's base of operations had been moved to Corinth. He had worked hard at Iuka, getting a vast store of supplies housed in a large building that had been confiscated from a "rebel." Plans were that Iuka was to be the supply point for the troops along the railroad, "as far east as Decatur." By the first week of September, Carpenter had his storehouse in good condition:

> I now have on hand over 800 Barrels of Flour over a 1000 Boxes of Pilot Bread, 500 Barrels of Pork, 200 Bbls of Mess Beef, 100 casks each of Bacon Ham and Shoulders, 300 Barrels of Salt, 200 Bbls of Sugar, 250 Bbls each of Beans & Peas, 100 Bbls of Rice 300 Bbls of Hominy, 500 Bbls of Roasted Coffee, 200 Sacks of Green Coffee, 50 half chests of Tea, 50 Bbls of Molasses 150 Bbls of Desicated Potatoes, 100 Boxes of Desicated Mixed Vegetables, and other things required for Hospitals &c &c besides several and sundry Bbls of Whiskey.[21]

Hardly had these stores been neatly arranged than all the work had to be undone. Word came that Confederate General Sterling Price was approaching Iuka from the south. Grant's forces, spread over too large a territory and depleted by the sending of reinforcements to Buell who was engaged in a race for the Ohio River, had been reduced to only 50,000 men.[22] Therefore, the order went out to evacuate Iuka. Carpenter's storehouse was emptied, and the goods piled along the railroad track to await transportation.

On the morning of Saturday, September 13, while this work was in progress, sporadic firing was heard outside the town. Still the train did not come. By nightfall it was evident that it would be impossible to save the foodstuffs, and Carpenter tried in vain to organize a force to destroy them. No teams were available, and the troop of cavalry delegated to fire the subsistence stores rode through town without stopping. Carpenter was forced to run for it himself. He lost all his personal papers and the commissary reports he had just completed. Along the line of retreat incredible

Carpenter as Union Commissary

confusion reigned. "Negroes old and young crowded both sides of the road and hung screaming and crying upon the rear of [the] retreating forces." About four miles out of Iuka, Carpenter came upon two small Negro children, lost by their mother in her flight. All he could do was give them a hard cracker from his pocket and try to assure them that soon friends would come for them. Soldiers dropped by the road from exhaustion, "and no kind hand picked them up and cared for them." A great cloud of dust marked the route of the retreating army, choking and blinding those caught up in the rush.[23]

Meanwhile, Grant gathered his scattered forces for an attack on Price. Carpenter was at Burnsville, with a new stock of 400,000 rations and 120 head of cattle and looking for Rosecrans, when he received orders from Grant to remain there and "issue to his army." Grant's attack on Iuka on September 19–20 was a success, but the "wiley old villain" Price escaped after inflicting heavy losses on Rosecrans's wing.[24]

After Iuka, Grant fell back on Corinth as the strongest point on the railroad, and Carpenter also moved to that Mississippi city, where he was to remain for almost a year. He was assigned temporarily to full charge of the commissary there in the absence of Captain R. E. Bryant, his senior officer who had gone home on furlough. Carpenter also hoped for a furlough, "[a]fter the fall campaign."

During a lull in the fighting, Carpenter settled down to enjoy the ease which Bryant's full "force of clerks" gave him.[25] But the fall campaign soon broke over Corinth. The Confederates, stopped at Iuka, turned their forces against Corinth on October 3–4, and Carpenter's leisure was over. He was "not much exposed" during the bitter two-day struggle for the city, but when the "dearly purchased" victory was achieved and the rebel army scattered, he walked over the battlefield littered with the dead of both armies and felt ashamed that he was "not more exposed and did not take as many risks as others." [26]

Shortly after this battle, Rosecrans was transferred to the Department of the Ohio and Cumberland, but Carpenter was retained at Corinth in charge of supplies. The District of Corinth was placed under the command of Brigadier General Grenville M. Dodge, and Carpenter became a member of his staff. Dodge "is an Iowa man," Carpenter wrote, "with whom I had a slight acquaintance before I came into the army and appears to have implicit confidence in me." [27]

Carpenter remained under Dodge for almost two years, and a lasting friendship developed between the two men. Dodge's future fame as a railroad builder has somewhat obscured his political role, but it was as a leader of Iowa politics in 1871 that the former general approved the candidacy of his former commissary for the governorship of their state. And, whatever might be the shifting political alignments in the future, Carpenter always remained loyal to his chief. In March of 1863, Carpenter wrote of Dodge: "I like him . . . very much and think he has a good opinion of me. He is a little fellow not much larger than I am. He walks along in a shuffling kind of gate [sic], bent over almost as much [as] I am." [28]

The winter of 1862–1863 dragged slowly along, with Carpenter only moderately busy at Corinth. As the spring approached, he found his attention divided between the coming military campaigns and the political scene in Iowa. Even a war could not long distract Cyrus from politics, especially in a gubernatorial year. Iowa's popular Governor Kirkwood was serving his second term; the "anti-third-term bogey" would prevent him from asking for another nomination.[29] Thus, there was a hurrying and scurrying among the political hopefuls. Carpenter's preference was for Elijah Sells, Iowa's Secretary of State since 1856. Not yet aware of the weight a military title would carry in coming elections, Carpenter preferred Sells to General Fitz Henry Warren. He wrote Emmett that the fact that Warren was "a Gen in the army will add nothing to his strength among the thinking intelligent people with whom capacity integrity and executive experience will be the test." It was a foolish thing, he thought, to nominate a man "because forsooth he has been in the army." [30]

When word reached him that the Republicans had nominated neither Sells nor Warren but had chosen William M. Stone, colonel of the 22nd Iowa Infantry, as their standard-bearer, Carpenter called the nomination "rather far-fetched." The ticket put up at Des Moines was a "kind of Kangaroos Concern with the weakest part being the head," he added. In spite of his fears, however, the Republicans triumphed in the election. Before long, rumors reached Corinth that there was a movement afoot to defeat Grimes, whose senatorial seat would be filled by the 1864 General Assembly, and that "the hollow brained Stone" was in on the conspiracy. Grimes had always been and would always be, even in his blackest days, Carpenter's hero. That anyone should try to defeat him would be a "national calamity," Carpenter stormed to Emmett.[31] The rumor was only a rumor, however, and Grimes was safely returned to the Senate.

At Corinth, as spring warmed into summer, Carpenter went on several short forays with the troops. On one of these they brought back about 300 Negroes, in accordance with the government's policy "to get within our lines all the negro's [sic] of Rebels possible." Plans were being made to build up some colored regiments, and Carpenter seriously considered applying for a commission in one of them, although his experience with contrabands had made him well aware of the problems such a command would bring: "I tell you the man who 'runs' a negro Reg, will be worried and teazed [sic] by his Reg, for passes to go and see their wives, for permits to visit their sweethearts, and for this, that and the other, until his life will be worn out." [32] He finally concluded to stay where he was.

Through the summer months Carpenter remained at Corinth, on the fringes of the campaign against Vicksburg. He came to admire Grant and to have "the utmost confidence" in him. "Grant is a man who never gets discouraged, he is a brave man, and a Patriot, & will continue to deal out blows to the Rebels, as long as he has an arm to strike *with,* or a country to strike *for."* Carpenter hoped that the North would be patient and not let the "Copperheads . . . ride into power over the necks of a discouraged people." [33]

As the fall of 1863 approached, Carpenter hoped to obtain a furlough. By October, he thought he could come home "in about a month." Things were in great confusion at Corinth, with the troops moving eastward from their victory at Vicksburg. But, just as Cyrus had "every thing ready to come home," Dodge's division was ordered to move out, and Carpenter had to move with them. [34] Rosecrans, in command of the Army of the Cumberland, had succeeded in getting himself besieged at Chattanooga after the disastrous battle at Chickamauga. Another defeat would ruin the effect of the victories of Vicksburg and Gettysburg; therefore the government had created a new "Military Division of the Mississippi," which included all the territory between the Alleghenies and the Mississippi, and placed Grant in command. Grant had gone immediately to Chattanooga and in a series of lightning moves had strengthened the Union position there and opened lines of supplies for the near-starving troops. [35]

Dodge, with his experience as a railroad builder, was needed at once to keep the railroad line open from Nashville south to its junction with the east-west Memphis & Charleston Railroad at Decatur, Alabama. The road was in a shambles; the Confederates had destroyed all the bridges and taken up and twisted the tracks. Dodge and his men, with no tools but axes, picks, and spades set out at once. Carpenter's headquarters were established at Pulaski, Tennessee, midway on the railroad between Nashville and Decatur, and teams were sent out to forage about the countryside for supplies. Grant himself described the achievement:

> Millers were detailed from the ranks to run the mills along the line of the army. When these were not near enough to the troops for protection they were taken down and moved up to the line of the road. Blacksmith shops, with all the iron and steel found in them, were moved up in like manner. Blacksmiths were detailed and set to work making the tools necessary in railroad and bridge building. Axemen were put to work getting out timber for bridges and cutting fuel for locomotives when the road should be completed. Car-builders were set to work repairing the locomotives and cars. Thus every branch of railroad building, making tools to work with, and supplying the workmen with food, was all going

on at once, and without the aid of a mechanic or laborer except what the command itself furnished. . . . General Dodge had the work assigned to him finished within forty days after receiving his orders. The number of bridges rebuilt was one hundred and eighty-two, many of them over deep and wide chasms; the length of road repaired was one hundred and two miles.[36]

Carpenter was the only commissary for the railroad builders—some 12,000 men in all. "I was up late and early and worked without ceasing," he reported to his brother.[37] To help out, Dodge gave him authority to raise a Negro regiment "for fatigue purposes." For officers, Carpenter chose a nephew of a Fort Dodge friend and a "boy I found in the 7th Ill who used to go to school to me in Johnstown Ohio." It took "superhuman efforts" to carry on his duties, but by December 10, Carpenter could report that within a few weeks the road would be open to Nashville, and then supplies could come in by rail.[38]

The New Year came, and Dodge's force was still at Pulaski. Carpenter had been in the army almost two years without a leave, and he was heartily sick of it. He constantly urged Emmett not to enlist. Emmett's health was none too good, and his eyes bothered him. Furthermore, Cyrus feared that his brother's "sensitive nature" could not stand military service. If he himself could get out of the service, Cyrus wrote, "I would do it, and feel like a caged animal escaped from my Keepers."

> I am not apt to complain, and consequently have refrained to tell you how sincerely and heartily I hate every thing connected with military life. Even with the Superior advantages which an appointment from the President gives me; I still despise my situation. The whole spirit of the army is unnatural and anti-Republican and calculated to crush the spirit of a man of noble impulses and a proud sensitive nature.[39]

Evidently Carpenter's furlough was long overdue. His attitude toward the Negro had changed from his first disgust with the ex-slaves. He was now ready to turn the whole Southland over to them, let them "march down through the Southern Confederacy, and crush out, and eat up every Green and living, thing." [40] Such bitterness was not characteristic of Carpenter and indicates a deep war-weariness.

Dodge must have sensed his commissary's depression, and he promised to do all he could to push through a leave for him. To add to Carpenter's woes, Kate had written that certain people in Fort Dodge were teasing her about her long engagement and suggesting that Carpenter would never marry her. Cyrus also was worried for fear Emmett might be drafted. He made one last "desperate effort" for a furlough and was finally granted a meager twenty days, including travel time.[41]

Early in March, he set out for home. On the 14th, he and Kate were married at Fort Dodge. He reported this fact to his brother in California in language singularly prosaic for a bridegroom:

> It was my first visit north of the Ohio River, for two years, and I made the best use of that twenty days possible. While at home I was married. It is a thing I have had in contemplation for some years, but have been deferring it, from time to time, until I should be better prepared. The woman I married is a plain, honest, true woman, of good natural sense, and good disposition. She has not been cultivated in the schools, and cannot play on a piano &c &c, but she is a good housekeeper, and an economical industrious woman, twenty seven years old, and healthy. She belongs to the Methodist church, loves her mother, prays every night to her God, belongs to a sanitary aid society, loves the soldier, especially the one now writing to you. . . .[42]

Kate and her soldier had time for only the briefest of honeymoons at Yellow Springs, Ohio, where they visited Kate's brother, Henry, and his wife. All too soon Carpenter returned to his post, while Kate stayed on with her brother. Almost her first letter to her husband—whom she always addressed as "Dear Carpenter"—was about a problem that faces every young matron—a new dress. She wanted more than anything else, she wrote, a "black silk dress"—the badge of gentility in the 1860s. "I have the money now," she assured him, "& I may never have it again & the dress will do me the rest of my life time." She was afraid he would think her terribly extravagant, but she "did want a nice new dress." A few days later, not having heard from Cyrus, she took the plunge and bought the material for twenty-five dollars. To take the edge off this display of extravagance, she reported that a friend had also bought a silk dress "which cost thirty-four dollars." Mails were slow during wartime, and Kate did not hear from Cyrus until sometime in May. "I am not a bit mad," he wrote, "but would have been mad I tell you if you had not got it. . . . I do not want you to go around and look like a country school mistress but on the contrary like a lady." [43] So the marriage started off on a happy note—a note, incidentally, which would continue throughout their lives—with Carpenter the indulgent husband and Kate the happy wife.

Back at Pulaski, Carpenter found orders from Dodge to proceed at once to Athens, Alabama, a few miles south of Pulaski in the direction of Decatur, where the north-south railroad, on which they had been working, joined the east-west road that ran from Memphis on the Mississippi to Chattanooga on the Tennessee. Other changes had occurred since Carpenter had left on his furlough. Grant had been called to Washington, given the re-created title of lieutenant general and, on March 9, placed in supreme command. Sherman had been moved up to Grant's old position in the West.[44] The war had entered its final year.

Dodge, now in command of the left wing of the XVI Army Corps of the Army of the Tennessee, was for the moment stationed at Athens. There were rumors that he might stay there for the summer, keeping the railroad from Nashville to Decatur open.[45] But, like most rumors, they proved false. New plans were in the making, and before long, Dodge's men headed for Chattanooga, the take-off point for Sherman's great offensive against the Confederate General, Joseph E. Johnston, then entrenched at Dalton, Georgia, some thirty miles southeast of Chattanooga. In mid-March, Grant and Sherman had met at Nashville, traveled together to Cincinnati, and there laid out their plan of campaign. "He was to go for Lee and I was to go for Joe Johnston," Sherman later reported.[46] May 5, 1864 was set as the day for the start of the great two-pronged offensive that would at last bring peace.

At Nashville, after his talk with Grant, Sherman began to mobilize his forces. He visited his commanders and laid out the plans for gathering some 100,000 men for the grand campaign. "The great question of the campaign was one of supplies," Sherman wrote. To keep the rail lines open and to keep the flow of supplies—both material and food—moving to his army as it advanced into enemy country was no simple task. On April 6, Sherman stopped all civilian travel on the railroads and ordered all his troops "destined for the front to march, and all beef-cattle to be driven on their own legs," while wagons were supplied for hauling each army's subsistence.[47]

By the end of April, with plans perfected, the armies began concentrating at Chattanooga. Dodge's men started on April 29, arriving at Chattanooga on the morning of May 5.[48] The troops were already moving out against Johnston's Confederate army at Dalton, and Dodge's left wing was ordered to Ship's Gap, some fifteen miles west and slightly south of Dalton.[49] The movement against Atlanta had begun.

Carpenter found time, in all the bustle of that busy day, to write Emmett that he thought there was going to be "a great battle." Remaining at Chattanooga for three days after Dodge had left, "to load and forward supplies," Carpenter then moved out to join his commander.[50] He had 160 mule-drawn wagons in the train, stocked with rations for the 13,000 men in the left wing of the 16th Army Corps.[51] Ahead of him lay a year of never-ending struggle to feed these men who were "marching through Georgia."

The ration of the Union soldier was specified exactly in the army "Circular" dated May 16, 1863:

> The ration is three-fourths of a pound of pork or bacon, or one and a fourth pounds of fresh beef or salt beef, twenty-two ounces of bread or flour, or one pound of hard bread, or one and a fourth pounds of meal, and at the rate to every one hundred rations of eight quarts of beans or

peas, and ten pounds of rice or hominy, ten pounds of green coffee, or eight pounds of roasted or ground coffee, or one and a half pounds of tea, fifteen pounds of sugar, four quarts of vinegar, one pound of sperm candles, or one and a fourth pounds of adamantine candles, or one and a half pounds of tallow candles, four pounds of soap, two quarts of salt, and four ounces of pepper. In addition to the foregoing, there is allowed twice per week one gallon of molasses per one hundred rations, and thrice per week, if practicable, an issue of potatoes at the rate of one pound per man. When beans, peas, rice, hominy, or potatoes, cannot be issued in the proportions given above, an equivalent in value shall be issued in some proper food.

Desicated potatoes, desicated mixed vegetables, at the rate of one hundred rations of one hundred and fifty ounces of the former, or one hundred ounces of the latter, may be substituted for beans, peas, rice, hominy or fresh potatoes. Where these articles cannot be issued or upon the requisition of the proper officer, and when the supply on hand will admit of it, they may be issued at the foregoing rate twice per week, in lieu of beans or peas, or in lieu of rice or hominy. Fresh beef may be issued as often as the commanding officer of any detachment or regiment may require it, when practicable, in place of salt meat.[52]

The desiccated, or dried, potatoes and vegetables were immensely unpopular with the army. A sergeant in the 15th Iowa thought "desecrated" would be a better name for "such fodder," which made him "the sickest" of his life.[53] The army recipe for preparing desiccated potatoes makes the sergeant's complaint understandable:

Mix the potatoe *thoroughly* with hot water, taking care that every particle of the potatoe is well moistened; mash well with a pounder, after being *well* stirred, turn off *all* the water that remains, and let the potatoe stand in a warm place for twenty minutes; half an hour would be better; mix a little butter if convenient, season to taste, and place it in the dish in which it is intended to be baked. If not intended for baking, mix as before; season and boil *very* slowly over a light fire, taking care that it is well stirred and does not burn.

The army had no other suggestion for the desiccated vegetables than that they be used in soup.[54]

Three years of war had taught the soldier how to exist on this fare, however. He foraged for himself when he could, his special favorites being fruits and sweet potatoes. By the time Sherman's "bummers" set off in May of 1864, they had learned many things about army living. During 1861 and 1862 when on the march, if the regimental cook did not catch up with the troops at nightfall, "no meat would be cooked, or coffee boiled, but the soldier would nibble hard tack, eat his sow-meat, swallow from his canteen some sickish warm water, and lie down upon the ground to curse his fate." Carpenter reported that "[n]ow the experienced campaigner carries his little coffee-boiler attached to his knapsack, and often when halting in the day-time boils a cup of coffee." A discarded canteen could be cut in two, by melting the solder, and carried on the pack for use as a frying pan.[55] The encampments along the hard road in Georgia were different from those in Tennessee and Mississippi the year before. Then the men had been citizens in uniform, unhappy and helpless; now they had become hardened soldiers, undergoing a rigorous campaign with a surprising amount of good humor. Carpenter reported the "evening bivouack" to Iowa news-paper readers:

> The whole atmosphere of an encampment is laiden with a kind of crowded hum. Every soldier will be doing something; either laughing, talking, whistling, singing, pounding something, or cutting wood. Two are extemporizing a bed. . . . Others will be kindling fires for the hundreds of different messes; others bringing rails for fires and bunks; others splitting wood; others pounding coffee in cups with the butt end of their bayonets or muzzles of their guns: others bringing water with a dozen canteens strung over their shoulders; others frying fat bacon; others picking chickens foraged during the day; and all at work.[56]

The task of keeping the soldiers fed was not an easy one, however. Many times during the "march to the sea" Carpenter rode all night, back and forth along the line, in order to keep his supply train together and his drove of cattle from straying. The road was littered with the debris of an army on the move—broken-down wagons, dead mules, stragglers sound asleep in the brush at the roadside, and refuse of every kind. Hard as the marching was, many kept their sense of humor. A wagon-master, one of a class held in great contempt by the foot-soldiers, came upon a whole field of stragglers one night. "What regiment is this?" he demanded with dignity. "Ninety-third stragglers," was the prompt reply. "You've got a d—d big regiment," said the wagon-master. "Yes," came the answer, "we used to have a bigger one, but those who straggled the worst have been promoted to wagon masters, so they can ride." [57] On another dark night Carpenter heard a group of the men discussing their possible destination, some thinking they were headed for the Atlantic, others claiming that they were going south to take Mobile. In defense of the latter belief, one soldier claimed that they had marched so far he was "afraid to take long steps for fear of stepping off into the Gulf." [58]

There was a reason for much of this good humor. On November 16, after having taken Atlanta, they began their triumphal march to the sea. Gone was the discouragement of the earlier years of the war. There was a feel of "victory in the smoke and dust laden air." The credit for this feeling Carpenter gave to Sherman. Although most of the thousands who marched across Georgia had never even seen their "Uncle Billy," he had somehow infused in them all a great self-confidence. "Ain't this a splendid movement?", "Ain't General Sherman a trump?" they said to Carpenter.[59] Confidence warmed to love, and love to hero-worship, as the campaign rolled on. By the time peace came, and the Army of the Tennessee marched down Pennsylvania Avenue in Washington, past the reviewing stand where Sherman stood with Grant, President Johnson, and the Cabinet, his "bummers" yearned to "give expression of their love, respect and confidence," but Uncle Billy had ordered them to march by in the old customary way, and they obeyed him.[60]

So, with confidence in their commander, the Union soldiers marched to the sea. At first, the countryside was so poor that it offered little in the way of foodstuffs to supplement the army rations, but as they progressed the forage improved. Vegetables, the popular sweet potatoes, chickens, and a large supply of sorghum added variety to the monotonous army fare, improving the soldiers' health as well as their dispositions.[61]

Marching was only a part of the campaign in Georgia. Sherman's army was ordered to destroy all railroads. "It is more work to destroy a R. R. than one would imagine," Carpenter wrote.

> In the first place the spikes have to be knocked out on the side of the rail—no easy job—then the rails are pried up, being frequently so imbedded in the ties as to be moved with great difficulty, then the ties are pried out of the hardened earth in which they have lain imbedded for years, being piled in heaps about every three rods. But as these ties have been hugged by the damp earth for years, they frequently will not burn without an addition of more combustible material, usually supplied from the neighboring fence. When this is done, and the fire kindled, the iron rails are laid across the burning ties, thus heating the middle of the rail, which causes the ends to sink to the ground from their own weight. The boys then take them off, put the heated centre against a stump, tree or telegraph pole, and bend the two ends together, and not infrequently drive them quite past each other.[62]

Even with the rails bent out of shape, to insure that they would not be used again, the men filled up deep cuts with the rails and brush and earth, and "commingled with them loaded shells, so arranged that they would explode on an attempt to haul out the bushes." The explosion of the shells, Sherman thought, would demoralize any gang of Negroes and thus prevent attempts to clear the roads.[63]

So, Sherman swept across Georgia, leaving destruction in his wake. In December, Savannah was reached and taken. Dodge, who had been "given a Confederate leave" by a bullet wound in the head in the fighting around Atlanta, had gone home in August, and his command had been broken up and divided between the 15th and 17th corps.[64]

In October, Carpenter had been promoted from captain to lieutenant colonel and ordered to duty with the 15th corps under the popular Major General John A. Logan.[65] This was a disappointment to Carpenter, as he had hoped to be reassigned with Dodge to the Department of the Missouri with headquarters at Vicksburg. Logan's corps was "going on a great campaign," and since that meant cutting off all communications, Carpenter knew it would be many months before he would hear from home.[66] He longed to be in Iowa, campaigning for "Old Abe" and for his brother Emmett who was running for district clerk.

Cyrus spent Christmas Day in Savannah, preparing for Sherman's next move and wondering about Iowa politics. "I would give $100 to-day to know your fate in the late election," he wrote extravagantly to Emmett.[67] Even in the field, Carpenter had done his bit for the campaign. In response to a request from Senator Harlan, he had sent a contribution to pay for the circulation of documents, instructing the Senator to send them to Emmett.[68] Such a large part did politics play in the hearts and minds of men that, even in the midst of a terrible and bloody campaign, politicians asked for and received help from the soldiers in the field.

At last, the long-delayed mails reached the army at Savannah, and Carpenter learned that Emmett was safely elected, although by only the small margin provided by the soldier vote. Webster County, a Democratic stronghold, had gone down fighting. Emmett's victory was the more pleasing since an *"infernal clique"* of Republicans had done their best to help the Democrats defeat him. Carpenter never held a grudge after his own political campaigns, but attacks on Emmett aroused him to an unusual display of vindictiveness. "I want you to tell me all the particulars about your election," he wrote, "and give me the names of the Rep's who turned the cold shoulder upon you. I want to know their names as I desire to think of them in my prayers." [69] His protective attitude toward Emmett also caused him more concern when another draft call went out. In September, Carpenter had written Kate that if Emmett were drafted he himself would resign and come home to take his brother's place. By January, with the draft scare still worrying him, he wrote Emmett that he would pay as much as $2,000 for a substitute, rather than let his younger brother go into the army. Carpenter felt Emmett would "suffer more than $2000 worth even if [he] should live it through." [70] His fears were groundless, however, as Emmett escaped the draft. Had Cyrus but known it, his own days as a soldier were numbered. The armies of Sherman and Grant were now moving to overwhelm the battered remnants of the Confederate army.

From Savannah, Sherman struck north in January, marching through South Carolina "without forming a line of battle." By the end of March, he was at Goldsboro in North Carolina, ready to push on to Raleigh, while Grant near Richmond closed the trap on Lee's army. With Grant in front of him, Sherman moving up rapidly from the rear, and only the remnants of Johnston's army in-between, Lee faced inevitable defeat.

On March 25, Sherman left his command at Goldsboro and went around by sea to confer with Grant at City Point. There the two generals called on President Lincoln, who had come down to the front on the steamer *River Queen*. They talked over the two campaigns and were later roundly scolded by Mrs. Grant because they had so far forgotten their manners as not to present their respects to Mrs. Lincoln. At a second conference the following day they dutifuly inquired for the President's wife, talked further on military affairs, and agreed on a plan of action against Lee. On March 30, Sherman was back at Goldsboro to begin preparations for an attack, set for April 10. But, on April 6, word reached him that Richmond had fallen, and Lee was in retreat.[71] "I seem to see the beginning of the end," Carpenter wrote to Kate. Guns were fired in celebration, while the soldiers rejoiced and bands played. It was good to hear "the deep toned cannon" and know that "they were not fired to kill any fellow men," wrote Cyrus.[72]

Hardly had this excitement passed when additional news reached Sherman. Lee had surrendered to Grant at Appomattox Courthouse on April 9. "We were all perfectly thunderstruck. . . . I ascribe the Glory to God and Gen Grant," rejoiced Carpenter. He so far forgot his usual reserve as to conclude the letter with a veritable burst of underscorings and exclamation points, such was his joy at the prospects of peace and home.

> Yes, *Glory to God!!* Praised be the God of Liberty!! . . . *How are you the Gold Speculators? You who have speculated off the hearts blood of American Soldiers. How are you Copperheads?* Miserable hissing traitorous Demons who have laughed at the death of Soldiers, and loss of Betters. How are you England & France? Sympathizers with a Slaveholders Rebellion. *How are you Last Ditch? How are you everybody & everything?* [73]

Carpenter wrote this from Raleigh, then occupied by Sherman's forces. But all was not quite over. Johnston's army still faced Sherman, who told his men that with only "[a] little more labor, a little more toil on our part, the great race is won." [74] The men's cheers were somewhat subdued after orders went out for preparations for a thirty-day march. It was "too too bad" for Sherman to do this, said Carpenter, but even as he wrote, a flag of truce was carried from Johnston to Sherman. The two men, after an exchange of letters, agreed to meet on April 17.

Just as Sherman left his headquarters on the morning of April 17, word came of the assassination of President Lincoln. Joy turned to gloom, and also to fear—fear lest the soldiers, who revered Lincoln, would turn the force of their wrath on the helpless people of the Confederacy. Keeping the news to himself, Sherman departed with a heavy heart to meet Johnston at Durham's Station, North Carolina. When the two had met, Sherman asked to speak with Johnston alone; he then showed him the dispatch.

"The perspiration came out in large drops on his forehead," wrote Sherman, "and he did not attempt to conceal his distress." The two men, victor and vanquished, talked over the problem, and Johnston agreed to try to get authority to surrender the remainder of the Confederate army. That night Sherman, back at Raleigh, broke the news of Lincoln's death to his men. His fears of an outbreak were not realized, and by the end of April, the final surrender of Johnston was accomplished. The long and dreadful war was over.[75]

Carpenter, saddened as were all the troops by the news of Lincoln's death, must have had some insight into Sherman's problem. On April 18, he wrote to Kate: "I pity the women & children of this confederacy if Johnston does not surender for if this army with its present feelings should march over the country they would raze every house to its foundation." Always the politician, Carpenter turned his thoughts from the immediate sorrow to the political future. Vice President Andrew Johnson had been an "old Dem Politician of the demogogical class, Pro Slavery until it became popular to be antislavery," and Carpenter feared that he was "but poorly fitted for the high duties which will devolve upon him." [76]

The war was over, but the marching was not. Sherman's army now prepared to march to Washington, there to be disbanded. "It will be the quickest way the army can get there in a body to march," explained Carpenter, "as it would take a month to embark this army on ships and cars, but I could get through much quicker as an individual, if I could get out [of] here. I do hate to march again 250 miles." The troops left Raleigh on April 29 and began the long movement northward. The weather turned very warm, and many soldiers died from sunstroke during the long marches. On May 7, Sherman's men reached Petersburg, south of Richmond.

At Richmond the two great armies met—the Army of the Potomac and the Army of the Tennessee. Now that the common enemy had been defeated, these two bodies of men, each jealous of the other from officers down to the meanest private, promptly clashed. Fights were common, and several men were killed. Carpenter rejoiced when orders came for his army to move out: "I of course do not partake of the prejudices and jealousies of most of our officers and men and try in every way to allay the foolish feeling but Gen Sherman shares the prejudice of his army I think to a large extent and that gives the men a supposed license to abuse the Potomac Army." [77]

At last they reached Washington, and on May 23 and 24, the two armies paraded in the "Grand Review" of the victors. Carpenter had hoped, once this ceremony was over, to be able to resign, but he was ordered instead to Louisville as Chief Commissary of Supplies. This post only delayed him for a few weeks, however; on June 20, "Lt. Col. C. C. Carpenter, of Gen.

Logan's staff, who was with Sherman in his brilliant campaign," came home to Fort Dodge.[78]

He had been in the army for three years, he was thirty-five years old, he was married, and he had no settled occupation or business. During the war he had been able to save most of his salary and had sent it home to Emmett for safe-keeping or investment. Carpenter's plans for becoming a lawyer had been changed by the war. "I am getting so far along in years that I give it up and only want to be happy and do a little good to my fellow men." He did not intend to "waste time in courting the admiration of men." Rather, all he wanted was a house with "sea room for a nice yard," with shrubbery instead of "gaudy furniture," and a chance to make up for the lost years of the war.[79]

Given his situation and inclinations, Carpenter inevitably drifted back into politics, in spite of repeated resolutions to the contrary. And now, added to his other abilities and assets for public office, he had acquired a new and important distinction—a military career and title. "Major," "Colonel," or "General" in front of a man's name carried political magic, in spite of Carpenter's earlier opinion that "being shot at will not be a passport to success." [80] George C. Tichenor, later to wield strong political power in Iowa, was on Dodge's staff at St. Louis. He expressed, in his characteristic vituperative fashion, the attitude of the soldier-politician toward the "stay-at-homes" who had had things their own way during the war:

> The present race of soulless, unscrupulous, grasping, greedy politicians have got to be dragged from place & power before we soldiers have any show whatever. They have, like craven cowards and petty sneaks & shirks, remained quietly at home enjoying their ease, filling their pockets & seizing & holding the offices—while the real patriots of the land have yielded up their lives—or hazzarded their all, for the country—and they are now holding with a death grasp to the places & power which thank God they will soon lose—by the decree of the people & the superior claims of the brave men whose valor, patriotism & sacrifices has saved the Nation, by crushing treason upon thousands of hard fought battle fields.[81]

The fact that Tichenor had just failed in a bid for the Des Moines postmastership certainly colored his opinions; nevertheless, he expressed an attitude which would have great influence in politics for decades to come.

That Carpenter was looked on by his party as a likely candidate was evident, even as he left for the war. "After his return, we propose sending him to Congress," wrote a Fort Dodge editor in 1862.[82] In the spring of 1864, on the eve of the "grand campaign," rumors had come to Carpenter that his name might come up at the party convention as a candidate for Congress from the Sixth District, in place of A. W. Hubbard, the incumbent. Carpenter promptly discouraged any such efforts on the part of his friends. He admired Hubbard and would not consider running against him. A year later, Tichenor urged Carpenter to go into the race for the state legislature in preparation for beating "Old Hubbard" in 1866, promising help from "our friends in Des Moines." That Carpenter then considered a return to political life is indicated in a letter he had written to his brother in California: "I am now pretty well established and acquainted in Iowa; especially the North Western Portion, and Senator Grimes who has always been my friend, has often told me, and written me, that I better stick to it, and eventually I would stand up the tallest man in north Iowa." [83]

Carpenter took Tichenor's advice—and Grimes's. Two months after he had returned home, he was nominated by his party for the state legislature.

SIX

Carpenter and Iowa Radicalism

———·•◦•·———

CARPENTER'S FRIENDS had convinced him that he could be elected to a seat in the Iowa House without any trouble. Therefore, rather against his own wishes, he allowed his name to be used; the district convention in August 1865, nominated him "with a unanimity that shows him to be the first choice of the Union [Republican] party for that position." [1] At the state gubernatorial convention Governor Stone received his second nomination—without too much enthusiasm on the part of many Republicans—and Carpenter's fellow townsman, Benjamin F. Gue, was chosen for the lieutenant-governorship.

Colonel C. C. Carpenter—he would never again be plain Mr. Carpenter—campaigned strenuously, speaking with Gue throughout the district and sometimes arguing issues on the stump with his perennial enemy, John F. Duncombe. To oppose Carpenter, the Democrats had put up a comparative unknown, Robert Alcorn of Homer, who had at least one necessary qualification—a military record. But it was Duncombe who ran the campaign and achieved the defeat of Carpenter by the slender margin of sixteen votes. Every issue was used to the utmost, including Carpenter's record in the 1858 legislature. The question of settlers on the lands claimed by the Des Moines Valley Railroad (the new name for the Keokuk, Fort Des Moines & Minnesota) was still unsettled, and Duncombe sought to blame Carpenter for not having accomplished that miracle seven years before. Gue's newspaper —the Fort Dodge *Iowa North West*—asked Duncombe why he himself, since he had served in subsequent Assemblies, had not done something about it. "Go slow, and be cautious where you tread, neighbor Duncombe," warned Gue. "Remember about 'glass houses.' " [2] But Duncombe did not "go slow," and the Democrats won.

"The Cops laid me out," [3] was Carpenter's explanation of his defeat, but there was more to it than that. There were four counties in the district— Webster, Buena Vista, Pocahontas, and Clay. Webster County, being the most populous, would naturally decide the vote, and Webster County was largely Democratic—or "Copperhead" as the Republicans preferred it. Gue, however, did not blame Carpenter's defeat entirely on the "Cops;" the "unaccountable treachery" of some of the Republicans of Webster County caused the defeat, he claimed. There was a factional fight within the party, one group led by Carpenter and Gue, the other by Fort Dodgers who wanted control of the local organization. Evidence of this split had appeared in Emmett's campaign for local office in 1864; it cropped up again in a struggle over delegates to the state convention in 1865, a fight won by Emmett and his friends even before Carpenter returned from the East.[4] This, then, was the opposition's revenge; they joined with the Democrats to help defeat Emmett's brother, and they succeeded.

Carpenter was not the only Republican rejected by the voters of Webster County, however. They gave a Democratic majority, small but sufficient, to all the state offices. Gue of Webster County was no more successful than Carpenter on his own home grounds, but Gue had the advantage of a statewide vote to carry him into office.[5]

In the pages of the *North West,* Gue lectured the apostate Republicans who had aided in Carpenter's defeat on the errors of their ways. According to Gue, their votes might jeopardize two Senate seats, cause the payment of a "rebel debt of $2,000,000,000," and affect the entire railroad and land interest of the Des Moines Valley.[6] The state and nation were spared this fate, however, because enough other districts hewed to the strict party line to place the Democrats in their usual hopeless minority at Des Moines.

Carpenter himself took his defeat with a "philosophical dont careativeness," and turned his thoughts to other things. He and Emmett had invested some of their money in a 160-acre farm near Fort Dodge and were debating the wisdom of specializing in sheep raising. But Cyrus kept his eye on the political arena. General Dodge was being considered for a seat in the Senate, and Carpenter lent himself to a short-lived boom for his old commander.[7]

Iowa's two Senators in 1865 were James Harlan and James W. Grimes. Harlan's term would expire in 1867; therefore, it would be the task of the 1866 General Assembly either to replace him or return him for another six-year term. But a complication had arisen: in March of 1865, Harlan had been appointed by Lincoln as Secretary of the Interior, thus vacating one Iowa senatorship. Governor Stone hemmed and hawed about appointing a successor to fill out the balance of Harlan's term. It was an open secret that ex-Governor Kirkwood wanted very much to go to the Senate, and it was no secret at all that Stone wanted renomination to the governorship. If, reasoned Stone, he appointed Kirkwood to Harlan's vacant seat, he would alienate certain anti-Kirkwood forces in the state and harm his own chances at the June convention. If he waited until after the convention to appoint, meanwhile dangling the senatorship before an eager Kirkwood, the latter's friends would see to it that Stone won renomination. He suggested as much to Kirkwood: "You will be Senator and I Governor again if our friends understand each other, and are *prudent* and *discreet* in their management." [8]

The convention came, and Stone won his renomination. But still he hesitated to choose a man to fill Harlan's post. Meanwhile, Harlan had let it be known that he was not happy in the Cabinet of Andrew Johnson, and that he would much prefer to return to the Senate. Here indeed was a dilemma. One appointment made by the legislature that met in January 1866 would be for the remainder of Harlan's term only; the legislature would then have the task of electing a Senator for the new term, which would begin in March of 1867. Iowa's strongest Republicans were of the ultra-Radical stripe, and since Lincoln's restraining hand had been removed, the Radicals were riding high. Already, after but a few months, Andrew Johnson was losing favor, and opposition to him was the standard that measured true party loyalty. Harlan's desire to leave Johnson's Cabinet, therefore, was all in his favor among Iowa politicos and gave him a strong edge for the full-term election.

As time passed, it became apparent that Governor Stone was going to dodge the whole ticklish problem of the senatorship by leaving the short term up to the legislature. This required some nice political juggling since Harlan and Kirkwood were not the only contenders. Practically every prominent Republican in the state was mentioned, at one time or another, for either the short or the long term, or both. Iowa's delegation in the House was a strong one—James F. Wilson, Hiram Price, William B. Allison, Josiah B. Grinnell, John A. Kasson, and Asahel W. Hubbard—and every one of them was a potential candidate for the senatorial seat.[9] Kasson, probably the strongest of the lot, did not display the proper amount of Radicalism to suit those in Iowa who wielded the most power. One of Kasson's most vocal and vituperative opponents was George Tichenor, who combined admiration for Grenville M. Dodge with hatred of Kasson. Kasson's failure to get Tichenor the Des Moines postmastership the previous year had not been forgiven nor forgotten. Therefore, Tichenor was sparking the move for Dodge for the Senate.[10] A few others, including Dodge's loyal ex-commissary, joined in the movement. "Gen Dodge is a candidate for U. S. Senate," Carpenter wrote to his brother Judd in California, "and I am doing what I can for him if he should be elected I think it would be to my advantage somewhat." [11]

Fortunately for his political future, Carpenter had aligned himself with the Radical wing of the Iowa Republican party. In practically every Northern state the national struggle for power within the party was reflected in miniature, and opposition to Johnson was the touchstone by which the "Vindictives" judged a man. Thus, defense of the milder policies

of the President was, at least temporarily, to cost John A. Kasson his place
of influence in Iowa Republicanism, as the factions within the party struggled for control.[12] In 1862, Carpenter had judged Kasson "the best man
in Iowa if you except Grimes;" by 1866, such a sentiment would have been
heresy from a follower of Grenville M. Dodge who, with George Tichenor,
was conducting a merciless political war on Kasson.[13] Carpenter was not
one to strike out for himself in politics; he remained unquestionably loyal
to the Radical Republican program. In this he was typical of the lesser
men who are the wheel horses of a political party. When, in later years,
Congressman Carpenter was introduced to Senator Zachariah Chandler as
being as "perpendicular" in his Republicanism as Old Zack himself, Chandler asked: "Does he lean over back a little? I wouldn't give a d—n for
a man that you have to inquire how he is going to vote." [14]

And Carpenter always did "lean over back a little." In the winter of
1865–1866, when the issue of the senatorship was being fought up and
down the state, Carpenter was in the Dodge camp, although his admiration
for Harlan, whom he considered one of the "noblest and best men" in Iowa,
must have called for some delicate maneuvering. But Carpenter always
seemed to be able to walk down the middle of the road of a Republican
party whose factions often fought with each other more bitterly than they
did with the Democrats.[15]

When the General Assembly met in January 1866, all the political pulling and hauling of the Republican aspirants for the senatorship was resolved by electing Harlan to the full term and giving the consolation prize
of the short term to Kirkwood—both Radicals. Dodge received only one
vote for the short term, indicating that he was not yet the political power
he would later be in Iowa. Dodge liked to claim in later years that he had
had no ambitions in this election, but there is evidence that he was certainly
not averse to the movement in his favor.[16]

With the senatorial question at last answered, Iowa politicians settled
back for a moment to rest and prepare themselves for the next election—
never far away in a time of yearly contests. Although the 1866 campaign
would be merely for minor state offices, the party men worked almost as
hard as they did in a presidential or gubernatorial year. The Republicans
had won in 1865, but by a reduced margin from that of the war years;
therefore, no efforts were spared to assure a stronger victory in 1866.

One of the offices to be filled was that of Register of the State Land
Office. The incumbent, Josiah A. Harvey, was completing his second two-
year term; tradition required that he withdraw from the contest. As early
as the first week in May, the Fort Dodge *Iowa North West* mentioned
Carpenter's name.[17] The office of Register had been established in 1855
"for the purpose of preserving a proper record of all lands belonging to

the state, and of their final disposition." [18] Because of Carpenter's experience as a surveyor, his work as a land agent, and the study he had made of the tangled Des Moines River land question during his term in the 1858 legislature, he was probably as well equipped as anyone to fill the office. "The salary of the office is $1500.00 per year," Carpenter wrote to his brother, "and it is said there are about $500.00 in perquisites connected with it. . . . I do not think I can make as much in money out of it as to remain where I am and raise stock; but it seems impossible for me to keep out of politics." [19]

Before announcing oneself for any state job, a prospective candidate sounded out political leaders around the state. This Carpenter did, once he had made up his mind that he could not "keep out of politics." The answers were more than gratifying. George Tichenor, with his usual ebullience, replied: "Bless your soul. We are all for you and will fight for you to the last hour. Palmer, Withrow, Godfrey, Cole, & all of us are for you, and are glad you are in the field." Since Frank Palmer, Tom Withrow, George L. Godfrey, and Judge C. C. Cole were among the leading Radicals of Iowa Republicanism, this sort of backing was just what Carpenter needed. Dodge also sent his blessing, explaining that he himself was "in a big fight" with Kasson for Congress, but that "the delegation from the west will be for you. I will see our delegates." James B. Weaver of Bloomfield promised his "enthusiastic support," and Frank Palmer was "quietly giving [Carpenter] a lick ahead in every quarter." [20]

Charles Aldrich, who was never happier than when managing a political campaign, had been among the first to suggest Carpenter for the position. The state convention was called for Wednesday, June 20, at Des Moines, and when Aldrich found that Carpenter did not plan to leave Fort Dodge until Monday he sent off an excited and protesting letter to Emmett:

> *This will not do.* He certainly ought to be at Des Moines Monday night, & it would be better to be there Monday morning. . . . [I]f Cyrus should not get down till Tuesday night he would certainly be defeated . . . In these political fights it is of but little use to go a-candidating after another man has got the inside track by being on the ground early. Jones, Cyrus' competitor, is *now* at Des Moines & so has a great advantage. I think you will agree with me that an early start is necessary, in fact, *indispensable.*[21]

As the nomination turned out, Aldrich need not have worried. Lieutenant Governor Gue nominated Carpenter; a man from Council Bluffs named an opponent, D. E. Jones. The first ballot gave Carpenter 503 votes to Jones's 259, and the nomination was declared unanimous.[22] Republican newspaper comment was, of course, favorable. Partisan newspaper editors almost always extolled the virtues of all their party's candidates, no matter what the office. The Waterloo *Courier* considered Carpenter "one of the best men in Iowa," while the Muscatine *Journal* editor went even further and called him "one of the best men we ever knew." [23]

Political campaigns were strenuous affairs. Carpenter was in demand to speak here, there, and everywhere. Dodge wanted him at Council Bluffs; the editor in Winterset suggested that he come there; dozens of other towns asked to be included in his canvass. Hardly a day, Sundays excepted, was free, from the close of the convention to the eve of election; within one two-week period Carpenter spoke in thirteen different towns in north-western Iowa.[24] Since he was only one of seven candidates for office, the appetite of Iowans for political speeches seemed insatiable, especially when it is remembered that no really satisfactory campaigner would think of talking for less than an hour, while a two-hour speech was not unusual.[25] Each candidate was expected to pay his own expenses and also to contribute to the party coffer; Carpenter's share was forty dollars.[26]

The technique of campaigning was fairly stereotyped. Little or nothing need be said about the particular office for which a man was running, or of local issues which might be awaiting solution. All Iowa Republicans, from Congressman to sheriff, ran against the Copperheads and Andrew Johnson in 1866. When Carpenter spoke in Humboldt County, the local editor's comment was that, "[h]e will do good service in fighting copper-heads led by Johnson now, as he did in fighting traitors led by Hood a few years ago." The editor did not think it necessary to explain that Car-penter's "fighting" had been done well to the rear: the title of "Colonel" was enough to carry the glamor of war and the smoke of battle into a political campaign. (Nor did the editor explain how the Register of the State Land Office of Iowa could fight either Copperheads or President Johnson from his post in Des Moines.) A Hamilton County editor also was enthusiastic about Carpenter. "The Colonel gave us a first-rate speech on the various topics which made certain ones of our democratic friends wince and leave the Hall scoring them right and left leaving scarcely a grease spot." [27]

None of Carpenter's 1866 speeches has been preserved, but from his later efforts it can be concluded that their theme was the sins of the Demo-crats—preferably called Copperheads—and the virtues of the Republicans. The doubtless dull and routine duties of the Register of the State Land Office were not considered of enough importance to warrant any discussion.

On October 10, under a rude picture of a flag and cannon, the Fort Dodge paper screamed: "GREAT REPUBLICAN VICTORY. FORT DODGE RE-DEEMED, REGENERATED AND DISENTHRALLED! . . . For the first time in the history of the world, FORT DODGE HAS GONE REPUBLICAN!" The fact that this outburst of enthusiasm was caused by a majority of four votes in the county did not detract at all from the excitement. Actually, statewide, the election had been a cheering one for the Republicans. In 1865, Governor Stone had been re-elected by only a 15,000 majority, which was a considerable decline from Kirkwood's previous vote. The 1866 local election, with the only national vote that for Congressman, showed a 35,000 Republican majority. Small wonder that Republican papers broke out their largest type.[28] Iowa was not only safely Republican, but safely Radical Republican.

Radical Republicanism had been on the increase ever since Lincoln's death. In fact, many of the leading members of Congress who considered Lincoln too soft toward the South had breathed a secret sigh of relief when Booth fired his fatal shots.[29] Andrew Johnson, they thought, had more of the necessary vindictiveness toward Southerners that would make him amenable to their plans. Those plans included control of Reconstruction by Congress, not by the President; enfranchisement of the Negro, who would then vote for his Republican saviors and thus enable them to keep control of the government through continuing defeats of the Democrats; and certain economic measures, such as a high tariff, and aid to the business and industry of the North and the railroads of the West. To insure the unquestioning acceptance of this progress by the rank and file of the voters, Republicanism was made synonymous with loyalty, Democracy with treason. The "bloody-shirt" orators of the Republican party hammered this theme home in every election.

When President Johnson proved an obstacle to their plans, the Radicals turned on him with such venom and vituperation as has seldom disgraced legislative halls and newsprint. In Iowa, Benjamin F. Gue, an ardent disciple of Thaddeus Stevens, ranted and raved and name-called with the best of them. In the *North West,* Andrew Johnson was "His Accidency;" he was "Booth's man" and had conspired with the assassin in the murder of Lincoln; he was a "maudlin, driveling, slobbering drunkard;" his initials, "A. J.," should not be confused with "A Jackass" because that would "come under the statute of cruelty to animals." [30] Hatred of Johnson, coupled with the desire for political victory strengthened the Radical program, the acceptance of which was the criterion of "true" Republicanism. Gue summarized it on the eve of Grant's election in 1868:

> Can any honest man, who will carefully examine the record of the two political parties for the last ten years, hesitate as to his duty in the approaching election Every Rebel leader, every Rebel sympathizer, every Rebel soldier, every Bushwhacker and Guerilla, every defender of human slavery, every apologist for rebel barbarity, every enemy of a Republican Government, every repudiator of National honesty and honor, is in full sympathy with the Democratic Party. Can the loyal, patriotic masses of the people; friends of universal Freedom, Humanity and political equality, consent to support such a party? Can Union Soldiers of the Republic,

ever consent to train in the ranks with unrepentant rebels, under Rebel leaders? . . .

Honest, law abiding men of Iowa, dare you hurl this party from power, and turn your Government over into the keeping of Rebel leaders? [31]

Carpenter's friend Charles Aldrich, not to be outdone by Gue, listed in his newspaper twenty-two "Arraignment[s] of the Democracy" in which he accused the Democratic party of instigating the war, murdering "300,000 of the nation's brave defenders," starving and torturing some 60,000 more in prison camps, assassinating Lincoln, attempting "to introduce a fatal and malignant disease" into Northern cities, "favoring fraud, corruption and malfeasance in office by endorsing . . . President Johnson," being a "treasonable, revolutionary and dangerous party," and causing high prices and high taxes.[32]

With the war over, Carpenter had forgotten his earlier distrust of emancipation and of the adaptability of the Negro to freedom, and had joined with the Radicals of his party in their demand for the passage of the Fourteenth Amendment and for the removal of the word "white" from Iowa's constitution. Less than ten years before, Carpenter's friend Pease had lost an election because he had voted for Negro suffrage in Iowa; now the pendulum had swung in the other direction, and Radical loyalty was based on acceptance of complete franchise for the black man, both North and South.

This change did not come about without objections, however. Gue, in the *North West,* was an early and strong supporter of the franchise for the Negro; but on the "slope" the Republican editor of the Council Bluffs *Nonpareil* fought the idea, preferring an intelligence test rather than a skin-color test for the franchise. "Let no man vote who cannot read, whether he be white, black or mixed," he urged. One correspondent in the Council Bluffs paper blandly suggested that it was all right for the Southern Negro to vote, "in order to neutralize the disloyal element among former slaveholders," but added that he did not think the Iowa Negro should be given the same privilege because it would lead to a great migration of the disfranchised Missouri Negroes into Iowa, and "plainly speaking, we do not wish to open the State to African emigration [*sic*]." [33] Other Iowa Republican newspapers in the 1865 campaign had argued over this issue; the Iowa City *Republican* carried on a debate with the Davenport *Gazette,* the former preferring caution on the franchise question, the latter considering it the "big issue." [34] The Iowa City editor took pleasure in publishing a letter from Senator Grimes to E. H. Stiles in which the Senator called the introduction of the Negro franchise into the campaign "both uncalled for and impolitic." Republican victory in the campaign was the important thing, wrote Grimes, and he was opposed to introducing issues which might tend to divide the party.[35]

Carpenter, not so cautious politically, joined with the faction of the Republican party favoring immediate enfranchisement of Iowa's Negroes. He considered the speeches of Thaddeus Stevens—the bitterest Radical of them all—"strikingly noble & majestic." [36] Shortly before Carpenter left Fort Dodge to assume his new duties at Des Moines on January 1, 1867, he explained his own brand of Radicalism to his brother in California:

> I declare things look somewhat gloomy to me. . . . I still hope however that we may come out of our present difficulties stronger, wiser, and purer than before. My own opinions are fixed and immoveable. They are politico-religious. We must do impartial justice to all men and all races looking to our Gov'mt for protection before we will ever have permanent peace. Some may call this fanaticism and hair-brained radicalism, but I am sure it meets the approval of my heart and judgment and I believe it to be approved of God.[37]

Thus the Radical oratory, which seems to a later generation mere political window-dressing in a struggle for power, was accepted by Carpenter, and no doubt by many others, as divinely approved.

Although a sincere Radical, Carpenter does not seem to have indulged in the popular practice of vilifying the President. Fragments of his political speeches, among the notebooks and papers that he preserved, contain only a little of the bloody-shirt phraseology; instead, there are long and dull passages of discussion, with facts and figures, of the financial situation of the government—hardly a topic to arouse much fanaticism. But even though he did not publicly attack Johnson, he had always distrusted him. On April 18, 1865, Carpenter was at Raleigh, North Carolina, waiting with the troops while Sherman met with Johnston to discuss the terms of surrender. Shocked by the news of Lincoln's assassination, Carpenter had passed the time in reading the congressional speeches of Lincoln and Johnson, made while both were serving in the House, "to try to see the difference of the two mens [sic] minds." "And in every line," wrote Carpenter in his diary, "of the one you see honor and candor while in the verbose declamations of the other you see all the ardor and flatery [sic] of the born demagogue." [38] Even while Iowa newspapers acclaimed the new President —"Thank God for Andy Johnson!" wrote a Council Bluffs editor—Carpenter expressed, in more dignified language it is true, the opinion of Johnson that would become current among Radicals within a year.[39] Within two years any man who questioned the sanctity of Radical opinion in Iowa committed political suicide; within three years the revered James W. Grimes, by his daring to vote against the impeachment of Andrew Johnson, was read out of the party he had helped to found, with vituperation only surpassed by that reserved for the President. It was an age of conformity. Fortunately for Carpenter's political future, he conformed.

SEVEN

Radicalism Triumphant

———•◦•———

WHEN CARPENTER entered the administration of Governor William M. Stone at Des Moines in January of 1867, he was welcomed into the inner circle of the party, even though his position might keep him for a time merely on the circumference of that circle. His job was to handle the several million acres of federal lands that had been turned over to the state for various purposes: among others, the 500,000-acre grant made to the state upon admission in 1846, to be used for internal improvements; the sixteenth-section grant, for education; the university and agricultural college grants; the swamp land grants; the Des Moines River grant; and the various railroad land grants.[1] Some 9,000,000 of Iowa's 36,000,000 acres were given to the state for these various purposes.[2] It was the duty of the Register and his deputy to keep track of this land and to prepare full reports for publication biennially.

Carpenter's first task had been to choose his deputy. He was not without applicants for the job. As early as December 1866, George Tichenor had hinted that he himself might be interested. He had, he wrote, "partly concluded to *rest* from active business . . . & engage in some light employment." But Carpenter, who had some idea of the work entailed in his new job, was not interested in someone looking for "light employment" and evidently was following the advice of John A. Elliott, the state auditor, who had suggested that Carpenter wait until he reached Des Moines before naming a deputy. The choice, if not the appointment, was probably made before Carpenter moved to the capital, however. The politically powerful Frank W. Palmer, state printer and editor of the Des Moines *Register,* had recommended John Davis, who was "an admirable clerk in the office of Secretary of State under Sells," and who was "needy." One of the party leaders had spoken: the "needy" John W. Davis became Carpenter's deputy at a salary of $1,000 per year.[3]

The reports issued by the Register of the State Land Office give some idea of the work done by that department. During Carpenter's two terms he published two full reports, one in 1867 and the other in 1869, plus a "Supplemental Report" published in 1868.[4] In addition to giving a brief background account of each of eleven types of grants, the reports contained long lists of every piece of land patented to the state by the federal government since the last report. Carpenter's first volume ran to 105 printed pages; the supplemental report, covering certain additional material on the swamp land and the Des Moines River grants, to twenty-four pages; and his final report of 1869 to 386 pages. In this latter volume, only about seventy-five pages were needed to list all the grants except for railroads; the rest of the book dealt with almost 4,000,000 acres reserved or already patented to seven railroads in the state.[5] The explanation for the great amount of space devoted to the railroad land grants, as compared with the 1867 report, is that the roads had resumed building after the lull in construction forced on them by the Civil War and were therefore becoming eligible for the grants provided for by the acts of 1856 and 1864. Thus, the work of the Register increased greatly during Carpenter's two terms.

The great proportion of the lands granted to the state by the federal government was handled without any controversy, but the lands for the improvement of the Des Moines River were the source of endless argument and litigation. Carpenter was particularly interested in this problem, not only in his position as Register, but also because the decisions regarding these lands seriously affected his neighbors in northwestern Iowa. During the rest of his political life, the troubles of the "river land settlers" would constantly harass him.

Confusion as to the meaning of the 1846 land grant for improvement of the navigation of the Des Moines River, conflicting railroad grants which brought the Des Moines Valley Navigation Company and the Dubuque & Pacific Railroad into litigation, and Supreme Court decisions in favor of the Navigation Company had left settlers on the odd-numbered sections of land above the Racoon Forks of the Des Moines River in the midst of what seemed a hopeless tangle. In 1868, it had at last become apparent that the settlers were going to lose out; by 1870, there was no question about it. In his special message to the legislature on March 28, 1870, Governor Samuel Merrill said:

> It is evident that the decision of the highest court in the nation in the case of Wm. B. Welles vs. Hannah Riley, lately announced against this pre-emption, settles the question that these pre-emptors can expect no relief from the court, and whatever they may obtain, for what, to most of them, comprises the accumulation of a life time of industry, must come from the mercy of a corporation and its grantees, or as a gratuity of the State or General Government.[6]

The *Welles* v. *Riley* case was only one of some half-dozen decided by the Supreme Court, all in favor of the Navigation Company or the groups to which that road had sold its lands above the Racoon Fork. The sentiment aroused by these decisions was another factor in the slowly growing animosity against corporations which would culminate in the Granger Law of 1874.

The case of Hannah Riley was typical of many that had aroused the settlers to organize in an effort to protect their claims. Mrs. Riley, a widow, owned a 160-acre farm in Webster County which her husband had pre-empted in 1855. In 1862, Mrs. Riley filed a pre-emption claim for her farm, which was included in the government lands opened for sale at the Fort Dodge Land Office that year; in 1863, she received her patent, signed by President Abraham Lincoln. Later, a New York capitalist, William B. Welles, bought Section 33 from the Des Moines Navigation Company, and Mrs. Riley's claim, included in that section, was contested. The case, decided in Welles's favor by the circuit court, was carried to the United States Supreme Court which confirmed the decision of the lower court. Thus Mrs. Riley, and many like her, found themselves dispossessed of lands they had bought in good faith, but to which the title had failed because of conflicting interpretations of the original 1846 grant to Iowa. The depth of the bitterness these decisions caused in northwestern Iowa was such that Benjamin Gue, writing a history of the state some thirty years later, could still remember and express his dismay: "This decision of the Supreme Court will always rank with the famous Dred Scott decree in ignoring the dictates of humanity and the principles of equity." [7]

The settlers on the river lands had organized into a "Settlers' Union" which helped finance the court cases, but to no avail. They next turned to the state legislature and to Congress for relief or indemnity. [8] During the 1868 term of the General Assembly, a bill to secure title to the lands passed the House by a vote of 77 to 21 but died in committee in the Senate. [9] Slight amends were made in the 1870 session by sending a Joint Resolution to Congress asking for a grant of land to indemnify persons suffering loss by the River Land decisions. In addition, the Assembly passed an act providing for "relief" of the settlers, when and if Congress voted indemnity lands. [10] This action only transferred the problem to Washington, where it rested, with intermittent attempts at revival, for twenty-four years before final action was taken. [11]

This plight of the river land settlers was a recurring problem for Carpenter. As Register, as Governor, and as a Congressman, he would spend long hours trying to work out a solution. Even though he would fail, his position on the side of the settlers was one factor in determining his political future.

The duties of Register, although heavy, were only a part of Carpenter's work during his four years in Des Moines. His position gave him standing in the party organization, and his talents as a speaker gave him statewide recognition. During the opening months of his first term, however, the political scene was fairly quiet. The legislature was not in session, the gubernatorial campaign was several months away, and no Senate seat would need to be filled for three years. Therefore, Carpenter could devote his attention, without too much distraction, to the duties of his home and his office.

By mid-summer, he and Kate grew tired of living in a "boarding place," and Carpenter bought a small house where they settled down to a quiet family life.[12] Personal joys and sorrows came to Kate's family during the years that she and Cyrus spent in Des Moines. In the spring of 1867, Emmett married Kate's sister, Matilda, thus strengthening the tie between the two Carpenter brothers and the Burkholders. The next year, an old tragedy was revived when the body of Kate's brother, William, who had been lost during the Spirit Lake Expedition of 1857, was found in Palo Alto County. In the fall, one of Kate's sisters-in-law died, leaving a ten-year-old daughter, Fanny. A year later, after a fruitless trip east with Cyrus in search of health, Fanny's father, J. D. Burkholder, died, and Fanny came to make her home permanently with her aunt and uncle. Although the Carpenters never formally adopted Fanny, she filled a warm and happy place in their childless marriage. Kate had lost two other brothers, Barton in the Civil War and Henry in a steamboat explosion in 1868.[13] Cyrus and Emmett Carpenter thus came to take the place of lost sons and brothers in the Burkholder household, and a close family relationship continued throughout the rest of their lives.

With home and family established and with his feet on the first rung of the political ladder, Carpenter could at last begin to feel some sense of security. Gone now were the discouragements of his early years, the long weariness of the war, and the first uncertainty of postwar readjustment. He was now regarded as a "coming man" in the party, and he worked hard. His circle of friends widened. Candidates for public office wrote to him for support, whether the correspondent wanted to be Governor or a clerk in the General Assembly. Marcus C. Woodruff, editor of the Iowa Falls *Sentinel*, asked for Carpenter's help in getting the appointment as Clerk of the House; E. W. Rice would like to be consul to Havana; Emmett sought his brother's help in getting a friend appointed Receiver at the Fort Dodge Land Office; and J. B. Grinnell wrote about his chances for the nomination for Governor in 1867.[14]

Grinnell's bid for the governorship was to prove futile. A Radical and a devout follower of Thaddeus Stevens, Grinnell was completing his second and last term as Representative from Iowa's Fourth Congressional District. In June of 1866, during a debate in the House, Grinnell and L. H. Rousseau of Kentucky, a believer in the Johnson program of Reconstruction, had exchanged insults that were continued in a more direct fashion outside the halls of Congress. The enraged Kentuckian had met Grinnell several days later and thoroughly caned him, an action which resulted in a reprimand by the Speaker of the House, on a vote of that body, and which seriously hurt the political futures of both men.[15] Iowa's first reaction had been in favor of Grinnell, and some Republican papers at once began a campaign in his favor for the governorship. A number of newspapers in eastern Iowa took up the idea with enthusiasm, and by the spring of 1867, Grinnell's campaign was making satisfactory headway. When Congress adjourned, Grinnell left for Iowa "head and tail up for governor," according to report.[16]

The party chieftains had other ideas, however. They had agreed upon Colonel Samuel Merrill of McGregor, a comparative unknown in politics. He was "right" geographically—the northern part of the state had long been clamoring for the governorship—and he had a military record and title, which made good campaign material. Possibly reflecting the wishes of the party leaders, many leading newspapers now changed their tactics and began to attack Grinnell for cowardice in not fighting back at Rousseau. Wendell Phillips, the old-time abolitionist from Massachusetts, saw fit to enter the fight, but his interference in what Iowa Republicans considered a family quarrel did more harm than good. Gue quoted Phillips's statement:

> General Rousseau alludes to the fact that Iowa has left Grinnell out of her Congressional delegation. To the utter and damning disgrace of that State, this is true. She enjoys the bad eminence of being the first free State that ever thus publicly endorsed a Southerner's insult to one of her Representatives. If I lived on her soil I should make an effort to raze out this stain, and, if I failed, quit the spaniel State forever.

In thus harking back to the 1866 nomination for Congress, Phillips erred in his interpretation of that event, an error repeated by Grinnell's biographer many years later. The nomination of William Loughridge to succeed Grinnell as the Fourth District's Representative in Congress took place in Oskaloosa on June 13, 1866; the famous caning occurred several days later in Washington, D. C. Thus, the "Rousseau affair" could have had no influence on Grinnell's defeat. Gue was at pains to point out this simple fact when he quoted Phillips's remarks and, in effect, told the orator to mind his own business.[17]

Grinnell's defeat for the gubernatorial nomination in 1867 may be attributed to a combination of things: the Rousseau caning, "locality," and the lack of a military title. In a letter to Carpenter early in the year, Grinnell had written that he believed the nomination lay between Merrill and himself. "In that case it will be only locality if I am not nominated," he admitted.[18] Aldrich recognized the growing importance of military honors:

"Grinnell will be strong," he wrote Carpenter, "unless some man prominent on account of military services takes the lead." [19] Grinnell also suffered from having opposed the Republican stand in 1865 in favor of Negro suffrage. In spite of his long record as an abolitionist, which had won him the nickname of "John Brown" Grinnell, he had "for reasons founded on policy" spoken against the adoption of that plank in the platform.[20] Now this action rose to haunt him. Whatever the combination of circumstances, the nomination went to Colonel Merrill. The informal ballot gave Merrill 426½ votes to 262¼ for Grinnell with four other candidates trailing. Grinnell at once moved to make the nomination unanimous for Merrill, a motion that was adopted "[a]mid the wildest enthusiasm." [21]

The Democrats nominated Judge Charles Mason to oppose Merrill. Mason had had a distinguished judicial career in Iowa, beginning as chief justice of the territorial supreme court, but he suffered from the stigma of having been not only a Democrat but a "Peace Democrat" during the Civil War. He accepted the nomination with some misgivings, realizing that he was a poor speaker and that the campaign would be strenuous and unsuccessful. The Republicans had had a 35,000 majority in the 1866 election, and the political picture had changed little since then. Mason saw a small ray of hope only in the restlessness of the Germans under the Radical program. "If this separation is real and permanent we shall give [the Radicals] some trouble," he said.[22]

The campaign was a rather dull affair. Carpenter's share consisted of a contribution of $20 to the party coffer (the chairman had suggested $25) and in filling a certain number of speaking dates.[23] The usual accusations and counter-accusations were exchanged, but the papers and politicians did not seem to have their hearts in the fight. One explanation may be that, with the railroads building at a furious rate after the long delay of the war years, people were more interested in the promises of transportation than of politicians.

The election was a victory for the Republicans, but with a decreased majority. Despite a larger electorate, the total Republican vote was the same in 1867 as it had been in 1866—around 90,000. Whereas their majority had been 35,000 out of 146,000 votes in 1866, in 1867 it fell to 27,000 out of a total of 153,000.[24] Satisfied with their victory, even if a smaller one, the Radicals at once turned their attention to 1868 and Ulysses S. Grant.

The year 1868, in contrast to 1867, was one of intense political excitement. Not only was it a presidential year, it was also the year of the impeachment trial of Andrew Johnson, who had come to be one of the best-hated men in Iowa and the nation. Attacks on the President had grown more and more frequent in Iowa Radical newspapers, reaching a new climax in August of 1867 when Johnson tried to remove Stanton from his Cabinet.

Carpenter left no record of his opinion on this controversy, but his two editorial friends, Gue and Aldrich, were among the bitterest of Johnson's critics. When, at what seemed like a very long last, the House voted impeachment of Johnson on February 24, 1868, the Iowa Radicals rejoiced. Governor Merrill wired words of commendation and support to the Iowa delegation in Washington, and the Iowa House voted a resolution endorsing the action.[25] Iowans followed the long trial with great interest, and the newspapers gave it full coverage. No Radical doubted for a moment that the Senate would uphold the impeachment voted by the House; the preponderance of Republicans in that body made this a certainty if the vote were strictly along party lines. But when, in April, rumors were heard that there were a few Republican Senators who might vote against conviction, and when the name of James W. Grimes was included in these rumors, the anger and dismay of Iowa's Radicals was boundless. E. W. Rice wrote to Carpenter from Washington on April 13: "I cant think for a moment that any Republican Senator can vote agst impeachment now yet there are rumors that Grimes Fowler and Sprague may do so. If they should they vote for their own impeachment." [26]

On May 16, when the vote was taken on the crucial eleventh article, and Grimes, who had suffered a paralytic stroke two days before, was helped into the Senate chamber to cast his vote against impeachment, there were few Iowa Republicans who would defend his action. In the eyes of the Radicals the impeachment was a purely political action; questions of judicial right or wrong were not even considered. But to Grimes, who had taken an oath "to do a man impartial justice according to the Constitution and the law," there was no other course open, as he saw it.[27] Iowa's editors outdid each other in vituperation: Grimes was a traitor, a Judas, he had been bought, he was "nothing but a cowardly political trickster." [28] How Carpenter, who had always admired Grimes, felt is not known; but when Grimes died at Burlington four years later, Carpenter wrote in his diary: "A great man has fallen; one who combined in his character a firmness of purpose, a personal integrity and a political independence such as distinguished but few men. He was among [my] earliest political friends and I never lost faith in him." [29] Carpenter was always loyal to his friends; it is hard to imagine him joining in the hue and cry of 1868. In 1872, as Governor of the state, he led the way in doing honor to a man whose sins had been forgotten.

Almost unnoticed in the excitement over the impeachment trial, the Republican state convention had met in early May and renominated the incumbents of the lesser state offices. "You of course know I was renominated," Carpenter wrote to his wife on May 7.[30] An officeholder needed to do little or no campaigning for a second nomination. Unless he had been flagrantly incapable of holding the office or had strayed from the strict path of Radicalism, he was granted a second term without question. The convention also adopted resolutions endorsing Grant for the presidential nomination and insulting the unfortunate Andrew Johnson by urging the delegates to the national convention, as a "guarantee of [Grant's] life and safety," to "secure as our candidate for Vice President a Republican of unswerving fidelity and unimpeachable integrity." [31] Thus, the Radicals of Iowa gave their endorsement to the worst of the accusations against Johnson—that he had conspired in the assassination of Lincoln.

All attention now turned to Chicago and the national convention, even though there was no question as to the outcome. As a curtain-raiser for the convention that was to open on May 20, a "Soldiers and Sailors Convention" was held at the German Turner Hall on the preceding day. Carpenter had been one of the many Iowans appointed as delegates to this meeting, but he had decided not to attend, concluding that it would not pay him "to spend the money it would take to go to Chicago." Carpenter was not much of a "convention politician" except for county and district meetings. Had he gone to more state and national conventions he might have learned more of the political tricks of such gatherings, thus saving himself from defeat in his district in 1882 and from failure to nominate his man, Jonathan P. Dolliver, in the latter's first campaign for Congress in 1886. Carpenter's forte was the hard work of campaigning. He took part in a Grant Union Rally at Des Moines on July 11, where "ten acres of Republicans" cheered Carpenter, Kasson, and several other orators in their efforts to arouse political enthusiasm for the ticket. Carpenter, said the *Register*, "[a]lways masterly and magnetizing . . . held his audience in close attention and earnest applause from the beginning to the end of his rallying, inspiring address." [32]

With Grant nominated, and the Radicals girding for the campaign with more than their usual determination, Carpenter had scarcely a free day from the middle of September to the eve of election on November 2. He spoke all over the state, concentrating in his own district but also making a swing to the Missouri River at Sioux City, down through southwestern Iowa and back to Des Moines for the windup of the campaign. In Sioux City he "mercilessly dissected the greenback fallacies of these small bored democratic orators who muddle their own brains, and their victimized hearers, by crude and unintelligible theories upon subjects they know nothing about," according to a Sioux City editor.[33]

Carpenter wrote out what he called "skeletons" of his speeches in a small black notebook. From these outlines it is evident that he spent little time on the traditional bloody-shirt type of oratory, but rather stressed the financial status of the country and the government under Republican rule. Of course, he repeated the customary Republican attacks on the Democrats, and it was here that he became the Radical orator. Let us ask ourselves, he said, whether "transfering this Government back into the hands of the men who brought on the war will give us peace & prosperity?" Then he would swing into a full attack:

> Would these men who to-day instigate the butcheries in the South do better if controlling Gov't and its army? Would Seymour who called the men who with bloody hands burnt down Orphan Asylums mobbed Newspapers offices and murdered innocent women and children, his friends? Call the Ku Klux Klan's of the South his friends or would he hunt them down like outlaws? Judge by his past record.

This is, indeed, very mild bloody-shirtism. The greater proportion of Carpenter's speech was devoted to the finances of government, with many figures by which he proved to his own satisfaction that the Republicans were able to run a cheaper government than had the Democrats under Buchanan.[34]

For some six weeks before election every Iowa Congressman, Senator Harlan, and all the state officers and candidates ranged up and down the state, speaking in cities and towns and in country schoolhouses; always, according to report, to "large and enthusiastic" audiences. When a locality could not obtain one of the big names for a meeting, local politicians filled in. For six days out of the week, every Iowan who was interested could find a political gathering somewhere within his neighborhood.

The campaign climaxed with a two-day barbecue in Des Moines where generals, Senators, Congressmen, and assorted orators fired their last broadsides. The meetings began on a Friday afternoon and continued through Saturday evening with such an orgy of speechmaking, torchlight processions, and parades as to have satisfied the most ardent partisan. On Saturday, three speaking-stands were set up on Capitol Hill—the *Register* claimed that each speaker had an audience of 6,000—and 800-foot-long tables "growing [*sic*] with the fat of the land" supplied food for the throngs who were given "twenty minutes for dinner." The demonstrations continued on through the evening, with other groups of speakers situated at strategic points around town. Carpenter was stationed on the "Savery Hotel corner," along with General B. M. Prentiss from Illinois, ex-Governor Stone, J. B. Grinnell, and several colonels and generals, who all made "ringing, stirring addresses." Two other stands were set up—one at the *Register* office and one at the courthouse—so that no one had to go far to hear a political speech. The *Register* concluded its account of the event rhapsodically:

> The meetings all closed by 10 o'clock to allow visitors time to reach the trains, on which they left—everyone of them, with the jewsharp of his soul playing a Te Deum of praise and hallelujah for the glories conquered and realized in the greatest demonstration which has been held in the West during the campaign.

The Republicans were masters of the art of stirring up enthusiasm for their cause. In all, forty-one different speeches were given—if not heard—during the two-day celebration.[35]

The Democrats did their best, but they fought a losing battle from the start. About 190,000 Iowans went to the polls on November 3, in contrast to some 150,000 the year before. Although the Republican papers anticipated at least a 50,000 majority—some hoped for 60,000—the result was more than satisfactory. Grant carried Iowa by over 46,000, while the majorities for the state officers on the ticket ran from 45,000 to 53,000. Carpenter must have felt great satisfaction when he found, after the returns were all in, that he had led his party's ticket with a majority of 53,324.[36]

With Johnson out of office and with Grant in the White House, the Radicals settled down to enact their program without executive interference. The Iowa Radical newspapers could find no fault with Grant, even when James F. Wilson of Fairfield did not receive the Cabinet post for which he had been slated. Rumors had been heard, early in January of 1869, that Wilson, who had represented the First Iowa District in the House from 1861 to 1869, would be in the Cabinet. When the first of Grant's many Cabinets was announced on March 5, Wilson's name was not included. In fact, the whole group of appointments was so bad that it "stupefied the politicians." At first they thought it was a mistake; when assured that it was not, Radical editors tried to make the best of it. They had built Grant too high in the public esteem to permit criticism so soon. The Des Moines *Register* put on a good face for public consumption, praising Grant for appointing men who were not obligated to any "political clique." That the politicians of Iowa did not know the story of the "deal" behind the appointment of Elihu Washburne of Illinois instead of James F. Wilson of Iowa as Secretary of State is incredible. Frank W. Palmer, former editor of the *Register,* was beginning his first term in Congress; his position in Iowa Radicalism should have made him aware of what was going on. Palmer wrote Carpenter on March 18: "We are very well satisfied so far with Ulysses;" possibly the Iowa delegation preferred unity of the party to justice for Wilson.[37]

The story of the Wilson Cabinet offer came out only by degrees. Two weeks after the first announcement, when Washburne had already been replaced by Hamilton Fish of New York, the *Register* carried a paragraph from "one of the leading politicians at Washington," explaining that Wilson had refused an offer of a Cabinet post. The story concluded: "The reason of his refusal of such proffered greatness approaches the unaccountable."[38] What this reason was "the leading politician" did not explain, nor did the *Register.* Two months later, in an obscure paragraph in a one-page supplement to the May 5 issue of the *Register,* a quotation from a Cincinnati

Charles Aldrich

John F. Duncombe

Benjamin Gue

James Grimes

paper appeared. Wilson had been offered and had accepted the State Department, but with the understanding that Washburne would be appointed "simply as a matter of compliment" and would then at once resign to be nominated Minister to France. While he held the office of Secretary of State, Washburne was to make no appointments. Such was the agreement, according to Wilson. Washburne broke the bargain by rushing through a series of appointments; Wilson then withdrew his acceptance and left Washington, in spite of urgings from Grant that he remain. "This statement may be taken as true," the *Register* commented, and then went on to lay the blame for the fiasco on Washburne rather than on Grant, who could have restrained his early Secretary.[39] Thus, Iowa Radicals early took up the line they would follow throughout the Grant regime—no criticism of the President was permitted, no matter how inept his policies.

Some Radical papers ignored the whole Wilson story, while the Iowa City *Republican* solemnly printed an account of Washburne's resignation "because of infirm health." Later, the editor published a letter from "Radical" in Washington, containing a story from a New York paper that Wilson had been offered several Cabinet posts but had refused them all.[40] Surprisingly, even the Democratic Iowa City *Press,* edited by the fiery John P. Irish, ignored the Wilson story.

Such was the partisanship of newspaper editors that the general reader, even if he read both sides of the political activities of the day (often unrecognizable as the same event, so biased were the accounts), could scarcely get a true picture. Republican papers far outnumbered Democratic, so that in many localities only the Republican story was told.

And it was a rosy story indeed. With Johnson gone and their man in office, the Radicals now seized the reins and set their program in motion. Congress quickly took the initiative away from the President on the belief that members of that body were the true voice of the people and that, in Kirkwood's words, "the President was but the executive, whose duty it is to execute their decrees." [41] Even the Supreme Court, in the eyes of some Radicals, should be subservient to Congress. Editor Brainerd of Iowa City contradicted the Cedar Falls and Des Moines papers when they claimed that the Court was a "new" foe to freedom. There was nothing "new" about it, said Brainerd; it had been a foe of freedom "for many long years past." Completely ignoring the tradition of checks and balances set up by the Constitution, some Radicals even called for the abolition of the Court. As late as April of 1868, Brainerd claimed that the framers of the Constitution had "lodged the sovereignty in the people, to be exercised through the Congress, and made both the executive and judicial departments subordinate thereto." [42]

Carpenter shared this low opinion of the Supreme Court. Writing to General Dodge in January of 1867, on the eve of Dodge's service as a Congressman, Carpenter hoped that Dodge could do something "to dispose of this miserable Supreme Court."

> I think the idea that one man just because he is clothed with the robes of an Associate Justice who perhaps before his appointment was a 2nd rate Lawyer holding wordy discussions in barrooms upon mooted points of law, as a Judge becomes suddenly so great and wise that he can set aside by his single will the deliberate judgment of the people and the best considered Laws of Congress is simply preposterous.[43]

The decisions in the River Land cases may have biased Carpenter's judgment of the Court at this time, but he also expressed, to one of Iowa's leading Radicals, true Radical doctrine.

Iowa was prosperous in 1869, and the Republicans took full credit for the good times. L. D. Ingersoll, a former Iowa newspaperman who wrote under the pseudonym of "Likensale," gave the reason for the wealth and affluence of the state. "It is agreed that in radicalism Iowa leads the column in the Northwest," he wrote, and this "superior Radicalism (as first-class patriotism and genuine statesmanship have got to be called) has brought about the superior growth." He then compared Iowa with Wisconsin, to the latter state's disadvantage:

> What is now called "Radicalism," and prosperity, go hand in hand. . . . The man who in politics is desirous of a better state of things for mankind, and more freedom and less "authority" and law, is apt to want to improve his farm also, or his shop. He thus preserves the general consistency of his progressive ideas. Well then, where these men of progressive ideas are greatly in the majority we should expect more improvement in that State than where they are not so greatly in the majority. And so the fact is demonstrated to be in the case of Wisconsin and Iowa, where the greater prosperity of the latter State is in just about the proportion of its great Republican majority.[44]

Thus was the Republican stand hammered home. Prosperity and loyalty were synonymous with Radical Republicanism; poverty and treason were credited to the Democrats. In this, Iowa reflected the line of reasoning that would be the battle cry of the party for many decades. The most popular device for keeping alive the charge of treason against the Democrats was the epithet "Copperhead," which could be found in Iowa newspapers as late as 1895.[45]

As in the nation, the Republican party in Iowa during the Grant years increased its hold on government. In the Iowa 1869 election for Governor, Merrill was returned to office with a comfortable 40,000-vote majority. The real struggles were no longer for the elections but for the nominations in convention. Often there was as much bitterness in these contests as there formerly had been between Republicans and Democrats, the only difference being that the intraparty fights were not so fully aired in the newspapers. The 1870 senatorial contest is a case in point.

The 1870 legislature had the task of electing two Senators—one to fill

Grimes's place which would become vacant in 1871, and the other to fill out the balance of his present term. The ailing Senator, after a second stroke in late May 1869, had concluded that he could not continue his work and had sent in his resignation to Governor Merrill. Although the deep anger at Grimes's betrayal in the Johnson impeachment trial had somewhat subsided by the fall of 1869, the announcement of his resignation received little attention and no regrets. Governor Merrill refused to appoint a successor for the few closing months of Grimes's term, judging that to be "a duty [which] belongs to the Legislature." [46]

No sooner was the fall election of 1869 over than aspirants for both the short and long senatorial terms began their campaigns. In fact, as early as September 29, William Vandever of Dubuque wrote to Carpenter that "Up this way, Judge Wright and Col. Allison are regarded as the leading candidates for the long term—and I know of no disposition on the part of any one to interfere with the contest." George G. Wright, a justice of the state supreme court, had strong support throughout the state. William B. Allison, then serving his fourth term as Congressman from the Third District, could claim many influential friends and the backing of the railroad interests. Vandever was annoyed that the Governor did not appoint a man to the short term, thus taking that office out of the political jockeying, and he hinted rather broadly to Carpenter that he would like to be that man. But the Governor himself had his eye on the Senate, and Vandever's personal ambitions were to be denied. [47]

One of Iowa's most colorful newspapermen and politicians entered the picture. James S. ("Ret") Clarkson (together with his father, Coker F., and his brother, Richard) had bought the Des Moines *Register,* and "Ret's" influence in Iowa Republicanism was soon felt. Writing under his nickname, Clarkson also served as Des Moines correspondent for the Chicago *Tribune.* In a long letter to the Chicago paper, dated November 19, 1869, Ret discussed the claims of the various Iowa candidates. Of the two leading contenders, he gave Wright a slight edge over Allison. He also had something good to say about every other man mentioned for the post, so that the article left the impression that Iowa's only problem was a choice among paragons of all political virtues. On the "locality" question, Ret divided the state by a "line from east to west midway between the North-Western road and the Sioux City road; what is south of the line you may practically call Wright's, and what is north Allison's." This explanation was challenged by Gue in the *North West;* northwestern Iowa, he claimed, was solid for Wright. [48] This was in December. As early as October, Vandever had written Carpenter that there was much dissatisfaction with Allison in his own home district. "It seems to me," he wrote, "that the Senatorial Contest is virtually settled for the long term, at least as far as Allison is concerned; for I cannot see that he stands a ghost of a chance—with several members from his own district dead against him." [49]

When the legislature assembled at Des Moines in January of 1870, Vandever was listed in the Wright camp, along with Thomas F. Withrow, a lawyer and former chairman of the Republican state committee, Judge Caleb Baldwin of Council Bluffs, and several other judges. Allison's "friends" included an imposing list of majors, colonels, generals, and the powerful Grenville M. Dodge. It seemed, on the face of things, a contest between the bench and the army. Contrary to the accepted belief that in the postwar years military men always had the edge in a political contest, the judge easily won over the colonel. Wright was only one vote short of nomination on the informal ballot; on the first formal ballot eleven of Merrill's twenty-four votes left him—three to Wright and eight to Allison. According to Vandever, the Allison people had hoped that they could get all of Merrill's votes. Had this happened, the contest would have been a tie between Allison and Wright with sixty-three votes each (one lone independent preferred Kirkwood). But Vandever had predicted that Merrill could not hold his delegation, and he was correct. Allison's strong support, "backed by the combined railroad influence of the State, with representatives of the Union Pacific, and three quarters of the prominent Federal officials of Iowa," was not sufficient in 1870. [50]

As in the case of the Wilson appointment, much went on behind the scenes before this election that was probably never made known to the average voter. Allison, backed by the growing strength of Dodge and his followers, made a strong fight for the nomination. But there was defection in his own home town: certain Dubuquers set out to defeat him, and they succeeded. Coupled with their activities were charges of corruption against Allison, charges which would haunt him during most of his political life. [51] His defeat was not fatal, however; two years later Allison would be elected Senator to succeed James Harlan, a victory which signaled the triumph of the Dodge wing of Iowa Radicalism.

The short-term contest was resolved after three ballots by nominating James B. Howell, editor of the Keokuk *Gate City*, to fill out Grimes's term until March 1871. Eleven men had been named on the informal ballot, with Grinnell and Howell leading. The contestants gradually dropped out until only John Scott and William Vandever remained in the balloting to garner a few votes away from the leaders. Grinnell made a good showing but did not have the necessary strength to overcome Howell. Clarkson, in his Chicago *Tribune* letter, had hinted that the only thing against Grinnell was the ill-fated Rousseau affair. Grinnell's biographer suggested that he was defeated because he had refused to desert Judge Wright and "make a deal" with the Allison forces. Whatever the cause, Grinnell had again failed to win public office from the Radicals. Two years later, he committed political suicide by joining the Liberal Republican movement.[52]

Grenville M. Dodge and his "ring," composed of James F. Wilson, George Tichenor, William B. Allison, Frank W. Palmer, and others, had been defeated, but their importance in Iowa Republicanism was growing. Dodge had feared the threat of his bitter enemy, John A. Kasson, or a combination of Merrill and Kasson, in the senatorial fight, but the threat did not materialize in the caucus, and Dodge & Co. had to be satisfied with Wright.[53] They would bide their time, and victory would come to them in great measure. Where Carpenter stood in this pulling and hauling is not known. By staying out of the "rings" developing within the party, he managed to find friends in both camps, no mean achievement in days of bitter party feuds.

Carpenter did not, however, keep out of the party fights in his own district, the Sixth. There things were building up to a rousing contest for Congress, and Fort Dodge animosities were the motivating factors. Battles for seats in Congress were often heated; in some district conventions, where several strong men had loyal and stubborn supporters, the number of ballots needed to nominate could, and sometimes did, run well over one hundred.

Charles Pomeroy had been sent to Congress from Carpenter's district in 1868 after a 77-ballot contest in the nominating convention. According to custom, he should have been renominated in 1870 without question. But a combination of circumstances had made him unpopular with a large segment of the Republican leadership and with an even larger segment of the electorate. To begin with, after his election he had allied himself with A. M. Dawley's wing of Fort Dodge Republicanism; the opposing Gue-Carpenter branch of the party, which had worked hard for Pomeroy's first nomination, did not take kindly to this. Then there were other things, such as the appointment of a township postmaster who had the support of sixteen Republicans, but the opposition of "over 100." Furthermore, northwestern Iowa, considerably aroused by the plight of the River Land settlers and by a quarrel with the Des Moines Valley Railroad, did not like Pomeroy's vote in favor of a subsidy for the Northern Pacific Railroad, since large grants to railroads were coming into disfavor. Emmett wrote to Cyrus that the feeling against Pomeroy was so strong that one of Pomeroy's supporters "could not have influenced his little girl to have voted for him." [54]

When the district convention assembled on July 20, there were some half-dozen candidates, with Jackson Orr of Boone County heading the list against Pomeroy. On the informal ballot Pomeroy led, but without enough votes for the nomination. The formal ballots then began and continued slowly, with but small shifts here and there, with four names most prominent: Pomeroy, Orr, Ford, and Couch. On the twelfth ballot Carpenter's name was introduced, probably as a diversion, and six men voted for him. By that time

Pomeroy's vote was slipping fast, while Orr's was gaining. On the fourteenth ballot the swing was completed, and Orr won easily—while two still remained loyal to Carpenter. As an anticlimax to the contest, Gue received a curt note from Pomeroy, asking that his subscription to the *North West* be discontinued. Gue printed the note and replied to it in a long public letter, writing more in sorrow than in anger and chiding Pomeroy for his desertion of his friends.[55] The aftermath of the contest left the Gue-Carpenter wing stronger in northwestern Iowa than it had ever been.

Carpenter was not a candidate for Register in 1870. He had served his two terms and was now ready to go on to bigger things. Nevertheless, he worked as hard as usual in the campaign, stumping the Fifth District with Palmer and the Sixth District with Orr. The victory at the polls gave the Republicans over a 42,000 majority for the state offices, an indication that the party was safely holding its own in the state.[56]

The electorate increased with the growing population of Iowa, and the state was due for reapportionment. Some suggested that the increased representation be supplied by Congressmen-at-large rather than by a change in the existing districts. Gue, as early as June, had mentioned Carpenter's name for one of the new seats. But even before that, a hint of what was in store for Carpenter had been bruited about in Fort Dodge. In January, Emmett wrote his brother that "an old Presiding Elder," who had been in Des Moines "to loby [sic] for Allison," had visited in Fort Dodge. "He told us that he heard a lot of fellows (Withrow of Des Moines among them) talking about running you for Governor." [57]

Withrow was in the upper echelon of the Republican hierarchy, and his word would carry weight. But perhaps just as important for Carpenter's future was the work he had done while Register in the battle between northwestern Iowans and the Des Moines Valley Railroad. This road had reached Des Moines in 1866, and Fort Dodge fully expected it to continue on its way up the river and into their city. When the Des Moines Valley decided to build some six miles west of Fort Dodge, sending their trains in on a spur, Gue, Carpenter, and Duncombe had combined forces with other Fort Dodgers to force the road to comply with the terms of their land grant which required them to build "into the city of Fort Dodge." Carpenter had been in the front of the fight for several years, writing letters to the newspapers, appearing before legislative committees, and serving on the boards of "paper railroads" drawn up at Fort Dodge to force the hand of the Des Moines Valley. At last, after four years of argument and threats, the Des Moines Valley agreed to build its main line into Fort Dodge, reaching there on December 22, 1870.[58] Although Carpenter had played only a minor role in this struggle, he had gained greatly in the esteem of his neighbors by his work in their behalf.

-EIGHT-

The 1871 Gubernatorial Campaign

WHY DID THE Republicans choose Carpenter for their candidate for Governor in 1871? Certainly there were more prominent men in the state who would have been willing to run. In fact, several made a fight for the post, but they were not of the upper crust of the party leadership. The office of Governor of Iowa is not a strong one; unless the incumbent is one of the top men in the party organization, he actually wields little power. If one of these top men did not hold the office, the man chosen would have to be one willing to work for—or at least not to hamper—the plans and program of the party.[1]

A Des Moines correspondent of the Democratic Dubuque *Herald* had his interpretation of the nomination of Carpenter:

> The men who manage Carpenter now and who will manage him should he be elected governor, know by experience how to manage their party in this state, when they wish to accomplish their ends. Carpenter himself is a good, clever fellow, but without the help of the capital clique, could not have made a ripple on the surface of Iowa politics. He would not have been heard of had they not picked him up and placed him at the head of their ticket. This, it is needless to say, was not done through any especial affection for him. They wanted a governor of their own, and they expect to have him.[2]

The story of Carpenter's selection and nomination would seem to bear out this opinion in some respects. As a loyal Radical, Carpenter could be expected to endorse the party program. What was this program in 1871? The platform tells little. It pointed with pride to the record of the Republicans and to the administration of President Grant, it favored economy in government, recognized the claims of agriculture, approved a uniform system of taxation, and endorsed "such protection" to American industry "as a fairly adjusted revenue tariff" would afford. In only one plank was there a new note: impelled by the pressure of public opinion, the Republicans for the first time called for "proper legislative enactment, as to effectually prevent monopoly and extortion on the part of railroads and other corporations."[3]

The popular picture of the Republican party in the age of "Grantism" is of a party filled with corruption and dominated by the interests of the corporations. Stories of dishonesty in the national and state governments were plentiful, while accounts of the buying of votes and the powerful influence of railroad lobbies were common. New York's "Boss" Tweed rode high in these years; in Illinois "there was a veritable orgy of boodle legislation" in 1867; in Wisconsin the railroad lobby had been able to defeat all unfriendly bills; and in Missouri a senatorial candidate was said to have spent $15,000 in buying votes.[4]

Iowa escaped most of these charges of corruption, although an effort was made by the Democratic press to play up the questionable activities of Governor Merrill's secretary in a swamp land deal. The Democratic newspapers never passed up an opportunity to repeat hints or outright accusations of lack of political morals among Republican officeholders, but no really headline-making scandal had yet erupted. As to the influence of the railroads, certainly the lobbies had been successful in Iowa in halting regulatory legislation, although the Doud Amendment, which spelled out the state's right to regulate railroad freight rates, still stood on the statute books —unenforced but a prevailing threat.[5] But there were rumblings of discontent, even in some Republican papers. Therefore, it was up to the Republican leadership in 1871 to provide a candidate who was above reproach and who had, in the public eye, a record of independence as far as the railroads were concerned.

The primary purpose of the Republican party was, after all, to win the election. Even the comfortable majorities of the last few years might melt away if they put up candidates not acceptable to the voters. And, by 1871, a strong undercurrent of revolt was building up in the Middle West, partly stemming from the growing Granger movement which was mobilizing the farmers, and partly a result of the widening split within the party—a split which would crystalize as the Liberal Republican movement of 1872. To court the votes of these factions, it was necessary to nominate a man who would appeal to all sides.

While Carpenter's opponents in the race for the gubernatorial nomination were bitterly attacked or stoutly defended by opposing elements, no Republican newspaper, in an age of often scurrilous journalism, could find anything to object to in Carpenter. Even the Democratic press had little to say against him; the caustic pen of John P. Irish of the Iowa City *Press* could only belittle him "as one of the best desk clerks that ever served the State." [6]

Another item needed to be considered in the nomination. Carpenter's district, the Sixth, comprising about one-third of the state, included the thirty-six counties in northwestern Iowa. No Governor had been chosen from this area, which prided itself on its large Republican vote at the polls, and the Republicans there were now determined that the next Governor should be from the "Big Sixth." The Cedar Falls *Gazette* announced in December of 1870 that "we propose to have our say in naming the next Governor." The Marshalltown *Times* threatened "a fuss in the family" if a candidate from the Sixth District were not nominated, while the Jefferson *Era* from Greene County was even more forthright: "The big Sixth speaks to be heard, not only for the present, but that the echo of her thunder tones shall reverberate down the corridor of time, warning the future Conventions that she demands a representative in the gubernatorial chair."[7] Thus, the question of locality was important in considering a candidate. Carpenter's opponents in the race came from Muscatine and Mitchell counties; until John Scott of Story County announced his candidacy Carpenter was unopposed as to locality.

Aside from the demands of honesty, railroads, and geography, the paramount issue in 1871 was the choice of a United States Senator. Grenville M. Dodge and his wing of the party were concentrating all their efforts on one thing—the defeat of James Harlan and the victory of William Boyd Allison. The voters in the fall, aside from choosing a Governor and the top state officials, would also elect a legislature that would pick a Senator to fill the expiring term of James Harlan. Allison had lost his bid in 1870; his backers had no intention of suffering a second defeat.[8] Much depended on whether Harlan or Allison chose the nominee for Governor.

All these facets of the Republican program for 1871 would determine the candidate to head the ticket. The man for Governor must have a sound reputation for honesty and integrity to offset the repeated charges of Republican corruption; he must be "right" geographically; he must not be either too "anti" or too "pro" railroads; and, if Dodge had his way, he must support Allison instead of Harlan for the senatorship. Did Carpenter fill these requirements?

He was certainly right geographically, and his nickname of "Honest Cy" expressed the prevailing opinion of him throughout the state. His public quarrel with the Des Moines Valley Railroad might have made him suspect in the eyes of the railroad interests, but was he actually as much of an enemy of the railroads as his activities would seem to indicate? The fact that Grenville M. Dodge, the head of the strongest wing of the party, and himself a recognized "railroad man," chose Carpenter for the nomination, with the consent of William B. Allison, would indicate that the railroads did not fear—or even worry about—Carpenter.

Early in January 1871, George Tichenor, with his usual excitement, wrote to Dodge:

We must fix upon our men for Gov & Lieut Gov *at once*. Harlan is looking to these matters already. . . . I think *you* are the man. Baldwin
{Caleb Baldwin of Council Bluffs} would be *my* next choice although I
cant promise much *open* work while John A. Elliott is a candidate as he &
I are good friends. It would simplify the matter if you would run.

Dodge sent the letter to Allison with a note on the back: "Cale dont want
to run. *I cant.* Suppose we put forth C. C. Carpenter of the 6th Dist. We
have no time to lose." Allison's reply sealed the bargain: "I agree with you
with reference to the Governorship substantially, and the 6th Dist. will
undoubtedly claim it, and from all you say, and from what Palmer says,
Mr. C. is the right man." But Tichenor was not so willing to accept Carpenter:

I think it would be better for all of us if either you or Cale Baldwin would
run for Governor. Carpenter is a clever man but not a strong man; and I
find that Gue, Orr and his other associates are opposed to Allison, some of
them bitterly, and I should want a positive pledge from Carpenter on that
question before supporting him.[9]

This, then, was the important point. The Dodge faction was determined
to win in the coming struggle between Harlan and Allison, and therefore
the gubernatorial candidate they chose—in addition to having the other
requirements—must be on their side in the senatorial contest. Carpenter
explained his position in a letter to Dodge on January 31. He could not
"afford to be a partisan" in the senatorial race, he assured Dodge, but his
preference was for Allison: "there is no one in Iowa that I regard more
highly than Mr. Allison, besides this he is comparatively my neighbor, and
being on the same line of road our interests are allied." [10] Was the latter
part of this statement a covert assurance to Dodge that Carpenter, in spite of
his recent quarrel with the Des Moines Valley, was not opposed to all railroads as such? Carpenter was seldom devious, but he was in a race for a big
office, and the experience may have made him cautious. Furthermore, he
knew Dodge and he knew what Dodge wanted to hear. At any rate, this
letter decided the issue and enrolled Carpenter in Dodge & Co. It also
allayed Tichenor's fears. Thus, it was, six months before the nominating
convention, that the choice of Carpenter was made. This did not mean
that there was no work to be done, however.

A candidate for office had to round up his delegates by writing innumerable letters, traveling about the state to meet with county leaders, and
wooing the support of influential newspaper editors. Only a few counties
had yet adopted the primary system of electing members to the state
nominating convention; a majority of the delegates would be appointed by
county caucuses. The man or men who controlled these caucuses controlled

the vote of the county. These were the men the candidate had to cultivate. In spite of powerful support, Carpenter was not without rivals.

Probably the first in the field, publicly, was Henry O'Connor of Muscatine. The "gallant Major" had an excellent background for the office. Of Irish birth, he had studied law in Cincinnati and emigrated to Iowa in 1849. A Free Soiler by conviction, O'Connor had been a delegate in 1856 to the convention that had organized the Republican party in Iowa. His ability as an orator had won him fame and popularity, while his services in the Union Army had won him a commission and a host of army friends. In 1867, he had been elected to the office of attorney general of Iowa, and he was still holding that office in 1871. Most active in support of O'Connor was the Muscatine *Journal* which came out strongly for his candidacy as early as December 1870. As the campaign progressed, newspapers in Davenport, Pella, Clinton, Mt. Pleasant, Vinton, Malvern, Tama, and Atlantic also gave him support.[11] Other candidates rose to prominence and declined, but O'Connor remained Carpenter's strongest opponent throughout the campaign.

John A. Elliott, state auditor from 1865 to 1871, was another serious contender. By January, he was "already busy at work."[12] A native of Pennsylvania, Elliott had come to Iowa in 1857 and located on a farm in Mitchell County. He was the only candidate without a Civil War record. Elected state auditor in 1864, he had served three terms in a manner apparently acceptable to the people and to the politicians.[13] However, his candidacy for Governor brought down upon him a storm of abuse and accusation from various Republican papers, a storm which eventually brought about his withdrawal from the campaign.

Hardly had Elliott announced that he was "available" than the Iowa City *Republican* attacked him, claiming that he had "made too much money out of his position of Auditor to be entitled to further honors from the people of Iowa." An insurance law, passed by the General Assembly in 1868, had provided that the fees collected under the law should be paid to the Auditor. The *Republican* and the other papers that joined in the attacks on Elliott implied that he had taken the fees illegally instead of turning them into the State Treasury. During January and February, the Iowa City *Republican,* the Council Bluffs *Nonpareil,* and the Marshalltown *Times,* in particular, stormed against Elliott, the latter paper warning that "should oily John be elected Governor he would clear at least $100,000 during his Gubernatorial term—and all in a perfectly lawful manner." The Des Moines *Register* was quick to point out that Elliott had acted in accordance with the law, that the salary of the Auditor was only $1,300 per year, and that the intention of the law had been for him to collect the fees to supplement this small stipend. The fact that the insurance business of Iowa was making rapid strides during these years had made these fees much larger than anticipated. This defense of Elliott by the *Register* quickly sent E. N. Chapin, editor of the Marshalltown *Times,* scurrying for cover with a wordy retraction that amused the Iowa City *Republican,* a paper not so easily intimidated by the powerful Des Moines journal.[14]

On February 3, Elliott wrote an angry letter to Carpenter, asking if he endorsed or encouraged these "attacks on an old friend" and suggesting that Carpenter had the power to stop them. "I can't be 'shelved' in that way," he concluded, "and such a course if it does injure me would *not* help you." "Shelved" he was, however, and rather quickly. Lacking any assurances of help from the politically powerful, Elliott retired from the contest on April 3, "owing to the pressure of my private business," as he phrased it. This had been a foregone conclusion to those who knew Iowa politics. Isaac Brandt, who claimed that he knew Elliott "as well as he does himself," had prophesied as early as February 15 that Elliott would "fly the track before the convention comes off." [15]

Thus, one strong contender was removed, and the way opened for some of the party leaders to work openly for Carpenter. It is significant to note that Tichenor's public support for Carpenter did not come until April 5, two days after Elliott had withdrawn. As Tichenor had written Dodge in January, Elliott was his good friend. He had to keep himself in "shape to control Elliott," he added. It was an "unpleasant and dangerous situation," but he did not intend to "shrink from anything" and suggested that Dodge, Allison, and James F. Wilson "make every possible show of friendship toward Elliott consistent with honor." [16] Now, with Elliott safely out of the way, the campaign could move ahead as planned. Tichenor wrote to Carpenter:

> I am now *openly* and earnestly at work for *you.* . . . I have to day written *13* letters in your behalf and can assure you I have my coat off and henceforth till the Convention, shall be 'on the war path' and you are aware that I am usually energetic if not efficient.
> Command me at all times.[17]

Long before Tichenor had added his blessing to the Carpenter candidacy, a strong support had built up for the nominee of the "Big Sixth." Early in January, Colonel George L. Godfrey, a Des Moines attorney active in political affairs, had written to Carpenter that if he really intended to be a candidate he should "have it understood *at once,*" since both O'Connor and Elliott were already in the field. "Now Carpenter," Godfrey concluded, "don't be to[o] *modist* [*sic*] in this matter, but come out, and let *every body* know that your friends intend to make a Governor out of the X Register." [18]

These friends were many. Most active was Charles Aldrich whose enthusiasm kept Carpenter constantly encouraged. He was the spark plug of the Carpenter campaign and together with brother Emmet and brother-in-law Arthur Burkholder, he worked ceaselessly. Spurred on by these friends and with assurances from Dodge, Carpenter at last agreed to come out publicly in his own behalf. Once the decision was made, he set to work. He wrote his wife on February 3: "I intend to fight the thing through just as manfully as I know how, and if I win I shall be glad, if I fail, I shall live just as long and die just as happy." [19]

Carpenter at once began to send a stream of letters throughout the state. The answers give a cross-section of the political life of the era as well as a good illustration of the methods in common political use at the time. The following letter to John McKean of Anamosa is a sample of Carpenter's campaign letters:

> My name, for some weeks, has been quite freely associated with the approaching Gubernatorial nomination. And while I did not originate my own candidacy, and in fact, at the first suggestion of my name in connection with it, shrank from its mention as a candidate, yet now that I have come to be regarded as in the field, I would like to succeed. You will therefore excuse me for writing in my own behalf. If you think my nomination would not be incompatible with the public interest, and if I am personally acceptable to you, it would highly gratify me to have your support. But allow me to say, that as much as I would prize that support, if from any cause you are not at liberty to aid me, I shall remain, as ever, your friend, C. C. Carpenter.[20]

Although McKean's answer was noncommittal, other letters revealed enthusiastic support for Carpenter, and many newspapers published favorable comments. As early as January 26, Gue, in the Fort Dodge *North West,* after quoting generously from other newspapers supporting Carpenter, concluded: "From a careful examination of our exchanges we are confident that Col. Carpenter would be acceptable to the great mass of the Republican party." Even this early endorsement, before Carpenter had even begun an active campaign on his own behalf, was not soon enough for Arthur Burkholder. He wrote Carpenter on January 20: "I was surprised that Gue didn't come out for you this week. Privately, I believe he's holding back, hoping to fix it so that, if he can't run in himself, he will defeat you, thus giving him a show for something else. He can do you a great deal of good, at large, by heartily supporting you, for a great many people, away from home, think he's 'a persimmon.'" But Arthur's worries were groundless; Gue supported Carpenter generously throughout the campaign.[21]

The influential Des Moines *Register,* most powerful Republican paper in the state, refused to support any one of the candidates, but Editor James S. Clarkson, leader of the "Des Moines Regency" and chairman of the Republican state committee, was secretly backing Carpenter. In April, Carpenter received a letter signed "Mum," written in the famous illegible scrawl of "Ret" Clarkson. "Mum" assured Carpenter: "I do not want to be known in this matter, but what stones I can throw in your yard, *will be there*." [22]

One letter, which would certainly have been a surprise to the Democrats of Iowa, came from Carpenter's perennial political enemy, John F. Duncombe:

> Happy to aid you all in my power. Wrote letters to Davis Cleghorn Smith & Ford of Sioux City for you—also to Platt Smith to write Allison.
>
> Hope your prospects are good Write all your friends, pitch in your best, rush the work & I believe you can make it.
>
> Dont be to[o] modest about asking your friends to aid you—*persistency* is the *true theory* in politics.
>
> Let me know when I can help you & I will do it freely & with all my heart & sincerely hope that you may succeed. [23]

This letter reveals at least two things about the political scene. First, whatever a Democrat or a Republican might say about each other for public consumption, they often cooperated most harmoniously in private. Duncombe, of course, realized that his party had practically no chance in the election; therefore, it would be greatly to his advantage to have his fellow-townsman in Des Moines. Secondly, his reference to Platt Smith and Allison is an indication that Duncombe would use his influence with the railroad men to reassure them—and Allison—that Carpenter was "safe" as far as the railroad interests were concerned. Platt Smith, a lawyer of Dubuque, had been attorney for the Dubuque & Pacific in 1860–1861 and vice president of the road from 1861 to 1868. He wielded wide influence both in railroad and in political circles, and his approval would serve to assure Allison of Carpenter's position. [24]

Thus, we have the picture of Carpenter and the railroads. Publicly, he had made a strong fight against the Des Moines Valley in the interests of Fort Dodge. [25] This made him, in the opinion of the average voter, who was growing more and more antagonistic to the great monopolies, an anti-railroad man. Privately, his supporters were assuring the railroad interests that Carpenter was "all right."

No doubt aware of Dodge's endorsement, many politicians were soon on the Carpenter band wagon. Iowa Adjutant-General Nathaniel B. Baker, Isaac Brandt, and the banker and State Senator B. F. Allen, who had himself been suggested for the governorship, favored Carpenter. Brandt, a Des Moines politican and deputy state treasurer, had written in February that he had "a nice little under current at work, that I think is doing good work," and added, "but remember we must *push things*." The popular General Baker, who could have had any Iowa office he desired "if he would only become a teetotler," was tireless in his work for and advice to Carpenter.

Arthur Burkholder wrote in January: "Gen. Baker announced this morning that he was a Carpenter man. I believe you said once that he would be for 'the coming man,' so you must be 'that fellow.' " State Auditor John Russell bolstered Carpenter's morale when his competitors pressed too closely by assuring him that Elliott was "blinded and brassey—and cant be Gov." [26]

Added to this strong support was Carpenter's popularity with the younger men who would, within a few years, themselves wield power. Joseph Dysart, to be Lieutenant Governor during Carpenter's second term, promised to work for his nomination. William P. Hepburn regretted that he had given a half-promise to O'Connor, which he felt obliged to honor—a promise he would not have given had he known Carpenter was to be a candidate. Lafe Young, editor of the Atlantic *Telegraph,* was strong in Carpenter's support. He was willing to "wager the *Telegraph* for one year that you get the nomination." William Larrabee, future Governor, promised help "with the understanding that your nomination will not prejudice senatorial interests in the northern part of the state." [27]

Support from the Des Moines "ring," from General Dodge, and from his friends and neighbors in Fort Dodge was not enough to elect Carpenter, however, unless the majority of the county leaders would also agree on him. Gradually letters from such men began to come in from other parts of the state, the great majority promising help and giving encouragement. James B. Weaver, whose break with the Republican party was still in the future, wrote in March that he would do all he could for Carpenter, adding that his own name had been mentioned in connection with the governorship but that he was not a candidate. On the other hand, ex-Governor Kirkwood, whose endorsement would have meant much, wrote in April that his support had already been promised to John Scott, although he would be satisfied with "either of you." He did not plan to take an active part in the canvass, Kirkwood said, and was sorry that he could not "go for both you & him." [28] Since Scott had not announced his candidacy until late, and since Carpenter's campaign was public knowledge long before that time, it would seem that Kirkwood was lending his powerful aid to a "johnny-come-lately" effort to defeat the "X Register."

Carpenter had been in Washington in early February, and while there he had been close to Iowa's Congressmen, the "men who can make or unmake Governors." Although support from these men was probably promised in some instances, since his stay in Washington had given him an opportunity to talk over his candidacy personally, the Carpenter letters do not reveal it. Iowa's two Senators, George G. Wright and James Harlan, were both friendly; the new Representative from the Sixth District, Jackson W. Orr, would naturally throw his influence to Carpenter; Frank W. Palmer of the Fifth District, a member of Dodge & Co., also favored Carpenter; Allison's position on the governorship had already been decided by Dodge.[29]

Senatorial support, however, was an explosive subject in 1871. Allison's bid for Harlan's seat would overshadow the gubernatorial contest, and Carpenter was acting with great circumspection to avoid the fight. Harlan wrote him on May 3, from his home in Mount Pleasant:

> On the subject of your candidacy I have had some difficulty to avoid being misunderstood, and to prevent some of my friends misunderstanding your position, so far as it may be supposed to relate even remotely to the election of U. S. Senator. I have written numerous letters to various parties to this effect: that you and I are personal friends of many years standing: that we have had a frank conversation on the subject of your candidacy, and the possible use of my name before the Legislature: that you wish to be nominated on your own merits without reference to the Senatorial question, and without committals, reserving your liberty to act in relation to the latter question as in your opinion the interests of the State, Nation and Republican Party may seem to you to require: and that I fully approved of your position.[30]

Thus, by cleverly placating both sides, Carpenter continued to win support from both the Allison and Harlan factions of the party—no easy task. General Dodge and Ret Clarkson were determined to defeat Harlan for re-election; other Carpenter friends were just as determined to defeat Allison.[31] Here again the question of locality came up. Generally speaking, southern Iowa favored Harlan of Mount Pleasant, and northern Iowa favored Allison of Dubuque, although there naturally were exceptions. According to Arthur Burkholder, a Des Moines correspondent of the Chicago *Times* had reported that "Harlan and Allison—whichever is the strongest—will make the next Governor." [32]

Emmett Carpenter felt that his brother was in a position that would not interfere with either senatorial contestant, since neither was from the Sixth District. M. M. Trumbull, who was collector of internal revenue at Dubuque, wrote in February that Jacob Rich, editor of the Dubuque *Times,* would be controlled on the governorship by its effect on the senatorial question—thus indicating that the fear in Dubuque was that a northern candidate for Governor might interfere with Allison's candidacy for the Senate. E. A. Teeling, clerk of the Floyd County District Court, wrote to Carpenter:

> . . . if it Should be the opinion that the Nomination for Governor Should fall to the 6th District and it would favor the election of Hon Wm B Allison as Senitor [*sic*] from this State I know of no Man who I would support more willingly than yourself and you must know that the republicans of this District and in fact this north part of the State desire the election of Allison to the Senate.

The postmaster of Monticello in Jones County, James Davidson, advised Carpenter that the Allison element was strong in his section; he hoped Carpenter would not "mix in" the senatorial contest. A. W. Hubbard, former Congressman from the Sixth District, warned Carpenter against an alliance with either Harlan or Allison. On the other hand, James M. Weart, an attorney of Independence in Buchanan County, hoped that the Sixth District would support Allison. Locality did not always determine the political complexion of a community, however. From Elkader in Clayton County, G. W. Cook, a lawyer, wrote to Carpenter that the delegation from his county preferred Harlan and would be controlled by the senatorial question in their support for the gubernatorial candidate.[33]

In March, the gubneratorial-senatorial campaign was complicated by the appearance of another contender for the Governor's chair. On March 20, after repeated rumors of his candidacy, John Scott of Story County in the Sixth District wrote candidly to Carpenter: "I have at last consented to take a 'weak hand' in the little game for Gubernatorial Honors. I want to see you, and talk over the situation. I expect you will want to win, and would rather beat two men than have one man beat you! How is that?"[34] Carpenter's answer to this proposal is unknown, but rumors of a "deal" were soon in circulation. In Marshalltown, shortly after his letter to Carpenter, Scott explained that he and Carpenter "and their respective friends, have agreed together, to work away till the Convention sits, and then determine which will withdraw in favor of the other." In April, Scott began "abusing" Carpenter, saying that the latter had *"arranged"* things and then gone back on him. Aldrich, who reported this incident, added that "I guess no one believes him."[35]

Whether Scott had deluded himself into thinking he had a deal with Carpenter, or whether he merely talked of such an arrangement for public consumption, is difficult to say. Two days after he wrote Carpenter that he was going to take a hand in the game, he wrote to Aaron Brown, Carpenter's successor as Register of the State Land Office: "I rather think I am in the race for Gubernatorial honors." On April 10, while accusations flew back and forth, Scott again wrote Brown:

> When I saw you last the understanding between Carpenter and myself was, at least with *me,* that neither of us would be announced without some further understanding—something definite. I hoped to arrange matters so that we would not both be in the field. I acted upon that understanding until the ground was largely occupied by him—and much of his territory I have studiously avoided, even yet. I was even disposed to yield the whole thing to him, after I saw what some of his friends were doing—but finally I concluded to say "yes"—and now am in the ring.[36]

Considering the fact that Carpenter had no need to make any "deals"—backed as he was by some of the most powerful men in the party—and that his candidacy had been announced early in February, Scott's late entry and his efforts at explaining his reasons for this are somewhat suspect.

Who was back of Scott's candidacy? This was the question that troubled Carpenter and his friends. Scott, a native of Ohio and a Civil War veteran, had served several terms in the Iowa legislature and had been Lieutenant Governor during Merrill's first term. Clarkson, in his "Mum" letter, hinted at "unseen causes . . . operating in the Scott interest—Masonry or Harlanism, or both." Aldrich had reported that there was undoubtedly a combination between Scott and Harlan, but J. B. Powers of Cedar Falls discounted this, at least as far as his county was concerned, adding that Harlan would know better than to enter into such a combination.[37]

There was a strong feeling, however, that some one was back of Scott. George W. Jones of Des Moines could "only guess at the source and projectors" of Scott's action, but he assured Carpenter that his friends in Des Moines were standing firm. Aldrich, who traveled about the state in Carpenter's interest, thought that Scott had been brought out by Elliott in order to defeat Carpenter. This information seems to have worried Carpenter, and he wrote to John Russell. Russell's reply, dated March 28, 1871, was in part a confirmation of the rumor, in part a reassurance of the efforts of Carpenter's friends in his behalf. In Dubuque, Editor Dennis A. Mahony of the Herald, said that it was a repetition of the "same shrewd policy" that Harlan had used "two years ago to kill off Allison." But, according to Mahony, O'Connor and not Elliott was the instigator. On a "divide and rule" policy, suggested Mahony, Scott had been persuaded to come out, thus splitting the Sixth District and assuring that the prize would then go to O'Connor. "Scott bites, of course—who ever knew a lean and hungry radical officeholder that did not bite—he is hard at work killing off Carpenter with good prospect of success, and meanwhile the wily and oleaginous O'Connor will probably step in and take the prize." [38] Mahony was wrong in his judgment of the result, but his explanation was plausible, as were all of the other interpretations of the Scott move.

During the rest of the campaign, rumors of alliances of Harlan and Scott, or of Allison and Carpenter, or even of Harlan and Carpenter, were plentiful. Trumbull of Dubuque wrote to Carpenter that "it was reported . . . that your friends and those of Mr. Allison had formed an alliance;" while Aldrich in April felt "no doubt that there is a combination between Scott and Harlan." From Chariton came a warning from William H. Gibbon: "If you are a Harlan man you had better keep that fact mighty dark so far as this part of the State is concerned." On the other hand, J. B. Powers of Cedar Falls reported that he was sure no combination of Harlan and Scott was working against Carpenter's interests. Carpenter, for his part, followed the advice of Elijah Sells, a strong Harlan man, to "Keep out of the Senatorial Contest," and his unofficial campaign managers did their best to quash all such rumors.[39] George W. Jones, state representative from Polk

County in 1870 and one of Carpenter's staunch friends, advised him in April:

> I wrote Senator Harlan a long letter a few days Since giving him my views of the Contest for Governor & telling him to Keep any of his friends from thinking there was any Combination between you & Allison because the North Seemed to be supporting you so strongly, told him that I know personally that you would not form any Combination even to secure the nomination. . . . This was a point I thought it very important to make just now, as I see evidences of an active & earley [*sic*] opening of the Senatorial campaign.[40]

Surface indications were, then, that Carpenter was able to steer clear of the troubled waters of the senatorial contest in spite of rumors and hints. However, the fact that both Carpenter and Allison were backed by Dodge and the Des Moines Regency—privately if not publicly—made it inevitable that much Allison support would go to Carpenter. Tichenor wrote Carpenter in May: "we can give you the Allison strength, I think *solid,* and can capture considerably from Harlans forces, unless they come up [to the convention] far better organized than they now are, or are likely to be by that time." [41]

On June 24, three days after Carpenter's nomination, Allison wrote him an interesting and revealing "Private" letter:

> Dear Carpenter: In the Hurley Burly at Des Moines, I did not get to see you, and now wish to sincerely and heartily congratulate you on your nomination for Govr. I feel certain that your selection by the Convention will be fully endorsed at the polls. At your Convenience I shall be very glad to see you and talk matters over with you. There are some things I wish to say that I will not trouble you about in a letter. It was claimed at D[es Moines] that your selection was a victory in a direction hostile to me. I am quite willing they should now hear such.[42]

This letter, plus several newspaper comments following the nomination, would indicate that the secret of Carpenter's position in the Allison ranks was well guarded. The Republican Marshalltown *Times* and the Democratic Dubuque *Herald* both misjudged the results, claiming that Carpenter's nomination was a victory for Harlan. Even after the election, Horace Greeley's New York *Tribune* sagely commented that the result insured Harlan's victory.[43] By clever and astute maneuvering the dominant wing of the Republican party in Iowa had succeeded in so confusing the issue as to hide their goal from all but those of the inner circle.

The senatorial contest was only one facet of the gubernatorial campaign, however. Equally important to the outcome of the canvass was the support of the local editors of the state. Journalism was intensely partisan in the nineteenth century Middle West. Most towns of any size had two papers—

Republican and Democratic—and some of the larger urban communities had two Republican journals, representing the two factions of the dominant party. Editorial feuds were the order of the day and became doubly bitter during a political campaign. John P. Irish reported in March that "Early in the year the canvass for Gov. on the radical ticket commenced with activity and in about three days degenerated into virulence." [44] Newspaper readers were bombarded with "puffs" for some candidates or with attacks on others. Since these county papers and their editors wielded great political influence, it was to the advantage of the candidates to win as many of them to their support as possible.

The editorial prize would be, of course, endorsement by the influential Des Moines *Register*. Clarkson refused to take a public stand, however. Each candidate received complimentary notices—that for Carpenter appeared early in January, praising his record as Register and closing with the words: "The people recognize in him a man of morals, convictions, intelligence, and experience, and not a few of them desire his promotion to the Executive chair." Replying to criticism from the Ottumwa *Courier* that he was not more forthright, Clarkson wrote that "the Register is not so fortunate as to have a candidate for Governor of its own. . . . The candidate of this paper for Governor will be the nominee of the party." Thus, although secretly backing Carpenter, the organ of the Regency maintained, in print, a strict neutrality, a course which Aldrich considered "peculiar." [45]

Other papers in the state were not so devious. As early as January the Algona *Upper Des Moines* endorsed Carpenter, "first, last, and all the time." C. V. Gardner, editor of the Avoca paper in Pottawattamie County, backed Carpenter without an *"if or a but."* Most northern Iowa papers, especially those of the Sixth District, were strong in his support, at least until the announcement of the candidacy of John Scott. In addition to the Fort Dodge papers, Carpenter received praise from the Marshalltown *Times,* the Storm Lake *Pilot,* the Independence *Bulletin,* the Cedar Falls *Gazette,* the Waukon *Standard,* the Monona County *Gazette,* the Webster City *Freeman,* and the Grundy County *Atlas.* M. C. Woodruff, editor of the Iowa Falls *Sentinel,* wrote Carpenter that *"you're my man for Gov. agst the State."* From Sioux City, George D. Perkins, editor of the strong Sioux City *Journal,* a Harlan paper, wrote frankly that he would support Elliott on grounds of long acquaintance, but that Carpenter's letter had raised him "several pegs" in his estimation. Andy Felt of the Nashua *Post* had wanted Ret Clarkson for Governor, he wrote, but Carpenter was his second choice. As the weeks passed, more northern Iowa papers came out for Carpenter; those of Monona, Hancock, Wright, and Plymouth counties among others. In May, the Waterloo *Reporter* carried an editorial urging Carpenter's nomination, and the Cedar Falls *Gazette* found "an almost unanimous expression that the Sixth District should go in solid for Col. Carpenter for Governor." [46]

Editorial endorsement of a candidate was not without its hazards, however. Samuel S. Haislet of the Decorah *Press* claimed that his backing of Carpenter caused foreclosure of a "Chattle Mortgage" on part of his equipment,[47] and A. M. Bryson of Osage, in Mitchell County, had some devious plans for overcoming the editorial rivalry of the two Republican papers in his county.[48] Letters of this type usually contained more or less subtle hints for money to help out the cause. Emmett warned his brother to "move *cautiously*" in such matters, advice that Cyrus no doubt followed.[49] He had little money to spend on buying editorial support.

Newspapers from other parts of the state came over to Carpenter's side as the campaign progressed. Charles Beardsley of the Burlington *Hawk-Eye* published favorable notices in his paper. From Birmingham and Bentonsport in Van Buren County came newspaper and personal endorsement. O. B. Brown of Bentonsport wrote that he would get the county delegation to agree on Carpenter, adding that "Last winter Ret Clarkson told me that you would probably be a candidate and since that time I have embraced every opportunity to say a word in accordance therewith." This is another indication that the "Des Moines ringmaster" had cast his powerful influence on the side of Carpenter early in the campaign. Aldrich, on one of his many trips throughout the state in Carpenter's interest, reported that Harlan's home town newspaper, the Mount Pleasant *Journal,* would "have a good notice soon," and that Carpenter could thus be sure of Henry County. From southwestern Iowa, T. V. Shoup, an attorney at Bedford in Taylor County, who, by his own admission, controlled the local paper, wrote that he would see that Carpenter received the "preference over others, *at once* if thought advisable to do so." The Iowa City *Republican* favored Carpenter over Elliott, but in March changed its support to Scott. The Clarinda *Page County Herald* and the Winterset *Madisonian* both backed Carpenter; H. M. Belvel, editor of the Lineville *Index* in Wayne County, promised to throw his weight to Carpenter; and in Warren County, the Indianola *Leader* "warmly favored Colonel Carpenter's nomination." [50]

The strong Ottumwa *Courier,* edited by General John M. Hedrick and Major A. H. Hamilton, could not be secured by the Carpenter supporters, in spite of constant efforts by Aldrich, Baker, and others to win the two Civil War veterans over to the support of their candidate. Major Hamilton wrote that Carpenter's nomination would please him but that there were others he could support with "equal zeal." Wapello County, Hamilton advised, might prefer Henry O'Connor, who was extremely popular there. Since Hedrick held "quite an important office which is a prequisite [*sic*] of the State and travels considerably," they had decided it was "proper to not mingle in the contest." D. M. Dimmick of Monona County wrote

Carpenter that a friend of his had heard Hedrick say that Carpenter seemed to be the favorite, but that was the only encouragement the Carpenter supporters could get. Aldrich wrote that "Hedrick will do nothing for anybody," and Baker, in Ottumwa on business, had "seeen no one, who knows anything. Genl Hedrick has gone to his farm or into the country. Hamilton has gone to dinner." With no definite promise from the leading paper of the county, Carpenter had to rely on the aid of Charles Dudley of Agency, farmer and member of the general Assembly, who would "cheerfully support" him.

The nominating convention was scheduled for June 21 in Des Moines. In the weeks preceding this date the counties held local conventions to nominate delegates. This was the crucial period, this was the time when the various candidates marshaled their strength and reaped the rewards of months of hard work. The most satisfactory result would be to have a county delegation instructed for you; the next best thing would be to have it uninstructed, thus leaving the way open for influence on the convention floor. As the various counties met and appointed delegates, word was sent to the favored candidates and notices appeared in the newspapers, claiming this or that county for this or that man. Carpenter, now in Des Moines, wrote his wife on June 8: "Tell Emmett or Arthur, if they hear of any counties which have gone for me, to drop a line to the *Register* and Mr Brandt. It will then be handled to my advantage." [52]

In Polk County, Carpenter's unofficial manager, Isaac Brandt, was chairman of the committee to nominate delegates to the state convention. Although the delegation was purposely uninstructed ("for you know Polk County has some enemies"), Brandt reported that he saw each man before he put him on the delegation, and each gave his pledge to vote for Carpenter. In Cedar County, the same technique was followed: "Delegates not instructed. . . . We run the convention in your interest and will give you the vote of this county for Governor." In order to keep the strong Wapello County delegation from being instructed for O'Connor, Carpenter made a flying trip to Ottumwa on June 10 and succeeded in getting an uninstructed delegation. Gue suggested that if Carpenter could get Ret Clarkson to go *"quietly* among the *uninstructed* delegations and confidently say that he thinks you will be nominated, it will have more influence than any other one thing." [53]

Instructed or uninstructed, the delegates began to gather in Des Moines by June 21. A week before, on June 14, the Democrats with much less fanfare had met in convention and nominated Joseph C. Knapp of Van Buren County for Governor and Moses M. Ham of Dubuque for Lieutenant Governor—both by acclamation. [54] This had been merely a formality; the chance of a Democratic victory in Iowa in 1871 was infinitesimal. Not so with the Republican convention, however. The men who met in Des Moines at Moore's Hall on Fourth and Walnut were going to name a Governor, and they knew it. The election in October would be an aftermath, with the only question the size of the majority.

As early as April, Colonel Godfrey had reserved rooms in Des Moines for Carpenter, whether at a hotel or in Moore's Hall is not clear from his letter.[55] The convention of some 600 delegates was the largest ever to assemble in Des Moines, and the hall was crowded to capacity. Called to order at 10 A.M. by State Chairman Clarkson, the business of the convention ran smoothly, as planned by the leaders. After the election of Marsena E. Cutts of Mahaska County as temporary chairman, the usual committees were appointed and a new state central committee named. At the afternoon meeting, Cutts was made permanent president, and the convention settled down to the business of nominating a Governor.[56]

J. A. Parvin of Muscatine, one of the founders of the Republican party in Iowa, nominated Henry O'Connor. Judge Alonzo Converse of Butler County then presented the name of Cyrus Clay Carpenter. John Scott was nominated by H. W. Rothert, mayor of Keokuk. Two "favorite sons," C. W. Slagle of Jefferson County and Ezekiel Clark of Johnson, were also named. The convention at once proceeded to the usual informal ballot—the test of strength—which gave Carpenter 375 of the total 616 votes, with 156 for O'Connor, 56 for Scott, and 14 and 15 respectively for Slagle and Clark. Before the final count was announced, counties began to change their votes to Carpenter, and Parvin moved that the nomination be made by acclamation without the taking of a formal ballot, a motion which was accepted and carried with "the greatest enthusiasm." [57]

The nomination of Dr. H. C. Bulis of Winneshiek County for Lieutenant Governor met with varying reactions in the press of the state. The Democrats, finding little to complain of in Carpenter's nomination or in his record, unlimbered their biggest guns on Bulis. Hints of Bulis's candidacy had produced bitter articles in the Dubuque *Herald* and the Iowa City *Press* as early as May. According to Irish, Bulis's nomination would "signalize the subserviency of the [Republicans] to the interests of the corporations." Bulis's record in the state Senate would seem to substantiate this charge. As a member of the Senate committee on railroads in 1870, he had consistently voted against bills to regulate freight rates or to equalize taxation of the roads. These bills, which usually passed the House, were defeated in the Senate by the action of Bulis and other "purple" Senators, according to Irish:

> And after the fight was over . . . [Bulis] sat down to the series of champagne suppers given by the railroad men to celebrate their victory over the people, won by his efforts.

Those banquets, in "Number 1," Savery House, will not soon be forgotten, either by the favored few who sat to them with Bulis and the
"purple" Senators, or by the people who sat outside and listened to the
revelry as the wine went round.[58]

The Dubuque *Herald*, calling Bulis either an "idiot" or a "scalawag"—they
were not quite sure which—claimed that he had not represented the people,
"but the railroad interests." [59]

Even some Republican papers expressed dissatisfaction with the party's
choice for the second place on the ticket. The Muscatine *Tribune*, classified
as a Radical paper, was furious over the nomination of Bulis, while a
"republican resident of Cedar Valley" wrote a long letter, published in the
Democratic Dubuque *Herald*, bitterly assailing the party and asking how
they could reconcile their platform with their candidate for Lieutenant
Governor.[60]

Whether Bulis could qualify for all the epithets hurled at him is not
certain. He had consistently opposed what were considered anti-railroad
bills in the Senate, and his leading opponent for the lieutenant-governorship, State Senator G. G. Bennett of Washington County, had voted in
favor of them. There was very probably influence on the side of Bulis by
the railroad interests of the state. After all, the Lieutenant Governor, as
president of the Senate, had more direct influence on legislation than did
the Governor. Tichenor had written Dodge in January: "We *must* fix on a
good man for Lieut. Gov. one who will . . . give us the Committees." [61]

Dodge & Co. and the railroads were satisfied with the choice of Bulis,
and after a few more flurries the newspapers, busy with other things, turned
their attention elsewhere. It should be noted, however, that by 1873, when
the pressure of the electorate against the railroads had increased considerably, the party did not dare offer even the concession of the lieutenant-
governorship to the railroad interests. In that year, the office went to an
avowed anti-railroad man, Joseph Dysart.

In 1871, however, General Dodge was well pleased with his ticket. He
wrote to Carpenter on June 28:

I can almost drum together an old staff of *Governors* and other officials.
You of *Iowa*, *Noyes* of *Ohio*, and likely another from Pennsylvania. . . .
No one feels better satisfied than I in the result, and it gives me no little
satisfaction to see the men who were so true to me in my struggles for
success in the war building themselves up in their own homes and reaping
the reward they are fully entitled to. If you come out here in your canvass
come to my house.[62]

The outcome of the October election was never in question; the work of
the campaign was to be concentrated on winning by at least a 40,000
majority, to hold the lead won in 1870. In fact, so widespread was this

hope that the Des Moines pastor, a Reverend Wilson, who gave the prayer before the Republican convention, carried away by political loyalty, asked Divine intervention for this majority, much to the amusement and delight of the delegates and to the righteous indignation of the Democrats.[63]

The canvass was a strenuous one. Despite the assurance of victory in October, and despite a popular and acceptable candidate, the Republicans had no intention of resting on their laurels. Beginning on August 15, Carpenter made one and sometimes two speeches daily (Sundays excepted) right up to the eve of the election on October 10. Starting at Council Bluffs, he covered every town of consequence in southern Iowa, concentrating his efforts there since the vote of the northern section of the state was practically assured. But speeches by the leading candidate were not the only political fare offered the voters of Iowa. The state central committee, with George C. Tichenor now chairman in place of Clarkson, arranged schedules for Harlan, Allison, the defeated but loyal O'Connor, ex-Governors Kirkwood and Stone, Senator George G. Wright, the Iowa Representatives in Congress, "and other prominent speakers." Gue claimed that "with two hundred speakers and as many Republican newspapers scattered throughout the State to aid in the work, the campaign will be one of the most vigorous and active that we have ever had in Iowa, and with the valuable assistance that the Rev. Wilson invoked at an early day, we expect to be able to 'give the usual 40,000 majority.'"[64] In a day when two, three, or even four-hour speeches were not only acceptable but expected, Iowa settled down to another season of politics.

The campaign "theme" had been decided by the Democratic platform, the so-called "new departure" of a party that still bore the onus of the rebellion. In their 1871 platform, the Democrats, following the leadership of Clement L. Vallandigham of Ohio, had "departed" from their old position in opposition to the various Republican Reconstruction measures so far as to accept the controversial amendments to the Constitution—the famous Thirteenth, Fourteenth, and Fifteenth—and to propose acceptance of the Constitution "as it now exists, without reference to the means by which the same became the supreme law of the land."[65] This "new departure" was the butt of many Republican witticisms. The Ottumwa *Courier,* torn between amusement and sarcasm, reported that the "genuine, simon pure, original old schoveltyfunk democrats, who never learn anything and never forget anything, are in as much of a flutter at Vallandigham's 'new departure,' as the historic old hen was, whose brood of new fledged goslings took to water as soon as they were hatched." The "new departure," as the *Courier* saw it, was an indication that the old Democratic party was dead. In Carpenter's acceptance speech before the nominating convention he had referred to the

Democratic position as a "reaching out one foot, feeling for the Republican platform." About one-third of one of his campaign speeches dealt with various Democratic "departures," likening them to the successive retreats of the Confederate armies before Sherman during the siege of Atlanta, an exposition which delighted his Republican audiences and "brought down the house" on several occasions.[66]

Carpenter's campaign speeches were not entirely devoted to poking fun at the Democrats, however; he reviewed the record of the Republican party and explained his strictly orthodox position on the controversial tariff question. "On the intricate question of tariff," commented the Des Moines Register, "a question he neither dodges nor blinks, it is among politicians admitted that he makes the best speech of any stumper we have in Iowa, making its dark ways plainer, going down into its mysteries deeper, and laying the whole subject barer to the view of the common mind, than any one who has brought the subject into the arena of debate in our State." [67]

Very little of Carpenter's two-hour speeches dealt with Iowa problems aside from a passing reference to the prosperity and growth of the state, a condition attributed to Republican rule. Nor did he waste time on his opponent. Campaign technique of the seventies required that the party, not the candidate, be elected. Although elections might be purely local, the appeal to the voter was on a national basis. Carpenter's orthodox Republican high tariff stand, while popular with the voters, would have little effect on congressional action and would seem to be out of place in a gubernatorial contest. Nevertheless, this form of campaign oratory was traditional in the seventies, and Carpenter was an expert at giving the voter what he expected. His frequent references to the Civil War, while more refined than some types of bloody-shirt oratory, were also traditional. The significance of this whole campaign of nomination and election is not that it was unusual, but that it was typical of the time—and Carpenter was also a typical candidate, except that he was probably more honest than some state officials who were being offered to the voters in that decade.

The campaign progressed through the hot summer and fall months. It was a canvass remarkably free from personal attacks. Only one effort was made to smear Carpenter, and that came from an Illinois paper, the Springfield Illinois State Register, and proved a miserable failure. Hardly had the candidate returned to Fort Dodge after the nominating convention, to be received with the usual brass bands and the inevitable speeches, before several Iowa papers, with or without comment, reprinted the Illinois paper's accusations, which impugned Carpenter's honesty while in the commissary department of the Union Army.[68] The story that Carpenter had come "out of the office a poorer man than he went into it" had often been quoted as an evidence of his unusual honesty. From a position where he had a chance for "what many considered honorable speculation," he had emerged with an untarnished reputation. When he ascended the rostrum for his acceptance speech before the nominating convention, one delegate remarked. "Now we will see the Commissary who didn't make any money!" [69]

Therefore, when the Springfield *Register's* article appeared, accusing Carpenter of favoritism in the issuance of rations and of profiting from his position, even the Democratic papers of Iowa exerted little or no effort to make political capital of it. John P. Irish's Democratic Iowa City *Press* reprinted the article without comment. The Keokuk *Constitution* remarked that there must be some truth in the story, since the Illinois editor had been in the Union Army. The Birmingham *Enterprise* immediately countered with the assertion that the Keokuk editor, Thomas E. Clagett, had served with Carpenter and should know that the statements were "false in every particular." To J. M. Shaffer, secretary of the State Agricultural Society, the newspaper story was merely *"villainous trash,"* and he advised Carpenter to ignore it. The Fort Dodge *North West* branded the accusations "absurd," while Jacob Rich, in the Dubuque *Times,* wrote that the "story looks like a lie, reads like a lie, and unquestionably is a lie." [70] Carpenter's reputation for honesty and sincerity was too well established in his home state to be tarnished by this type of political muckraking, and the story was soon forgotten.

The election, on October 10, was all that the party could have wished. Carpenter's majority (in a total vote of 177,427) was 41,029. Only seven counties—Allamakee, Audubon, Dubuque, Fremont, Jackson, Johnson, and Lee—showed Democratic majorities, and some of these by very small margins. [71]

With the election over, Carpenter settled down at Fort Dodge to prepare himself for his new office. He was, of course, flooded with mail asking for support and for favors and giving a great deal of gratuitous advice. Adjutant-General Baker took it upon himself to play the role of adviser-in-chief. "Don't make any promises about Sup. Court Judge, if Cole resigns." "Be extremely careful about the University at Iowa City." "Be wise as a serpent & harmless as a dove." "Keep yourself out of all combinations on state printing, state binding, new newspapers & new editors." "Be 'keerful.' " [72] As chairman of the inauguration program, Baker bubbled with ideas:

> How would it suit you to have a little display on your inauguration? We have had too little heretofore. I should like to do like some of the older states. Have an escort, have a little artillery practice, escort the Governor elect from his residence, and as he takes his oath, "let the cannon roar."
> Now Col Olmsted would give me his Zouaves for escort, he would turn out his artillery detachment (old Veterans). That would cost nothing.

The state has powder. I can get an order on Merrill for that. The state
would have to pay for powder bags & a little other contingencies not
exceeding in all $50. We ought to do it. . . .
    What do you say? [73]

Baker was not the only man with ideas for a "little display" for the
inauguration. Edward Russell, postmaster at Davenport, and Joseph Shields
of the Davenport Woolen Mills decided that the new Governor should enter
office clothed in a suit made of Iowa woolen. Russell informed Carpenter
of the plan, assuring him that "acceptance should be easy" because Shields
was a Democrat. Carpenter thus took the oath of office clad in a suit of
"bluish broadcloth" made from wool clipped from Iowa sheep, woven at an
Iowa factory, and made by a Fort Dodge tailor.[74]

Among the many letters of congratulation and advice that Carpenter
received during the waning months of 1871 was one that may have influenced him to preserve his papers. A former Fort Dodge friend,
W. Oakley Ruggles, now living in New York, reminded him that most public
men leave "only a barren legacy of recorded votes on the questions of the
day, or a list of the official papers sent from their hands." Ruggles then
pointed out the importance of the papers preserved by Jefferson, Hamilton,
Madison, Jay, the Adamses, and others, "from which the history of the
Country will be re-written and better written than now." "The lesson of
this is," Ruggles continued, "that every man holding high official station,
living in the busy scenes of politics should carefully keep his correspondence." Also, he "should keep a private journal in which fair criticisms of
prominent men are found . . . The doings of political cabals and cliques.
. . . A record of the secret springs which induce Men to act as they do—
and of all facts which do not come to the public through the press." [75] An
indication that Carpenter took this suggestion to heart is evidenced not
only in the great mass of letters and papers that he preserved, but also in
the fact that from the day of his entrance into the governorship until he
left his seat in Congress in 1883 he kept a diary in which he jotted down
the doings of the day. Unfortunately, his daily entries were brief and often
contained little of real interest; the "doings of political cabals and cliques,"
the "secret springs which induce Men to act," are largely missing from this
record. However, these diaries do give a fuller picture of the life of a
Governor and a Congressman than could be discovered without them.

Early in December, Carpenter sent his brother-in-law, Arthur Burkholder,
down to Des Moines. Arthur was to act as one of the new Governor's
secretaries, and Merrill had suggested that he come early in order to "learn
the ropes." Carpenter himself moved to Des Moines late in December and
together with the retiring Governor and Henry Bulis made a "swing around
the circle of the various state institutions." [76]

On January 11, 1872, Carpenter took office and entered upon a term which was to be as full of political wrangling as any in Iowa's history. The militant Granger movement was building up rapidly; the Liberal Republicans would split with the Radicals; the financial panic of 1873 with its resulting depression would bring political and economic discontent into sharper focus than for many years; and the taint of corruption would reach into the Governor's immediate political family. Because of the over-riding importance of the farm protest of the seventies the years from 1872 to 1876 in Iowa and the Middle West can be called the "Granger Years." The voice of the farmer spoke loud, and Governor Carpenter listened.

NINE

First Year as Governor

———·•·———

IN DES MOINES, on New Year's Day of 1872, Governor Carpenter began to keep a diary:

January 1

Spent this day at the Jones House. Could not get anybody to help move or clean House. Our goods came at 10 o'clock and we got them unloaded & moved by dark. Between the confused manner of doing business of RR officials and draymen it was next to impossible to get done to-day.

January 2

Spent to-day moving. Putting up beds. Fixing carpets and finding the proper places for furniture. Had a hard time in finding a Restaurant where we could get dinner. Tired to-night.

January 3

Still arranging things about the House. We now begin to live at Home. Got our meals at our own table to-day. The Senatorial Lobby begins to pour in. To-day Senator Harlan, Col Allison and Judge Wright called at our house.[1]

There was no "Governor's Mansion" in Iowa in the 1870s. Therefore, the Carpenters had found a house to rent on Court Avenue at Eleventh Street, just a block from the statehouse and had done the "fixing" themselves.[2] The new chief executive of the state received little attention—at least not until the "Senatorial Lobby" began to arrive, and the chief contenders paid their duty calls on the Governor-elect.

The main topic of conversation and interest in Des Moines in the first two weeks of 1872 was not the inauguration of a Governor but the election of a Senator. Not even at church could one escape the excitement. On Sunday, January 7, Carpenter, after his regular Sunday ritual of "performing ablutions," attended the Fifth Street Methodist Church. "The House was full of politicians & preachers from different parts of the state, in attendance at the senatorial fight."[3]

James Harlan, completing his third term in the Senate, had served Iowa in Washington since 1855, with the exception of the one year he had spent in Johnson's Cabinet. He was only fifty-two years of age in 1872, and he wanted another term. Many of his friends throughout the state were determined that he should have it.

Just as determined that he should not return to Washington were the members of the Dodge-Clarkson-Allison wing of the party. Dodge had made a good fight for Allison in 1870 and had failed; this time he intended to win. He had acquired a strong ally in the person of James S. Clarkson of the Des Moines *Register,* who "came out" for Allison on December 13, 1871. In fact, the senatorial fight of 1872 had caused a change in management of the *Register* when "Father" Coker F. Clarkson, a strong Harlan supporter, had sold out his interest in the paper to his two sons, Richard and James, rather than have the paper, under his ownership, support Allison.[4] The change in emphasis in the paper was noticed as early as August 1871 by the Democratic editor of the Dubuque *Herald,* although the *Register's* open support of Allison did not come until December. Wrote the Democrat:

> The Register is some neutral. . . . The senior Clarkson is a hot Methodist, a warm friend of Harlan, but he stays on the farm in Grundy county. Many think he controls the paper. This is a mistake. He is seldom here—writes but little, and then nothing but innocent articles on agriculture, or morals. "Ret" is the brains of the institution, and I don't think has any special love or admiration for Harlan.[5]

Mention of Father Clarkson's Methodism illustrates one phase of the political wars of the time. A Methodist minister and chaplain of the Senate, J. P. Newman, had written a letter to Iowa Methodist ministers urging support for Harlan. In some fashion the anti-Harlan wing of the party obtained a copy of the letter and gave it wide publicity, with many sanctimonious comments on the evils of mixing politics and religion.[6] This had been in July; as the campaign progressed other accusations took precedence, but references to the "Newman Letter" continued to crop up from time to time.

The fight descended from innuendo to accusation, and Harlan's record as Secretary of the Interior came in for an unusual amount of probing. Charges of corruption were plentiful; manipulation of the county and district nominating conventions for members of the legislature was practiced on both sides; and the struggle became, according to a Dubuque Democrat, "the most disgraceful affair ever witnessed in Iowa politics."[7]

William B. Allison, who had served eight years (1863–1871) in the House of Representatives from Iowa's Third District, was forty-three years old in 1872, just Carpenter's age.[8] He had the backing of the young, strong wing of the party, out to gain control at any cost. They managed local conventions, spread scandalous stories about Harlan, and worked without ceasing up to the eve of the election. They were not always successful, however, and lost several counties by too much interference. According to a Democratic editor, the Allison support of Carpenter for Governor had been a mistake since Allison had thereby lost the friendship of Henry O'Connor. "Carpenter will not lift a finger for [Allison], being as much indebted to Harlan as to Allison for his nomination." Writing in December, this same editor thought he saw Allison's impending defeat:

> [Allison's] management of the campaign in behalf of himself has been a stupendous failure. Six months and even three months ago, his chances were decidedly the best. Now, even the most sanguine of his friends will claim nothing of the kind. Everybody calls him a good clever fellow, and so he is; but this is dish-water. He never stands up for a square fight, but shuffles and shirks and smiles and smirks, and like the Irishman's flea, when you put your finger on him he is not there.[9]

Three weeks later, Allison, whose political obituary had thus been written, was elected to the United States Senate.

The Dubuque editor was not alone in his lack of foresight. On the eve of the Republican caucus John P. Irish wrote from Des Moines: "Harlan has a clear majority and the Allison men are struggling desperately to break his line." The legislature was due to convene on Monday, January 8. On the Saturday before, wrote Irish, the Savery Hotel was a "sea of politicians" and lobbyists. "The crowd got larger and the talk louder. Far into the morning the lobby tramped and tore, and at day-break Harlan's lieutenant assured me they counted sixty-three votes, or two more than necessary for success." Allison, however, was "as bland as ever and his champions as active." [10]

At 7:30 on the evening of Wednesday, January 10, the rough and muddy hill up to Capitol Square was filled with a rushing mass of lobbyists, legislators, and the general public. One hundred and twenty Republicans filed into the House chamber, while John P. Irish stationed himself at a "crack in the post office door" and prepared to eavesdrop on the proceedings. Sixty-one votes were needed to nominate; on the informal ballot Allison received sixty, Harlan thirty-eight, and James F. Wilson twenty-two. Then came the first formal ballot: fifty-nine for Allison, forty-two for Harlan, and twenty for Wilson—a total of 121. Commented Irish: "Some man's hand had been bold enough and sufficiently steady to cast a fraudulent ticket." Again the votes were collected, and the clerk began the count. Irish described the scene as he saw it through the crack in the door:

> Harlan and Allison were neck and neck to 25, then Allison went ahead, Harlan came slowly up while Wilson took the odd votes untill [sic] the two leaders panted side by side. Again Allison goes ahead to 55 and the pencils record 56–7–8–9, 60—"Harlan," "Wilson," "Harlan," and so on

for eight counts it goes. Does the hat hold one precious vote? The teller takes up a ballot, the last one. In the pencil marks on that crumpled scrap are scrawled two men's fates! Unrolling it, every ear is alert and— "Allison" rings through the silent Hall and immediately is echoed in a roar that shakes the roof and almost crumbles the foundation stones of the New Capitol that lie piled just over the way.[11]

That night Carpenter wrote in his diary: "To-night the Senatorial Caucus took place. Allison was nominated and the long agony was over." Eight days later the Governor "commissioned Wm. B. Allison USS to succeed James Harlan Mch 4th 1873." The following day he added this comment: "While not taking any interest in the Senatorial Contest the result indicates that the people of this Republic dont believe in a too-long tenure of office."[12] This sentence indicates that Carpenter had both a considerable amount of political naiveté and a woeful lack of ability as a political forecaster. Allison, on "Mch 4th 1873," entered upon a tenure of office of thirty-five years in the United States Senate, one of the longest on record.

The turmoil attendant on the senatorial caucus had been distasteful to Carpenter. In spite of a lifetime spent in politics, he never could quite adjust himself to the pulling and hauling, the trading and influencing necessary for political success. In particular, the attacks on Harlan's honesty had disturbed him. He wrote to the defeated Senator:

> I desire to say: that while I did not think it proper for me to take an active part in the contest, I nevertheless deeply regretted and disapproved the personal attacks made upon you. I know them to be baseless fabrications and regarded them then, as I do now, as entirely untrue. Although you were defeated I shall never cease to regard your career in public life as worthy of the people you so faithfully served.[13]

Iowa City's fiery Democratic editor, John P. Irish, who did not take so kindly a view of Harlan—who was, after all, a Republican and therefore fair game for a Democrat—saw a chance to embarrass the opposition in the attacks made upon Harlan during the contest. On January 16, Irish, a member of the House, introduced a resolution asking the United States Senate to investigate the charges made against Harlan and, if the charges were found to be true, to impeach him. The Republicans blandly tabled the resolution, thus showing, according to Irish, "that the radicals either fear investigation or that the Allison men confess to falsehood and slander in the charges made against Harlan."[14] With the election over and won, the attacks on Harlan's honesty subsided.

On the day following the senatorial caucus, Carpenter, dressed in his all-Iowa suit, made his way with due pomp to the Capitol and there took the oath of office.

> To-day I was Inaugurated. During the A. M. and on the way to the capitol I felt many misgivings. But after getting on the Platform although

Grenville M. Dodge

James (Ret) Clarkson

William B. Allison

Isaac Brandt

in the presence of an immense audience and surrounded by all the dignitaries of the State I seemed to loose [*sic*] all trepidation and only thought
of doing my duty in a manly way.[15]

After paying the traditional respects to the good condition of the country
under the administration of President Grant, Carpenter presented his ideas
on some of the topics that the General Assembly would or should consider.
First, he endorsed the establishment of a "Normal Institute" for the training
of teachers. Carpenter always felt strongly on the subject of education. His
own lack of more formal training was a constant regret. Actually, wide
reading had provided him with a store of knowledge equal to that of his
contemporaries who held college degrees, but throughout his life he nursed
a sense of inferiority because of the scanty years of his schooling. Therefore, he stressed the need of expenditures for schools in all his messages.
A government must practice a "wise economy," he argued, "but retrench-
ment in any reasonable expenditures for educational purposes would not be
economy."

> If citizens of large wealth would place a guard over their treasures, more
> reliable than locks or bolts or safes, and cheaper than the iron bars of
> prison cells, the *per diem* of jurors, or the salaries of sheriffs and judges,
> that safeguard will be found in enlarging and perfecting the common
> school system of Iowa, until no citizen can reach maturity without obtain-
> ing a fair education.

Carpenter also touched briefly on the problems of capital versus labor, a
question still not too pressing in nonindustrial Iowa. Here again, he thought
that education would solve more of the capital-labor conflicts than would
statutes governing hours of labor or scales of pay. The state needed more
manufacturing, he added, and suggested that it was up to the Board of
Immigration to attract industries to Iowa.

The railroad question naturally came in for a good deal of attention.
Iowa needed railroads, but that fact should not make her subservient to the
demands of the corporations. Even though retiring Governor Merrill, in
his closing message to the General Assembly the day before, had carefully
avoided the issue of regulation of the roads by the state, the new Governor
made his position abundantly clear:

> I do not regard the pretense that railways are beyond the control of law,
> in respect to fare and freights, as worthy of more than a moment's con-
> sideration. It cannot be conceded that a corporation, when asking the
> right of eminent domain, may avow the purpose of building a public
> highway, for which purpose alone it could hope to acquire this preroga-
> tive of sovereignty; and, when the right has been conferred and accepted,
> and is enjoyed, may declare itself independent of statutory control, in the
> limitation of fare and freights, on the ground that a railway is private
> property. . . . There can be no clearer duty . . . than for the State to

maintain its power over railways and all other corporations of her own creation. And if Iowa ever abdicates this sovereignty, she will have proved herself unworthy the dignity of a free commonwealth.

Carpenter admitted the difficulty of finding a method of correction and at the same time of doing justice to both sides. In this view he expressed an unorthodox opinion. A popular theory of the time was that competition between railroads would adjust freight rates. "But this cannot be true," said Carpenter. "George Stephenson once said, 'where combination is possible competition is impossible;' and that this was true to-day. Indeed, competition not infrequently proves a source of oppression to the people."

Carpenter's solution for the railroad problem was the appointment of a "tribunal" to study the question and "report facts and conclusions with a spirit of judicial fairness." But he warned that an attempt to fix freight charges "by arbitrary statute" would be neither wise nor just. Railroad taxation also needed study, and Carpenter admitted there was no simple solution; rather, he left the problem to the "wisdom" of the legislators.

The plight of the settlers on the Des Moines River lands was discussed at length in Carpenter's inaugural. The Iowa delegation in Washington was trying to get through legislation providing indemnities for those dispossessed of their lands. In preparation for the passage of this legislation, Carpenter suggested that the state appoint an agent to investigate the many claims that would be presented.

Showing himself to be a middle-of-the-roader, Carpenter concluded his address by warning against too much legislation. Change for the sake of change is not wise, he said, and "all changes are not reforms." "When the people come to know the law, and their habits are conformed to a system, unless it can be materially improved, it is unwise to confuse public business with needless innovations." [16]

A Governor, in his first term, did not give a "condition of the state" message to the legislature. That task was left to the retiring Governor. So not until 1874 could Carpenter present more detailed plans for needed legislation. His first term was spent in settling into his job, learning the duties of a chief executive, and getting to know his colleagues.

Constitutionally, the Governor of Iowa does not have much power.[17] Politically, his power varies with the individual; if he is adept at playing politics and is a member of the inner ring of the party, his influence can be very great. But in Carpenter's day the party bosses were seldom found in the executive or legislative branches of the state government. Men like Dodge and Clarkson controlled the party and the state through their friends at Des Moines and at Washington. Actually, the members of the Iowa delegation in Congress, with the patronage jobs at their disposal, could and did exercise more power in Iowa than the Governor. The accepted practice, nationally and locally, was to put straw men in the White House and in the state capitols.

Was Carpenter a straw man? The answer is not clear, but the weight of evidence is in the negative. There is no record in his papers that he went to the bosses for orders; rather, the indications are that he made up his own mind and acted accordingly. By the end of his second term, his popularity was so high throughout the state that, had he been more of a politician, he might have been able to mobilize personal support for election to the Senate to succeed Wright, whose term expired in 1877. That he made no effort to do so, because he thought that a man serving in one public office had no right to campaign for another, was certainly politically unorthodox. By 1875, he could expect no support from the Dodge faction for such a bid. Rather, they shunted him off to a well-paying but minor post in the Treasury Department at Washington. Again, the reasons for this are not clear. The Washington job could have been a reward for services rendered or the burial of a potential senatorial rival to the ambitions of Samuel J. Kirkwood.

All this was in the future, however. There is no evidence that the party leaders were dissatisfied with Carpenter during the years of his governorship. When, at the end of his first year in office, he spoke out strongly in favor of the rights of the people against the demands of the railroads in his famous "Skeleton in the Corn-Crib" speech, Clarkson was among the first to praise him for his stand. The traditional concept of the Dodge-Clarkson-Allison ring as dominated by the railroad interests is too simple an interpretation. During Carpenter's tenure of office agrarian unrest was mounting. When, aroused by an issue, the voters speak with one voice, it is political wisdom for the leaders to listen. A party that ignores an aroused electorate in favor of the desires of special interests will soon find itself voted out of office. To remain in power, the Republican leaders became followers for the time being and awaited a turn in the tide of public opinion.

Fortunately for the Iowa Republican leadership in the 1870s, they had a Governor who spoke for the people; his popularity kept them in office in 1873, a year when Republican heads were rolling throughout the Middle West. An Iowa historian wrote of Carpenter years later: "No better representative of Lincoln's 'plain people' of the West ever sat in the executive chair." [18] Jonathan P. Dolliver, who owed much to Carpenter, wrote of him:

> Governor Carpenter gave the State a coherent and intelligent guidance, which has saved us from the disasters that have afflicted other Western communities. It was a time when we needed a leader who could be trusted both by the people and by the strangers who had invested their capital in Iowa. He had the confidence of the people because his own experience

identified him in thought and sympathy with them. He could speak to them in terms which in other men would have struck the note of insincerity and affectation. His public utterances are filled with homely wisdom, and are as compact and full of sense, as the maxims of the ancients. The people believed him because he told them the truth. He had no patience with the street-corner statesmanship that was abundant at that time. . . .

It was a fortunate thing for the State, in that time of the adjustment and settlement of old quarrels between the people and the railroads that a man having thus the confidence of both parties, was in the executive chair.[19]

Granted that this was written in the emotional aftermath of Carpenter's death and by a man who loved Carpenter almost as much as he had loved his own father, a cooler estimate of the man, based on what he did and wrote both privately and publicly, would seem to show that Dolliver gave a true picture of Governor Carpenter.

The inaugural address was a good start. Charles Aldrich, whose enthusiasm was colored by friendship, considered it "the best that has ever been delivered in Iowa." Grinnell thought it was "a paper . . . which will be regarded with favor in every respect." Frank W. Palmer, Dodge's man in Congress, praised the speech as showing "on its face that the subject of political philosophy is not a new topic to its author." And many others wrote in a similar vein. Even Democrat Dennis Mahony of Dubuque had words of praise: "I am very much pleased with your Inaugural, and hope nothing will direct or influence you from living up to its principles and recommendations." [20] All in all, the new Governor had cause to be happy over the reception of his first public statement.

Among the Governor's duties, that with the most delicate political overtones, and the one to cause the most trouble, was his power to fill by interim appointment certain elective posts which became vacant by death or resignation of the incumbent. On Carpenter's first full day in office and before he had even reached the statehouse, he was waylaid by David Wilson, an aspirant for the circuit court judgeship in Dubuque that had just been vacated by the death of Judge Winslow T. Barker. Carpenter moved swiftly in this appointment and thus caused a minor whirlwind of criticism. Barker had been a Democrat; Wilson was the Republican whom he had defeated in the last election. When Carpenter appointed Wilson, Democrats at once clamored that a member of their party should have been chosen. John P. Irish was particularly incensed and wrote that "Allison's debt to one man is paid." The editor of the Dubuque *Herald* was equally caustic in his criticism of Carpenter's action. On the other hand, Dennis A. Mahony, now editing the Dubuque *Telegraph,* wrote to Carpenter that "you should not be asked to appoint a person on the score of his being a democrat, as some persons have been claiming you ought to do." Carpenter's own explanation of his action was that "There was no general expression among the Lawyers of the Dist in behalf of a Democrat, and it was my judgment if a Republican was appointed I should select the man whom the party had endorsed by the nomination."[21] There is no indication of any influence from Allison on the appointment, but there may well have been, since Allison would naturally prefer a Dubuque Republican to a Dubuque Democrat.

The other side of the picture appeared when Carpenter appointed a Democrat, John A. Hull of Boone County, to a commission to study the River Land settlers' problems. Letters promptly arrived criticizing his choice; the Governor replied that he wanted a nonpartisan commission, had chosen the best men, and if the commissioners could get justice for the settlers, he would be satisfied. He added, somewhat tartly, "If I can do that, I dont care who makes political capital out of it, or who gets the credit."[22] Carpenter was, early in his term, finding out the political hazards of his appointive power.

There is no doubt that General Dodge asked for and received, two appointments in Council Bluffs. On January 23, he wrote Carpenter a "strictly confidential" letter asking him to appoint his brother, N. P. Dodge, and Judge Caleb Baldwin to the board of the Deaf and Dumb Asylum. Carpenter at once complied with the request. That one of the appointees did not find the job a pleasant one is indicated by Baldwin's request, within a year, to be relieved of his commission.[23]

Many other minor appointments faced Carpenter, but one of importance came up when he had been in office scarcely a month. Henry O'Connor, his opponent in the race for the gubernatorial nomination, was still serving as Attorney General, an office to which he had been elected three times. On February 12, he wrote Carpenter that he intended to quit; three days later, the Governor received his formal resignation. O'Connor was retiring from the Iowa political scene to accept an appointment from President Grant as a solicitor in the State Department.[24]

Carpenter here was faced with his first real political decision. The attorney generalship would be filled by election in the fall, but in the meantime an interim appointment must be made. Traditionally, a Governor chose the man most likely to be selected by the party in the coming convention. Nomination of another man would be a repudiation by the Governor of a prospective candidate and a reflection on his political sagacity, and no man not a candidate for the job would want to take it for only a few months. Therefore, it was necessary for the Governor to sound out the party leadership. But Carpenter was not always orthodox. He was more interested in appointing a good lawyer than a good politician. The first man he sought out for advice was C. C. Cole, Chief Justice of the State Supreme Court.

Meanwhile, Carpenter's office was flooded with letters of petition and recommendation and with visitors, each pleading his or another's qualifications. The first letter came from Marsena E. Cutts of Oskaloosa, who very frankly wanted the job. "I have been making arrangements to be a candidate before the State Convention for the nomination," he wrote, "and if there is to be an appointment would of course like *to be the man,* for the appointment of another would be disastrous to my hopes at the hands of a convention." [25]

Carpenter would have preferred to appoint one of his personal friends to the office—Cutts was a "cold-blooded, selfish cuss," according to Aldrich —and so, he waited and listened to arguments and read letters. A telegram arrived from Harlan, asking Carpenter to hold up his appointment until a letter could reach him. When the letter arrived, however, Harlan had changed his mind.

> I intended to recommend for your consideration the name of a friend for Aty Gen. But on reflection have concluded that this might be embarrassing to you; I will not therefore give any indication of a personal choice, other than to express the hope that you may not find it to be a duty to appoint any one who has made himself offensive to my friends in the recent Senatorial contest; as I feel almost certain you can serve the State as well by selecting some one who has been at least honorable in his opposition to me. Of course I would rejoice if it should hit a friend.

Senator Wright was not so circumspect—he wrote recommending Cutts.[26]

When Carpenter, on February 23, appointed Cutts, the response throughout the Republican press was favorable, and the Governor decided that he had "hit the nail on the head." He had found a happy combination of professional and political agreement. The following day he wrote to Harlan: "I do not know what Mr. Cutts' relations are with you but hope agreeable. This was an appointment in which I thought or sought to have a good Lawyer and the recommendations of those interested in the courts largely influenced my judgment." That Cutts was a member of the Dodge ring no doubt had great influence on his selection by both Carpenter and the nominating convention, but this facet of the case is not mentioned by the Governor, nor is there any written record of pressure brought to bear on him from Dodge or any others of the ring.[27] Cutts was chosen the party nominee at the 1872 convention and again in 1874; thus, politically, Carpenter's choice had been a success.

The threatened resignation of Chief Justice C. C. Cole of the State Supreme Court created quite a tempest for a time, but Carpenter managed to persuade Cole to stay in office until after the election, thus neatly sidestepping an unpleasant situation. Kirkwood had warned Carpenter of the possibility of Cole's resignation in December 1871 and had offered advice.

Carpenter gratefully acknowledged help from one who had "been there," and who knew something of the "embarrassments which surround any question of this kind." He promised Kirkwood that he would try to do what he thought "best for the state and its jurisprudence." While the issue of Cole's resignation was in doubt, rumors flew about the state, and letters swamped Carpenter. His office was crowded with men "with Supreme Judge on the brain." A letter from J. D. Wright of Chariton, protesting a rumor that an appointment was being "arranged" by a certain group, threatened that "it will be very unfortunate for the state & for *you* if the appointment is made." Carpenter, on the surface a mild and gentle man, could show a strain of iron when pushed. He did not take kindly to threats, and he informed Wright that "Judge Cole has not yet resigned, and when he does, I am under the impression that a few Gentlemen who have some ulterior object in their own behalf in view, will hardly control the appointment of his successor."[28] Whether the correspondent realized that he was being snubbed for his impertinence is not indicated, but the Governor had made his position quite plain.

Cole did not resign, much to Carpenter's relief, and for a few months the Governor's appointment difficulties were over. In the summer of 1872, a letter from David B. Henderson of Dubuque, reporting rumors that Allison and others had opposed a circuit judge appointment made by Carpenter, again drew from the Governor an emphatic and annoyed answer: "In reply I will say, that no protests were received by me from Mr. Allison, or Shiras, *or any other person,* at any time, before or since the appointment of Mr Poor. No *word,* or *telegram* or *letter,* or *petition* or *remonstrance* from any one has even been *spoken,* sent, or *presented* to me in opposition to such appointment." The appointment, which was for only four months, had been made at the suggestion of Platt Smith, Carpenter added.[29] He did not often emphasize his words with underscorings; only when he was really aroused did he succumb to that popular habit. Evidently the constant bickering, rumormongering, and accusations over appointments had worn his patience thin. Furthermore, wanting to scotch any stories that would indicate friction between himself and Allison, he brought Platt Smith's name into the letter. Smith would be the last man to suggest an appointment that would be opposed by Allison.

Perhaps the briefest letter requesting an appointment came to Carpenter from B. F. Reno of Marengo, an old friend. "Dear Governor If you think I would make a good 'Aid,' to his Excellency. Please say so." Carpenter "said so" on January 17, when he appointed Reno and a number of other ex-soldiers, "all good boys," as his military aides.[30]

Of more importance and interest during Carpenter's first months as Governor than his appointive troubles was the activity—or lack of it—of the Fourteenth General Assembly. Seldom has a legislature in Iowa received so much criticism, not only from Democrats but from Republicans as well. The Democratic Dubuque *Herald's* opinion, by March, was that "The present legislature is about as big a failure . . . as ever turns up.—It has now been in session for eight weeks, or at least has drawn pay for eight weeks, and can any living men tell what it has done, or what it will do?" [31] Republican E. N. Chapin, editor of the Marshalltown *Times,* was even more forthright:

> We are sorry to record the further fact that the Iowa House of Representatives have made themselves notorious, and some say infamous, but we do not subscribe to so strong a denunciation of them. They certainly have done very little in the way of legislation, and the cause is more attributable to ignorance, we think, than wickedness. . . . It is nevertheless true that the Lower House have become notorious for their inaction and that a large number of the members are new men who have come to the surface through local causes or ignorance in their constituents, and that so many of them are representatives that they are really BARNACLES, impeding the business of legislation, and are simply waiting for the usual third house to arrive with the necessary spondulicks to grease the wheels of legislation.—Thus far no corruptionists have put in an appearance, and these men are like wild geese in a storm, billiting around from place to place and wanting to be owned. . . . there never was an assembly of legislators in Iowa that contained so much stupidity, ignorance and obstinacy, as this present House.

After another column in like vein, Chapin suggested that one "step across the hall and look in upon the Senate, and what a contrast greets the eye. . . . A more dignified body of men we do not recollect to have seen before in the Senate chamber." [32]

Chapin's comments on the ignorance and inexperience of the House members are hardly borne out by the record. At least one quarter of the 100 members had served in previous legislatures. Outstanding among the Democrats were John F. Duncombe and John P. Irish, neither of whom could be considered ignorant or inexperienced even by the most partisan observer. The Republican side of the House contained two future Governors —John H. Gear and Joshua G. Newbold. The Speaker was "Tama Jim" Wilson, already well on the way to a distinguished career as Congressman and Secretary of Agriculture. And there was John A. Kasson, storm center of the Republican party, and one of the most brilliant men ever to serve the state.[33]

Kasson, a native of Vermont, had come to Iowa in 1857 and had within an unbelievably short time climbed to the upper reaches of the Republican party. In 1860, as a delegate to the Republican national convention at Chicago, he had helped Horace Greeley write the platform on which Abraham Lincoln was elected. He had served as Lincoln's First Assistant Postmaster General in 1861–1862, had been the sparkplug of the International Postal Conference in Paris in 1863, and had represented the Fifth Iowa District in Congress for two terms, from 1863 to 1867, but had been defeated for a third nomination by Grenville M. Dodge. The Dodge-Kasson feud was to keep Iowa Republicanism in turmoil for several years. Failing in his effort to return to Congress, Kasson had been elected to the Iowa legislature; in 1872, he was beginning his third term in spite of all that Dodge and Clarkson could do to stop him. During the Thirteenth General Assembly he had pushed through, against mighty opposition from some in his own party, the bill for a new capitol building. Now, in the Fourteenth Assembly, he was chairman of both the powerful ways and means committee and the rules committee, and was a member of the committee on federal relations.[34]

Although Kasson never succeeded in taking over complete leadership of his party—the Dodge ring was too strong for him—he served constantly as a threat to the top men. Carpenter admired Kasson's intellectual powers but could never quite accept him because of Kasson's divorce in 1866, a scandal that would have meant political death to a lesser man. Dodge, who had been a party to the worst of the attacks on Kasson after the divorce, in 1872 had the Governor, the Lieutenant Governor, the Speaker of the House, and the strongest newspaper in the state on his side; but he could not, in spite of his power, silence Kasson completely.

Of the many issues which faced the legislature in 1872, those dealing with railroads overshadowed everything else. In fact, the "railroad problem" led all others throughout the Middle West in the 1870s. Carpenter's administrations came at the peak of the agitation for state regulation of railroad rates. Iowa, Illinois, Minnesota, and Wisconsin, in particular, were seeking solutions to the economic problem of falling prices and high freight rates. Each state in turn passed so-called "Granger Laws" incorporating some type of rate schedule during this period, and each, with more or less alacrity, repealed those laws with the return of good times. When Carpenter took office in 1872, the Iowa sentiment was building to a climax, spurred on by the Granger movement. In 1874, the regulatory law was finally approved; Carpenter's last year in office was colored by the struggle with the roads to enforce the law, and when he left office in January 1876, the movement for repeal was well under way. In 1878, the law was replaced with a railroad commissioner system such as Carpenter—and the Grange—had recommended in 1874, and Carpenter was appointed to the first board of commissioners.[35] All other issues took second place to the railroad problem during Carpenter's four years as Governor of Iowa.

The belief that a state could control its chartered corporations antedated Iowa's statehood. The first constitution drawn up by Iowans—in 1844—

incorporated this Democratic idea. The second constitution—of 1846 and the one under which Iowa entered the Union—somewhat modified the regulatory provisions in deference to Whig principles, but still retained the Democratic theory of the supremacy of the state over corporations of its creation.[36] In 1857, Iowa revised her constitution, and the article on incorporations contained the following firm statement:

> Subject to the provisions of this article, the General Assembly shall have power to amend or repeal all laws for the organization or creation of corporations, or granting of special or exclusive privileges or immunities, by a vote of two-thirds of each branch of the General Assembly; and no exclusive privileges, except as in this article provided, shall ever be granted.[37]

It was on this section that the proponents of railroad regulation based their appeal in the postwar years, when high freight rates and low farm prices contributed to a growing sentiment for more state control over the railroads.

Quite naturally, the roads had fought every effort at regulation through several sessions of the General Assembly. So far they had been successful, with the exception of the Doud Amendment to a railroad bill passed by the 1868 legislature, an amendment that declared the state's right to prescribe "rules, regulations, and rates of tariff for the transportation of freights and passengers." [38] Efforts by the 1870 legislature to control freight rates had been successful in the House, but were defeated in the Senate by close votes. Now, in 1872, the anti-railroad forces were ready to try again, and the "Third House" gathered in Des Moines. "The railroad lobby is gathering in," Irish reported to his paper. "The familiar faces that sat around the banquet board two years ago with the 'Purple Senators,' are seen again, reinforced by others." [39]

The question of revising the system of taxing the roads came before the General Assembly first. Dissatisfaction with the taxation of railroads as established by the Ninth General Assembly in 1862 had long been voiced. By the act passed in that session of the legislature, the state taxed the roads on a basis of "one per centum" of their declared gross receipts, while the real and personal property of the roads was taxed locally by the counties where it was located. In 1868, the Twelfth General Assembly had revised this system somewhat by requiring the roads to report not only their receipts but their mileage in each county; the rate of one per cent remained. The agitation for higher taxes on the railroads continued, however, and in 1870, the legislature again revised the act, this time providing for a one per cent tax on the first $3,000 of gross receipts, two per cent on over $3,000 and under $6,000, and three per cent all over $6,000. Instead of one-half, the new law provided that four-fifths of the tax should be apportioned to the several counties through which the roads ran. Local taxation of the "real or personal" property of the roads within the counties was left with the county authorities as in the original act.[40]

With the convening of the Fourteenth General Assembly another attempt was made to revise the taxing system on railroads. A fight at once started that cut across party lines. Geography and economics, not politics, determined positions for or against the proposed bill. The contest with the railroads which raged during most of the seventies and eighties has long been considered almost wholly farmer-inspired. The role of the businessman in this struggle has only recently been assessed, and new light thrown on the movement in Iowa.[41] The efforts to tax and to regulate the freight rates of railroads in the Fourteenth General Assembly illustrate the fact that the businessmen of the Mississippi River towns of Iowa "voted their pocketbooks" on these subjects. Whereas they fought furiously to push through the bill regulating the freight charges of the roads, they fought just as furiously to prevent a revision in the system of taxation. Under existing law the municipalities along the river, where there were large concentrations of railroad property on valuable land, taxed the roads according to their local schedule. "Here is the secret of the fight," wrote "Cato" to the Ottumwa *Courier.* "By the present law, cities are allowed to tax Railroad property for municipal purposes, which the people living in the country have to pay, and it is the effort to remedy this, that gives rise to such a fight." [42] Newspapers that favored revision of the taxation system sought to convince the rural voters and their representatives that placing taxation of all railroads wholly under the state government would equalize the tax burden on all the people. Farmers paid the heavy taxes charged by the cities, they pointed out, through increased freight charges. Thus, during the discussion of the tax bill in the Assembly, the issue developed by newspaper prodding into an urban-rural fight.

The bill, as finally passed, provided that all railroad taxation should be assessed by the Census Board, which consisted of the Governor, the State Treasurer, the State Auditor, and the Secretary of State, on all railroad property except the "lands, lots, and other real estate of a railroad company not used in the operation of their respective roads." The roads were required to report to the Census Board the number of miles they operated, the amount of property located in each county, a "detailed statement" of their rolling stock, and their gross earnings in the state. From these figures, the Census Board then had the job of assessing the railroad property and pro-rating it per mile of track. Each county would then collect tax from the road based on the number of miles of track within the county. Delinquent taxes due under the previous laws were canceled, a provision that aroused a storm of protest and was eventually declared unconstitutional by the State Supreme Court.[43]

Criticism of the tax law, as passed, was heard on all sides. That railroad taxes were too low had long been recognized, but agreement as to the proper method of assessment varied. Governor Merrill, in his last message to the General Assembly, had endorsed the existing mode of taxation, but had agreed that the tax should be increased. In 1870, he reported, $186,-722.04 had been collected from the railroads, whose property was estimated as worth some $75,000,000. On this basis, said Merrill, the average property tax paid by Iowans, which was about three and one-eighths per cent of the assessed value, was five times that paid by the railroads; he concluded that "a great disparity exists." Governor Carpenter, in his inaugural, also had tackled the question of taxing the roads. He agreed with Merrill that the railroads should pay a larger tax, but he was "not able to see that the same mode of assessment should be adopted as is applied to the assessment of private property." The state constitution provided for equal taxation, which was right and proper, he continued, but if railroads were assessed "in the same *manner* as other property, a few townships in each county will reap the benefit of all local taxes, and a few towns in the State of all taxes upon rolling-stock and other propety." The value of a railroad, Carpenter pointed out, was not in its "right of way, embankments, masonry, bridges, ties, iron, machinery, locomotives, cars, buildings, &c., &c., but in the essential franchise," which was dependent on dividends. To assess railroads in the same manner as other property was "very nearly impracticable." [44]

Many men in the state did not appreciate the reasoning behind Carpenter's position, and his political enemies used this part of his inaugural against him for many a campaign to come. In fact, Irish seized on this portion of the address at once and accused Carpenter of going against the Republican platform, which, he said, stood for taxing railroad property by the same method as other property was taxed. Carpenter's statement that such a system of taxation for railroads was "very nearly impracticable" showed, according to Irish, a "wonderful ignorance." What Irish did not point out was that the Republican platform was much more circumspect on the subject than he claimed; the plank on railroad taxation favored a "uniform system of taxation, so that all property . . . shall bear its just share of the public burden." This, of course, did not lay down a hard and fast rule for a method of taxation, as Irish claimed. [45]

The fight on railroad taxation in the legislature had not been on political lines. One prominent Democrat, John F. Duncombe, introduced and fought for the new tax bill; the equally prominent Democrat Irish fought just as hard against it. Votes against the new system came almost entirely from the eastern counties, with the largest proportion in the so-called river counties, where a concentration of railroad property had meant a profitable tax revenue for those localities. The only western vote in the lower house against the bill came from Democrat Washburn A. Stow of Fremont County, who sarcastically moved, after the passage of the bill, an amendment "setting forth that it was a bill to exempt rail roads from taxation." [46] Eleven of the twenty-two Democrats in the House were among the eighteen who voted against the bill, while two prominent Republicans, John H. Gear of Burlington and John A. Kasson of Des Moines, opposed the revised system of taxation. Two protests were entered in the House *Journal,* one calling the bill "inequitable" and "unjust," the other claiming it was unconstitutional.[47]

In the Senate, the fight against the taxation bill had been carried by Gear's colleague from Des Moines County, Charles Beardsley. The bill passed the Senate with but seven dissenting votes, only one of which came from a Democrat.[48] It was a "bill of abominations," stormed the Burlington *Hawk-Eye.* The bill was drawn up by the railroad lobby and bore the name of the "chief representative of the railroad interests in this general assembly . . . Hon. John F. Duncombe," echoed the Dubuque *Herald.*[49] The editor of the Marshalltown *Times* put his finger on the real conflict by pointing out that it was the river towns who were fighting the new tax law out of "the promptings of self and self-interest." The reason "our river friends howl so terribly," he continued, was that they could no longer tax the railroad property within their borders. This might seem unfair, but the railroads had made the river towns what they were, had brought them wealth by building from their gates to the interior, and therefore they had "no right to complain." [50] But complain they did most bitterly, although in a hopeless minority against the votes of the interior counties that would profit by the new system.

Carpenter seems to have been satisfied with the action of the General Assembly in this case. He signed the bill without comment, but his inaugural address had favored some such system. Early in the session he had received a letter from A. W. Brownlie, a prominent farmer and stockman of Scott County, who had taken the position that roads should be taxed on their profits. Carpenter, in his reply, agreed with his position as "the only true theory." [51] While the bill did not quite incorporate this system, it did set up a new basis for railroad taxation, a basis that proved satisfactory in the long run in spite of the bitterness it engendered at the time of passage.

Hardly had the excitement over the taxation bill subsided, than a new railroad freight bill stirred up the river-interior conflict anew. But this time the river towns were for the bill, while many interior areas without railroads opposed it.

In the House, Fred O'Donnell, Democrat from Dubuque and a mighty opponent of the railroad tax bill, had already introduced a bill to establish maximum rates of freight on the railroads. On the day after the tax bill passed, Samuel T. Caldwell of Ottumwa, chairman of the railroad committee of the House, reported the tariff regulation bill back with recommendations that it pass. Caldwell's home town newspaper had predicted that the bill would surely pass this time, "as the backbone of the present members is stiff enough not to bend beneath the pressure of a railroad corporation." [52] The writer's judgment of the strength of the legislative backbone was over optimistic.

An immediate vote to postpone consideration of the bill for several days passed the House, fifty-eight to thirty-two, with ten not voting. "The reasons for the postponement are manifest in the great influx of railroad lobbyists on tonight's train," reported Irish to his paper. Both sides were gathering their forces. "What a pity," Irish lamented, "the *people* cannot send a lobby here." [53]

The editor of the Dubuque *Herald* was even more forthright than Irish on the subject of lobbyists. The railroads had favored the tax bill—some editors even claimed they had written it—and the *Herald,* representing Dubuque's interests, had opposed it. Now, the railroads were fighting against the regulation bill; the *Herald,* again reflecting the interests of a river town that would profit by cheaper Iowa rates, strongly supported the theory of regulation. "Monday night was diligently improved by the railroad attorneys who enliven the lobby," wrote the *Herald*'s Des Moines correspondent on March 12. "They hold caucuses in the Savery house, of various degrees of secresy [*sic*]." The writer further hinted at "corrupt use of money," but piously refused to elaborate. A month later he was no longer so evasive; he flatly reported "shameful buying of votes," accused several senators of having "flopped" into the "arms of the railroad attorneys," and speculated on the expenditure of some $7,000 by the railroad lobby.[54]

In the House, John F. Duncombe, the sponsor of the taxation bill, fought long and hard against the regulation act. Irish, O'Donnell, and others who had opposed the tax bill now supported the regulation bill. Efforts to write the commissioner system into the several bills under consideration failed in the House but succeeded in the Senate. The debate was long and, in some cases, able on both sides. In spite of dark talk of bribery, many of the legislators obviously took their stands from honest conviction. Senator William Larrabee, a future Governor who would have a long career in dealing with railroad problems, argued that the bill as proposed was unjust and would "defeat the very object for which it was intended," and he quoted Governor Carpenter's inaugural and the Republican platform in support of his stand. Logic clashed with emotion, and tempers grew short. But the bill passed the House by a vote of 80 to 13, with 7 not voting. In the Senate, the bill, with an amendment providing for railroad commissioners tacked on, passed 39 to 10, with one senator absent. Three conference committees failed to reach agreement on the amendment, however, and the bill finally failed.[55]

The railroad men were pleased; regulation had again been staved off. But businessmen of the river towns and farmers dependent on rail transportation for shipping their produce to market grumbled and threatened. We must send our own men to the legislature, wrote a farmer to William Duane Wilson of the *Iowa Homestead.* "We are not careful enough to select men whom we know to be right on this question," he continued, "—men who have back bone stiff enough to stand up to the rack and with ability enough to carry out what the people want." [56]

What Carpenter thought of the failure of the bill is not known. The Senate had adopted his recommendation for a board of railroad commissioners, and on that amendment the bill had foundered. Likewise, there was little newspaper comment on the failure. Other interests, in particular the ever-fascinating game of presidential politics, absorbed their attention.

Compared with the turmoil over railroad legislation, the rest of the activities of the General Assembly engendered little emotion. An effort to save money by eliminating the publication of the laws in the newspapers of the state caused a minor tempest. The bill was referred to the ways and means committee, where Chairman John A. Kasson approved it. This added fuel to the intra-Republican conflict. Clarkson of the *Register* could not seem to control his own local branch of Republicanism, which insisted on giving honors and offices to Kasson, whom Clarkson hated.[57] Thus, the bill, as endorsed by Kasson, and which seemed an attack on newspapers, was fought furiously by Clarkson and other editors whose papers would lose revenue by the act. Nevertheless, the bill passed both houses and was soon forgotten.[58]

Of more interest to the Governor was a bill before the Assembly to abolish capital punishment in Iowa. The reform sentiments of the seventies touched all phases of life, public and private, and the agitation for prison reform was strong. A murder in Story County brought the movement for the repeal of the death penalty in Iowa to a climax. Two years before, a man by the name of George Stanley had murdered one William Patterson. The evidence was circumstantial, but Stanley was tried and convicted at the April 1871, term of the Story County district court. The case was appealed to the Iowa Supreme Court, which affirmed the decision of the lower court on February 24, 1872. Carpenter, as Governor, reviewed the case and set the date of execution for April 12. No sooner had he acted than he was besieged from all sides with petitions for leniency. The Quakers of Springdale in Cedar County sent a petition with 750 signatures.[59] A Catholic priest, Father P. M. Delaney of Boone, was particularly insistent in his appeals. Carpenter replied in a letter to Father Delaney in which he set forth the reasons for his action and for his refusal to commute Stanley's sentence. The letter, published in several newspapers, throws light on Carpenter's interpretation of his position and on his firm belief in a strict adherence to the law—both its letter and its spirit.

> But you will tell me that I have the power to commute his punishment to imprisonment. This is true. And this is the point upon which more particularly I desire to write you. . . .
>
> The Governor may have the *power* to commute punishment, as he has the power to pardon, but that is a power which he cannot abuse. . . . He would certainly err, if only consulting his sympathies; and it would hardly Satisfy the public mind for him to give as a reason for commuting the death penalty: "That he did not believe in capital punishment." . . .
>
> I cannot but regard the policy of making it a rule to commute penalties affixed by law to certain grades of crime, to some lighter punishment, as fraught with evil to the State and as dangerous to the well-being of Society. If the execution of the penalty affixed to a crime is So habitually ignored or evaded as to produce the belief that in no instance will the highest penalty of violated law be executed where the Governor may intervene to prevent it: it Seems to me that it cannot but destroy confidence in executive firmness and loosen all respect for law itself.
>
> I believe, myself, crime is more effectually prevented by the *certainty* of punishment, than by its *severity*. . . . But while capital punishment remains a part of our Statutory law, and its operation is only prevented from humane considerations, by executive clemency, it is natural for men . . . to reason: that if one Governor will commute the death penalty to imprisonment for life, from considerations of humanity, in the course of a few years, when prejudices have worn away and the enormity of the crime is softened by time, Some Governor will come into office who will grant an unconditional pardon. Any system of executing the law which encourages, Suggests, or gives plausibility to such a course of reasoning cannot but weaken the effect of all laws and all penalties.[60]

Meanwhile, the legislature considered various bills dealing with capital punishment, and at last, in the closing days of the session, agreed upon a bill that abolished the death penalty, substituted life imprisonment, and prohibited the Governor from granting a pardon unless recommended by the General Assembly.[61] Carpenter was relieved. He had watched the debate in the legislature anxiously, and, hoping that "a man's life will be saved," had, on April 9, suspended the execution of Stanley's sentence for one month.[62] Now the burden of decision was lifted from his shoulders, and a life was saved. "The state can now go out of the hemp business and take her place in the very front rank of progressive, humane, enlightened communities," exulted one editor. "Exit, The Iowa Hangman!" was the *Register's* headline.[63]

On April 23, the legislature recessed until January 1873, when it would meet in adjourned session to consider the revision of the Iowa Code, upon which a joint committee had been laboring during the session. The Governor "had his arm lamed in shaking hands" with the legislators as they prepared to depart for home. They had done "faithful and manly work," according to Carpenter.[64]

The legislature, whether manly or stupid, had shown one last trace of the bitterness of the Johnson era when, on March 15, a proposal had been introduced to purchase a portrait of Senator James W. Grimes to be hung in the new capitol building. Grimes, a stricken man since the day of the impeachment trial of Andrew Johnson in 1868, had returned home to Burlington from a sojourn abroad in September 1871. Apparently improving in health, he had suffered a severe heart attack on February 7, 1872, and had died within a few hours.[66] "A great man has fallen," Carpenter wrote in his diary upon hearing the news. "He was among [my] earliest political friends and I never lost faith in him." [67] The *Register,* in whose columns the mildest epithet for Grimes in 1868 was "a false son of Iowa," now devoted a half column to him, headed "A Statesman Gone!" [68] Carpenter, ex-Governors Merrill and Lowe, and several other state officials went at once to Burlington to attend the funeral, while the papers of the state indulged in an orgy of praise for the man they had so recently vilified.[69]

Thus, when the resolution suggesting the purchase of Senator Grimes's portrait was introduced in the Senate, no opposition was expected, but a few bitter-enders fought the action for most of a morning before surrendering. In the final vote of the Senate, two Democrats joined nine Republicans in opposing the purchase.[70] As though ashamed of this final display of Republican animosity, the papers of the state ignored the debate, merely reporting that the resolution had passed. Only Irish, ever ready to put the Republicans in a bad light, gave a short paragraph in his report to his newspaper on the debate.[71]

With the adjournment of the legislature, Carpenter had passed his first test as Governor. No legislative problems would present themselves until 1873, but in the meantime the politicians were busy. Grant's first term was drawing to a close; in the normal course of events his renomination by the Republicans would have been a certainty. But a rift had appeared in Republican ranks. The Radicals, whose control of the party had been firmly secured, suddenly found themselves challenged by a minority calling themselves "Liberal Republicans." Meanwhile, the Democrats of Iowa and the nation, weakened and almost leaderless, watched and waited.

When J. B. Grinnell wrote Carpenter on January 13, 1872, congratulating him on his inaugural address, he added a sentence that foretold his future actions: "You do not say Grant should be re-nominated and I am of the number who think the Clan [*sic.* Ku Klux Klan] States would defeat

him." Just a week later Grinnell publicly opposed Grant's renomination
in a letter to the newspapers.[72] He thus cast in his lot with the "Liberals"
of his party—political suicide in Radical Republican Iowa.

Grant was a brilliant general but a naive politician, and having accepted
Radical principles and control, he was the natural candidate for renomination in 1872. But he had alienated certain powerful members of his party
such as Charles Sumner, Horace Greeley, and Carl Schurz, and a revolt,
beginning in Schurz's Missouri, was in full tide by the early months of
1872. The Liberals demanded civil service reform, amnesty to the South,
state's rights, and free trade—the latter having a strangely Democratic
ring.[73]

The Des Moines *Register,* Iowa's voice of Radicalism, was both amused
and shocked at the defection of Grinnell, one of the original Republicans
in Iowa. Editor Clarkson's explanation was that the Ginnell was only a
disappointed office seeker and "sorehead." [74] In spite of public jibes and
sneers at Grinnell and his followers, however, the Radical leaders were
worried. They called their state convention in March instead of May in
order to avoid any chances of revolt against their planned endorsement of
Grant, a move that did not go unnoticed or unchallenged by the Liberal
editors of the state.[75]

Five days before the Republican state convention met, Grinnell spoke
to a Des Moines audience that included the Governor and many of the
state officials. "It hardly came up to my expectations," Carpenter commented. What he had expected is hard to understand, since by that time
there was no secret about Grinnell's Liberalism. Possibly the Governor,
who was a polished orator, was disappointed in the manner of delivery
since Grinnell read his speech from a manuscript, oratorical heresy in those
days. Whatever the style of delivery, the speech denounced Grant and called
for the nomination of Iowa's James F. Wilson or a "Reform" candidate. If
Grinnell thought that by suggesting the nomination of Wilson he could
win his support or could placate Clarkson, who was active in a Wilson-
for-Vice-President move, he was mistaken. The *Register* had been agitating
for the nomination of Wilson to the second place on the Grant ticket ever
since January, possibly in an effort to assuage Wilson's feelings because
of his loss of the senatorship to Allison. Clarkson did not take Grinnell's
bait, of course, but continued his attacks on the Liberals.[76]

Meanwhile, several leading Democratic editors in the state suggested
that their party join with the Liberals in a coalition dedicated to the
defeat of Grant and the Radicals. Republican editors retaliated by warning
the Liberals that the Democrats would take over control of any such
coalition. The movement toward fusion continued, however, and even after
the Liberals chose Horace Greeley as their presidential candidate, the Demo-

crats meekly swallowed the bitter pill and endorsed him at their own convention at Baltimore.[77]

However obvious the ineptitude of the Liberal-Democratic fusion of 1872 may have looked from the vantage point of election day, in the spring months of 1872 the Republicans were disturbed. Even the nomination of Greeley did not quite allay their fears. "What do you think of the Greeley party," Carpenter wrote to Charles Aldrich on May 13. "I regard Greeley's candidacy as calculated to injure the Republican Party, but I still believe it will re-elect its candidate this fall by an overwhelming majority. . . . I shall fight for the party that saved the country and of which Lincoln, Colfax, the two Wilson's and others are better types than Greeley." [78] It is interesting to note here that Carpenter did not mention Grant among the "better types" of the party. Could it have been that the growing hints of scandals in the Grant administration were disturbing to the honest Governor of Iowa?

Carpenter was not a delegate to the Republican convention at Philadelphia. The doubtlessly weary job of being a delegate was passed around to the lesser lights in the party in those days, probably on the theory that the thinner the jobs were spread, the more votes would be brought into the party. One or two big men usually dominated the delegation, however —in Iowa's case, Grenville M. Dodge was the man—and delivered the state's vote at the convention. But the Governor went along, to lend dignity to the delegation and to work for Dodge if any of the members showed signs of independence. Not that he was needed in the latter capacity; the convention was a cut-and-dried affair with only a slight contest over the second place on the ticket. The James F. Wilson boom from Iowa was completely swamped by the Henry Wilson boom from Massachusetts. Carpenter realized this on the day before the convention opened: "It now looks very much as though Henry Wilson would be nominated for the vice Presidency," he wrote. James F. Wilson's name was but little mentioned, reported the *Register* on the eve of the convention.[79] Thus ended the Wilson candidacy.

Meanwhile, in Iowa, the Radicals' warnings were coming true. After the "marriage" of the Liberals and Democrats had taken place in a public and touching ceremony in Des Moines led by the aging Augustus Caesar Dodge with tears in his eyes, the Democrats proceeded to take over the new party. Three of the five men chosen for the state offices on the ticket and eight of the nine congressional candidates were former Democrats. The hybrid party waged a listless campaign, turning its biggest guns on Grant and almost ignoring its own local slate.[80] The Republicans, on the other hand, were well organized. Masters at campaigning, they put their best men in the field, sending them on extensive speaking tours that covered the state from end to end. The Governor, the two Senators, the nine Congressmen, and every candidate for office went through a grueling two-month canvass.

Carpenter had played only a minor role in the preliminary skirmishing at the local conventions, but now his real work began. From September 9 until election day, he traveled back and forth across the state, speaking almost daily at towns and hamlets, in schoolhouses and in picnic groves, in good weather and in bad. He traveled by passenger train if lucky, or by freight if nothing else were available. Where there was no railroad, some loyal party worker might transport him to the next town by buggy or carriage. Wherever possible, he was "put up" at somebody's home so that expenses were not too heavy and the strain on Carpenter's perennially thin purse not too great. Physically, however, the canvass took a toll. On September 21 his voice gave out, and he returned to Des Moines for a rest. Four days later he was back on the road, but by October 4 the doctors had to put him to bed with a bad cold, caught while speaking in the rain. Up again, he was back at it on October 9 and continued without a break until November 3, speaking from Fort Dodge to Council Bluffs and back. "I am glad the contest is over," he wrote on election day.[81] Carpenter loved the hurly-burly of campaigning, but he was understandably glad when the work was done.

Orators of the day usually had one address that they used throughout a campaign, either in whole or in part. Carpenter's has been preserved in the small black notebook in which he outlined his speeches. In 1872, he chose for attack the Democratic theme, "Anything to beat Grant," and he rang the changes on that phrase in every possible way, climaxing his talk with a slogan of his own. Quoting a telegram Grant had sent Sheridan during the closing days of the war—"Push things"—Carpenter urged his hearers to "Push things." The beginning of his speech was a combination of historical background, praise for the great work of the Republicans under Grant, and comments on the decreasing national debt (with many figures quoted). After this serious talk as an introduction, Carpenter launched into his main attack on the Liberal-Democratic coalition. Here he displayed the usual bloody-shirt tactics of the Radicals; here the useful word "Copperhead" was used time and again. First he told a story that Greeley had written, of finding an owl and a snake in a prairie dog hole while traveling in the West. The conclusion to this was obvious to a Radical: Greeley was the prairie dog who "had but very little influence in his own castle." Then, said Carpenter, if you compare the owl to the Ku Klux Klan, and the snake to a Copperhead, "you can conceive of the average influence Mr. Greeley would have in the White House surrounded by his new political associates." This led to another story:

> The position of the Liberal Republicans in this New Party is well illustrated by another bit of natural history. It is said, there is a kind of snake, which, when followed by its young, at the approach of dangers

swallows the little ones, and when the danger is past the old one has a way of spitting them out of its mouth. You have heard democrats talk of the nauseating mouthful they found in Greeley but still protesting that they will swallow him. It was just so with the Democratic convention at Des Moines the other day, when it went up to the Court House and swallowed the Liberals. Now these Liberals may think if such an untoward event as the election of Greeley should transpire that when the distribution of offices comes to capacious maw into which they disappeared will be opened sufficiently to give them a glimpse of day-light, but in this they are mistaken. If [this] should happen, however, the parallel of the snake will hold good. The little ones will all be just like the old one—all snakes—all little "Copperheads!" [82]

This was standard stuff, of course, dressed up by natural history and must have delighted an audience that had just sat through a long period of the reading of facts and figures. Carpenter would then swing into his attacks on the theme of "Anything to beat Grant," and close with a moving appeal for his hearers to "Push things."

When Carpenter spoke in Webster City, leading farmers from many miles around attended the meeting especially to do honor to the Governor, "who is one of their chief favorites," according to one editor.[83] Discounting the partisan bias of the newspaper, this report still gives a clue to Carpenter's political success—his popularity with the Iowa farmer. In January 1873, his famous "Skeleton in the Corn-Crib" speech would further endear him to the agricultural population of the state.

Radical Republicanism has been traditionally viewed as a cold-blooded movement of the political tools of the industrial magnates of the East for control of the politics and the economy of the nation in their own interest. That the farmers of the West accepted this program, which offered them little, is one of the mysteries of political behavior. One explanation is the equating of Republicanism and prosperity, Radicalism and patriotism. However specious these arguments may now seem, during the 1870s they were used with telling effect in every campaign. That Carpenter sincerely believed in the great mission of the Radicals is unquestioned. There is no evidence in his letters or papers that he was anything but a devoted and devout believer in that mission. And he was able to put this sincerity into his speeches and convince his listeners. Stump speakers, such as Carpenter, no doubt played a great part throughout the nation in keeping the Radical Republicans in power.

Election day of 1872 came, and Carpenter and his party had cause to rejoice. The Liberal-Democratic coalition in Iowa had been snowed under, and the Republicans emerged with a 56,000-vote majority, an increase of 10,000 votes over the majority given Grant in 1868. The state offices were all carried by the Republicans by about the same majority, while the entire

Republican congressional delegation was elected. But the Republicans ignored or did not notice that, although their victory was substantial, their vote had actually declined in some 30 counties in the southeastern half of the state. Whereas the voting population between 1868 and 1872 had increased by about 45,000, the total votes cast in 1872 increased only about 10,000. Thus, not only did Democrats stay away from the polls (one of the explanations of the defeat of the coalition), but Republicans also had failed to vote. Declining Republican voter-interest should have warned the Republicans that they might run into trouble, but for the moment they were satisfied with their victory.[84]

When State Chairman Jacob Rich praised Carpenter for his work in the canvass and offered to pay his expenses, the loyal Republican Governor replied, "I do not think I have done more than I ought to have done, and have no bill against your committee." That a party should pay the expenses of its campaigners was a new idea in politics. Carpenter felt obligated to the party which had done him honor, he wrote. He was working for the success of the party to which he was devoted, and he wanted no compensation for his labors.[85]

After the election things quieted down, and Carpenter turned to his duties in Des Moines. He lectured at several Teachers Institutes and worked on a speech he was scheduled to give before the State Agricultural Society in January. On December 9, he "received information" about the State Treasurer, Samuel E. Rankin.[86] Carpenter's prompt investigation brought about the famous "Rankin defalcation" scandal that almost destroyed the good name of the Carpenter administration.

-TEN-

Scandal and Politics in 1873

——•◦•◦•·——

SAMUEL E. RANKIN, state treasurer since 1867, was an honest man, said his friends. The fact that he had been making unusually large investments since holding office disturbed them from time to time, but they trusted him. Governor Samuel Merrill had told Carpenter of these misgivings when the latter took office, but at the same time had "expressed . . . unbounded confidence in [Rankin's] integrity as a man and officer." [1] In addition to his office as state treasurer, Rankin had been serving as treasurer of the funds of the State Agricultural College and Farm at Ames—without bond for the last two years of his term as it was revealed later.

The suspicions, voiced from time to time, finally came into the open, with disastrous results. On December 9, 1872, Isaac Brandt, then serving as deputy state treasurer, came to Carpenter and told him that he was afraid that Rankin was behind in his accounts. He had no positive knowledge, he hastened to assure the Governor, as he himself had nothing to do with the College fund, but he was suspicious. Carpenter promptly went to see Rankin, told him what he had heard, and asked for an accounting. Rankin, faced with bankruptcy, confessed that "he had appropriated some of the College funds" but assured Carpenter that his friends in Des Moines would stand back of him by replacing the money. Two days later Carpenter went to Ames, met with President A. S. Welch and the board, and told them what he knew. [2]

Several days passed, while the College officers and the Governor mulled over the best course; finally, they confronted Rankin and made arrangements to take over his property to cover the loss of some $38,000. "'Tis a bad job," Carpenter wrote. "This is not the end." [3] Nor was it the end, indeed. Rumors were soon flying, and on December 31 the *Register* published the story. Republicans read it with apprehension, Democrats with delight. The facts were distorted by the opposition press, but Clarkson made every effort in the *Register* to put as good a light as possible on the whole affair and to defend Carpenter from the attacks which immediately turned from Rankin to the Governor and his administration.

The legislature, sitting in adjourned session, took over. A committee was appointed to investigate the matter, and Carpenter, ex-Governor Merrill, Rankin himself, President Welch of the College, Brandt, and a host of other state officers testified. Some of the sordid story came out now, but not all of it. Rankin had juggled state and College funds about in a most unorthodox manner but had always managed to have money in both funds at the quarterly check by the State Auditor. At some time during his term of office he had invested money (borrowed from one account or the other) in a school desk factory which had not proved profitable, and he had been unable to replace the funds. How many other borrowings there were was never cleared up, but when the entire affair was exposed (on the eve of Rankin's retirement from the treasurer's office) the College fund was short $38,000. This the legislative committee reported, and there the matter rested. No punishment was meted out to Rankin, but deeds for his property were accepted by the College.[4]

Carpenter's name was constantly linked with Rankin's during the investigation—on purpose by the Democrats, who hoped to make political hay out of the scandal—unavoidably by the Republicans. First, there was the fact that Carpenter had broken the story. When Clarkson, on December 30, went to him to determine the truth of the rumors, Carpenter took him to Rankin and insisted that the latter give the *Register* the whole story. Reluctantly, Rankin did so.[5]

Then, in the midst of the investigation, a "missing bond" was found by the College authorities. Rankin had given no bond for the last year or so—they trusted him—and his first bond of 1869 had expired. I. P. Roberts of the College, who had been instructed to make another search for a more recent bond, wired the chairman of the investigating committee, Senator John Shane, on February 1: "Bond for the amount of one hundred thousand dollars, date May 4, 1870. Will send copy to-day." [6] When the bond arrived it was found to have been signed by Rankin, Brandt, John A. Elliott, Ed Wright, John M. Davis—and C. C. Carpenter. The fact that Carpenter did not remember having signed such a bond was hard to explain, but it seems that he honestly had forgotten it. An entry in his diary, where he had no reason to dissemble, proves both his innocence and his honesty: "heard to-day for the first time that another bond has been discovered given by Maj Rankin in 1870, & that I am one of the bondsmen. If this is true I hope that I will survive to pay and that the College will be made whole out of it." [7]

Two days later, Carpenter wrote to Attorney General Cutts: "I do not remember signing a bond with the Major, but I had such confidence in his ability and integrity three years ago that if he had asked me to sign a bond with him, I should have done so without a second thought; and it is therefore not strange that I should have forgotten it." He continued:

. . . I desire to say now, that if you regard this bond as valid and as covering any portion of Rankins defalcation, I hope you will take prompt steps to collect upon it. And should you be in doubt as to its legal affect, in view of the time which has elapsed since it was given; I desire you to give the state the benefit of the doubt, and proceed to the collection; or at least to the determination of the doubt through the courts. The only thing that will give us an administration of public affairs in the interests of pure government; is to promptly explore every delinquency, no matter who it may involve, and to rigidly enforce the law in the collection of forfeited securities no matter who may suffer; and notwithstanding my circumstances are such that the payment of any considerable sum would take all I have; yet it will not hurt me more than anybody else in the same situation, and I desire to see the law enforced to the end.[8]

This stopped the Democrats, who were preparing to use the bond to attack the Republicans in the coming election. The letter was published widely throughout the state, and the *Register* rejoiced that Iowa had such a man as Governor—"the truest and ablest man sitting in the Executive chair since the days of Grimes." [9] Fortunately for Carpenter, the bond was declared invalid, having been good for only one year. The important thing growing out of this, however, was that by his quick acknowledgement of his responsibility under the bond, Carpenter had saved the Republican party from the attack being readied by the Democrats. Even Richardson of the Davenport *Democrat* had to confess that "the letter has an honest ring, and I for one, glory in the old gentleman's late found pluck." [10] (The "old gentleman" was forty-four at the time.)

But the Rankin scandal was not over. It would crop up from time to time for the next two years, until other matters pushed it into the background. One event occurred during the first days which was a well-guarded secret until 1875, when the story leaked out, and Carpenter had to explain it to squelch the garbled accounts going the rounds.

Clarkson's first story about Rankin, published in the *Register* for December 31, 1872, had concluded with the words: "It is proper, also, since the name of Mr. Isaac Brandt, Deputy Treasurer of State, has been connected with the above matter by some, for us to add that we are informed that the gentleman is not now interested in the school furniture factory, and has not been." This comparatively mild statement, seeming to exonerate the deputy treasurer, infuriated Brandt. Later the same day, while Carpenter worked alone in his office, Brandt stormed in, waving a gun at the astonished Governor. According to Carpenter's story, written two years later, Brandt was "pale with rage." He shouted and swore, until the mild little Governor bristled, told Brandt he was not used to being spoken to in such a manner, and demanded to know what it was all about. It seemed that Brandt was outraged that his name had been mentioned in the *Register* story, that he considered Carpenter to blame for it, and that he was going to kill somebody, either Carpenter or Clarkson or both. "My name was just lugged in there to set inquiry on foot in regard to me, and for the purpose of connecting my name with Major Rankin's in the public mind," said Brandt. Carpenter replied that if Brandt could interpret that from the story, he was reading more into it than he himself could see, and if he had any complaints, he should see Clarkson. With that, Brandt suddenly left Carpenter's office and headed across the river to the *Register* and Clarkson.[11] Whether he ever reached there is not known. Why Brandt was so sensitive to a seemingly harmless statement puzzled Carpenter at the time. Two years later he knew why. The hands of the deputy treasurer were no cleaner than those of the treasurer; but during the Rankin investigation of 1873 this did not come to light.

In the midst of the excitement over Rankin's swindling of the College, Carpenter had found time to work on an address he was to give at the annual meeting of the State Agricultural Society. Not only was the speech one of his better efforts, striking straight at the problem troubling the farmers of Iowa and the Midwest, but it went far toward saving the Republican party itself in the coming election. Falling prices and high freight rates were combining to bring on a farm revolt in the Middle West in 1873. The Granger movement and the Anti-Monopoly party, which tried to profit by this unrest, sent many Republicans toppling throughout the nation, but in Iowa the popularity of the head of the Republican ticket in the fall election possibly saved the party there from the same fate.

The State Agricultural Society, which managed the State Fair each summer, held a meeting in January at which officers reported on the affairs of the Society and at which speeches were given by prominent farmers or by some well-known public figure. Carpenter had been invited to speak at the evening meeting on January 8, 1873.

His topic was indeed timely. The demand for regulation of freight rates, agitated in Iowa since 1866, had reached a crescendo by January 1873. Prices for farm produce had been falling steadily since the postwar boom of the late sixties, while freight rates had remained high. The Order of the Patrons of Husbandry, or the Grange as it was generally called, had grown strong in Iowa. The third annual meeting of the State Grange would be held in Des Moines, January 28 through February 1, 1873, just a few weeks after Carpenter's speech to the State Agricultural Society, and there they would petition the General Assembly for a law "prescribing maximum rates" on railroad freight shipments.[12]

Therefore, when Carpenter chose to speak to the farmers on the subject of freight rates, he was talking about the most agitated question of the day. He had been turning over in his mind the important opening sentences of his speech for some time. On the flyleaf of his 1872 diary he had worked and reworked several sentences, until he had developed what came to be a famous passage:

> There is a tradition that diligent search will discover in every house a hidden skeleton. . . . If, then, to-day, there is a shadow resting upon the prosperity of the Great West, which it is no exaggeration to compare with the fleshless fingers, the rattling joints, the eyeless sockets, and the grinning teeth of a skeleton, it is found in the cost of exchanging commodities over long lines of communication, by expensive agencies, and at exorbitant charges for transportation. *This is the skeleton in every Western farmer's corn-crib.*[13]

This gruesome phrase delighted the farmers, plagued with falling prices. A hog that would bring $7.54 per hundredweight in January 1870, sold for only $3.14 in January 1873. Corn had dropped in the same period from 47 to 20 cents, oats from 35 to 20 cents. Other prices were holding fairly steady, but the products that were the mainstay of the Iowa farmer hardly repaid the cost of producing them.[14]

At the time Carpenter spoke to the farmers in Des Moines, corn was selling there at 16 cents a bushel. In Chicago, it brought 31 cents, while in New York the price was 67 cents. Wheat, which sold in Des Moines for 95 cents a bushel, brought $1.25 in Chicago and $1.65 in New York. Quoting these prices, Carpenter pointed out that it cost the Iowa farmer one bushel of corn to "lay another down in Chicago," and three bushels to get one to New York. The problem therefore, as the farmer and Carpenter saw it, was purely one of the high cost of rail transportation. Several solutions were suggested by the Governor: more corn should be fed to hogs and cattle and sold as meat; more sheep should be raised; production could be varied and diversified; and home markets could be cultivated. By these "modifications" the farmer could help himself, "but modifications are demanded on the other side of this transportation business," Carpenter added. There were competing agencies that could be used, he suggested, such as water transportation or the building of narrow gauge railroads. But even this competition would not solve the problem. As he had shown in his inaugural address, Carpenter did not subscribe to the popular theory that the way to bring freight rates down was to build more railroads. The roads would retaliate with combination or consolidation. Thus, the "last hope of the producer must be in legislation." This, of course, was what the farmer wanter to hear—this was the course he advocated through his Granges and through pressure on the legislature.

Carpenter, however, did not hesitate to point out the dangers and pitfalls of establishing rates by state law:

> I am not prepared to say that a legislature can successfully and wisely fix a schedule of tariff charges upon the commodities exchanged and dis-

tributed by means of railroad transportation, and in fact am inclined to the opinion that it is impracticable, as it seems to me no such arbitrary enactment would either be sufficiently flexible to meet the changing processes of commerce, or the increasing wants of the country.

Here Carpenter showed himself a good prophet. When Iowa did enact a stringent regulation law, it was almost at once found to be unworkable. Pointing out that railroads, since they cross state lines, are not "national" but "international," Carpenter advised: "Let Congress settle it by national legislation."

He then went on to suggest another solution which, to modern ears, sounds unbelievable, coming from a Radical Republican, but which was seriously considered by many in the seventies:

The time will come when a system of national railroads, built at government expense, and monaged [sic] by the government, as a department of the civil service, will extend from the Atlantic to the Pacific oceans. This I know will startle gentlemen who are deeply imbued with the Jeffersonian, "let-alone principle," in respect to government; but the country will be brought to it by force of necessity, and necessity is always the controlling power with men when they are brought to a point where they voluntarily knock down their own idols.

Belgium had tried this system, he reminded his hearers, and it had worked. Then he quoted Lincoln's famous phrase—"government of the people, by the people, and for the people"—and concluded that the people will promote their own prosperity best "by making their government subserve their pecuniary interests and social happiness when they see a necessity and an opportunity to do so."

But such schemes could only be in the future. What of the present? Here Carpenter had some advice for the railroads. Lower freight rates and you will make more money, he told them. If the farmer could ship his corn to market cheaply, even if the railroads lost money on that one item, he would have more money to spend on better homes and more machinery, and the resulting expanding market would give added business to the railroads. Carpenter elaborated on this suggestion with many illustrations, quoted Gladstone on the transportation of coal in England, and then concluded with a plea to the Iowa farmer to "go forward." [15]

Carpenter had worked long on this speech, "reading up" for it in the intervals of quiet during the turmoil of the Rankin affair. "I suppose," he commented in his diary, "this Major Rankin matter will continue as the skeleton of my administration." But he worked away at his speech, hoping through it "to take the lead in giving direction to the public mind on this question of transportation." He had spent the last two days before the meeting going over it, correcting errors, and polishing sentences. [16] Thus the speech was a carefully worded effort to meet the question of the hour, a question that was rapidly pushing all other considerations into the background.

The reception given the speech was gratifying. Not only did Clarkson print it in full in the *Register,* and praise it editorially, but he wrote Carpenter a highly complimentary letter. "I never saw anything come in more timely, & rarely have I seen a thing so squarely and directly 'hit-the-spot,'" he wrote, adding that he hoped the speech would be widely published "so it would reach more farmers, to the end that they may see we now have a Governor who is awake to their interests & who is able to defend them. We had a dummy for Governor so long, that I am anxious for all to see for themselves that the period of a putty man for Governor is not now." [17]

This was high praise indeed, and coming from the "Des Moines ringmaster" was extremely pleasing to Carpenter. Clarkson had found only one thing to criticize in the speech—Carpenter's suggestion for a government railroad—but he hoped this mild objection would not be considered "unkind." On the contrary, Carpenter "felt quite well over the notice." [18]

Comments in other papers were equally flattering, and letters poured in on the Governor, praising him for his stand on transportation. Altogether, January 1873 brought Carpenter to the depth and the peak of his administration. The Rankin scandal threatened him, but almost simultaneously the "Skeleton" speech brought him new popularity. Democratic attacks on the Governor dwindled, drowned out in the chorus of Republican applause.

Carpenter's troubles were not over by any means. The year 1873 was one of such political turmoil that only the most loyal of Republicans could stand up to it with any enthusiasm. "It seems almost impossible to awaken in my own mind anything like an interest in the crooked politics of this year," Carpenter wrote. "Too much claptrap." [19]

The Crédit Mobilier scandal in Washington—touching such high-placed Iowans as Senator Harlan, Senator-elect Allison, and ex-Congressman James F. Wilson—was a background for the minor Rankin scandal in Des Moines. The national unrest over falling prices—storm warning of the crash to come in September—was reflected in the growing numbers and influence of the Iowa Grange, voice of the discontented. And over all rose the increasingly shrill demand for legislative action against the railroads—the symbol of the evils of monopoly. This was an election year, which meant that the Republican party must somehow find solutions to the political and economic questions no longer to be avoided or obscured by bloody-shirt oratory.

The State Grange of the Patrons of Husbandry, meeting in Des Moines on January 28, 1873, took advantage of the fact that the General Assembly was sitting and petitioned that body for passage of a law "prescribing maximum rates for passengers and freights on the railroads of Iowa." The Grange represented 40,000 Iowa farmers, it reminded the legislators.[20] Practically every newspaper in the state, Democratic and Republican alike, joined in this plea and urged the lawmakers to listen, at last, to the voice of the people rather than to that of the railroad lobbyist. And the lawmakers tried, but too many of them "sat too close to the lobby," according to John A. Kasson, and crippling amendments again killed railroad legislation —and snuffed out the political life of many of those who voted against it. These fatalities included Lieutenant Governor Bulis, whose refusal to vote to break a tie on several of the amendments insured his defeat for re-nomination.[21]

Almost before the Rankin case was concluded, and the railroad bill buried, a Des Moines newspaper war came to a head. In 1872, Ret Clarkson's *Register* had acquired a rival—the Des Moines *Republican,* supposedly the organ of the anti-Clarkson wing of the party. The usual caustic editorial exchanges followed, and on February 10, 1873, the *Republican* published an anonymous letter, signed "One That Knows," accusing the Des Moines banker, Rock Island director, State Senator, and part-owner of the *Register,* B. F. Allen, of disbursing some $68,000 among the legislators "last winter" and thereby defeating the railroad legislation of the 1872 session of the Fourteenth General Assembly.[22] Allen's was a name highly respected in Des Moines financial circles. He controlled the banking business of the city, owned most of the *Register* (according to some), dominated the Clarkson wing of the Republican party in the city, and was the chief "railroad" member of the Iowa Senate.[23] In addition to rivalry from the Des Moines *Republican,* Allen had recently been challenged in the banking field by no less a political figure than ex-Governor Samuel Merrill.[24] An attack on Merrill in the *Register* had prompted the counterattack on Allen in the *Republican.*

Allen promptly rose to a question of personal privilege in the Senate and denied the accusations in the letter. The Senate appointed an investigating committee, and the editor of the *Republican,* George W. Edwards, was called to testify. When asked the name of the letter-writer, Edwards refused to answer and was cited for contempt of the Senate. Not knowing quite what to do with the "recalcitrant witness," as Carpenter called him, the Senate, in good parliamentary tradition, put off the decision for a day.[25] That was on a Friday. On Saturday morning, the Senate, endeavoring to extricate itself, offered Edwards a "parole" from the contempt charge, an offer that Edwards blandly refused. He did, however, testify that Samuel Merrill had told him that J. K. Graves of Dubuque had told Merrill that Allen had had $68,000 from the railroad companies to use in preventing regulatory legislation in the session of 1870 (not 1872). From here on the testimony became confusion confounded. Merrill was called; he refused to answer any questions until Monday, hinting that he would then have information on the lobbying of 1870. After a good deal of haggling, the committee agreed to this delay and adjourned.[26]

That evening Carpenter had hoped to stay quietly at home reading, but visitors descended upon him with "so much talking to do" that his usually quiet Saturday night was profoundly disturbed. Evidently he learned some of the facts of lobbying by the railroads, although his only comment was, "I have heard ugly stories about the RR investigation." [27] The Governor, whose adult life had been spent in politics, seems always to have avoided the shadier affairs of the professional politicians and to have been constantly surprised and shocked when unsavory deals were explained to him.

The veiled hints in the Saturday testimony, plus Merrill's promise to return Monday and discuss the railroad legislation of 1870, seemed to throw the Allen men into a panic. According to one reporter, they had "an elephant on their hands" and were seeking some way to get rid of it.[28]

Merrill spent Monday, before being called back to the Senate committee, in Carpenter's office. What the Governor said to him is not known, but when Merrill appeared before the Senate committee no mention of 1870 was made, although Merrill corroborated Edwards's statement about Graves. J. K. Graves, a banker and capitalist of Dubuque, was then called; he promptly denied the story of the $68,000, but admitted that he had been sent to Des Moines by the people of Dubuque "to secure the passage of a tariff bill" in 1870. He had talked to Allen about it then, offering to trade votes for a tariff bill for votes for the capitol appropriation that was at that time before the legislature. Further testimony showed that the people of Dubuque had chosen a very weak reed: Graves frankly stated that he himself was opposed to railroad regulation. He added a long story of a conversation with Merrill on the previous Saturday, in which Merrill had begged Graves to back him up. Graves further testified that Merrill had insisted that Edwards himself had written the letter in question.[29] Among other names brought into the testimony was that of George C. Tichenor. When called, Tichenor piously assured the committee that Allen had never disbursed money for a railroad lobby.

The committee then adjourned and submitted its report to the Senate for action. Before the full Senate, Merrill suddenly changed his whole garbled story and read a statement, admitting that the letter originated only for the discomfort of Senator Allen. Allen, anxious to forget the whole dangerous subject, rose and moved that Merrill and Edwards be excused from answering the question as to the authorship of the letter.[30] Since the motion came from the aggrieved principal in the case, the Senate—glad to forget it—agreed to the motion.

Carpenter, evidently accepting Merrill's last testimony as the truth, sorrowed over the "humiliating spectacle" of his predecessor admitting "complicity with a boy's trick." [31] And so the Allen affair was ended, raising more questions than it answered. How much the public knew of what really went on is unknown. The Allen newspapers gave Merrill the full treatment, while some Merrill papers found it unnecessary to mention the ex-Governor's testimony at all. The partisan press of the seventies again demonstrated its unreliability as a source for the facts of a case. Three days later the legislature adjourned, much to the relief of all concerned. Its real job of rewriting the Code had been done in the intervals of investigation and scandal, but that work was too dull for much press attention. The legislature had skirted too close to a public exposure of the activities of the "Third House" for comfort.

Although the Allen case seemed to have been forgotten in the ensuing months, at least publicly, it must have been one more straw added to the mounting burden of anti-railroad sentiment. Scarcely an issue of a newspaper appeared without at least one editorial or letter to the editor demanding reduction of railroad freights by legislation, either state or federal. Even the *Register,* supposedly the voice of the railroad ring in Iowa, urged regulation. In fact, Clarkson was disappointed that the adjourned session of 1873 had not taken advantage of public sentiment to push through a regulatory bill. Early in February, he had suggested that since there would only be a year before the next legislature met, this would be a good time to "try out" a regulatory law; if it did not work, then the Fifteenth General Assembly could revise it. Clarkson preferred regulation by Congress, not by the states, but he was certain that "this question will meantime never be at rest in Iowa, nor the people satisfied, till our State Legislature attempts such control." Better try it now, he urged, than wait until 1874. Then, if a bill were passed, it would be two years before it could be changed.[32]

While editors clamored for regulation—listening to the voice of the people rather than to the demands of the lobby—the Grangers continued to agitate antimonopoly and antirailroad sentiment. In this election year the Governor, the Lieutenant Governor, and members of the General Assembly would be chosen. All other political issues were pushed into the background by the demands for railroad regulation. One editor warned the lawmakers, during the session of 1873, that "overwhelming defeat will be the lot of every railroad leech that offers his name for re-election." Another demanded that "no man should be permitted to receive a nomination for a seat in the State Legislature . . . unless he will publicly pledge himself to the interests of the people, and that he will not aid powerful corporations in trampling on the rights of the masses." [33]

During the meeting of the State Grange, Carpenter had been visited by many of the members; he found them "fine looking men" and heartily approved their organization. "Anything that tends to awaken thought, and bring men together socially, helps." [34] When, in April, the Governor and Mrs. Carpenter were invited by William Duane Wilson, editor of the *Iowa Homestead* and secretary of the State Grange, to become members of the Capitol Grange of Polk County, Carpenter accepted, although "in doubt as to the propriety" of his action. But he had talked it over with Brandt—the incident of the pistol now forgotten—and Brandt, an active Granger, had advised him to join. [35] As Carpenter had expected, the opposition press promptly attacked him and kept up a running fire of criticism during the summer and fall. On the other hand, invitations to address various Granges poured in on the Governor, and he accepted as many as he could. Probably the largest group he spoke to was at Mount Pleasant, where the Grangers held a Grand Jubilee on June 12. Carpenter doubted if many of the audience of some 6,000 heard his speech, which was given out of doors, but he did his best. His talk, he explained to brother Emmett, was an effort to "tone down and give a wiser direction to the Grange business than I fear they will take." [36] By June, the Grangers were definitely flirting with politics—a subject supposedly banned from their meetings—and a group of Democrats and Liberal Republicans, disguised as "Anti-Monopolists," courted them assiduously.

In April, a local Grange at Waterloo had passed a resolution endorsing the retiring State Master of the Grange, Dudley W. Adams, for Governor. This caused a minor tempest both in the Republican party and in the Grange. Adams himself, however, promptly squelched any such movement in a public letter rebuking the Grange for political action. [37] Charles Aldrich had become both excited and depressed over the Waterloo nomination. It was ungrateful, he stormed to Carpenter, to suggest an opponent to the Governor who had been such a firm friend of the farmer. Aldrich remembered the Know-Nothing agitation and "how clannishly men run wild over such matters." Carpenter reassured his excitable friend that he was not afraid of the Grangers; rather, he was more afraid of the "undisguised and bare-faced disregard of a reasonable public sentiment by the last Congress." [38]

The increasing exposure of corruption within the Grant administration disturbed the local Republican organizations, who would have to explain away these disclosures during the coming campaign. Carpenter had informed Jacob Rich, state chairman, that he would defend no such "devilment" as the salary grab "on the stump or anywhere else." [39] Congress had just voted itself a retroactive pay increase that brought disapproval from all sections of the country. Congressmen who had voted for the "Salary Grab" would have to do a lot of explaining during the coming campaign.

Carpenter became more and more disgusted and discouraged over the political outlook. "Since Congress played the fool and knave," he wrote to a friend in April, ". . . I have sometimes thought it would not hurt my feelings much, if I should be relieved of the responsibilities of public life." It might be better to "avoid all responsibilities," he suggested to Elijah Sells, thereby maintaining one's "self respect and peace of mind." [40]

These periods of depression were temporary, however. Carpenter was too much of a party man to give up his political life, even in the face of what looked like sure defeat. During the months following the adjournment of the legislature he worked steadily at his job. Part of every day was spent in answering his mail, all by hand. Very few of his letters were written by his secretary, William H. Fleming, or by Kate's brother, Arthur Burkholder, who also worked in the Governor's office. Carpenter made various trips inspecting building stone for the new Capitol, and he sandwiched in various speeches, most of them to Granges. On Sundays, official business was put aside, however, and the Governor attended church at least three times—in the morning at the Wesley Methodist, of which he and Mrs. Carpenter were members, in the afternoon at Sunday school, where he taught a class, and in the evening at some other Des Moines church. Visits or reading took up the rest of the day. On Monday, he was back at his desk in the Capitol.

One task facing him and the members of the Census Board was assessing the railroads for taxation purposes, as provided by the new law. The Board met almost daily during March, going over the figures sent in by the railroads, and trying to find an equitable method of assessment. George Tichenor, underestimating the integrity of the Governor, tried to convince him that the Board should "materially reduce the taxes on the main lines," but his efforts were in vain. "We however fixed them as we thought nearest right taking their gross as a basis," reported Carpenter. The task was a thankless one; both the railroads and the people found much to criticize in the work of the Board, but the Governor was stubborn. It had been difficult, he admitted, but he hoped they had "approximated the right basis." [41]

The interval between the comparative quiet after the adjournment of the legislature and the opening of the political campaign was short. As early as April, Jacob Rich asked the Governor for his suggestion as to the best time for holding the state convention. Remembering the objections to the early call in 1872, Carpenter warned Rich against holding the convention too soon: "the Patrons might regard it as an attempt to forestall their influence." [42] Practically every political move of 1873 was made with the Grange—supposedly a nonpolitical organization—in mind.

The Grangers were not the only ones to pose a problem for the Republicans, however. The Liberals of 1872 were no longer organized; the

Democratic party was in its usual undecided confusion; and in Polk County a movement was growing that would cause trouble. In May, fifty men met at Des Moines and sent out a call for a county "Anti-Monopoly" convention of those opposed to the "encroachments of the rings and monopolies on the rights of the people." They proposed "consultation as to the propriety of nominating candidates to be supported by the people at the October election." [43] The resulting county convention, meeting on June 7 in Des Moines, sent out a call for a state convention for August 13. As other counties joined in the movement, calling conventions to name delegates to the state meeting, the Republicans began to worry. Some Democrats, led by John P. Irish, showed a decided interest in the Anti-Monopoly movement, and the Republicans warned that this was a repetition of 1872—the Democrats and the defunct Liberals would take over the new party and control it.[44] When the state convention met and when John P. Irish attended and pronounced the Democratic party dead, "hopelessly bankrupt," and "having outlived its day," the Republicans said: "We told you so." [45]

Carpenter, recovered from his disgust of the early spring months, was not much worried. He described the gubernatorial nominee of the Anti-Monopolists, Jacob G. Vale, as a "vain old man," while D. W. Prindle of Hamilton County, nominated for superintendent of public instruction, he considered a "scrub" and a "sweet-scented reformer." The other nominees were "young men of ability," but he did not regard the movement as dangerous.[46] The Governor should have been a little more wary; this opposition came close to defeating him.

Meanwhile, the Republicans had held their convention at Des Moines on June 25. They renominated Carpenter by acclamation, and chose Joseph Dysart, an anti-railroad man, as his running mate to replace Henry C. Bulis, the avowed pro-railroad man. Ex-Governor Lowe had nominated Carpenter amid general enthusiasm. Traditionally, an Iowa Governor who had proved satisfactory to the party was accorded a second nomination without contest. The nomination of Carpenter, wrote Clarkson, was "simply the due of the man who had already made himself the peer of Grimes and Kirkwood." [47]

"Tama Jim" Wilson, one of Iowa's most respected politicians, placed Joseph Dysart in nomination for the lieutenant-governorship; James Hamilton of Buchanan County named Dudley W. Adams, the Granger; and a third named M. M. Walden, editor of the Centerville *Citizen*. That Dysart won nomination on the first ballot was not unexpected, although Adams made a good showing. As early as April, Carpenter had discussed possible candidates with Jacob Rich in a letter that clearly shows the Republican tactics. Carpenter thought both Adams and Dysart excellent men, but seemed to lean toward Dysart, who was a farmer and "would be regarded by the Grange element as a representative man." Several people with whom he had discussed the problem had said that Adams would also be "a very fit candidate" for the job. Either one, said Carpenter, would be "satisfactory to the farming population." Here was the crux of the problem. The Republicans could not, this year, cater to the railroads by giving the second place on the ticket to one of their choosing. So definitely had the anti-railroad sentiment developed since 1871 that a man, known to favor railroad regulation, must be chosen to preside over the Senate. Both Rich and Carpenter, together with the leaders of the Regency in the state, realized that victory in 1873 depended on pleasing the farmers.[48]

The ensuing struggle between the Republicans and the Anti-Monopolists for the vote of the farmer was a rather dull affair, in spite of the issues at stake. Many Democrats, remembering the fiasco of the Liberal Republican "marriage" of 1872, were not enthusiastic about the Anti-Monopoly coalition of 1873. While the Republicans tried to forget their party differences and present a united front, the Democrats, masquerading as Anti-Monopolists, were torn by indecision and factional quarrels, especially in John P. Irish's home town of Iowa City. Carpenter made his usual strenuous campaign, speaking to as many Grange meetings as possible, and stressing his own anti-railroad stand as expressed in his first inaugural and in his now famous "Skeleton" speech.

Actually, Carpenter and the Republican speakers and editors paid more attention to the real issue—railroad regulation—than did the so-called Anti-Monopolists. The reason for this was that the Anti-Monopolists, dominated by Democrat Irish, really did not care too much about regulation of corporations. Irish was what was then known as a "Bourbon" Democrat—a democrat of the old school who opposed any interference by government with what were considered the sacred rights of localities. Not really concerned over the agrarian protest movement, they had accepted the Anti-Monopoly agitation as a means of winning an election. Once having adopted the name, they proceeded to ignore the principles and to concentrate their attack, such as it was, on the evils of Republicanism.[49] Candidate Vale was hardly heard from after his nomination, while the Rankin defalcation case was brought out and aired at every opportunity. This meant that Carpenter had to talk about it—a thing he hated to do. "I will necessarily have to say much about myself," he wrote on the eve on the canvass. "That is a thing I have never done and I dread it." [50]

The other speakers were no more enthusiastic about the campaign. R. H. Dutton, secretary of the state central committee, wrote Carpenter a month or so before the campaign opened: "Our Speakers are very much loth to take the field this year. And we shall have hardly enough to make an effective canvass of Six weeks." [51] A. H. Neidig, the new state chairman, had to go to Iowa City personally to persuade Governor Kirkwood to take an active part in the campaign, while efforts to get out-of-state speakers to help them were fruitless.[52] The usual long lists of speaking engagements for the various leading Republicans were strangely absent from the columns of the *Register,* probably because their paucity would have indicated the sparseness of the Republican campaign. Weak as it was, however, the Anti-Monopolist canvass was weaker, and the campaign ground to a weary close.

Election day finally came on October 14, and both sides settled back to await the counting of the ballots. Carpenter expected to be re-elected, but by a reduced majority, and in this he was right. His 1871 majority of 41,029 was reduced to 26,112, and Dutton congratulated him that it was no worse. Even Carpenter's home county of Webster gave Anti-Monopolist Vale a majority of fourteen, a disappointment that may have been somewhat offset by the fact that Vale's home county gave Carpenter a majority of eleven.[53]

The governorship and the state offices were safe, but trouble lay ahead. When the votes were all in, it was found that the Republicans had been able to win only half of the 100 House seats in the legislature; a combination of Democrats and Anti-Monopolists held the other half. For the first time since the Civil War, the organization of the Iowa House of Representatives by the Republicans was in question. Geographically, the Anti-Monopoly vote had come from the southern and eastern counties—those longest settled and with the largest concentration of railroads. In northwestern Iowa, where railroads were few and more were needed, the anti-railroad sentiment was weakest; there the Republicans won by good majorities in most localities. In spite of the fact that the Republican platform and the head of the ticket favored railroad regulation, the newer areas of the state preferred the traditional party to the new venture of the Anti-Monopolists.

Fortunately for Republican control of the General Assembly, only six of the twenty-seven holdover Senators were Democrats, since the Anti-Monopoly-Democrats won ten of the twenty-three seats up for election in 1873. However, on the important issue in the coming General Assembly—railroad regulation—this party split made no difference, since it was not really a party issue. Both platforms had called for railroad regulation by the state; all candidates had paid at least lip-service to the demand. A railroad law of sorts was a certainty when the legislature met in January 1874.[54]

The election fulfilled the forecast of 1872. In the presidential year of 1872, the Republicans had won by a vote of about 130,000 to about 77,000. This, on its face, was satisfactory, except for the fact that the vote had been less than an increased electorate would have indicated. Taking into account the smaller vote in a nonpresidential election, the Republican total of 105,000 in 1873 could be explained; but in that same year the Anti-Monopolists received a total of 81,000—a decided increase over the vote for the Liberal-Democratic coalition of 1872. Whereas in 1872 only three counties had shown a Democratic majority, in 1873 twenty-two counties "went Democratic"—or Anti-Monopoly, as the case might be.[55] In spite of a divided and weak opposition, the Republican strength in Iowa was on the decline.

The Anti-Monopolists were jubilant. Democrats who had approached this hybrid party with misgivings now added their voices to the rejoicing. Even Edward H. Thayer of the Clinton *Age* and Sam Evans of the Ottumwa *Democrat,* who had supported the Liberals in 1872 but had mistrusted the Anti-Monopolists in 1873, editorially threw their hats in the air and cheered. With a passing nod to the "monstrous usurpations of the railroad companies" and what the coming legislature would do about it, they turned their attention at once to 1874 and the chance they now saw of cutting into Republican control of the Iowa congressional delegation.[56]

Carpenter wrote to Emmett, now visiting brother Judd in California, and unburdened himself after the election. His reduced majority showed, he claimed, that "there is great dissatisfaction among the people and that unless new issues should compact the Republican Party it is on the high-road to disintegration." He would not have lost a night's sleep if he had been defeated, he continued, but now that he was re-elected, he would try to give the people the best he could, and leave office with "an honorable record." "One thing, however," he added, "I am going to quit. I do not intend to be made the victim of dead-beat politicians to the extent that I have been, nor do I intend to spend so much money canvassing and paying election expenses in the future as in the past." [57]

Of course he did not quit. He would fill out his two more years as Governor, spend four years as a Congressman, even serve another term in the state legislature, and then devote the rest of his life as an "elder states-man" to furthering the political career of Jonathan P. Dolliver. As dissatisfied as he became with the unsavory scandals of the 1870s, Carpenter could never stay away from politics for long. He loved the game, he loved the Republican party, and in his later years he loved Jonathan P. Dolliver like a son. The year 1873 had been a bad one for him; he had had to cover up for "dead-beat politicians," and his honest soul rebelled. He could not help but feel that his reputation for integrity was being used as a cloak behind which actions he could never condone were taking place. A stronger man might have pulled away the cloak, disclosed the hidden corruption, and taken over control himself. But Carpenter was not that strong. He was a loyal party man, and some of those he would have exposed were his friends. He could only grouse to his brother and go on with his job, doing his own task as well as he knew how, trying to overlook the unlovely aspects of "practical" politics.

The rest of the year Carpenter spent in working in his office, answering correspondence, meeting with the Capitol Commissioners, making speeches throughout the state, visiting the state institutions in his official capacity, and preparing for the coming session of the legislature. He did not leave the capital and return to his home and business when the legislature was not in session, as did many of Iowa's Governors at that time. His evenings were spent in reading, visiting with friends, and now and then attending lectures or concerts. The Carpenters led a simple life, being quiet, modest people who disliked most social events. When an eastern publisher, who was preparing a biographical book to be brought out by subscriptions from the biographees, invited Carpenter to participate, Iowa's Governor declined. "I am too poor for a place in your book in order to gratify my own vanity," he explained.[58] This sentence, as much as anything he wrote, characterized Carpenter: honest, straightforward, not afraid to admit he was "poor," and not the least interested in the type of self-advertising the editor offered.

The year, which had begun so bleakly, ended on a note of low comedy, although the serious-minded Carpenter saw nothing funny in it. Prize fighting, then looked upon as the lowest form of sport, was not actually illegal in Iowa but was frowned upon by the authorities. In mid-November, rumors began to circulate in Council Bluffs that two "bruisers" planned to stage a fight—or "mill" as the papers called it—in that vicinity. On November 16, the Council Bluffs *Nonpareil* reported the details: the Kansas City, St. Joseph & Council Bluffs Railroad was selling tickets in Omaha, "Good for one passage from Council Bluffs to ——— and return," for $5.00 each. The purpose of this excursion was to attend a fight between Tom Allen, "somewhat noted as a pugilist," and a certain Hogan, "without particular record." The train was to leave Omaha on Tuesday morning, November 18, cross the river to Council Bluffs, pick up an Iowa contingent, and then proceed to some unidentified spot on the tracks of the railroad, where a ring would be set up and a fight staged.[59]

The authorities at Council Bluffs were in a quandary, realizing that the local sheriff could hardly stop a whole train by himself. Therefore, on Monday, a group of citizens wired Governor Carpenter, asking for "military force" to prevent the fight. Carpenter replied that he would have to have a direct request from the sheriff, a request that came at once. The legal amenities thus complied with, Carpenter instructed Adjutant General N. B. Baker to dispatch the militia to Council Bluffs. This Baker did, sending parts of two militia companies under command of Colonel F. Olmsted by train to Council Bluffs with instructions to aid the sheriff there "with all the force at your command." The troops reported to Sheriff George Doughty, and on Tuesday morning they assembled at the tracks in Council Bluffs to stop the train.[60]

When the train arrived, filled with "roughs" but without the two principals, Allen and Hogan, the sheriff was at a loss. He had a warrant for the arrest of the fighters, but there were no fighters on the train. When the sheriff proposed boarding the train with his militia, he was told that they could not do so without tickets. The sheriff and the militia had no tickets; therefore, he and his men "stood back from the cars and the train passed on to its destination." [61]

Colonel Olmsted, furious at this lack of aggressiveness on the part of the sheriff, at once tried to telegraph Baker, but found that the railroad telegraph office, by some strange quirk, was closed. He had to send a man a mile and a half to get the telegram on the wire, thus giving the train a chance to get under way. "Train now loading with roughs bound for the fight," Olmsted wired. "Sheriff Dougherty [*sic*] does not wish to take the responsibility of following them. What shall I do?" Baker's answer, received after the train had departed, told Olmsted to do nothing without orders from the sheriff.[62] Meanwhile, Carpenter had been told of the sad outcome of his military expedition; he sent Fleming on the run to the telegraph office with a peremptory wire to disperse the rioters regardless of sheriff or anybody else. But at the telegraph office Fleming heard that the train had already left Council Bluffs, so the Governor's wire was never sent. Thus ended the fiasco. Carpenter was furious and mortified. The Council Bluffs sheriff, he decided, was a "putty-head." [63]

The fight itself was actually an anticlimax. The fighters, Allen and Hogan, had crossed the river from Omaha early in the morning in a carriage and had joined the train after it had left Council Bluffs. Proceeding to a likely spot near the Pottawattamie-Mills County line, the promoters set up a ring and the fight took place, with Hogan, the popular underdog, being soundly trounced by the professional, Allen. But the fury of the Hogan admirers, some armed with pistols and knives, convinced the referee that the fight was a draw, and the crowd boarded the train and returned peacefully.[64]

Actually, as Carpenter pointed out in his message the following January, there was no law against prize fighting in Iowa, and if the state wanted to prevent further such brawls, a punitive law should be passed. Such legislation was, in fact, introduced in the Fifteenth General Assembly, but the bill died in committee.[65]

Several Democratic editors, always eager to find fault with a Republican Governor, tried to place the blame at Carpenter's door, but Republican editors promptly came to his defense, and the affair was soon forgotten. The hapless Council Bluffs sheriff came in for his share of criticism and accusations of bribery, and the Council Bluffs *Nonpareil* did its best to defend him. Admitting that the sheriff certainly lacked the nerve necessary in such a case, the paper pointed out that the prominent citizens, including Judge

Caleb Baldwin, who had called on Carpenter for help on Monday, were strangely absent from the scene on Tuesday.[66]

During the political excitement of 1873, only casual attention had been given to the failure of the banking house of Jay Cooke in New York and the subsequent bank failures in New York and Chicago. Iowa farm prices did not at once reflect the panic, but remained at about the same level, some even showing slight increases during the winter months of 1873–1874—a natural rise during nonproductive periods.[67] The State Grange met in Des Moines in December and again discussed the transportation problem and urged state and national legislation on freight rates.

Meanwhile, Governor Carpenter worked on his inaugural address and the message he would give at the opening of the Fifteenth General Assembly in January 1874. In his diary, on New Year's Eve, he listed all the work he had done during the year, which he decided had been the busiest of his life. "So good bye 1873," [68] he wrote, probably with the hope that his worst year was behind him. And it was. His career now lay in pleasanter paths.

ELEVEN

The Iowa Granger Law of 1874

———•━•●•━•———

AS THE MEMBERS of the Fifteenth General Assembly arrived in Des Moines early in January 1874, one question predominated: who was going to organize the House? For the first time in sixteen years, according to a reporter for the Estherville *Vindicator,* "the Iowa Legislature had begun its session with the stormy contending of political parties." Of the 100 members of the House, forty-seven were avowed Republicans, forty-eight claimed to be Anti-Monopolists or Democrats, and five called themselves "Independents." "It will be seen that all the face cards are in that hand of five," reported Irish, who was in Des Moines as an observer for his paper.[1]

Who the "five" were, Irish did not say, but in the counting of votes for Speaker they evidently split, three and two. The first vote for Speaker, taken on the second day of the session, January 13, resulted in fifty votes for Republican John H. Gear and fifty votes for Anti-Monopolist Jacob W. Dixon.[2] This was the first time in Iowa legislative history that such a tie had occurred, and the lawmakers seemed unable to bargain themselves out of the impasse. For ten days and some 130 ballots they stubbornly refused to compromise.[3] Each side blamed the other, and every motion for recess or adjournment, when deals might have been made, was blocked. Irish reported "dark rumors" of bribes offered for a vote for Gear, while the editor of the Keokuk *Gate City* accused Irish of dictating the long deadlock in order to "get up a partizan [*sic*] feeling that shall cement and solidify the new party in the State." When the House settles down to work, he continued, the Anti-Monopolists and the Republicans will be working together to put through the desired railroad regulation, and party differences will be forgotten. Therefore, in order that the "chance results of last Fall's election shall be worked up into a solidified party that shall at last, after so long waiting give them a chance to get office," Irish, Sam Evans, Judge Clagett, and others were manipulating and controlling the Anti-Monopoly votes on the Speaker.[4] Carpenter evidently subscribed to this theory, for he commented, after the deadlock had been broken by a compromise on January 23: "It has been a long struggle and has ended by the crystalization of the opposition element into a party which in the years to come will fiercely contest for power, place, and pelf." But finally "this fool General Assembly," as the Governor called it, came to an agreement.[5]

Whatever the efforts of the Democrats to build a party out of the Anti-Monopoly protest movement and the speakership deadlock, the Republicans actually came out ahead. Gear was elected Speaker, and the Anti-Monopolists took the other offices. The Republicans also won the chairmanships of the committees, while the membership of each committee was to be equally divided between the two parties. As a final gesture, the Anti-Monopolists were given the chairmanship and a majority on all investigating commit-tees. Both sides grumbled. The Speaker had lost most of his power over committee appointments by this agreement, complained certain Republican editors; the Anti-Monopolists gave up the Speaker for a few clerkships, commented Mahony.[6]

Actually, the deadlock had little effect on present or future politics. Once the Speaker had been seated and the Governor had sent in his message, the House settled down to work, and the struggle was forgotten. As far as "solidifying" the Anti-Monopolists, the effort was a failure. True, the party had some fair success in the fall elections of 1874, actually winning one seat in Congress, but the victory was an empty one. The Democrats quickly sloughed off the Anti-Monopoly principles and label and returned to their old program and name.[7] Possibly the fact that the legislature had been elected for only one purpose—whatever the party label—had already made impossible the creation of a new, lasting party out of the Anti-Monopoly protest.

The deadlock had been broken in the morning session of the House on January 23; in the afternoon, the Governor sent in his message, which had already appeared in most of the newspapers. Four days later, Carpenter was at last inaugurated for his second term. He spent the morning in his of-fice; at noon he went home to prepare for the ceremony. Adjutant General Baker, with a company of militia and a band, called at the Governor's house and escorted him to the Capitol, where the other state officers were gathered. The ceremony took place in the House chamber, a band playing "Hail to the Chief" as the dignitaries entered and took their places. Chief Justice C. C. Cole administered the oath to Carpenter and to Lieutenant Governor Dysart, and then Carpenter delivered his inaugural address. "I was a little too anxious to do my best," he complained, but the general reaction was favorable. The ceremony had been carefully staged, and even John P. Irish, who seldom had anything good to say about a Republican, admitted that the inauguration ceremonies were "the most imposing that have been for several years." [8]

"Started to-day upon my new administration," Carpenter wrote in his diary the next day. "I feel the necessity of hard work and constant application. Unless I do so, with my limited education & lack of early training I will not meet the expectations of my friends. I am anxious to succeed, not so much on my own account as on account of my party and personal friends." [9] Herein he displays both his weakness and his strength. His lack of formal education was a constant regret to Carpenter, and this regret contributed time and again to a self-depreciation which would keep him from reaching a position of real political power. Actually, by constant and serious reading and study, the Governor's grasp of affairs was as good as, if not better than, that of many of his friends who had college diplomas. Perhaps if Carpenter had not worked so hard at every job he had, and had spent more time in political maneuvering for his own advancement, he might have risen faster and farther, but it was not in him to slack any work he had to do. He spent not only long hours at his desk in the Capitol, but often was there in the evenings as well, answering letters and "reading up" for his many speeches. During the tense days of the House deadlock, he relaxed at home by reading Macaulay's essays or serious articles in *Harper's* or the *Atlantic*. Thus, as the years passed, Carpenter became widely read and acquainted with the best in the literature and thought of his time, but his political fences often fell into disrepair. Most governors spent their second term in building up support for a higher office; Carpenter, with becoming modesty and unusual reticence, did not believe that a man serving the people in one office should spend his time campaigning for another. His state papers reflect this attitude, and none more so than his message and his inaugural of 1874.

In his inaugural address, after the usual amenities, Carpenter spoke of the dignity of free labor and warned against a "constant widening of the space between labor and capital," reminding his hearers that it took "the blood of three hundred thousand patriot martyrs to wash out [the] stain [of slave labor] from the escutcheon of free labor in America." He praised President Grant for his efforts to prevent further wars, he devoted a paragraph to mild criticism of Alexander H. Stephens's defense of the "salary grab" act, and then he advanced to the problems facing Iowa herself. This naturally led him to the question uppermost in everyone's mind—railroad regulation. The section of his address dealing with this question illustrates not only his grasp of the situation but the smooth facility with which he handled the English language, without the bombast so popular with orators of the time:

> It has become a habit of American thought, which rises almost to the character of a mania, to believe that, for all the political ills to which human economy is heir, either a new statute, or an amendment to some existing statute, will be an effective cure. Almost every man has a panacea which in his judgment will improve the business prosperity of

the country, and secure the future against the recurrence of those financial disasters which have heretofore periodically affected all commercial nations. In Iowa these disturbances have increased the former grievances of agriculture, and have set inquiry on tip-toe in search of a remedy. . . . Are the railroads responsible for any portion of this complaint? They are subject to the control of the power to which they are indebted for life; and in many particulars they should be controlled. . . . They should be treated so fairly and so consistently, and yet so firmly, by our law-makers, that they will feel no temptation to employ lobbymen to besiege legislatures.

The solution, he continued, was not only regulation—a setting of maximum rates—but the introduction of diversified industry into Iowa, industry that would use the products of the farm. Iowa needed capital and labor, as well as agriculture, for a well-rounded economy. It was up to the legislature to encourage capital and investments by wise legislation and sensible taxation.

Carpenter concluded his short address—short by the standards of the day—with a warm tribute to the man he had long ago set up as an idol, the man who so recently had been reviled in the Iowa press for his vote in the Johnson impeachment trial—James W. Grimes.[10] And Clarkson took particular notice of this part of the inaugural, praising the "graceful words" of the Governor, words that were "true . . . and fitting," words that were "due to the man who stands in history as our greatest man, and who rests in death with his record revered and his name treasured in love by all our people." [11] Iowa was doing her best to erase the stain of her vicious attacks on a man whose courage had meant his political death.

The inaugural received the usual praise from Republican editors and was on the whole ignored by the Democrats. In the evening, the Carpenters entertained at a reception in a "plain, unostentatious manner so characteristic to them both." Although it was a stormy night, there was a "perfect jam," reported one observer. Carpenter thought it a "nice reception." Because of the storm, he was sure that those who came really wanted to see the Governor and his lady.[12]

Carpenter's biennial message, longer and more detailed than the inaugural, had been sent to the Assembly on January 23. Because of its length, few papers printed it in full, as was the custom, and not a few poked gentle fun at the Governor for his long-windedness. Carpenter took scant note of this criticism; those who objected were either "too lazy" to read it through or "lacked the enterprise and the means to print it," he commented.[13] When published in the official documents of the state, the message ran to forty-eight pages and covered every phase of government operations. The section of most interest to legislators and the public alike was that dealing with railroads. Whereas Carpenter in his first inaugural address had hedged on the issue of a law regulating railroad charges ("That we can, by arbitrary statute, fix the price for freights upon all articles, and on all roads, and do justice to the community and the railways, seems almost impossible"), he now came out flatly for such regulation:

> In my judgment the time has arrived when a limit to freight charges on our Iowa railroads should be fixed by law. . . . I will make no attempt to indicate the details of the law required. From the consideration I have given the subject, my mind has been led to the conclusion, that a law fixing maximum charges, thus affording opportunity for the effects of competition below the time established, is the true theory of restriction.

Answering one of the favorite arguments of the opponents of railroad regulation—that capital would not be invested in roads where the state exercised control over freight rates—Carpenter suggested that whereas uncertainty as to what a state might do could discourage capital, once a law was passed and the capitalists knew what to expect, money would immediately again be available for investment. "It is human nature to exaggerate the effects of a blow which is threatened by an uplifted arm, the blow as it falls being generally tempered by the power which directs it, lest the concussion be as serious to the force that gives as to the force that receives it," he explained.[14]

At last the legislature could settle down to work. Farmers, who had always been a factor in the House, were in almost complete control. Whereas forty-nine of the 100 House members in the 1872 Assembly had been farmers, seventy-nine of the 100 in 1874 were, or claimed to be, agriculturists. The second group, lawyers, had been reduced from eighteen in 1872 to ten in 1874. Although the occupational balance returned to normal in 1876, with twenty-one lawyers and fifty-six farmers among the membership, the 1874 Assembly was clearly a farmers' legislature. In the Senate, a better distribution occurred. Of the fifty members, fifteen were farmers, twelve were lawyers, and eight were merchants, with scattered professions claiming the rest.[15] Nevertheless, it was unquestioned that this legislature would pass a railroad regulatory law.

Numerous bills were at once introduced into both houses and referred to the committees. On February 6, in response to a resolution passed by the adjourned session of 1873, Governor Carpenter sent in a voluminous report he had had compiled on transportation.[16] The makeup of the railroad committees reflected the attitudes of the two houses. In the more conservative Senate, the thirteen committee members—eleven Republicans and two Anti-Monopoly-Democrats—were divided occupationally between two merchants, two lawyers, three farmers, three physicians, two editors, and one college president. The committee was definitely stacked in favor of regulation. Ten of the thirteen had had previous legislative experience, and nine of them, including the chairman, Frank T. Campbell, were known to favor railroad regulation.[17] In the House, the committee of twenty-seven, evenly divided between the two parties, consisted of twenty-one farmers, four lawyers, and two others.[18]

Both committees struggled to produce an acceptable bill and to ward off the influence of the railroad lobby. As early as February 5, the Senate committee asked the State Grange for recommendations, a request that the Grange at first declined. Ten days later, however, the Grangers agreed to meet with the railroad committee and present their suggestions. The bill they proposed, providing for a board of railroad commissioners, was a surprise to everyone, since the Grange had long led in the demand for a stiff law regulating freight charges. Now they opposed a "cast iron tariff bill" as unjust both to the people and the railroads; instead, they recommended that a board of commissioners make a complete study of the problem before any definite legislation was passed.[19] Thus, Iowa's railroad law as finally enacted cannot be called a "Granger" law, although that is the name by which it is known to history.

Most of the bills introduced into the Senate and the House called for an exact schedule of rates, while only one or two incorporated a provision for a board of railroad commissioners such as the Grange and Governor Carpenter favored. The railroad committees in both houses wrestled with the accumulation of bills, and at last, on February 13, the Senate committee reported out a bill which was a combination of no less than eight of the measures introduced into that body. Scheduled for debate in the Senate on February 26, the bill passed the following day with a modicum of discussion and was sent on to the House for consideration.[20]

The House, "touchy and frisky as an old maid," was not going to be rushed. Its railroad committee added a number of amendments and reported back to the full House on March 2, where a desultory debate took place, after which the bill was again sent back to committee. On March 6, the committee came up with another version which was debated for two days and finally passed by a vote of ninety-three to four.[21]

"I do not know how it will work," commented Carpenter, "but I think if we had three practical, honest, brave men, who could exercise a kind of semi-Judicial power over Railways it would be far better." [22] Both the Governor and the Grange had been ignored in the matter of a board of railroad commissioners. Some Representatives and Senators had favored the commissioner system, but the majority of both houses refused to consider the suggestion. According to a reporter for the Keokuk *Gate City*, the "House Committee got into a wrangle, and came near busting up . . . over the Granger's bill, which provided for a Board of Commissioners." [23] Carpenter put his "fist" to the bill on March 23 with many misgivings. "So at last the State has a Rail Road Law fixing Maximum rates," he wrote in his diary that night. "I have doubted as to whether the people would reap all the benefit from this that they expect but I hope for the best." [24]

The reaction in the press of the state was cautious. After eight years of agitation for a law regulating railroad rates, there was little enthusiasm when the goal had finally been reached. The bill will pass, predicted Irish on February 28, "not because it is just what it ought to be, but because they had the same law in Illinois, and if passed it can hereafter be adapted to the requirements of this State." The reporter for the Estherville *Vindicator* agreed with Irish that the bill had been modeled on the Illinois law and that it would produce "disastrous" results for both the state and the railroads. Several editors in the state, not completely satisfied with the law, claimed that it had been drafted in a "railroad office in Cedar Rapids." [25]

Ret Clarkson, in the Des Moines *Register,* tried to be judicious. "What it is, how good it shall prove to be, remains to be tried," he wrote. The legislators had "honestly tried to do what was best," and if they failed it will "prove an honest failure." After all, he concluded, the people did not really know what they wanted, so they should not expect too much from their representatives.[26]

Contrary to the accepted interpretation of the "Granger" laws of the Midwest, the farmers were not wholly responsible for this legislation. The shippers of Iowa's Mississippi River towns, who were losing business to Chicago and the East because of the more favorable rates for long hauls, fought just as fiercely for regulation of freight rates as did the farmers. When, in 1878, repeal of the law was up before the Iowa legislature, these same businessmen voted to keep the law on the books. Not one representative from the eastern counties of Iowa voted against the 1874 bill. Legislation respecting railroad rates was promptly and inaccurately dubbed "Granger" legislation by the railroads, and the historian has taken up the useful and colorful phrase, but it is a misnomer. The very fact that the Iowa Grange did not recommend the type of law passed in 1874 should have indicated to observers that a "cast-iron tariff bill" was passed in spite of, and not because of, the Grange. In Iowa, the struggle was one of farmers and small businessmen against the large corporations. The Midwestern railroad laws would have passed when they did had there been no Grange organization. Economics and geography determined the passage of the law, not the existence of a farmers' social group.[27] True, the Grange helped to mobilize sentiment for some sort of railroad regulation; farmers and businessmen, through their representatives in the legislature, carried on from there.

The Iowa legislators, for the most part, voted geographically. In both the Senate and the House, the men from the "western slope" opposed the bill. According to the Estherville *Vindicator,* northwestern Iowa could see nothing in the bill of "encouragement to either the farming or mercantile interests" of their area. Although the new rates might benefit the eastern half of the state, where railroads were plentiful, the western half, in need of more railroads, generally opposed any legislation which might discourage the roads from building through their counties.[28] Three of the four Senators and four of the nine Representatives who voted against the bill on final passage were from western Iowa. Politics played no part in the vote; only one of the total of thirteen men in both houses who opposed the bill was a Democrat.[29]

The most surprising vote against the law was that of William Larrabee of Fayette County in northeastern Iowa. A member of the Senate since 1868, Larrabee was considered an anti-railroad Republican. He had favored the board of commissioners system recommended by Carpenter, and he did not think the law as passed was the right one. He courted political suicide by voting against it, but his neighbors stood by him and continued to send him to the Senate for many years. During the debate over the "Granger" law, Larrabee at one point said that "he was not willing to hold the Republican party responsible for a bill containing so many errors." He "advocated the prevention of extortion and discrimination, but called this bill a demagogue measure." [30] As indicated in the running debate in both houses, many legislators agreed with Larrabee, but few had his courage in voting against a measure that had popular support, whatever its defects.

The bill was to go into effect on July 4, 1874.[31] Iowa waited anxiously to see what the railroads would do about it. Having lobbied furiously against such regulation for years, the roads could not be expected to comply with the new law without some sort of protest. As early as April, the Dubuque *Times* reported from New York that the North Western and the Milwaukee roads would fight the "Granger" legislation of Iowa, Wisconsin, and Minnesota. The roads had failed in the legislatures; now they proposed to carry the fight to the courts.[32] The ground for contesting the law was, of course, its constitutionality. Benjamin R. Curtis of Massachusetts, a former justice of the United States Supreme Court, and William M. Evarts, a prominent New York lawyer, both insisted that railroad regulation was beyond the power of a state because it impaired a railroad's contracts with its bondholders.[33] Curtis and Evarts were but two of the imposing list of counsel employed by the roads to fight their cause.

In May, James S. Clarkson went to Chicago to attend the Northwestern Associated Press convention, and while there he interviewed the managers of the various Iowa roads to sound them out on their reactions to the law. At the Burlington offices he received little information. They did not know yet just what they would do. It might depend, they said, on what the Rock Island did. From the Illinois Central and the Rock Island offices came hints that, because of the loss in revenue from the new law, they planned to make it up in interstate traffic charges. The North Western managers flatly announced that they planned to contest the law. A decision would be reached in June, said representatives of the other roads. Ret closed his report with a warning to Iowa and to the Governor:

> The people of Iowa, in grappling with the iron-armed monster of monopoly, may as well expect business. The railroads have not gathered within their employ vainly the best brains and the shrewdest managers and the most eminent legal talent that the country affords. Against this day they, in their might have been long preparing. They will have all their rights and all that they can get besides. Our Iowa people are now nearing the real railroad crossing, and Gov. Carpenter, even before he hears the bell ring, may as well be looking out for the cars.[34]

And the Governor was "looking out for the cars." The legislators had done their work; now it was up to the Governor and the Attorney General to enforce the law against the expected opposition of the railroads. Late in May, the Melrose Grange of Grundy County had passed a resolution calling on the Governor to enforce the law strictly and promising to stand by him in the fight. Coker F. Clarkson sent Carpenter a copy of the resolution, and the Governor prepared a careful reply, knowing that it would be published. He wanted to write such a letter that it would "make some political capital for the Republican Party as everything now is attempted to be turned to the account of the Anti-Monopoly Party." [35]

"Father" Clarkson sent Carpenter's letter to son Ret, who immediately wrote Carpenter, asking if he had any objections to its publication. Clarkson was "sure it would have a good effect with the people while there is nothing in it that the railroads can object to." [36] Naturally, Carpenter agreed to publication of the letter, since he had written it with that in mind, and so Clarkson printed it in the *Register* on June 12, with a complimentary editorial, praising the way the Governor had dealt with the question, "without palaver and frankly."

Carpenter hoped the railroads would conform to the law and would trust the people to eliminate any injustices that might appear. Should the companies not abide by the law, however, he wrote, "I shall not hesitate in the duty which will then be upon me, to see to it that all the authority possessed by the executive is invoked to secure its enforcement." Impressed by the eminence of the counsel employed by the railroads, the Grange had suggested that the Governor employ men of "equal ability" to "write opinions in support of the power of legislative control over railways." This he could not do, said the Governor, because he had insufficient funds for such expensive legal aid. Besides, he did not think it would be necessary; he did not believe the "written opinions of the paid attorneys of railroads will have the effect to lead astray either the people or the courts upon the question of the right and power of the Legislature to retain control of railway companies." Thus the Governor defied the legal opinions of some of the top lawyers in the country and reiterated his belief in the right of the states to control corporations within their borders. He would rely on the ability of Attorney General Marsena E. Cutts, wrote Carpenter. Should the railroad law be "resisted or evaded," he continued, he was sure that Cutts would "perform his duty in respect to it with an alacrity, ability and persistency that will insure justice to the people." Carpenter refused to be stampeded into trying to match the legal talent employed by the railroads, depending instead on the legality of the law as he saw it.

Eastern newspapers now took up the argument. One Iowa paper quoted the "Wall Street View of the Railroad Question," as published in the New York *Bulletin*. "Grangerism," wrote the New York editor, ". . . is . . . an attempt at one of the most stupendous acts of injustice ever undertaken in the name of law." The "Granger" laws of the Midwest would confiscate property, he said, and this "cannot be sanctioned by the Supreme Court of the nation." Corporations would have no security for their investments should the law sanction appropriation of their property "without due compensation." People who approve such laws are not to be trusted, continued the New Yorker, warming to his subject. If Americans will commit acts "of such glaring injustice and bad faith," then "there is a fundamental dishonesty in the hearts of large masses of our people." In that case, "the basis of our hopes of commercial greatness is gone, and the future of the Republic is imperiled." All that the people will gain by such laws, he concluded, is a "permanent degradation of character." [37]

The lines were now drawn, with Carpenter standing on the rights of the people, the railroads countering with opinions as to the prior rights and privileges of invested capital. The "magnitude of the question," wrote Clarkson, "is shown by the fact that it is exciting as much attention in the East as in the West." According to the New York *Graphic,* he continued, the question boils down to this: "whether the railway corporations exist for the convenience and use of the people, or whether the people exist for the convenience and profit of the railway corporations." The sooner this question is settled by the courts, the better, Clarkson concluded.[38]

Rumors as to compliance or noncompliance with the law multiplied, as the date for enactment neared. On June 29, Hugh Riddle, vice president and general superintendent of the Rock Island, wrote Carpenter a lengthy letter in which he lectured, complained, warned, and quoted statistics. The letter was published in the Des Moines *Register* on the eve of enforcement of the law. The tenor of Riddle's complaint was that the Iowa law would make it impossible for the Rock Island to pay dividends to its stockholders. Surely, he said, the people of Iowa do not really wish to "confiscate the property of companies owning railways in that State." That the people even had such a power, he "respectfully, but firmly and persistently denied." However, while questioning the constitutionality of the law, he was "disposed to subject it to the test of actual experiment before assailing it in the courts." [39] One railroad had agreed to the law, under protest.

Other roads fell into line, also under protest. Albert Keep, president of the North Western, wired Carpenter on July 5 that since the classification of the road was not received until July 4, it would take several days for them to put the new rates into effect. John Given of the Keokuk & Des Moines also telegraphed his acceptance of the law. James Grant of Davenport, speaking for the Illinois Central, wrote that his road would comply with the law, but that it would contest the validity of the statute in the courts. Carpenter replied that he was pleased that they would "pursue the litigation in no factious spirit but with the sole view to obtain a correct decision from the court in respect to the legal questions involved." He had no doubt as to the constitutionality of the law, Carpenter added, but if there were defects, they would be removed by legislation.[40]

What would the powerful Burlington do? Iowa's southernmost railroad, the Burlington & Missouri River, was leased to the Chicago, Burlington & Quincy. The B&M charter did not have the Doud Amendment attached, and on this the Burlington based its refusal to comply with the Iowa law. On July 24, the *Register* reported on the situation:

> The Chicago, Burlington & Quincy Railroad has not yet issued any tariff to conform with the law, nor have any orders as yet been given to get up such tariffs. It is generally believed in railway circles that this road has no idea of complying with the regulations made under the new law, and that the president, in asserting that he would comply, merely wanted to imply that he would obey the law, but not these regulations.[41]

How a road could comply with the Iowa law without accepting the rates of that law was not explained. While, on the one hand, the other roads were meeting the rates set forth in the law, on the other, they were preparing suits against the validity of the law. The Burlington preferred to defy the law from the first, and the managers at once set about seeking an injunction in the federal court against any attempts by the state to force them to comply with the law.[42]

While Iowa's "Granger" legislation was going through these early stages, all eyes were on the Wisconsin "Potter" law, which had gone into effect on May 1 and was being tried in the district court. When the decision in favor of the state came in early July, the news "fell like a bombshell" on the railroad men. The Chicago papers reported a "perfect state of demoralization." [43] The railroads' claims of unconstitutionality had received their first setback, but the Burlington moved ahead stubbornly with its Iowa injunction.

Several suits had been instituted by individuals against the Burlington for failure to comply with the rates specified in the law. According to that act, $10,000 had been appropriated to "employ suitable counsel" in such cases, subject to the approval of the Executive Council. Carpenter kept a tight rein on this appropriation, however, refusing to draw on it in several cases. His position was "somewhat delicate" in this matter, he explained to John Teesdale, because if he did not agree to pay the expenses in all cases he would be accused of favoring the railroads, whereas if he complied with every request, he would soon "fritter away the appropriation . . . and accomplish no good purpose." [44] There was no doubt that if the roads did not succeed in the federal courts, they would carry the suits to the Supreme Court, and thus Carpenter felt constrained to husband the meager $10,000 appropriation for use in the expense such suits would entail. In November, Orville H. Browning of Illinois and Judge David Rorer of Burlington, counsel for the CB&Q, called upon the Governor with a copy of the writ of injunction they were requesting, which would restrain the Attorney General from commencing any suits against the company. [45] The judicial battle would soon be joined.

Rather than face a number of suits in the local courts, where the sentiment would be against them, the railroads had decided on seeking an injunction aginst Iowa's Attorney General in the federal courts. Their argument was based on three points: that the law impaired the obligation of contract; that it was an attempt by a state to regulate interstate commerce; and that it did not act uniformly on all railroads in the state, since the roads were divided into three classes. [46] The suit came up before Judge John F. Dillon at the session of the United States District Court for Iowa at Davenport early in January 1875. On May 12, 1875, Judge Dillon, with Justice Samuel F. Miller of the United States Supreme Court concurring, handed down his decision, denying the injunction and confirming the constitutionality of the Iowa law. Clarkson, in reporting the decision, considered that "the question is to be settled for all time to come," and immediately suggested that a part of the $10,000 appropriation for counsel be used to plead the case of Iowa when the Dillon decision was appealed to the Supreme Court. [47]

In spite of urging from the newspapers and from various correspondents throughout Iowa that he hire other counsel for the state, Carpenter clung to his faith in the ability of Attorney General Cutts to handle the case. This was a "very delicate matter." Unless Cutts himself asked for additional counsel, Carpenter wrote one correspondent, he would not employ other lawyers.

> [Cutts] has spent much time and labor upon the case which has been decided, and if I should propose to take its future management away from

him, he would doubtless feel that he had shaken the tree and other attorneys were picking up the fruit. I want our case well managed, and I have a good deal of confidence in Mr. Cutts as an Atty and as a man, and I think he feels the responsibility of his position before the people so keenly in this matter, that if he doubted the result he would suggest to me the propriety of employing other counsel.[48]

Thus it was that the relatively obscure Attorney General of Iowa, with the backing of an equally obscure Governor, appeared before the Supreme Court of the United States to face a galaxy of legal talent that was the best the country could afford. The Burlington had employed William Evarts, who had been Attorney General under Andrew Johnson and would soon be Hayes's Secretary of State; Orville H. Browning of Illinois, formerly Secretary of the Interior under Johnson; F. T. Frelinghuysen, who would be President Arthur's Secretary of State; William G. Goudy of Chicago; C. B. Lawrence, a former Chief Justice of the Illinois Supreme Court; and Burton C. Cook and John W. Cary, leading corporation lawyers of the Middle West.[49] These were the men Marsena E. Cutts of Iowa faced when the case reached the Supreme Court.

Yet, in spite of the preponderance of big names on the side of the railroads, the Supreme Court, in March of 1877, confirmed Judge Dillon's decision, thus denying the elaborate legal pleadings of the Burlington counsel.[50] Carpenter had gambled on his Attorney General and on his conviction that the Iowa law was constitutional, and he had won. However, even had he been wrong, and the case had gone against Cutts and the Iowa law, probably there would have been little adverse reaction. By the time the Supreme Court, through Chief Justice Morrison R. Waite, had spoken in the case, Carpenter was no longer Governor of Iowa, and interest in railroad regulation had almost reached the vanishing point. Less than a year later, in the 1878 session of the General Assembly, the 1874 statute was replaced by a Board of Railroad Commissioners—the type of law that Carpenter had recommended in 1872 and the Grange had proposed in 1874.[51]

The Court's decisions in the "Granger" cases—the Iowa suit was only one of eight—has long been looked on as a "turning point in American history." Actually, recent research has shown that the decisions were traditional, "surprisingly old-fashioned." That a government could control corporations of its own creation had long been an accepted principle of American and British law. The arguments put forward by the railroad attorneys were radical constitutional innovations. But times were changing, the industrial interests of the nation were gradually assuming more and more control of both business and government, and by the turn of the century their ideas would prevail.[52] Carpenter, Cutts, and the majority of the Supreme Court in 1877 endorsed an interpretation of the police power of the state which would soon be outmoded.

-TWELVE-

Last Years as Governor

———·•◦•·———

THE GRANGER LAW and railroad problems dominated Carpenter's second administration, but there were other matters to be dealt with. The Rankin scandal grew into the Brandt scandal, the Anti-Monopolists put up a last hard fight for office, and the question of a successor to Carpenter had to be met and solved.

The grand jury of 1873 had quashed the indictments against State Treasurer Samuel E. Rankin; the grand jury of 1874 reviewed the matter, after an investigation that disclosed some startling new facts, and returned six indictments against Rankin and eight against his deputy treasurer, Isaac Brandt. The introduction of Brandt's name shocked the Republican party, the Governor, and the state. Carpenter had been called by the grand jury on March 26, 1874, to testify in the "Rankin case." That night he wrote in his diary:

> I was told of a feature in the business which had not before come to light and to which, at first I could hardly give credit. It has developed that [Rankin] and Brandt had been carrying on a Speculation with the funds of the Bank [*sic.,* probably meant "State"] for years & had divided the proceeds. This astonishes me as I supposed Brandt had too much honor & political pride to become a party to such business. . . .

Now Carpenter knew why Brandt had been so enraged as to come into his office waving a gun when the Rankin story first appeared in the *Register.* For over a year Brandt's role as a speculator in state funds had been kept secret; now, Rankin disclosed the whole sordid story, and Brandt faced disaster. As early as February 4, the Republican Dubuque *Times* had hinted that Rankin's testimony would "seriously implicate other parties." Once the story was known, the spotlight turned from Rankin to Brandt.

Inevitably, during the excitement over the Brandt exposure, the story of his visit and his threat to Carpenter in December 1872, came out, and the papers made much of this brand of "pistol politics." Carpenter wrote letters and gave interviews, trying to gloss over the "miserable affair," which received undue attention in an election year.[1]

Two days after Carpenter discovered the Brandt story, the ex-deputy himself came to the Governor's office with an explanation. It was the custom, he told Carpenter, when there was a surplus in the state treasury, for the treasurer and his deputy to place the money with various banks, for which they received bank drafts which they held until the funds were needed. For this use of state funds, the banks paid the treasurer, or his deputy, a "bonus" which those officials, according to Brandt, used to make up shortages, dividing the residue between them.[2] This "residue," however, was rumored to amount to some $40,000 that had found its way into Brandt's pockets.

On April 2, the day the Brandt indictments were made public and Brandt was arrested and released on $24,000 bond, Carpenter wrote to Attorney General Cutts, instructing him to institute civil suit at once. Cutts replied that he had sent for copies of the bonds given by Rankin and Brandt, and that he would commence suit as soon as they were received. He was of the opinion, Cutts added, "that somebody owes the state forty thousand dollars, more or less, 'possibly more.' "[3]

The Republican press was in a quandary as to how to approach this new exposure. Several editors urged that judgment be withheld and "immediate censure suspended." Carpenter at first felt sorry for Brandt, who spent some time with the Governor "talking . . . about his troubles." But when Brandt tried, without success, to get the Governor to stop the civil suit instituted by Cutts, Carpenter's opinion of the man underwent a change.[4] Brandt had helped Carpenter in his first campaign for the governorship, and the Governor felt that he had an obligation to the deputy treasurer, but he could not condone dishonesty in anyone.

Faced with ruin, Brandt and his editorial spokesman, the Des Moines *Journal,* turned to the attack. Brandt was being made the scapegoat of the Republican party, they claimed; he had only been "following a precedent" of other state officers, and now certain "influences . . . have worked this case up" against him.[5] There may have been some truth in this suggestion; Brandt had been a Kasson supporter and as such had defied the power of Clarkson and the "Des Moines Regency." Innuendoes, but no real facts, were repeated by several editors, some of whom tried to implicate the Governor himself. Carpenter believed they were all inspired by Brandt, and by mid-June his compassion for the unfortunate deputy treasurer had turned to disgust. The editorials attacking the Governor showed Brandt's "villainy and adroitness," said Carpenter.[6]

The case dragged on through the summer and fall months of 1874, overshadowed by the political campaign, and finally came to trial in November, after the election had safely returned Republicans to office. Brandt's attorneys first entered demurrers, claiming that the indictment was faulty because of the illegal method of empaneling the grand jury, but the court overruled them. They then succeeded in getting a postponement, because of the inability of B. F. Allen, now in the banking business in Chicago, to attend as a material witness.[7] Not until April 1875, when the gubernatorial campaign was gaining momentum, did the Brandt case come to trial. He was then found guilty of embezzlement of $2,000—a sharp and surprising reduction from the original charge of $40,000. A year had changed the guilty man. Whereas in April 1874 he had looked "badly" and had constantly sought help from Carpenter, now he was the "Napoleon Bonaparte of equanimity," and he accepted the verdict without flinching.[8]

Did Brandt know even then that he would never serve his sentence? Was he being used as a scapegoat, as some Republican and most Democratic editors claimed, to prove that the Republicans were willing to wash their linen in public? His case was appealed to the State Supreme Court, and in September 1875 that body ruled that his conviction was void because of the illegal empaneling of the grand jury. Chief Justice William E. Miller, who had called on Carpenter a day or so after the first indictment and expressed more concern for the political than the legal aspects of the case— he was "very anxious about the civil prosecution for the sake of the Republican Party"—delivered the opinion, in which Justices C. C. Cole and James G. Day concurred. Justice Joseph M. Beck dissented at length.[9]

The reactions of the Republican press would seem to belie John P. Irish's claim that Brandt was the whipping-boy for election purposes. The decision came a month before the 1875 gubernatorial election, in plenty of time to have damaged the Republican party. The papers gave the story full coverage, and the *Register* quoted a long opinion from an unnamed Iowa jurist attacking the decision. Cutts, who considered the Court's action "an outrage upon common sense, common law and common honesty," immediately moved for a rehearing. Carpenter read Cutt's argument and wrote the Attorney General that he was sure it would "have the effect to re-open the case," unless the Court were "proof against logic, Law, and common-sense." But the court was proof against what the Governor and the Attorney General considered reasonable; Justices Miller, Cole, and Day refused a rehearing, and again Justice Beck dissented.[10] Thus ended the Brandt scandal.

The Rankin trial, almost forgotten in the excitement over Brandt's embezzlement, was an anticlimax. Carpenter testified, as he had in the Brandt trial, and even Brandt, then under indictment, was called. On May 14, 1875, Rankin was acquitted, a decision that was "greeted with a loud burst of applause." Carpenter, who had turned against Brandt in disgust, felt sorry for Rankin—"the poor old Major"—and was no doubt pleased that Rankin had been exonerated.[11] After all, Rankin had paid for the error of his ways with practically all he had, while Brandt repaid nothing to the state.

In spite of the Rankin-Brandt scandals, the Republican party did not suffer much in the 1874 and 1875 elections. Only moderate interest could be aroused in the off-year politics of 1874, when minor state officers were elected; the congressional races of that year were the only ones to arouse much interest. Most of the excitement among the Democrats was caused by the efforts to make over the Anti-Monopoly party of 1873 in their image, while the Republicans looked on with tolerant amusement. N. M. Ives, state chairman of the Anti-Monopoly party, tried to discard the name for the more resounding "People's Party," but the Anti-Monopoly label clung to them throughout the campaign. On January 1, 1874, Ives had sent out a call for a state convention to be held on February 25, for "consultation." Evans of the Ottumwa *Democrat* endorsed the call as appealing to "old line Democrats, Grangers, old line Republicans; everybody opposed to Salary-grabbing monopolies and Rankinism." Thayer of the Clinton *Age* also approved, but suggested that the delegates to the state convention should be chosen by county caucuses. He saw no reason why the Democrats could not tally themselves with the new movement, but he wanted a hand in the alliance. "The Democratic party will not consent that somebody else shall build its platform," he commented.[12]

The Republicans pretended great amusement at the Anti-Monopoly-Democratic union and were delighted when wide rifts appeared in the hybrid party. In Iowa City, home of John P. Irish, strong opposition to his brand of Anti-Monopolism had developed on the eve of the election of 1873 with the publication of the Iowa City *Anti-Monopolist* by J. B. Sehorn, a Grange leader and former Democrat who had left his party and fought stubbornly through 1874 for what he considered true Anti-Monopolism. Ives's call for a state convention, Sehorn considered, was "made for the purpose of organizing the Anti-Monopoly party, or rather to turn the Anti-Monopoly party and Grange organization over to the chief fuglemen and political demagoges [*sic*] of the dead Democracy." "If the Anti-Monopoly movement is to be run in the interest of the broken down politicians of either party," Sehorn asked, "where is the sense in changing the name, except to deceive the people who are working for reform?"[13] A newspaper war developed in Iowa City that resulted in contesting Johnson County delegations to the Anti-Monopoly convention and a general weakening of the new party.

When the state convention met in Des Moines on February 25, the *Register* reported that it was dominated by a "brigade of old Bourbons" who played the "Democratic game of kicking out half of the Anti-Monopoly delegation from Johnson County, and admitting half of the Democratic delegation." The platform, continued the *Register,* had "a pure Democratic essence." Carpenter, in his campaign speeches that fall, called it a platform of *"generalities* without even sufficient vitality to *glitter."*[14]

The two parties held their state conventions in mid-summer, nominated their tickets, and settled down to the usual routine of a campaign. Meanwhile, the congressional district conventions met to nominate their candidates for Congress. The only real struggle developed in the Seventh District, where John A. Kasson was up for renomination. In a last-ditch effort to stop Kasson, some Republicans in Des Moines and the Seventh District wanted Carpenter to move his residence permanently to the state capital and run for the congressional nomination in that district, in the hope that the popularity of the Governor might overcome the vote-getting abilities of the hated Kasson. Carpenter was much too sensible to be drawn into such a fight, however, and he assured one and all that his residence was in and would remain in Fort Dodge and that he would, under no circumstances, consider running for Congress in 1874.[15] John H. Gear had written him in May 1874, asking if he was going to be a candidate for Congress from the Des Moines district after his term of office as Governor was over. Carpenter replied emphatically and in terms he would use again and again in the following two years in answer to similar questions:

> I shall not be a candidate for Congress either in this Dist or the 9th [the Fort Dodge district]. But I think I ought to serve out the time as Governor, for which the people elected me, without "nosing" around and trying to make it a stepping stone to something else before my time is out. The people have honored me beyond my deserts, and I ought to be satisfied; still I have been so long living on a salary, and have accumulated so little, and withal have such a taste for public employment, that if the people should think I could serve them to advantage in Congress I could not be indifferent to the honor. But upon one thing I am determined; it has been the rule of my life in respect to office, and I believe the partial cloud under which we are, as a party, today, is the result of not observing this principle among many of our leading politicians—and that is this; the candidates of a party should be the men whom the [one word illegible] of the party want, and not just the men who want to be candidates. This being my view, it seems to me if I should be nominated for Congress while Governor, it would injure the party.[16]

Seventh District Republicans, failing to interest Carpenter in their nomination, had to try other methods to defeat Kasson. Clarkson filled the columns of the *Register* for weeks before the district convention with attacks on the Congressman—attacks so bitter in fact that Kasson later sued Clarkson for libel. But Clarkson was no more successful in 1874 than he had been in 1872. When Kasson won renomination, the *Register* came out in support of J. D. Whitman, his Anti-Monopoly rival. Kasson must be "a child of star-eyed destiny," marveled Carpenter, who was torn between dislike of Kasson personally and admiration for his "brains & industry."[17]

Early in September, as was customary, the campaign went into high gear. On September 7, Governor Carpenter attended a speech given by W. C.

Flagg of Illinois in behalf of the Anti-Monopoly cause. Flagg used a manuscript, "to which he seemed quite closely confined," Carpenter reported, adding that Flagg was "rather a young man . . . but evidently thinks himself old enough to tell the world a great many new things in politics." [18]

Certainly Carpenter could not be accused of telling his audiences any "new things" on his 1874 canvass. His speech was traditional—he praised the Republicans, damned the Democrats, and tried to soften the embezzlement charges of the opposition by pointing out how quickly the frauds had been uncovered. He had worked on the speech for several weeks before starting his canvass. "Ghost-writing" was a rarity in the 1870s, and Carpenter not only composed all his speeches but wrote them out in longhand himself. His 1874 effort ran only about thirty pages, a fairly short speech for the time.

From September 14 to election day on October 13, Carpenter stumped the state, giving his speech in each place he stopped. On October 13, having just returned to Des Moines that morning, he went to the polls to cast his ballot and then to the statehouse to resume his routine duties. His listeners for the past month might have been surprised at his diary entry for that day: "Voted the straight Rep ticket. I believe Rep's are better than Dem's [even] if they are a little shady." [19]

The Republicans carried the state offices by a comfortable margin of about 30,000, an improvement of some 4,000 over Carpenter's majority of the previous year. In the congressional races they lost one seat—that of the Third District—to the Anti-Monopolist-Democrats by the narrow margin of forty-nine out of a total of 22,083 votes. Lucien L. Ainsworth, a former Democrat and lawyer who had served one term each in the Iowa House and Senate and who had been a captain in the Sixth Iowa Cavalry during the Civil War, defeated Charles T. Granger, the Republican's choice after incumbent William G. Donnan had declined renomination. Ainsworth was the first Democrat elected to Congress from Iowa since 1854, and he had won the seat once held by William B. Allison.[20]

This one victory was slight comfort to the Anti-Monopolists, however. Their defeat in the state had been complete. With indecent haste, the Democrats started running for the shelter of their old party label. "On Tuesday, Oct. 13th the Democrats of Iowa closed their engagement with the Anti-Monopoly Troupe and on Wednesday Oct. 14th entered into business on their own account," reported Sam Evans in the Ottumwa *Democrat*. "We have seen the last of 'Anti-Monop' and other ephemeral organizations. We will settle down, now, to straight Democracy." Evans can be excused for his haste —he had been only lukewarm toward the Anti-Monopoly coalition during the 1874 canvass—but other Democratic editors were just as anxious to get back to traditional Democracy. Thayer wrote in the Clinton *Age,* ten days after election: "There seems to be a disposition all over the State to turn 'anti-monop' out to grass. This is wise. Such a name is enough to destroy any political organization. It ought never to have been adopted; and the democracy ought never to have been caught with a hook so miserably baited." [21] In Iowa City, Irish, who had once declared the Democratic party dead, hedged and hemmed and hawed and called for a "palingenesis . . . a resurrection in better form of that which was buried." Sehorn, the true Anti-Monopolist, asked weakly for a "new and pure political workingmens party to save the country." After the usual calling of committees and conventions, the Democrats emerged in the 1875 campaign as the "Democratic-Liberal Party," evidently in a last effort to attract other than Democratic votes.[22]

The big question of 1875 for the Republicans was the choice of a successor to Carpenter. No man had yet been elected to a third term as Governor of Iowa, and no suggestion appeared that Carpenter should try to break that tradition. But there was a Democratic tide running elsewhere in the nation, and the Iowa Republicans had to be sure that the man they chose could win.

The Democrats, torn internally because of the Liberal Republican and Anti-Monopoloy splits of the last several years, did not really pose too much of a threat, but the Republicans were leaving nothing to chance. They not only wanted to win, but they wanted to boost their majority, and they had to insure control of the Iowa legislature, since 1876 was another senatorial year.

Trying to put up a facade of unity, the Democrats indignantly denied all charges of a split in their ranks. A Des Moines correspondent of the Chicago *Times* wrote of the Democrats as "not utterly without hope, but as is their custom always when they have a semi glimpse, or half a chance, they waste as much energy in quarreling over the best way of improving it as if applied directly would improve it well nigh to absolute success." Evans of Ottumwa scoffed at this and claimed complete agreement among the various elements of the party, although he himself was at the same time contributing to the disagreements. There were two schools of thought among the Democrats in 1875: some wanted to accept all comers, whatever their political backgrounds; others, like Evans, wanted to exclude all but tried and true Democrats of the old school. This, said the Chicago *Times* correspondent, was a conflict between those who wanted "open communion" and "close communion." [23]

The "open communion" wing of the party won out, since the call for the state convention invited "liberal-Republicans, Democrats, and Anti-Monopolists . . . to unite on a common ground and combine in a common organization, against the common enemy." At the convention the clash came, with Evans and Irish leading opposing wings. Evans insisted that the name "Democratic" was sufficient; Irish wanted it to be "Democratic-Liberal," pointing out that Governor Samuel J. Tilden had won in New York on a "Democratic-Republican" ticket and in Connecticut a ticket called the "Democratic-Liberal" had won. After considerable debate, Irish won, and during 1875, the Democrats campaigned under the label of "Democratic-Liberals." One delegate, in disgust, said it really did not make any difference what they called themselves, since the Republicans would give them "some epithet"—probably "the bastard party." [24]

Whatever the name of the party, the platform was a standard Democratic document: favoring adherence to the doctrines of Jefferson, Madison, and the Constitution; repeating the states' rights stand of the party; opposing banks and tariffs; calling for repeal of prohibition; and arraigning the Republicans for corruption, extravagance, and mismanagement. For a candidate to head their ticket, they chose sixty-year-old Shepherd Leffler who had begun his state service in 1839 as a member of the first territorial legislature.[25]

Six days after the Democratic convention, the Republicans met in Des Moines in one of the most exciting conventions in their history. As early as February, the newspapers had begun speculation as to the possible successor to Carpenter. Several names soon appeared. Auditor John Russell had some support; Hiram Price, Representative from the Second District from 1863 to 1869, was favored by many. But the majority of the delegates had settled upon James B. Weaver of Bloomfield. Here the question of the senatorial election of 1876 came in. George G. Wright had tired of the Senate and wanted to quit, and ex-Governor Samuel J. Kirkwood had decided that he wanted the job. If Weaver, who was a Harlan man, won the gubernatorial nomination, Harlan would have a great deal to say about who would be chosen Senator, or, as it turned out, he would want the office himself. Thus the Dodge wing of the party, in order to control the senatorship, had to have their own candidate for Governor. Flying in the face of custom, and against the wishes of their chosen candidate, they settled on Kirkwood, who had already served his allotted two terms as Governor and who definitely did not want a third.[26]

When his name was first mentioned publicly for the governorship, Kirkwood hastened to disclaim "most emphatically" any aspirations for the job. He wanted to succeed Wright in the Senate and had no intentions of runing for the governorship. But the Dodge men were not to be denied. When the convention met, and Weaver, Russell, John H. Gear, and several others were placed in nomination, the "ring" made its move. The gathering was electrified by the strong voice of Dr. S. M. Ballard of Audubon County placing the name of Samuel J. Kirkwood in nomination "by the authority of the people of the state of Iowa." Russell and Gear quickly withdrew their names, but Weaver and others refused to be thus stampeded. The informal ballot gave Kirkwood 286 of the 307 votes needed for the nomination; Weaver trailed with 200. When, on the first formal ballot, counties began to change from Weaver to Kirkwood, the former withdrew, and the nomination was made unanimous. It took a hurried train trip to Iowa City to convince the former Governor that he should accept, and it also took assurances from the leaders of the Dodge wing that his inauguration as Governor in January 1876 would not preclude his election as Senator in the same month.[27]

Carpenter, who had had no part in the behind-the-scenes choice of his successor, was not pleased. "I do not know how this will work but am disposed to think it a mistake," he wrote in his diary on the day of the convention. "Time will show, however, but I believe it would have been better to have nominated one of the candidates." [28] Carpenter never had much of an opinion of Kirkwood; they had known each other since the General Assembly of 1858, but there is no indication of friendship between them. In 1871, Kirkwood had refused Carpenter support and had thrown his influence behind John Scott, the late-comer from Carpenter's own district. But Carpenter was not petty nor did he hold grudges. His probable objection was that he knew Kirkwood did not want to be Governor and would not work at it but would spend only a few months of his term in preparing for the Senate. One other feature of the politics of the time might have made Carpenter a bit disgruntled at the turn of events. He surely knew that Kirkwood would not be denied the senatorship, which he wanted, even after election to the governorship, which he did not want. During the year, many friends had suggested to Carpenter that his next step should be into the Senate, and although Carpenter had persistently denied any such ambition, he would have been less than human had he not cast longing eyes toward Washington while knowing full well that the leaders of the party had chosen someone else.

The Governor knew that William B. Allison had the power to select his colleague in the Senate, and no word or nod came from that direction. Carpenter was a party man, and he knew that his party—or at least the Dodge-Allison wing of it—did not want him in the Senate. In February of 1874, he had replied to a letter from brother Judd in California, in which Judd had prophesied that Cyrus would one day go to the Senate, that he "hardly" thought he would be a Senator ". . . very soon if ever. The ground is occupied now in a way, that I do not believe the occupants could be displaced . . . without the expenditure of a great deal of money. This I have not, nor would I with my sense of what constitutes a man, spend it in that way even if I had it." [29]

In March 1875, when Wright had made it known that he did not want renomination to the Senate, several of Carpenter's friends suggested that he try for the office. Al Swalm of Fort Dodge wrote that "our ticket for Senator reads 'C. C. Carpenter,'" and H. B. Van Leuven of McGregor promised help from his part of the state, should Carpenter be a candidate. M. D. O'Connell, an attorney of Fort Dodge, wrote that he would rather see Carpenter in the Senate "than any other man that has even been named for the place." Emmett, watching things at Fort Dodge, wrote his brother that he did not doubt his friends were eager to put him in nomination and that if Cyrus decided to make the try, "whatever of worldly possessions *I* have are at your service." [30]

Carpenter could not help but be flattered by all these letters, but his replies were always a cautious negative. He told Swalm that the senatorship "should neither be sought nor declined;" to Van Leuven he suggested that the people alone should choose their candidate, without any effort on his part; O'Connell's advice was appreciated, but Carpenter pointed out that his location, in northern Iowa, would conflict with Allison's residence in that part of the state, that too much money was being spent on the senatorship, and that he regretted the "strife and bitterness" that the struggle for the office always engendered in the party. [31]

He had neither the money nor the temperament to make the kind of fight for the position that would be necessary, wrote Carpenter. "I dont know what to think of this matter," he commented on March 20, "but will let it drift." It was very soon evident that the "drift" would not be toward him. Some newspapers published endorsements, but no word of encouragement came from those in high places in the party—a word without which no man could expect to succeed. In September, Carpenter wrote to a friend, "I am not a candidate for the U. S. Senate. . . . I do not think a person ought to fish up a candidacy for himself unless there seems to be a pretty strong leaning toward him voluntarily in the public mind." [32] No such leaning developed, and the Governor, although frankly admitting that he would like to be a Senator, continued to refuse to make any effort in his own behalf.

Of course, had Dodge or Allison approached him with the suggestion that he be a candidate for Wright's place, Carpenter would not have refused. He had been their candidate for the governorship four years before, and he would have been glad to be their Senator. But Carpenter was not the man for the Senate. He was too modest and retiring to join that exclusive club, where men fought ruthlessly for place and power. Allison needed a strong man as his colleague, and probably neither Allison nor Dodge ever thought of Carpenter for the post.

Meanwhile, Carpenter played his role in the gubernatorial canvass faithfully, speaking throughout the state for Kirkwood and the ticket. On August 18, Kirkwood had opened his campaign in Des Moines, and Carpenter had introduced him as "the great War Governor, who in about six months will be the peace Governor of Iowa." [33] Kirkwood was elected in October by a 30,000 majority, and the politicians of the Republican party turned their full attention to the senatorial contest, which grew hotter as the year ended.

Kirkwood's senatorial ambitions were not unopposed. Harlan was making one more try for the seat that Dodge and Allison had taken from him in 1872; William W. Belknap, Grant's Secretary of War, had some support; Hiram Price and George W. McCrary had to be considered. On December 14, Carpenter received a letter from Harlan:

> Is it your purpose to permit the use of your name as a candidate for the U. S. Senate? If not, I would be glad to know that you would not exert your well known influence gainst the success of such of my personal friends as think I ought to be elected. [34]

In reply, Carpenter assured Harlan that he was not a candidate for the Senate and did not expect to be. He then added, cautiously:

> And I may assure you, that if it were possible for me to exert any influence in the General Assembly towards securing the choice of any candidate, it would not be against you. I think, however, that it is due to the office I hold, that I should remain silent as to my choice between the candidates. I feel under personal obligations to you; for when I was in Washington, four years ago, upon a mission of mercy, endeavoring to secure some legislation in behalf of the poor settlers on the Des Moines River lands, you treated me with great kindness, and you were really the only member of the Iowa delegation that exerted any special influence in behalf of the object I sought. I have before acknowledged this to you; but I suppose you do not ask any special acknowledgment, as whatever you did in this connection, was done in the line [of] your duties as a Senator. Still, I do not forget these things, and want you to know that, personally, my regard for you is the same to-day that it has been in all the past. [35]

Harlan immediately wanted to publish the letter, but Carpenter refused permission. "One or two expressions" were "unfortunate," he explained to Harlan, and would lead to "unfriendly criticisms upon me." Allison and McCrary had been members of the House in 1871 when Carpenter was in Washington; the reference to Harlan as the only member who had "exerted any special influence" at that time would certainly cause hard feelings now. Harlan could do nothing but accept Carpenter's decision, and the Governor decided that "a man can never be to[o] careful in writing to an aspirant for any office." [36]

Carpenter now had only a few more weeks in office. His future was uncertain until December 30, when Senator Allison wired him:

I am authorized by Secy of Treasury and president to offer you place of second comptroller of Treasury. . . . salary five thousand and at present one thousand additional. You should in case you accept come immediately after the close of your term. An Early answer by telegraph is desired. I hope it will be favorable. This communication is confidential.

This sent Carpenter into a "brown study." The next day he wired Allison: "Think I will accept. Would like till to-morrow to determine." But before Allison had received this wire, he again telegraphed Carpenter: "Did you receive my telegram yesterday? It is very important to have immediate answer." Meanwhile, Carpenter had telegraphed to Emmett for advice: "The President offers me the position of Second Comptroller in the Treasury Dept. Salary $5000. Dont like to go to Washington. But $5000 is tempting to a poor man. What would you do?" Emmett's answer came in mid-afternoon: "I dislike to have you go but believe it best for you. I will stay and do all in my power for our interests here." Carpenter's final message that day was to Allison: "Have your last telegram. I will accept." [37] Thus, quickly was the Governor's future decided.

Within the next few days telegrams and letters began to come in. Secretary of War Belknap wired on January 2: "I congratulate you and wish you a Happy New Year. When can you come? Bristow [Secretary of the Treasury Benjamin H. Bristow] desired to know & asked me to telegraph you;" and another from ex-Governor Ralph P. Lowe, who was in Washington: "Have seen Belknap. Dont fail to accept. All right." Charles Aldrich, also in Washington, had seen Allison and knew of the offer. He wrote enthusiastically, urging Carpenter to accept. "Go for it," he wrote, "for it is a good place, & it needs just such as you are." [38]

Carpenter had served his party as Governor for four years, he had not interfered with the leaders' plans for the senatorship, and now a place had been found for him in his retirement. After accepting the office, Carpenter closed his diary for the year:

This is the last day of 1875. As usual I am at work. I have tried to make the past year one of moral & mental progress to myself. . . . And as I am about to enter upon a new responsibility I pray God that more than ever I may be guided by the rule of right. Do nothing for effect nothing for praise of men but everything for duty.[39]

The reaction to Carpenter's appointment in Iowa was varied. The Dubuque *Times* headlined its story: "HONOR TO IOWA! President Grant Wanted to Find an Honest Man to Make Him Second Comptroller of the Treasury and Sent for Gov. Carpenter, of Iowa." A group signing themselves "15th Army Corps" wrote to the *Register* that "President Grant might have looked the United States over without finding a more suitable man for the position." The letter continued with a glowing and flattering account of Carpenter's army service, but concluded with the suggestion that the people of Iowa could ill afford to let the Governor serve in even such an honorable position when they needed him in the United States Senate. The Burlington *Gazette* thought Carpenter had "sold himself too cheap" in accepting the Treasury post, and the Missouri Valley *Times* considered it a "well devised and well executed scheme to buck the Governor off of the Senatorial course." This the *Register* indignantly denied, claiming that the office, "only subordinate to that of a Cabinet officer," had come to Carpenter "solely through parties who are neither concerned in, nor taking the least part in the present Senatorial contest." [40] Either Clarkson did not know of Allison's part in the appointment, which is hard to believe, or he was making a deliberate attempt to gloss over what was obviously a reward for services rendered. The members of the "ring," whom Carpenter had served faithfully, must have felt obligated to find him a comfortable, even if obscure, post. They knew he had no money, and faithful party workers must be taken care of. In his haste to deny that Iowa influences had brought the offer to Carpenter, Clarkson even claimed that "it came unexpectedly to the parties through whom the President tendered it." [41] Since Allison was the "party" in question, a letter from Senator Wright to Carpenter indicates that Clarkson's report of the appointment was, to put the best light on it, in error.

Wright had been on his way to Washington when the appointment was announced. He immediately wrote Carpenter, congratulating him and explaining how it came about:

> The facts are, that Allison happened to be in Bristow's office, when the first knowledge of the vacancy came to the Secretary—who told him that if he would give him a good name from *Iowa,* he would let us have it. Allison at once suggested your name. Bristow said he must have immediate action & Allison telegraphed you. *No other person knew a thing of it—nor did they until after Allison had telegraphed to & received your second despatch except that Bristow had mentioned the matter to the President, who at once concurred.* Allison as soon as he could, mentioned the matter to our delegation who of course heartily favored the move. *So that let no one deceive you by assurances that they secured the place— for it was Allison & the delegation & none others.*[42]

Allison had written Carpenter on January 3, telling him that Bristow wanted him to come as soon as possible, and that his name would go to the Senate immediately. On January 7, Allison wired: "You are confirmed today. Come as soon as you can." [43] Five days later, Carpenter gave his second, and final, biennial message to the legislature, closing with the hope that "the prosperity of the past may symbolize the glories of the future." [44] The following day, Samuel J. Kirkwood was inaugurated for an unprecedented third term as Governor of Iowa.

But even before he took the oath as Governor, Kirkwood had been elected to the United States Senate. Carpenter had been visited in the days preceding the caucus by the various candidates and had in turn called on them. "I am glad I dont have to be cat-hauled the way these candidates are," he commented, possibly with a hint of sour grapes. On the evening of January 12, the day before inauguration, the Republican caucus had met. Harlan, Belknap, and Hiram Price were Kirkwood's rivals for the post, but Harlan withdrew at the last moment, sensing defeat and pleading as an excuse the illness of his son. Kirkwood won on the first formal ballot.[45]

On January 14, Carpenter began the task of cleaning up his desk preparatory to the move to a new life, and on Thursday, January 21, he took the train for Washington. He left Iowa amid a chorus of praise and well wishes. Fort Dodge had wanted to give him a reception, but his haste to reach Washington, and the death of Mrs. Carpenter's mother just at this time, prevented his friends from this expression of their admiration for him. Clarkson in the *Register* was fulsome in his praise for the retiring Governor. "Among all the people who have held high offices in Iowa, none have retired from office with a better fame or a cleaner name than Gov. Carpenter," he wrote on January 21. He was "as good a Governor as ever has occupied the Iowa chair," Clarkson continued. "God save the Commonwealth! and give it always as noble and true and strong a man for Governor as Cyrus C. Carpenter." On the following day the *Register* was again *"Carpenter* all over," according to Arthur Burkholder.[46]

Praise of a retiring state officer is traditional. How good a Governor had Carpenter actually been? In the light of the record of the previous occupants of the office, his administration had been satisfactory both to his party and to the state. He had exerted little direction on legislation; time and again he had refused to "lobby the legislature" for a bill, considering such action beneath the dignity of his office. Some of the measures he had suggested in his messages were considered, some ignored. The outstanding piece of legislation during his administration, of course, was the Granger Law, which he had approved although it was not entirely satisfactory to him. But such a law would have been enacted in 1874, whoever the Governor might have been.

Carpenter's chief value, during his administration, had been to his party. He had stumped the state during every campaign, and because of his personal popularity and his ability as a public speaker, had brought out the vote. His recognized integrity and his quick action, when the Rankin and Brandt scandals were uncovered, served to remove some of the onus from his party. Carpenter was not one to blaze new paths. He had handled the routine administrative affairs of his office faithfully and efficiently. His reward was high praise throughout the state, great popularity with the people, and appointment to a minor patronage job in Washington.

-THIRTEEN-

Election to Congress

———•—•—•———

CARPENTER SPENT twenty months in the Treasury Department at Washington, and he hated every minute of it. Constantly harassed by the struggle for appointments and the bickering among clerks in his office, Carpenter became more and more "astonished at the intrigues constantly in progress from top to bottom of official life." By May 1, 1876, when he had held office scarcely four months, he was so "impressed with the misery of those who are dependent upon the Government in subordinate offices" that he concluded that he would not stay in Washington any longer than he could help.[1]

Early in his career as Second Comptroller of the Treasury, Carpenter had dismissed a clerk to make way for his brother-in-law, Arthur Burkholder. This seemed at the time a perfectly natural procedure, but when the clerk begged pitifully for his job, Carpenter almost relented. The "poor fellow had no friends among Congressmen," so there was no other place open for him. "If this is to be the effect of every dismissal," wrote Carpenter, ". . . I can begin to smell grief." [2]

On January 24, 1876, Carpenter was sworn in as Second Comptroller of the Treasury, and the following day he took up his duties in the great white Treasury Building across from the White House, in an office so large that it looked to him like a "trackless desert." [3] The duties of the comptrollers of the Treasury were divided between a "First" and "Second" officer. Carpenter's job, as Second Comptroller, was to examine, revise, and certify the accounts of the various branches of the armed forces, the Indian service, bounties to Negro soldiers, the Soldiers' Home, and the National Home for Disabled Volunteers. Three auditors were under the Second Comptroller, two under the First, who handled all other government accounts.[4]

Carpenter's days were filled with the routine of his office. In the evenings he usually stayed at home in his boarding house on New York Avenue, reading or visiting with friends. In March, Mrs. Carpenter and Fannie, accompanied by Arthur Burkholder, arrived in Washington. The Carpenters did not join in the Washington social whirl. Now and then they entertained or were entertained at small gatherings, and once in a while they attended the theater, a lecture, or a concert. Carpenter enjoyed most of all visiting with Senator Allison and the other members of the Iowa delegation and gossiping about Iowa politics. As his acquaintance with Allison grew, Carpenter came to admire the Senator more and more. "Among the public men of Iowa I believe that Allison is as clear handed & useful as any," he wrote in his diary on March 10.

This comment was no doubt occasioned by the shock of the Belknap scandal. On March 2, 1876, Carpenter had read a Baltimore paper that gave him the "first intimation of the terrible charges against Sec. Belknap." That night, at home, he mused over the shattering news that one of Iowa's favorite sons had been selling appointments to the traderships at the army posts under his jurisdiction. "My mind goes back now 18 years when in Des Moines we were in the Legislature," Carpenter wrote, "and I liked him." [5]

William Worth Belknap, one of the most popular men in Iowa, had been Grant's Secretary of War since 1869, the appointment coming as a result of the recommendation of General W. T. Sherman, under whom Belknap had served during the Civil War. Everyone liked the Secretary. A large, handsome man, with a brilliant war record and a host of friends, he had come to Washington from an obscure government post in Iowa, and on a salary of $8,000 a year—meager by Washington standards—had lived on an increasingly grand scale, entertaining lavishly.[6]

The Committee on Expenditures in the War Department of the Democratic-controlled House had uncovered the scandal.[7] Spurred on by a story in the New York *Herald* of February 10, 1876, the committee had instituted an investigation that led to one Caleb P. Marsh of New York City. Marsh's testimony revealed that Belknap had received from him, since 1870, some $20,000 in payment for an appointment as post-trader at Fort Sill, Oklahoma. Faced with these revelations, Belknap went to President Grant on the morning of March 2 and resigned. Grant—too hastily—accepted the resignation "with regret." Late on the same afternoon, the House committee recommended that Belknap be impeached.

Belknap's quick resignation had saved him from conviction but not from disgrace. Although the House voted unanimously to impeach him, the Senate failed to convict the Secretary by five votes, most of the Senators who voted "not guilty" claiming that his resignation had removed him from their jurisdiction.[8] This vote did not come until August 1, five months after the impeachment in the House. Thus, the "Belknap scandal" was a continuing sensation through the summer months, during the national conventions, and to the eve of the presidential campaign, adding fuel to Democratic charges of Republican corruption.

"It is too bad that the Rep Party has got to bear this burden," mourned Carpenter. On March 7, he had gone to see Belknap:

> I had wanted to see him for days but felt a delicacy and dread about going as I knew it would be impossible for me to control my feelings. I mustered courage and went however, and having to go in through guards and policemen and finding him broken & sad, I was affected just as I expected and bawled like a calf.[9]

Naive and sentimental, Carpenter could not see beyond admiration for the man he had believed Belknap to be to the pervading evil of corruption in government that was bringing the Grant administration to a close in almost complete moral collapse.[10]

Carpenter reflects, in this and other instances, the Republican disposition to exonerate Grant from any connection with the evils of his administration. The President, whom Carpenter thought "a great man," was not held responsible for the scandals in his official family, nor for the constant shufflings and reshufflings of his Cabinet. When successive Cabinet changes brought Don Cameron, who had absolutely no qualifications for the post aside from the fact that he was the son of Senator Simon Cameron, into the War Department, Carpenter commented: "It is plain that this has been done at the dictation of Simon Cameron and it will subject the President & the Rep Party to a torrent [of] abuse simply terrific. It only evidences the supreme selfishness of Sen Cameron." [11] The fact that the appointment might "evidence" the weakness of President Grant did not occur to Carpenter, the devout Republican.

Although Carpenter was always loyal to his party, there were times when he did not follow the Republican line faithfully. In 1876, Grant was completing his second term, and the fight for the succession was bitter and merciless. Some members of the Radical wing of the party were strong for James G. Blaine. In Iowa, Clarkson and his *Register* never swerved from admiration—almost adulation—of the Senator from Maine. When Blaine's questionable railroad transactions were exposed by a House committee, Carpenter thought the Senator was "a dead duck" and that, if he were nominated, the Republican party would "go to the dickens." [12] But Blaine brazened it through and was placed in nomination at the Republican convention as the "Plumed Knight." Carpenter, who had wept at Belknap's downfall, was not so charitably inclined toward Blaine. He was not sure that Blaine had explained everything, nor could he bring himself to believe that Blaine was the right man for the nomination.[13] Needless to say, Carpenter kept these unorthodox opinions to the privacy of his diary; his Iowa friends and supporters were Blaine men, and it would not do for Carpenter to express contrary opinions publicly.

Much to Carpenter's relief, the Republican convention rejected Blaine in favor of the relatively obscure Rutherford B. Hayes of Ohio. Watching the proceedings from Washington, Carpenter was pleased with the convention's choice: "I think [Hayes] is one of those modest sensible men who will call around him the best men of the country, and will have no vanity as to who secures the credit of control." [14] Carpenter was satisfied that with Hayes the Republican Party would not "go to the dickens."

One of Blaine's—and Hayes's—opponents in the convention had been Carpenter's superior, Secretary of the Treasury Benjamin H. Bristow. Here again Carpenter was not in agreement with the majority of his party. He had liked Bristow at once, had thought he had a "very practical turn of mind," and had admired his honesty. [15] But Bristow was out of favor with the President because of his role in the exposure of the connection of Grant's secretary, Orville E. Babcock, to the Whiskey Ring frauds. The reform element in the Republican party, because of Bristow's work in uncovering this scandal, favored him for the presidency and had put him in nomination at the convention. To Radicals like Clarkson, Bristow was "unscrupulous and treacherous," and his supporters were the "kid-gloved and hair-oiled crowd, composed of Horace White, the blue-blooded Adams, the toney Schurz, and others of the same kidney. . . ." Carpenter had boldly tried to tone down the Iowa attacks on Bristow by writing to Clarkson and to Frank Hatton, editor of the Burlington *Hawk-Eye,* but his efforts were futile. Iowa had sent a delegation to the national convention for Blaine. [16]

Bristow left the Cabinet after the convention, and Carpenter was sorry that he had felt constrained to resign. [17] But regret over Bristow's resignation was soon forgotten in the excitement of the presidential campaign. The Republicans, so long in power, had a real fight on their hands in 1876. With the House already controlled by the Democrats and with national unrest over the continuing exposures of corruption within the Grant administration, it behooved Republicans to get out and work for the party if they were not to be defeated. Carpenter's friends suggested that he resign his position and run for Congress from the Ninth District. S. Addison Oliver of Onawa, who had been elected to Congress in 1874, had proved unsatisfactory to some of his constituents, and many of them felt that Carpenter was the man to defeat him. But Carpenter made no effort to get the congressional nomination, and Judge Oliver was renominated on the first ballot. [18] Friends then urged Carpenter to come home during the canvass and stump the state for the ticket. Al Swalm, editor of the Fort Dodge *Messenger,* thought it would "be a wise thing for yourself politically to make a canvass of the 9th District" with a view to entering the race for Congress in 1878. Oliver had been granted the traditional second term; "two years hence" Carpenter should be the candidate. Brother Emmett was also sure that Cyrus could have the nomination then if he wanted it.[19]

Never one to pass up a chance to do a little campaigning, Carpenter returned to Iowa on October 23 and canvassed daily until election on November 7. Thoroughly convinced of the appointed mission of the Republican party, Carpenter thought election day one "upon which the destinies of this country are determined." The returns, at first indecisive, later seemed to favor the opposition, and Democrats "swarmed upon the street corners with hard grins upon their faces." When Carpenter left for Washington a few days later, the verdict was still in doubt.[20]

The disputed election of 1876, when Rutherford B. Hayes won only by the partisan count of the votes of Florida, Louisiana, and South Carolina, held the attention of the country from November until the final decision of the Electoral Commission on February 16, 1877. Carpenter watched the debates in Congress avidly, attending some of the sessions, and to him the decision of the Commission was "for the public weal."[21] To dedicated Republicans such as Carpenter, a Democratic victory was unthinkable, and they conveniently overlooked the questionable tactics by which their party had retained the presidency.

With the change of administration, conditions in the Second Comptroller's office became more and more unpleasant. Even before election day in 1876 Carpenter was "tired almost beyond the power of endurance by the pleadings of the discharged clerks,"[22] but his worst troubles were ahead of him. Grant had replaced Bristow with Senator Lot M. Morrill of Maine, and Carpenter had been satisfied with the new Secretary and hoped Hayes would keep him. But Hayes chose Senator John Sherman of Ohio for the Treasury post, and Carpenter soon realized that he could not remain in the Department under the brother of General W. T. Sherman.

Carpenter's relations with Secretary Sherman had been pleasant enough at first, but he disagreed with the Secretary about claims on the government and about the treatment of clerks in the Department. "I almost wish I was away in Iowa," wrote Carpenter, as early as April 16, 1877. The next day he approved of a settlement that Quartermaster General Montgomery C. Meigs objected to. "I seem to be in a chronic antagonism to the Heads of the Depts in my judgment of what is right and proper," Carpenter commented, adding stubbornly, "I know of no other way, however, than to go forward in the path which seems to me right and let consequences take care of themselves."[23]

On April 25, Carpenter talked to his old friend George W. McCrary, now Hayes's Secretary of War, about leaving the Treasury. Two paths were open to him. He could either return to Iowa and run for Congress from his district, or he and Emmett could buy the Fort Dodge *Messenger*, which was for sale. This second choice was eliminated, however, when Judge William N. Meservey of Fort Dodge outbid the Carpenter brothers for the newspaper.[24] Thus, if Carpenter were to leave his lucrative but unpleasant post in Washington, he would inevitably return to the Iowa political scene. He had been too long "in politics" to do anything else, now that his hopes of a newspaper career had been dashed.

By early May, Carpenter's proposed resignation was no longer a secret, and by the middle of the month the newspapers had the story. Clarkson, before hearing the real account of why Carpenter had resigned, commented that "any mistreatment of [Carpenter] at Washington would be very generally resented in this State." [25] Immediately upon reading this in the *Register* Carpenter wrote a long letter to Clarkson, explaining just why he had resigned. This account, however, was "not for the print." He did not want a "controversy," nor did he want to "injure the Republican cause." [26]

The demands of patronage had given Carpenter a good excuse for withdrawing gracefully, an action which, quite unintentionally on his part, resulted in a good deal of favorable publicity. In the juggling of positions that always accompanied a new administration, the Secretary had decided that Iowa had too many political plums in the Treasury and that some one would have to go. The choice fell on Stephen J. W. Tabor of Independence, then fourth auditor in the Treasury, since the party leaders could hardly dismiss an ex-Governor without unhappy political consequences in his state. Carpenter, hearing of this when Tabor came to him and explained "the difficulties in which it would place him to go out," offered to resign at once if it would save Tabor's job. This action was not entirely generous, since Carpenter had already decided to resign. He told Clarkson of the other reason why he had wanted to leave:

> I had come to feel that I was not altogether in harmony with secretary Sherman, and I must exercise my own judgment and cannot be a sycophant. In the first place, the Secretary came in with a flourish of trumpets on questions connected with the manner of doing business, which was really a criticism upon most of the officers in the Department. I do not believe that my views in respect to public expenditures are extravagant. In fact I have always tried to act upon this principle where I have controlled public moneys: to discourage extravagance and not even encourage liberality, *but to be just*. And when I thought I saw a tendency, not even to be just to public creditors, I could not refrain from saying so. Or in other words, giving my judgment in matters within the jurisdiction of my office of what I regarded as justice and the Law. . . .

Sherman, continued Carpenter, seemed to have two aims in view: one, to show larger reductions of the public debt than his predecessors; and two, to return to a specie basis "regardless of the temporary interests or wishes of the people." If he can do this, said Carpenter, he thinks he can "fix his place" in history as a "second Alexander Hamilton." Furthermore, Sherman desired places in the Department for "persons for whom the administration wanted to provide." Carpenter was to bear the "onus" of the dismissals but was to have "no voice in filling the vacancies." At last the demands of patronage were too much for Carpenter; he resigned. There was one more thing that made him "uncomfortable," he told Clarkson:

> Just as soon as a new administration comes in all the Whipper-snappers in these Departments, and all the old *Factotums,* auditors, &c &c, who have been here since the flood begin to smell around to see what the new powers want, and then they begin to operate accordingly. . . . All these things disgust me and I think Iowa is big enough for me.[27]

The newspapers spread the story that Carpenter had resigned to save the job of another employee, to Carpenter's chagrin but to his political advantage. The Chicago *Inter-Ocean* thought it was an example of "refreshing" news in "these days of office-hunting." Tabor, who had held his job for eighteen years, had been saved by the generosity of Carpenter, said the Chicago *Times.* Clarkson reprinted these favorable notices, with glowing comments of his own. The action was "characteristic of Cyrus C. Carpenter," and an evidence of the "noble impulses of his always manly heart." [28] Nowhere in the *Register* is there any indication of the real reason why Carpenter had resigned.

Even before his announced decision to leave his Treasury post, Carpenter had received much encouragement from Iowa friends to run for Congress from the Ninth District.[29] The two-term tradition, although weakening, still held as to congressional offices, and Oliver was expected to decline renomination. Carpenter now felt that his time had come. This decision was probably behind his plan to resign his office in the fall of 1877 so that he could be free to return to Iowa to begin a campaign for the 1878 nomination.

Leaving Washington on September 27, 1877, with no regrets, Carpenter stopped off at Harford, Pennsylvania, on his way west, for a visit with his boyhood friends. He reached home on October 9, just in time to cast his vote for John H. Gear in the gubernatorial election. Two weeks later, Congressman Oliver replied to an inquiry from Carpenter: he had decided after his second election that he would not again be a candidate and so Carpenter was "at perfect liberty to go to work." [30]

There followed the usual writing of letters, visiting about the district, and collecting promises of support. By February 1878, the tide ran so strongly in Carpenter's favor that the race seemed to be almost over. Here and there were murmurs of discontent, and other candidates made their appearance, but on the whole Carpenter's campaign seemed almost too easy.[31] It would not remain so for long.

Several opponents had appeared, in spite of Carpenter's popularity. The most persistent was M. D. O'Connell of Fort Dodge, district attorney for the Eleventh Judicial District, who was "working like the devil," according to Charles Aldrich. Other men were mentioned in the newspapers, but most of them either declared publicly, or privatly to Carpenter, that they were not in the race.[32]

Meanwhile, the Sixteenth General Assembly, in session in Des Moines, took action which affected Carpenter's campaign. For four years the railroads had agitated for a change in Iowa's Granger Law of 1874, and in 1877, they had seen to it that their own man was elected Governor. According to that perennial governor's secretary, William H. Fleming, the railroad corporations were behind Gear's nomination and election in 1877.[33] When the General Assembly convened, the question of repealing the 1874 railroad law occupied the attention of the legislators almost to the exclusion of all other matters. And this time the railroads were successful. A new law passed the House on March 7, the Senate on March 19, and was signed by the Governor on March 23, 1878. In addition to repealing the Granger Law, the act provided for the appointment of a board of three railroad commissioners "to have the general supervision of all railroads in the state. . . ."[34]

On March 21, Carpenter received a telegram from Fleming: "Will you accept the office of Rail Road Commissioner if tendered you? The appointment to be for one year, with reappointment for three years. Please answer." These few lines upset Carpenter's plans and led to a mistake that almost ended his political career. "It makes me feel strangely as I am in such a quandary as to what I better do," he wrote in his diary that night.

The following day, Carpenter went to Des Moines and told the Governor that he did not want the appointment. Gear would not accept his decision, however, and begged him to reconsider. Finally, Carpenter suggested that they take it up with the delegation in the General Assembly from his district; he would abide by their decision, he said. Gear promptly called in the Republicans from the Ninth District, explained his reasons for wanting Carpenter on the commission, and asked for their opinion. They at once agreed with the Governor, and Carpenter "felt bound almost to accept." He was unhappy about his decision, and when he returned to Fort Dodge he found his family and friends disappointed. "But I did what I thought was right," said Carpenter. His sense of duty had overcome his own wishes, although he was troubled about his decision and its effect on the congressional race and on the friends who had been working so hard for him.[35]

What arguments had Gear and the delegation used to persuade Carpenter that he should give up a sure nomination to Congress for a troublesome job in Des Moines? According to Clarkson, the Governor wanted the "best men" in the state as commissioners to inaugurate the new law, which was a "departure in our system of government." Therefore, quite naturally, he had turned to ex-Governor Carpenter, and Carpenter had accepted, although with "very great reluctance." Clarkson admitted to the people of the Ninth District that "the interest of the State at large in this matter has been secured at great expense to them." [36] Such were no doubt the arguments made to Carpenter by the Governor. One explanation from Carpenter himself has been preserved in a letter to a young nephew in California, his brother Judd's son Prentiss, written on May 11:

> I was a good deal disturbed to know what my duty was, when offered this position, as I suppose if I had kept out of it, I would have been nominated for Congress in our Dist by acclamation. But I rather shrank from the turmoil of a candidacy for Congress, & then a struggle for a position after I was elected; and as the salary of this position is practically better than that of a Congressman, & I am relieved of political assessments and expenditures, I thought I could save some money out of it, which is something of an object to me, while at the same time it would afford me a wide field for usefulness, if I properly performed its duties, so I took it. Many of my friends did not like it, and others thought I acted wisely. I suppose time will tell.[37]

Carpenter was no doubt rationalizing in this letter. His sense of duty had been appealed to, and he had been flattered by assurances that he was the one man who could make the new law work. The commission established by the law had little power; the only way to make it successful would be through the appointment of strong and honest men to the board. Carpenter and the two other appointees—Peter Dey of Iowa City, a railroad builder, and James W. McDill of Afton, a former district judge and Congressman—were men of impeccable reputation.[38]

Reactions to Carpenter's appointment varied. Although most of the newspapers in the state reported favorably on his acceptance, his friends were unhappy about it. They had wanted to send him to Congress; now it seemed that his new job had removed him from that race. Ira N. Kidder of Boone reported great discontent in the district; he feared that Carpenter had been "bluffed" into acceptance by men who wanted him out of the way. The fact that one of the Ninth District delegation in the legislature—John J. Russell of Jefferson—announced his own candidacy after Carpenter's appointment seemed to Kidder to prove this point. A correspondent from Humboldt County thought the appointment "unsatisfactory" if it took Carpenter out of the congressional race; George D. Perkins had "serious doubts" that Carpenter's friends would permit him to withdraw from the canvass; and the Pomeroy *Journal* considered this effort to dispose of Carpenter as "a little off color." [39]

The other candidates, O'Connell in particular, doubled their efforts, reporting that Carpenter had withdrawn. There is no evidence that Carpenter formally stepped out of the contest, but several letters imply that he had told certain Republicans in his district that he would not be a candidate. O'Connell claimed that Carpenter had told him he was *"out of the field,"* and C. W. Lowrie of Boone, who entered the contest in May, asserted that he did so after Carpenter's withdrawal. It is thus evident that Carpenter, in the first few weeks after his appointment, had told friends and foes that he was not to be considered as a candidate.[40] His foes accepted this gladly; his friends at once set to work to convince him that his appointment did not preclude his consideration as a congressional candidate.

During April and May, the politicians of the Ninth District were in a turmoil. O'Connell pushed his chances "like a tiger;" State Senator John J. Russell and C. W. Lowrie added their names to the list; and Carpenter's friends pressed him constantly to let them go ahead with the campaign. O. J. Jolley of Rockwell City expressed the general attitude of Carpenter men: "We will nominate you notwithstanding." Others began to circulate petitions, to which they found ready signers, and these were sent to Carpenter and to the newspapers.[41]

Faced with this situation, Carpenter, in spite of promises made, changed his mind. Since accepting appointment as a railroad commissioner and being elected president of the board, he had spent about half of his time in Des Moines, trying to get the work of the commission organized. The rest of the time he stayed at home in Fort Dodge, with little to do but help Mrs. Carpenter with spring house cleaning or take trips to his farm just outside of town. And he was bored. The pleasures of a political campaign were too attractive to him to be ignored.

At last, in answer to a petition from a number of Fort Dodge supporters, Carpenter wrote a public letter on May 13 and sent it to the papers. He had not sought the nomination originally, he claimed, but had let his name be used when his friends had insisted. Then, when the Governor had urged him to accept appointment as a railroad commissioner, "insisting that I owed a duty to a whole State which had greatly honored me," he had accepted and had urged his friends to support some other candidate. But when the letters and petitions became "so numerous and so urgent," he had been forced to reconsider his position. "I therefore say to you, that while I have at no time been over-anxious about this candidacy, and feel embarrassed now at the position in which a nomination would place me, yet I am a citizen of this district, and a Republican, and if in your judgment it will be the best and wisest thing to do, I shall accept the candidacy." [42]

In a long letter to George D. Perkins, editor of the Sioux City *Journal,* Carpenter explained some of the private reasons why he had written his public letter. His action was not motivated by a desire to hurt the Russell campaign, he wrote, but rather to stop O'Connell. Many of the Republicans of his district feared that O'Connell, "a persevering and unscrupulous worker," might be nominated if Carpenter did not run. Both Russell and O'Connell had asked him to write letters withdrawing from the race, Carpenter continued, but he had not replied because, although Russell would not use such information unfairly, O'Connell "would have rode over the District declaring that I wrote it out of my high regard for him." Carpenter's main objection to O'Connell, aside from his "unbounded audacity and unscrupulousness," was based on the fact that, in his opinion, O'Connell would use the office of Congressmen, as he had used the office of District Attorney, for his own benefit and not for service to the people. "He would regard all its patronage and influence as simply a personal perquisite to be used for his own individual aggrandizement." He had a "retinue of adherents ready to perambulate the prairies in his interest," and he also had an entire "lack of appreciation of the great responsibilities of the office and the true dignity of a candidate." Rather than run the risk of having the nomination go to O'Connell, Carpenter had concluded, on the urging of his friends who were anti-O'Connell, to re-enter the race.[43]

Now the positions of friends and foes were reversed. Friends gleefully set to work to see that Carpenter men were sent as delegates to the district convention; foes angrily fought harder for their own men as delegates. Carpenter, who had been a factor in Iowa politics for almost twenty years without making any real enemies, had now aroused a solid core of opposition.

From mid-May until the district convention at Cherokee on August 7, Carpenter divided his time between his duties as railroad commissioner and his active campaign for the nomination. In June, a new opponent appeared on the scene when Judge Isaac Pendleton of Sioux City announced himself as available. Lowrie had withdrawn by this time, and when the convention met, Carpenter's opposition had dwindled to Pendleton, Russell, and O'Connell. Pendleton, evidently backed by George D. Perkins, soon outstripped the other contestants and became Carpenter's most serious rival for the nomination. O'Connell's chances, on the other hand, fell almost to the vanishing point when Webster County chose a Carpenter delegation. Russell stayed in the race to the end, but without much hope.[44]

When the Carpenter party arrived at Cherokee on August 6, in a special railroad car chartered by Carpenter with the help of Senator Allison, they found Pendleton and his supporters "on the ground and busy as bees." Carpenter's men immediately rounded up their delegates and agreed on a course of action. The opposition was strong, however, and Carpenter lost the organization of the convention when Pendleton men were elected as president and secretary, a sign that the ex-Governor was not going to have an easy time.[45]

Balloting began at 1:30 in the afternoon of August 7, with 112 delegates present, making fifty-seven votes necessary for the nomination. The informal ballot showed at once that Carpenter, although leading, was in for trouble. He received 52⅓ votes; Pendelton followed with 32⅔; Russell and O'Connell trailed with sixteen and ten respectively. On the first formal ballot Carpenter and Pendleton each gained one vote, O'Connell lost four and Russell picked up two—making a total of 112. The Pendleton votes had reached their peak, but his supporters were loyal, and four more ballots were necessary to put Carpenter over. Having reached a stalemate after the fourth ballot, the convention adjourned until 7:30, giving the candidates a chance to do some trading. On the fifth ballot the break came. When Carpenter's total had built to 56⅚, Kossuth County changed two votes from Pendleton to Carpenter, Buena Vista followed, and the nomination was declared unanimous.[46]

For the first time in his political life, Carpenter had had to fight for votes. Five ballots was hardly a contest, compared with some convention battles that ran to a hundred or more, but it was something new for Carpenter. His popularity in the district had saved him from the defeat that his inept handling of his candidacy might have caused.

Carpenter's chief opponent in the election race was the Greenbacker, Lucian Q. Hoggatt of Story County, a colorful character whom John P. Irish described as "so ugly he sours milk when he looks in the pan." [47] The Greenback party, organized in Iowa in 1876, was a continuing expression of the unrest that had brought about the Granger, the Liberal Republican, and the Anti-Monopoly movements. The panacea for the economic ills of the time was now inflation—more greenbacks—a solution opposed by the conservatives in both major parties. Although many Democrats were willing to support a Greenback candidate, John P. Irish, having failed in his search for a new combination for his party, had now returned to complete loyalty to the Democrats and was violently anti-Greenbacker. Many of the Democrats of the Ninth District felt the same way. John A. Hull of Boone wrote Carpenter that at least 1,000 Democrats in his county would rather vote Republican than support Hoggatt. As a result, some of them met and named Walter H. Brown as their candidate. Six other districts had three tickets in the field in 1878; only in the Sixth and Seventh Districts did the Greenbackers and the Democrats agree on a single candidate to oppose the Republican nominee.[48]

From August 26 until election day on October 8, the candidates canvassed the state diligently. Carpenter's speeches inevitably dealt with the money question, and according to partisan reports his arguments were "bringing men to their senses and knocking Greenbackers and Democrats right and left." But the Greenbackers were strong, and Republicans in many sections were concerned over the outcome. Carpenter, the conservative Republican, "without the least equivocation . . . held up . . . the standard of honest money." [49]

On some of Carpenter's trips he was accompanied by a new resident of Fort Dodge, Jonathan Prentiss Dolliver, who had come to Iowa from West Virginia to practice law. Carpenter had met Dolliver at church one Sunday in early April, and he was at once impressed with the young man. Dolliver, more interested in politics than in law, entered into the Carpenter campaign with enthusiasm, and a friendship developed that was to have great importance in both their lives. [50]

Election day came at last. Carpenter worried a bit during the day, but as the returns came in the prospect brightened. Final results gave him 16,489 votes; Hoggatt, 12,338; and Brown, 1,202. The Republicans won in seven of Iowa's nine congressional districts, but in the Sixth and Seventh the fusion of Greenbackers and Democrats had defeated the Republican candidates. James B. Weaver, who had left the Republican party and called himself a "Greenbacker-Democrat," won in the Sixth; Edward H. Gillette, an out-and-out Greenbacker, was the victor in the Seventh. [51]

The election was over, but the Republicans had little cause to rejoice. On the state ticket their majority had shrunk from a comfortable 51,000 in 1876 to a mere 8,500 in 1878. The warning of the 1877 gubernatorial election was now realized. [52] The Democrats saw that if they had embraced the Greenback program wholeheartedly in 1878 they might have broken the strong Republican hold on Iowa. It had been a close call for Republican rule in the state.

To add to Republican troubles, the question of the legality of the election now faced them. Even during the canvass, agitation had been started regarding the correct date for congressional elections. According to the Iowa constitution and the Iowa Code of 1860, elections were held in Iowa in October, except in presidential years, when they were held on the "Tuesday next after the first Monday in November." [53] In 1872, Congress had passed a law providing that after 1876 all state congressional elections should be held in November. However, in 1875 a proviso was added: the law did not apply "to any State that had not yet changed its day of election, and whose constitution must be amended in order to effect a change in the day of the election of State officers in said State." [54] Iowa had made no change in her law, and since the date had been set in the constitution, many believed that an amendment would be necessary. A legal argument, with political undertones, had been developing for several months.

In August, the Des Moines *Register* brought the debate into the open with an editorial on "The Double Election Question in Iowa," and Clarkson concluded to his own satisfaction that the October date was the legal one for Iowa, both for state and for congressional offices. A few days later the Iowa City *Press* published a letter written by Edward Campbell, Jr., the chairman of the Democratic State Committee: he believed that the "prevailing notion" that there should be two elections in Iowa in 1878 was a mistake. The Dubuque *Times,* a Republican paper, agreed with the *Register* and with Campbell. Since other leading Republican and Democratic papers accepted the October date, there seemed no further cause for argument.[55]

But Democrats and Republicans could not long remain in agreement. When, in September, Governor Gear and Attorney General John F. McJunkin announced that the October date was the legal one, the Democratic Dubuque *Herald* at once took issue with them, hinting rather broadly that if the Governor and the Attorney General were wrong, the Representatives elected in October would not be seated by the House.[56] After Democrats had studied the October election returns, certain leaders among them came out strongly for a November election.

Their reasoning is obvious. In the seven districts where there had been three tickets in the field, the Republicans had won, although by narrow margins. In fact, in three of the districts the Republican had been elected by a minority of the total votes cast. In the two districts where the Democrats and Greenbackers had combined to oppose the Republican candidate, the fusion candidate had won.[57] The Democrats therefore concluded that if they had joined the Greenbackers on a single candidate in every district, they would surely have won three more seats and possibly four.

John P. Irish, who had been consistently anti-Greenbacker during the campaign, now adopted Weaver and Gillette as his own and began urging Iowa Democrats to hold November elections in all the districts. As a result, a few Democrats met in Burlington on October 23, and Chairman Campbell (forgetting his earlier decision against a November election) pushed through a resolution claiming that "the first Tuesday in November is the only legal election day for Congressmen in this State." A week earlier Carpenter and the other Republicans just elected to Congress had met with party leaders in Des Moines and, "after some talk," had resolved to ignore the November date. Only Hiram Price of the Second District refused to go along with his colleagues, insisting that he would not risk a contest for his seat but would enter the November election seriously.[58]

On November 5, the "snide" election, as the Republicans called it, was held in scattered precincts throughout the state. It was consistently boycotted by the Republicans with the exception of Price. In the Ninth District a few Greenbackers and Democrats had united on John J. Wilson of Algona as a forlorn hope, according to Clarkson. Certain Republicans in the district were worried, and they wired and wrote Carpenter, urging him to enter the contest. But Carpenter stood firm, refusing to recognize the election, and as a result Wilson polled 228 votes in a few scattered areas, while 96 Republicans cast ballots for Carpenter. Similar returns came in from the other districts; the candidates contesting the October winner received a few hundred votes each, thus "defeating" the Republican ticket. Only Hiram Price polled more votes than the opposition.[59]

Democratic rejoicing was short-lived, however. Samuel J. Randall, Democratic Speaker of the House, told "an Iowa Gentleman" that "the Democratic majority in Congress could not afford to, and would not, take advantage of a legal quibble to exclude the October delegates" elected in Iowa.[60] Thus ended the fiasco of the November election, although repercussions would continue for some time, and John J. Wilson would follow Carpenter to Washington and contest his seat in Congress.

Unfortunately for Carpenter, he would enter a Congress where for the first time in twenty years both houses were controlled by Democrats. In the normal course of events, Carpenter would not have taken his seat until December 1879, but President Hayes called a special session of the Forty-sixth Congress for March 18, 1879, so Carpenter had only a few months to wait after election before returning to Washington.

He spent the intervening time in reading, answering a mountain of correspondence, and in home cares. The Fort Dodge home that the Carpenters shared with Emmett and his family was a busy place, and the "Governor"—as he was always called now—was often needed to "mind the baby," Emmett's son, Clay. On January 13, 1879, more than the usual bustle of activity filled the modest home when Carpenter's niece, Fanny Burkholder, was married to Byron Allen of Ottumwa.

Carpenter was a tireless but rather uncritical reader, enjoying practically everything he read. Each day he went through the newspapers thoroughly, and hardly a day passed that he did not spend some time with serious books and magazines. On Sundays he attended church twice and taught his Sunday school class, just as he had done for years. From this quiet and studious life he was about to be plunged into what would seem to him a madhouse of activity—the United States Congress.

FOURTEEN

Congressman Carpenter

———•◦•◦•———

> . . . I dont believe I will ever be able to do anything on the floor. It dont seem as though I could any more go in and fight for recognition among that howling hooting mob than I could fly to the moon. I dont believe that anybody who does not have a great voice and aggressive manners has any business in a modern Congress.[1]

Such were Carpenter's reactions as he watched the closing days of the Forty-fifth Congress. He had arrived in Washington on February 21, 1879, a month before the special session of the Forty-sixth Congress was due to open, and had obtained a card that admitted him to the floor of the House. There he observed the day-to-day business of Congress going forward, or standing still, while legislators wrangled, and he was frightened.

Carpenter would never make his mark as a Congressman. As he realized, he did not have the "great voice and aggressive manners" necessary to win attention. Nor did he have the drive for power that makes a leader. He would be one of the great majority of Congressmen who serve for a term or two; men who run errands for their constituents, parcel out the patronage jobs in their districts, vote as the party leaders dictate, and retire to private life without having made a ripple on the current of their times.

The thirty-eight states of the Union in 1879 had sent 293 Representatives and seventy-six Senators to Washington. In the House there were 148 Democrats, 130 Republicans, and fifteen Greenbackers; in the Senate, thirty-three Republicans, forty-one Democrats, and two Independents. Almost all the great names of the past decades were gone from the House, their places taken by lesser-known men who had yet to make their reputations. James A. Garfield of Ohio, minority leader of the House, was just two years away from the presidency, but no one suspected that in 1879. An Ohio colleague just starting his second term would also move to the White House—William McKinley. Two future Vice Presidents were there: Democrat Adlai E. Stevenson of Illinois (listed among the Greenbackers in 1879) and Republican Levi P. Morton of New York. Three members of the Forty-sixth House would become Speakers: J. Warren Keifer of Ohio; Joseph G. Cannon of Illinois; and Thomas B. Reed of Maine.[2] Of the 122 "freshmen" in Congress in 1879, the one with the brightest future was probably Nelson W. Aldrich of Rhode Island, who after one term in the House would move on to the Senate and national prominence.[3]

On the Democratic side of the House in 1879 were many ex-Confederates, men whose fame was in the past rather than the future. Chief among them was the venerable Alexander H. Stephens, Vice President of the Confederacy. From the military came Joseph E. Johnston, the general who had surrendered to Sherman in the waning days of the war. In fact, of the sixty-nine Democrats from the eleven Confederate states, fifty-nine had fought against the Union, while several had served in the Confederate Cabinet or in its Congress. The war was indeed over, although many Radicals—men like James S. Clarkson of Iowa—still found this hard to accept.

The men of the Senate overshadowed the men of the House, partly by length of service and largely by the power they had built up over the years. Chief among them was James G. Blaine, who inspired much idolatry and almost as much hate. Carpenter had distrusted Blaine in 1876; possibly he still did, but his position as a member of the Iowa delegation now forced him to join that segment of his party known as "Half-Breeds" (followers of Blaine), who struggled for power with the other faction, the "Stalwarts" of Roscoe Conkling.[4]

The notorious Roscoe Conkling, boss of a powerful political machine in New York, alternated between political battles with Blaine and with President Rutherford B. Hayes, and these battles dominated Carpenter's first term in Congress. The President was now almost as unpopular with his own party as he was with the Democrats. One of his first acts as President had been to remove the federal troops from Louisiana and South Carolina, the last two Southern states under Republican-dominated "carpetbag" governments. This "Southern Policy," part of the bargain by which Hayes had won the disputed election, had aroused the anger of the Old Guard Radicals, who seem not to have known the terms of the famous Compromise of 1877.[5] Within six weeks after inauguration day in 1877, the Republican papers had begun the attack. In Iowa, Clarkson had at first reported the President's actions more in sorrow than in anger, but by April 27 he had thrown aside all pretense, and his mildest term for Hayes's policy was "Conciliation by Betrayal."[6] Carpenter's echo of Clarkson's attack had been milder but definite: "It is a crime."[7] Conkling turned on Hayes when the President interfered in the appointments to the New York Custom House, Conkling's private property, or so he thought. Hayes had won— Conkling's man Chester A. Arthur had been removed from his lucrative and politically powerful job as Collector of the Port of New York—and Conkling never forgave the President.[8] When Carpenter first met Conkling on March 20, 1879, in Allison's office, the New York Senator proceeded to give the new Congressman from Iowa "his view of the administration." [9] Although Carpenter did not explain what this "view" was, it is not hard to imagine the tone of it.

When Conkling was not warring with Hayes he was searching out ways to block the ambitions of his other enemy, Blaine. The battles of these two men colored the political scene for a decade or more. In 1876, Conkling had won by defeating Blaine's bid for the presidential nomination; in 1880, Conkling would lose in his effort to nominate Grant for an unprecedented third term, but Blaine would also lose in that a deadlocked convention turned from him to James A. Garfield; in 1884, at long last Blaine would win the nomination only to lose the election. And Conkling, even then, had the last word. When Blaine, driven by fear of losing New York State, and thereby the election, sent his friends to Conkling, then in retirement, to ask for help, Conkling's reply carried the last insult: "Gentlemen, you have been misinformed. I have given up criminal law." [10]

There were other prominent Senators during Carpenter's four years in Washington, not so pompous as Blaine nor so flamboyant as Conkling, but equally powerful in their own right. Some were the great ones of the past: Hannibal Hamlin of Maine, Lincoln's first Vice President; old Zachariah Chandler of Michigan, one of the founding fathers of Republicanism; Justin S. Morrill of Vermont, father of the agricultural college land-grant act of 1862; and the "Webster of the West," Matthew H. Carpenter of Wisconsin, now near death but still fighting. (One wonders if Cyrus Carpenter of Iowa and Matthew Carpenter of Wisconsin knew that they shared a common ancestor in the first William Carpenter who had come to America in 1640.[11]) Among the younger men, soon to be the rulers of the Senate, there were Iowa's William B. Allison, Orville H. Platt of Connecticut, George F. Hoar of Massachusetts, George F. Edmunds of Vermont, and many others. On the Democratic side were such familiar Confederate names as General John B. Gordon, who had led the last charge at Appomattox; Lucius Q. C. Lamar of Mississippi, Confederate colonel and diplomat; and General Wade Hampton of South Carolina, who had become Governor of his state after Hayes withdrew the troops in 1877.[12]

Such were the men surrounding Carpenter in the Forty-sixth Congress. Small wonder that he and many like him were obscured. But in spite of the ability of these party leaders, the issues they dealt with were minor compared with the great problems of the past. The war had reunited the nation, the Southern states were back in the Union, and Radical Reconstruction was a thing of the past, although the scars it had left would be long in healing. People's interest lay less and less in Washington and the doings of their Congressmen, and more and more in the great expansion taking place all over the nation. America's Industrial Revolution was at high tide in the 1870s.

The United States had grown rapidly in population and wealth since the Civil War; industry and manufacturing had expanded; great fortunes had been made. Watching and taking part in this development, the American people now had little time and less concern for the issues of government. Rumblings of labor discontent, bursting into the violent railroad strike of 1877, aroused only temporary interest; most people had applauded Hayes's use of the troops to put down this unprecedented revolt of the working class. Businessmen—some would later call them "robber barons"—ran the country. They wanted no interference from government, and they saw to it that Senators and Representatives in Washington let them alone. And the Congressmen were amenable, some by purchase, many by conviction. The individualistic doctrine of laissez faire was accepted by the politician and the businessman without question. The legislator's job was to pass the necessary legislation to keep the government going, to provide patronage jobs, and—every four years—to do battle for his party at the polls.

In spite of election-year oratory, there was little difference between the two parties during the closing decades of the nineteenth century. The issues of state rights and the tariff were, for the time being, almost forgotten, and the minority voices of liberals and reformers were not heard above the clamor for place and patronage. The new social and economic ideas stirring in the world did not reach into the United States Congress. Nowhere in his writings or speeches does Carpenter, a typical minor politician of this era, reveal any awareness of the significance, or the problems, of the changing economy of the day.

The special session of Congress, called for March 18, 1879, had not been summoned to deal with any great national issue but merely to provide money to run the army. The Democrats, having won a concession from Hayes by the removal of the troops in the South, now demanded another— the repeal of the federal election laws which allowed the President to use troops at the polls to protect the rights of voters. For the past two Congresses, Democrats had tried to repeal these laws by attaching to the army appropriation bills "riders" that would eliminate this vestige of Reconstruction. Republican Senates had blocked the bills so far, and the Forty-fifth Congress had adjourned without providing any money for the army.[13] Thus Hayes had been forced to call the extra session, but since it was controlled by Democrats in both houses, a stalemate seemed inevitable. The Democrats had the votes to pass the law, with the rider, but they did not have the necessary two-thirds majority to over-ride a presidential veto.

The result could be foreseen. No member of either party was likely to vote with the other side on issues. The age has been called one of individualism, and so it was in the world of business. But in the halls of Congress, and in the statehouses throughout the country, it was an age of conformity. Old Zach Chandler had said to Carpenter that he "wouldn't give a d—n for a man that you have to inquire how he is going to vote." John F. Duncombe, Fort Dodge's leading Democrat, expressed his opinion of this tendency: "In my judgment, at the present time, the greatest curse of this country . . . is, the almost absolute necessity that any man is under in politics, who is ambitious or desires to maintain his position to cooperate with *his party*." [14] Caucuses decided the position the party would take on issues, and the vote of each member was there determined. Carpenter, like so many other lesser members of the House, never deviated from the decision of the party leaders.

When the army appropriation bill, with the Democratic rider attached, came up in the Forty-sixth Congress, the orators put forth their best efforts, not with any idea of changing anyone's vote, but just to be heard. On April 24, Carpenter stood for almost three hours at the back of the Senate Chamber, with a crowd of other Representatives (even Speaker Samuel J. Randall "deserted his post") to listen to Roscoe Conkling in one of his more dramatic efforts. Since no seats were available, Representative Omar D. Conger of Michigan "sat upon the floor at Conkling's feet," and even members of the Cabinet crowded in to hear the "gentleman from New York." [15]

Conkling's speech, well advertised in advance, brought crowds not only to the floor of the Senate, but to the galleries as well, which were packed with the well-known society people. The "queen of the day's tournament," according to one reporter, was Mrs. Kate Chase Sprague, Salmon P. Chase's daughter, whose name had been romantically and scandalously linked with that of Conkling.[16] Attired in "dark purple silk, over which sparkled jet ornaments," Mrs. Sprague must have presented a colorful sight. Her hat, of black lace with a scarlet rose, "perched jauntily upon her auburn hair." Her gloves were lavender, and she held a black fan and a bunch of scarlet and yellow roses. Conkling, dressed with "studied simplicity" in a black business suit instead of his usual frock coat, began his speech promptly at one o'clock.[17] A reporter for the New York *Sun* gave a word picture of the handsome Senator in action:

> Mr. Conkling had upon his desk a handsome portfolio, within the covers of which were sheets of foolscap paper, with the notes of his discourse carefully written thereon. As fast as he exhausted one page of notes he crumpled it up in his hands, tore it in shreds, and cast the pieces upon the floor. Before he had half finished his speech the carpet under his feet was almost concealed from view by bits of paper. . . .
>
> He spoke slowly, deliberately, and with emphasis. Every syllable of every word uttered could be distinctly heard in every part of the chamber.

He moved about much while talking, turning from the President pro tem.
of the Senate toward his colleagues; now facing the Democrats, then raising
his face toward the galleries, stepping back and forth from his desk to
the centre of the main aisle. . . . He uttered the last word of his speech
as clearly and calmly as he spoke the first word.[18]

The speech, a combination of an attack on the Democrats and an un-
mistakable bid for Grant as the candidate for 1880, was a carefully staged
drama, and Republican listeners were impressed. It was a "grand effort,"
wrote Carpenter, and "did not leave an inch of solid ground for Democracy
to stand on."[19] Solid ground or no, on the following day the Democrats
passed the army appropriation bill that Conkling had been attacking.

Other Republicans agreed with Carpenter. Some time later Jonathan P.
Dolliver wrote to him, asking for a copy of "Mr. Conklings great speech
in the Senate," and expressing his opinion of the "congress of deadbeats
and democrats" then in session.[20] This judgment of the Congress was generally accepted by Republicans. Just before adjournment on July 1, 1879, the
editor of the Cedar Rapids *Times* wrote its epitaph:

> Congress is dragging its weary length along without effecting anything,
> except that of making for this congress a history which for worthlessness,
> disgusting demagogism and Democratic damphoolishism has never been
> equaled in the history of any country. Roll-calling, wrangling, bourbon
> bull-dozing and boys' play generally has been the character of the sessions
> during the past week, some of them continuing all night. How long, O
> Lord, how long?[21]

Carpenter took no part in the "damphoolishism" of his first session of
Congress. As a freshman Congressman he did not enter into the debates,
although many of his first-term colleagues did. He sat through the sessions
of the House, ran errands to the various Departments for his constituents,
sent government documents to those who wanted them, and voted on
amendments and bills as the party caucus had dictated. Congressmen did
not have offices in the 1870s, unless they were committee chairmen, and as
a result they either took care of their correspondence at their hotels or
boarding houses or at their desks on the floor, while debate and argument
whirled around them. "I begin to see how much I need a clerk," Carpenter
decided on April 17. "There is no let up in the letter writing and nothing
for me to do but write and run to the Depts."[22]

The Army Bill, with the Democratic "rider" attached, passed the House
on April 5, the Senate on April 25, and was vetoed by President Hayes on
April 29. On May 1, the House voted again on the measure, but since the
Democrats could not command two-thirds of the vote, the President's veto
was sustained.[23] In June, with the rider somewhat modified, the bill again
passed the House. This time the Iowa members, and a majority of the Re-

publicans, voted for the bill, although Carpenter confessed to himself that it was "Crow," but that he thought it best and right "under the circumstances." The watered-down version also passed the Senate, but here the Republicans, including Allison and Kirkwood, would not accept the "Crow" that the Iowans in the House had swallowed. Hayes signed the bill, and the army was at last provided for.[24]

Meanwhile, the Democrats had pushed through a separate bill to prohibit military interference at elections, which Hayes promptly vetoed. His message, read to the House on May 12, 1879, was "frequently interrupted by applause on the republican side of the House," a new and pleasant experience for the President. The Democrats were "fearfully enraged," said Carpenter, adding that he had to admit that the message was the best he had ever read "as coming from the present administration." [25]

And so it continued throughout the first session of the Forty-sixth Congress. The Democratic majorities in the House and Senate were able to pass legislation but not able to over-ride the vetoes. Thus little was accomplished, except that Hayes won back some of the Republican support he had lost in his first two years in office. "I am now experiencing one of the *'ups'* of political life," Hayes commented on July 3, adding realistically, "Of course, it will not last." [26]

Almost unnoticed by many, but well understood by his enemies, Hayes had begun to restore the prestige of the American presidency. Since the death of Lincoln, the country had been ruled by a congressional oligarchy that over-rode the presidential prerogatives at will. Andrew Johnson had done his best but had been impeached, and only a stubborn eight among the Republicans had blocked his conviction. Grant, the choice of the Radical oligarchy, had kept his place and taken his orders from them. But with Hayes things began to change. The old and bitter Radicals were almost all gone now, and a new generation, "indifferent to war hatreds," had arisen. Even Blaine and Conkling, who could sometimes almost forget their mutual hatred in fighting Hayes, could not take the place of Thaddeus Stevens. Hayes defied both Republican and Democratic attempts at "coercion of the Executive," and in so doing, returned the presidency to its proper place in the separation of powers laid down by the Constitution.[27]

When Congress adjourned on July 1, 1879, Hayes could say, complacently, "I have . . . I think vindicated the power of the National Government over congressional elections and the separate authority of the Executive Department of the Government." [28] Evidently, even Hayes did not see the full importance of what he had done. The election laws, which he had "vindicated" with his veto, were doomed to failure and were repealed in 1890. On the other hand, his defiance of Conkling and those who had supported him in the patronage fight had begun the re-establishment of presidential power and the restoration of the balance between the three branches of the government.

Carpenter's active role in the Forty-sixth Congress consisted of introducing minor pension bills and petitions on various subjects. His only committee appointment was on the Committee on War Claims. "Dont like it," was his brief comment. The other members of the Iowa delegation fared little better, since the Republican minority had few choice places for new Congressmen.[29] Had it not been for the contest for his seat by John J. Wilson, Carpenter's presence in the Congress could have passed unnoticed.

On March 28, 1879, Democrat William M. Springer of Illinois, chairman of the Committee on Elections, rose "to a question of privilege," presented a memorial from Wilson contesting Carpenter's right to represent the Ninth Iowa District, and asked that it be referred to his Committee. A wrangle immediately ensued as to whether Wilson's memorial was actually a question of privilege. With nothing better to do, Congressmen delighted in these parliamentary discussions which solved nothing but gave the more vocal members of the House a chance to air their views. Congressman Conger considered the whole thing a "farce," and he was echoed by Hiram Price. Springer promptly reminded Price that he himself had not considered the November election a farce, since he had taken part in it, and Price tried to explain away this embarrassing point with many words but little light. The argument then descended to the problem of whether the memorial should be referred to the Committee on Elections by the House, or whether it should merely be placed in the petition box and in that way eventually reach the Committee. After a great deal of senseless argument, the memorial was finally referred to the Committee by a vote of 108 to 99.[30]

Republican papers, for the lack of other news, at once took up the case and tried it in their columns. " 'Snide' Wilson seems determined to steal a seat in Congress from Iowa," the Des Moines *Register* reported, "and the Democratic Congress seems very willing to aid him to do so. . . . The Confederates are desperate, and will hesitate at nothing." A few days later Clarkson continued his attack on the "Confederate House," and other papers argued the issue. The Chicago *Tribune* thought it "would not be surprising" if the Democrats stole Carpenter's seat, since they needed to bolster their small majority in the House. The New York *Tribune* considered the contesting of the seat an "outrage." Actually, the Democrats may have contemplated such action, but the realities of the situation restrained them. By invalidating Carpenter's election, they would immediately unseat the whole Iowa delegation, including the two Greenbackers who were voting with them on legislation. As early as April 1, 1879, the Democratic *Dubuque Herald* admitted that the November election had been "irregular and wanting in all the legal forms of an election. . . ."[31]

The House Committee on Elections, consisting of eight Democrats, five Republicans, and Greenbacker James B. Weaver of Iowa, held several hearings on the case, and Carpenter testified a number of times.[32] No report came from the Committee during the session, however, probably to the disappointment of the Republicans, who were spoiling for a fight on the issue. In fact, the Committee made no report until January 31, 1881, when Carpenter had already been re-elected for another term. Wilson's claim was rejected. "So that settles the question of the Oct. election," Carpenter could write then, over two years after the event.[33]

After adjournment, Carpenter returned to Iowa for the gubernatorial campaign. Jonathan P. Dolliver, the young lawyer of Fort Dodge, joined the "Governor" on some of his stumping tours, and Carpenter, hearing Dolliver speak for the first time, found him to be a "marvel as a talker," "a natural born orator." [34] Through Carpenter's influence, Dolliver soon became known to the party leaders in Iowa.

The Republican state ticket won in 1879 by a 25,000-vote majority, and John H. Gear returned to the governorship for another term. "Now comes the fight with the Bourbon Democracy in 1880," Carpenter wrote, seemingly with relish.[35]

Carpenter attended the meetings of the second session of the Forty-sixth Congress faithfully, becoming more and more disgusted with the waste of time, the long arguments, the bitter fights, and the general "foolishness of grown men when the spirit is on." [36] He introduced several bills on pension requests; he brought in petitions and memorials from his constituents and the Iowa General Assembly on a number of subjects; and he voted dutifully with the Republican minority. During his spare time, he worked on a speech he hoped to deliver on finance, but William P. Frye of Maine, one of the Republicans on the Ways and Means Committee, finally told him that there would be no opportunity for him to give it. Therefore, to Carpenter's disappointment, he was forced to publish the speech in the *Congressional Record* without having delivered it on the floor. Not one to join in the running debate on issues, and unable to get the time to make a set speech, Carpenter decided that he would not again spend so much time in preparing his remarks. His only words on the floor during the second session were his eulogy of Rush Clark, the Iowa Congressman who had died during the first session. Even this small effort "embarrassed" him.[37] Carpenter, perfectly at home on the stump in Iowa, was tongue-tied in the halls of Congress.

Congressmen were more interested in politics than in legislation in 1880, and the House had considerable trouble maintaining a quorum. After the Republican National Convention opened in Chicago on June 2, so many of the House members were "in the lobby receiving dispatches from Chicago" that no work of any kind could be accomplished.[38] It was the old issue of Blaine against the field, and Iowa, as usual, was firmly behind Blaine. A "National Blaine Club" had been organized in Washington, D. C. as early as February, with Hiram Price of Iowa as president.[39]

Fortunately for himself, Hayes had long ago announced that he would not run for a second term, thus avoiding the public embarrassment of being rejected by his own party. At the convention Conkling fought to nominate Grant, who was not averse to the honor, but the convention deadlocked, with Grant, Blaine, and Secretary of the Treasury John Sherman the top runners. At last, on the thirty-sixth ballot the delegates turned to a dark horse, James A. Garfield, who had been managing Sherman's campaign. Iowa had resolutely clung to Blaine for thirty-five ballots but on the thirty-sixth joined the Garfield parade when it became obvious that neither Blaine nor Grant, Iowa's second choice, could win.[40] Possibly as a sop to Conkling, second place on the ticket went to the notorious Chester A. Arthur. "I think [Garfield's] nomination a good one the best that could be made," Carpenter wrote, adding that he hoped the nomination of Arthur would "suit N. Y." [41]

After adjournment of Congress on June 16, Carpenter set out for home and his own campaign for renomination. Carpenter's friends had assured him that he had no opposition, and on July 8, at Sioux City, he was renominated at the district convention by acclamation.[42] The only Republican who did not like Carpenter's renomination was Robert Buchanan, editor of the Cherokee *Times,* whom Clarkson considered the "sweepstakes donkey in Iowa journalism." Buchanan had opposed Carpenter in 1878; in 1879, he had suggested that bygones be bygones and that a certain appointment would be satisfactory. "Gov Carpenter of course did not pay the fellow his price," said Clarkson.[43] Therefore, Buchanan nursed a grudge.

As in 1878, Carpenter's opposition was split between a Democratic and a Greenback candidate, but this was true in all the congressional districts except for the Sixth and Seventh, where fusion candidates had won in 1878. Moses A. McCoid, Thomas Updegraff, Nathaniel C. Deering, William G. Thompson (Rush Clark's successor), and Carpenter won renomination in their districts without trouble. In the Second, Sewall S. Farwell of Monticello was nominated for Hiram Price's seat, after Price had declined to run again. Marsena E. Cutts, Attorney General during Carpenter's governorship, was chosen in the Sixth District to oppose John C. Cook, the Democratic-Greenbacker who ran in place of Weaver, now a presidential candidate on the Greenback ticket. In the Seventh District, Greenbacker Edward H. Gillette—whom Clarkson delighted to call "Our Congressional Idiot"—was faced with Republican John A. Kasson, now returned from four years in the diplomatic service. Kasson's nomination had come with the blessings of his old enemy, Clarkson, who now forgot past hatreds and supported Kasson to the hilt. Only in the Eighth District did the incumbent seeking renomination lose out. Here William F. Sapp lost an almost un-precedented 346-vote convention fight to William Peters Hepburn of Clarinda. "Hepburn is a good fellow," Carpenter thought, "but I doubt whether he will make as good a Rep as Sapp." [44] Here Carpenter was not much of a prophet. Hepburn would serve twenty-two years in the House and become one of its leading members. [45]

Carpenter made his usual active canvass. Since it was a presidential year, the Ninth District was treated to many outside speakers, including Senator Kirkwood. Jonathan P. Dolliver, now rapidly gaining fame as an orator, stumped the district for the ticket and for Carpenter. During the campaign the *Register,* in true bloody-shirt fashion, fought the war over again in each issue. Although both Garfield and his Democratic opponent, Winfield Scott Hancock, had been generals during the war, Clarkson concluded that Garfield's claim was better, since he had been a volunteer while Hancock had belonged to the regular army and had to fight anyhow. Clarkson also attacked Hancock for everything from drinking and kindness to rebels, to the question of his father's paternity. [46] This was campaign journalism at its worst, and Clarkson was a master of invective.

The Iowa Republicans worked hard and were rewarded with a handsome victory, making a clean sweep of the nine congressional races, with ma-jorities ranging from a gratifying 11,000 for Carpenter (compared to his 2,500 margin in 1878) to a slim 97 for Cutts in the Sixth District. [47] In fact, Cutts's seat was contested by Greenbacker John C. Cook, but a dilatory Republican House did not get around to deciding the issue—in Cook's favor—until the closing day of the Forty-seventh Congress. [48]

Nationally, the Republican party also fared well. Garfield won by an electoral vote of 214 to 155, although his margin in the popular vote of over 9,000,000 was a slim 7,000. Iowa's James B. Weaver, the Greenback presidential candidate, managed to win 307,000 votes in the nation at large, but no electoral ballots, while his home state gave him only 32,000 votes out of a total of 322,000. In the congressional races, the Republicans won back control of the House by a satisfactory margin, while the Senate was evenly divided, requiring the vote of the Vice President to give the organiza-tion to the Republicans. [49] For the first time since 1875, the Republicans held the executive and both houses of Congress.

The opening of the "lame-duck" third session of the Forty-sixth Congress, like other openings, took on the form of a happy reunion of school boys after the summer vacation. Flowers appeared on the desks of House mem-bers, probably sent by a "fair decoy in the employ of the lobby," or by their "fair clients in the government offices." The galleries were also filled with the "fair," and in the Senate the members of the diplomatic corps, "with faultless hair and gloves," looked down on the American legislators gathering for another session. What the reporter saw in the House brought back memories of the war. There was the Vice President of the Confederacy, a member of Jefferson Davis's Cabinet, and General Joseph E. Johnston—men who "yesterday . . . could have been in Washington only as conquerors or prisoners." That that "yesterday" was fifteen years in the past seemed more a matter of regret than of history to this "Special Correspondent" of the Des Moines *Register*—could it have been Ret Clarkson? [50] How many other Republicans looked back nostalgically on the days when they ruled the country without interference from Democrats and ex-Confederates?

During this final session, the interest of Carpenter and the Iowa delegation centered on H.R. 1067, a bill to "quiet title of settlers on the Des Moines River Lands," originally introduced in the second session by William F. Sapp. Hearing that the bill would come up on Monday, January 17, 1881, Carpenter prepared to speak on it, going so far as to stay home from church to work on his remarks. When George L. Converse of Ohio, Democratic chairman of the Committee on Public Lands, reported the bill with a recommendation that it pass, Republican John Van Voorhis of New York immediately objected, calling it "one of the most villainous bills ever presented to this House." Opponents of the measure used every possible parliamentary delaying tactic, but finally the bill was debated, Carpenter "made some remarks with fair success," and Van Voorhis retaliated with a long history of the whole River Land controversy. He spoke for the New York investors who owned much of the land under dispute, but his efforts failed. The bill passed by a *viva voce* vote, and another bit of legislation was added to the long story of the Des Moines River lands. [51]

The Forty-sixth Congress adjourned on March 3, 1881—or rather, at 3 A.M. on March 4, after a long session delayed, said Carpenter, by "two or three Dem's in Whisky." [52] Instead of returning at once to Fort Dodge, Carpenter remained in Washington for a few weeks, sometimes observing the special session of the Senate, called to confirm Garfield's Cabinet and appointments, and sometimes making the rounds of the Departments in the interest of Ninth District Iowans.

Garfield had chosen Senator Kirkwood for his Cabinet, after Allison had rejected the President's offer of the Treasury. [53] This had left one Iowa Senate seat vacant. Since the legislature would not meet until January of 1882, Governor Gear had appointed James W. McDill to fill in for Kirkwood, so that the even split between Republicans and Democrats would not be upset. To the Carpenters, who crowded into the Senate gallery to watch the fight over organization, the speeches were "exciting and interesting." [54] After the Republicans had won the committees, by the vote of the Vice President, the Senate proceeded to other business.

Conkling had lost one enemy—Hayes—and gained a new one—Garfield.

Blaine, now Secretary of State, had the President's ear, while Conkling did not. And in this special session of the Senate, Garfield succeeded in destroying Conkling by the simple expedient of sending to the Senate for confirmation the name of William Robertson for Collector of the Port of New York. A long-standing Conkling-Robertson feud made this nomination a direct slap at Conkling and a declaration of war between the President and the Senator. Even Carpenter was shocked. "The discrimination made against Conkling by Garfield is utterly mean on his part and ridiculous as a civil service reform experiment." [55] Senators begged Garfield to reconsider, but the President held firm, even going so far as to withdraw the names of certain Conkling-approved appointees in New York. The result was dramatic, in true Conkling fashion. On May 16, the Vice President read to the Senate a letter from Conkling; he had notified the Governor of his state of his "resignation as Senator of the United States from the State of New York. . . ." [56] So ended the career of Roscoe Conkling, and some of the drama went out of the United States Congress.[57]

Carpenter spent the months between March and December at home, busy with all the multitude of details of a Congressman's life: writing letters, receiving calls from office seekers, sending out government documents and seeds to his constituents, speaking at fairs and celebrations of one kind and another. In addition, he did the "chores" around the house, helped Mrs. Carpenter "whip" the carpets at house-cleaning time, made daily trips "down street" for the mail, newspapers, and the latest political gossip, and watched the operations on his farm on the outskirts of Fort Dodge. During the late summer months, he walked out to his farm almost daily, unless some more prosperous neighbor with a carriage happened to be going his way, and helped with the harvesting of the crops. This year he also bought a number of blooded cattle for his farm, possibly with an eye toward the day when he would retire from public life.[58]

On July 2, President Garfield was shot by Charles J. Guiteau, a disappointed office seeker. After a long summer of suffering, the President died on September 18, 1881, and Chester A. Arthur became President of the United States. Carpenter has left no comment on Arthur; perhaps this in itself indicates the general Half-Breed distrust of the man who had been Conkling's friend. But Arthur's elevation to the presidency came too late for Conkling. Arthur now disavowed any connection with the Stalwarts, rejected Conkling, and proceeded to stand on his own feet. Blaine was retained in Arthur's Cabinet, while his old enemy, Conkling, sulked in retirement and defeat in New York.[59]

As a member of the majority party in the Forty-seventh Congress, Carpenter received much better committee appointments, being assigned to the committees on agriculture, improvement of the Mississippi River, and education and labor. His colleague, John A. Kasson, did even better. Returning to the House after an interval of four years, Kasson was appointed to the powerful Ways and Means and the Foreign Affairs committees. These positions were only consolation prizes for Kasson, however. The Iowa delegation had backed him strongly for election to the speakership, but after fifteen ballots in the Republican caucus, the post went to Joseph Warren Keifer of Ohio. "This was brought about by the fellows calling themselves *Stalwarts* & skillful playing upon the sectional issue," wrote Carpenter. "I was disappointed in the result but hope for the best." [60]

Having overcome his first-term reticence, Carpenter now entered more vocally into the work of the House, speaking on several bills. In February 1882, he joined in the debate on an apportionment bill and found that "in voice and matter" he could "command the attention of the House." During the long arguments on the Chinese exclusion bills, sponsored by Californians, Carpenter had his say, although briefly, doing "reasonably well," he thought.[61] His longest speech was in favor of a bill to raise the Department of Agriculture to Cabinet status. The Department, established in 1862, had been growing in importance and usefulness, and petitions favoring an expansion of its work had been numerous. Several measures, introduced into the Forty-seventh Congress and referred to the Agriculture Committee, had been combined into H.R. 4429. As such, after much debate and oratory, the bill passed the House on May 10, 1882, with only a handful of dissenting votes. The Senate debated it several times, but took no action. Not until seven years later would Congress finally add the Agriculture Department to the President's Cabinet. The House was "thin" during Carpenter's remarks on the bill on May 8, 1882, but his conclusion was greeted with favorable remarks, so he again decided that he had done "reasonably well." [62]

For several years Senator Allison and other Iowans had been trying to get the state of Iowa divided into two judicial districts. While in Fort Dodge, Carpenter had studied on this type of legislation, prepared a bill, consulted with Allison about it, and on December 13 introduced it in the House. The Judiciary Committee reported the bill out in revised form, and after considerable debate, in which Carpenter joined, the measure passed the House. The Senate added amendments, a conference committee ironed out the differences, and at last both houses approved the bill. This action had been agitated in Iowa since 1870; at last the Iowa delegation had succeeded.[63] Carpenter was especially pleased with the measure, since two cities in his District—Fort Dodge and Sioux City—were given terms of the court. "It gratifies me that I was able to do a thing for Fort Dodge which Burlington, Davenport, Ottumwa, and Cedar Rapids have kept lobbies here working to secure to their own cities," he wrote to Dolliver.[64]

Carpenter took little vocal part in the other issues that came before the House, but he continued in his steady way to attend sessions, vote on bills, answer letters, send out "Doc's" to those who wanted them, and look after the interests of his constituents. When the first session adjourned on August 8, 1882, he returned to Fort Dodge to look after his political fences, which were in very bad repair. He had written to his brother Judd in June:

> The life of a member of Congress, who tries to do his duty, is a dogs life. There is a canvass going on in my district in respect to the coming nomination. I shall be a candidate, but I have some considerable opposition and may not succeed. If I dont, I am going home, and going to work to try to make some money.[65]

Owing to the long session of Congress, Carpenter did not return to Fort Dodge until August 11, 1882, where he found at least half of his District organized against him.[66]

-FIFTEEN-

Defeats and Victories

————•◦•◦•————

THE IOWA GENERAL ASSEMBLY had reapportioned the state in 1882, increasing the congressional districts from nine to eleven. Carpenter's old Ninth had included twenty-six counties in northwestern Iowa; after reapportionment, six of these counties (Kossuth, Humboldt, Webster, Hamilton, Boone, and Story) were combined with seven from the old Fourth (Winnebago, Worth, Hancock, Cerro Gordo, Wright, Franklin, and Hardin) to make a new Tenth.[1] This was the district from which Carpenter now sought nomination to Congress for a third term.

The nominating convention was not called until August 30, 1882, but during the summer months rumors had reached Carpenter in Washington that all was not well. From Northwood, in Worth County, as early as June 30, Carpenter received word that, although the Worth delegates would be uninstructed at the convention, some people there supported John D. Glass of Cerro Gordo County, "he being so close home."[2] Other candidates also appeared throughout the district, while in Fort Dodge, Dolliver and Carpenter's friends worked hard for the "Governor." It looked to him, wrote Carpenter, "as though the fight you boys have been carrying on for me, was a fight with the beasts of Epheus."[3]

Who were these "beasts" contesting for Carpenter's job? By the time Carpenter reached Fort Dodge, after the adjournment of Congress, the claimants had sifted down to Major Adoniram J. Holmes of Boone County, Colonel John Scott of Story, Captain Rufus S. Benson and Colonel Arthur T. Reeve of Franklin, David Secor of Winnebago, John D. Glass of Cerro Gordo, and Corydon M. Nagle of Wright.[4] The other counties in the Tenth (Kossuth, Humboldt, Webster, Hamilton, Hancock, Worth, and Hardin) had elected delegations wholly or in part for Carpenter. On the eve of the convention, which would have 139 delegates, making seventy votes necessary for the nomination, Carpenter could be sure of only between fifty-five and sixty.[5] This presented no unsurmountable problem, however. Favorite-son candidates were common in nominating conventions, and after receiving a complimentary vote on the first ballot, they usually withdrew in favor of their county's second choice. In 1880, the second choice of almost all the counties with favorite sons was Carpenter. But this was to be no ordinary convention. Things were going to work out differently.

Since reaching Fort Dodge on August 11, Carpenter had been scurrying around his new district, talking to the party leaders in the counties and sounding out the situation. In Fort Dodge, aside from Dolliver, there was another young man interested in Carpenter's future. This was George E. Roberts, only twenty-five years old at the time but already editor of the Fort Dodge *Messenger*. Roberts, who had just been elected state printer and was rising rapidly in Republican circles, took Carpenter in hand and shepherded him around the district.[6] They visited the leading men in the various counties, getting promises of support, ironing out difficulties, soothing ruffled feelings, hearing complaints, and promising appointments where possible. Carpenter made the most of the short time allowed him before the convention met on August 30 at Webster City. Arriving there two days early, he spent the time talking with those of his supporters who had already arrived. Something was wrong. "Does not look right," Carpenter wrote in his diary two nights before the convention opened.[7]

Knowing that they could not defeat Carpenter by the usual methods, the opposition met on the day before the convention and evolved what they thought was a foolproof plan. Each county with a favorite son sent a stated number of delegates to a caucus, with the understanding that these men could choose one of the several candidates to oppose Carpenter. They could command between seventy and eighty votes, and that was enough. Agreement was not easy to get, however. After voting most of the afternoon of August 29 without reaching a decision, the caucus adjourned until six o'clock on the morning of August 30. After some four hours and seventy-four ballots, the delegates at last agreed, to the satisfaction of very few, to cast their lot with Colonel John Scott of Story County. This decision was only reached, however, after the delegates had agreed to a provision, unfortunate for Scott, that left a door open for the other contenders. Should the Carpenter men, facing defeat, throw their strength to one of the other candidates, thus giving him enough votes so that his home county ballots could put him over, then that home county could break the agreement and support its own candidate.[8] It was on this proviso that the plans of the anti-Carpenter men foundered.

John Scott of Nevada in Story County was the same John Scott who had tried to get the gubernatorial nomination away from Carpenter in 1871. Perhaps this old defeat still rankled. Whatever the reason, aside from the understandable one of wanting to be a Congressman, Scott had put on a strong and bitter campaign against Carpenter and thereby had won the enmity of Carpenter's friends. They were determined that if Carpenter were to be defeated, it would not be by John Scott.[9]

Well aware of what was going on in the caucus of their opponents, the Carpenter men promptly laid plans to block the Scott nomination. What resulted was the "most brilliant political *coup-de-etat* [*sic*] that ever occurred in the annals of the republican party in this state," according to one editor, while the *Register's* "Special Correspondent" described it as "an anomaly in the history of nominating conventions." [10]

When the convention opened at one o'clock in the afternoon of August 30, Carpenter had fifty-five votes, while the caucus had eighty-four pledged to Scott. The outlook was a quick defeat for Governor Carpenter. When the balloting began, the votes were delivered to Scott on schedule, until Hamilton County was reached; there, four of the eleven votes of the county went to Scott, seven to Carpenter. This was expected. But when Hancock, a "Carpenter" county, was called and its seven votes were cast for Holmes, the Scott men pricked up their ears. As the voting continued, and all the rest of the Carpenter votes now went to Holmes, some few may have sensed what was happening, but the others were too busy cheering for Scott. At the end of the balloting, and before the result was officially announced, Scott had eighty-four votes, Holmes forty-eight, and Carpenter seven. While the Scott men shouted and stamped, the tellers slowly checked the totals.

Sure of victory, the Scott men had allowed a Carpenter supporter, W. J. Moir of Eldora, to be elected chairman of the convention. In addition, one of the assistant secretaries was C. H. Moore of Fort Dodge, who, at a very convenient moment, could not add his figures correctly. When the chairman rose to give the totals, this Fort Dodge secretary called him back to help find a mistake in the tallies. Moore's obviously faulty mathematics corrected, Moir again went to the front of the platform to read the results.

Then, and only then, did the Carpenter men make their move. Holmes lacked twenty-two votes to put him over. Even his home county's nineteen votes would not do this, and the agreement had been that if the Carpenter votes went to a man who could then win with the addition of his own county's vote, that county was released from the caucus agreement. Holmes needed three more votes than Boone County could give him; Carpenter held seven votes in Hamilton County.

As Chairman Moir approached the edge of the platform a second time, a delegate from Hamilton County rose: "Mr. Chairman, Hamilton county wishes to change her seven votes from Governor Carpenter to Major Holmes." The Scott men were stunned into silence. Major Holmes now had fifty-six votes, within fourteen of the nomination. Then came the move that brought victory from defeat: the Boone County delegates, freed from their pledge to the caucus, happily changed their nineteen votes from Scott to Holmes, cutting Scott's total to sixty-five and giving Holmes seventy-five votes and the nomination.[11]

Carpenter, unable to find enough votes to win himself, did have enough to defeat Scott, and in so doing he had actually won, since he had blocked the ambitions of his old enemy and had named the man he preferred, out of the list of candidates. His "friends," who had fought Scott during the campaign, would have suffered politically had Scott won; therefore, Carpenter had protected them by giving his blessing to their scheme.

A report of the convention, written years later, describes Carpenter as sweating blood the night before the convention met, as "humiliated . . . his countenance white as marble" after the victory for Holmes.[12] This dramatizes the story but hardly fits the personality of Carpenter. According to a contemporary account, Carpenter appeared before the convention, after his defeat, mounting the platform with "his quiet, pleasant manner," completely "master of the situation." His brief speech was "a marvel of manliness. . . . He is a wonderful man, a statesman with a heart, and is greater in defeat than in victory." [13] Certainly the speech, as quoted in the newspapers, gives no indication of humiliation:

> You have done the work which your constituency sent you here to do, and I think you do not care to hear from me. I congratulate you upon this day's work. It did not turn out exactly as I would have had it [Laughter and applause]. But it has turned out well for the district and for the State, and for the Republican party [Applause and cheers]. There will be no more enthusiastic supporter of the gentleman you have nominated to-day than your humble servant [Applause]. I have stood by the Republican party for the last 25 years; fifteen years of that time it has stood by me [Cheers and applause]. I am thankful for the past, and I will be the same C. C. Carpenter, the same Republican, the same citizen, the same man, the same friend to Major Holmes and to Col. Scott, and to everybody in the future that I have been in the past. . . . I know that when you take things at a short range truth doesn't always seem to be a reality, but when you look over the years, like the events of history and at long range, I believe there never was a truer saying than that "What ought to happen, will happen." [Applause]. It has been the philosophy of my life, and is the philosophy which makes me so cool and comfortable now. [Applause and cheering].

Carpenter's "happy" remarks left the convention in high good humor. Holmes also spoke briefly, but Colonel Scott, although called for, did not appear.[14] Evidently he was not as "cool and comfortable" as Carpenter.

That night Carpenter wrote his account of the day in his diary:

> I felt pretty sure this morning that the fates were against me. The opposition were caucusing and from all appearance were nearing a conclusion. When this became apparent my friends went into a caucus on the question of changing front for Holmes. I told them to do as they thought best for the District for the party & themselves. They therefore changed and made Holmes the nominee. I made a speech before the convention & left for home.[15]

Why had Carpenter lost? Why had so much opposition developed to a man whose popularity in his own district and throughout the state was unquestioned? For lack of any concrete proof, the answer can be only supposition. One story has it that a Kossuth County mail agent, A. A. Brunson, had lost his job in the summer of 1881 and had blamed it on Carpenter. However, a diary entry in September, 1881, seems to exonerate Carpenter from blame in this: "In the evening I received a letter from the P. O. Dept. giving the reasons for the removal of Mr. Brunson as a Route Agent." [16] Since the "P. O. Dept." told Carpenter why Brunson had been removed, it hardly seems likely that Carpenter had caused the dismissal. Furthermore, Brunson owed his original appointment, in 1879, to Carpenter. During the summer of that year, Congressman Carpenter had been deluged with letters, some urging the appointment of James Patterson, others pressing the claims of A. A. Brunson. After several weeks the balance swung to Brunson, and Carpenter sent in his recommendation. Gratitude for this first appointment may have been forgotten when Brunson was dismissed two years later, evidently without the knowledge of Carpenter.[17]

Whatever the cause for his removal, Brunson made up his mind that Carpenter was "having too soft a job in Washington," and he set out to stir up opposition. Finding several "sore spots" resulting from jealousy over postoffice appointments, Brunson built up a hard core of malcontents who were determined to defeat Carpenter in 1882.[18] So runs the story, written years after the event, but it can not be given undue credit, since it would take more than a few disappointed office seekers to control a convention.

Another reason for the opposition to Carpenter may have been the redistricting of the state and the creation of a new Tenth out of remnants of the old Ninth and Fourth. Perhaps some politicians of the area had dreams of power that they had not been able to achieve before. Three of Carpenter's opponents came from ex-Fourth District counties, two from the ex-Ninth District counties of Boone and Story. And it was Carpenter's old district counties that defeated him. Local political rivalries and jealousies often play more of a part in congressional nominations than the record of the Congressman. New men no doubt wanted to take over the control of the party from Carpenter and the young men around him. And Carpenter was determined that his young supporters should be protected. Two in particular, whose political futures may have been saved by Carpenter in the convention of 1882, were George E. Roberts and Jonathan P. Dolliver. Certainly Dolliver owed his first steps up the political ladder to Carpenter; Roberts, already chairman of the Webster County Republican Committee, had served as an alternate delegate to the 1880 national convention, and had been elected state printer in 1882, would soon be secretary of the State Republican Committee, would develop into an outstanding economist, and would become director of the mint by appointment of President McKinley. Carpenter had two "up-and-coming" young men on his side in 1882, and he protected their immediate futures by his action at the convention. His opponents soon slipped back into obscurity.

Many years later George E. Roberts wrote of Governor Carpenter:

> I lived in Fort Dodge from boyhood and knew Governor Carpenter intimately, first as a boy knows and looks up to a leading citizen of his home town, and later as the editor of the local paper would naturally know the most important local leader of his own political party, its candidate for important offices, etc., and knew him also as a neighbor and fatherly friend and counselor. I loved him for his kindness and helpfulness to me and for his sterling worth as I knew it in close contact. . . .
>
> Governor Carpenter was an unusual man, intelligent, reflective, wise, sincere, absolutely reliable in every statement, public-spirited and patriotic in the highest degree, keenly interested in the preservation of the Union and the development of Iowa.[19]

One other facet of the political scene of the time should be considered, and that is the slowly dying two-term tradition. Of the forty-two men who had represented Iowa in the House from 1846 to 1879 (the year Carpenter entered Congress), only ten had served more than two terms: sixteen had served two terms; the remaining sixteen, one term each. In Carpenter's district only one man had gone to Congress for three terms—Asahel Hubbard, who was in the House from 1863 to 1869. Of the others, Charles Pomeroy had served only one term (1869–1871); Jackson Orr, two terms (1871–1875); S. Addison Oliver, two terms (1875–1879). Carpenter had now had his allotted two terms; no doubt many felt that he should step aside for someone else. The idea that a long term in Congress would profit a district and a state more than the passing around of honors every four years was only slowly gaining ground. In the eastern "river counties" the two-term tradition had been broken: Hiram Price of the Second had had five terms; William B. Allison of the Third, four terms before being elevated to the Senate; George W. McCrary of the First, four terms before he advanced to the Cabinet; James F. Wilson of the First, four terms, and he was soon to follow Allison into the Senate. In central Iowa, John A. Kasson had represented the old Fifth (later the Seventh) District from 1863 to 1867, again from 1873 to 1877, and would serve it again from 1881 to 1884, when he would resign to return to the diplomatic service in which he had already begun a brilliant career. Thus Carpenter's colleagues in Iowa politics who had been given longer terms of service in the House had brought honor and power not only to themselves but to their state as well.[20] But local rivalries often clouded this new idea, and in 1882 these rivalries had helped to defeat Governor Carpenter.

Carpenter himself later put the blame on "the schemes and combination of a few local politicians who wanted Post Offices." This did not make him a "sore head," he added, "yet it led me to consider more than I ever had before whether a man could retain his self-respect and keep up a struggle of that kind." [21]

Whatever the cause or causes, Carpenter had been rejected by his district. The newspapers of the state outdid each other in an unprecedented chorus of praise for the loser. "He had failed, we presume," wrote the editor of the Keokuk *Gate City*, "to satisfy those who think that a congressman should be a bully boy." But no matter whether in the House or in private life, continued the article, "C. C. Carpenter has record enough that he will be held in all good Iowa thought as a man who honored Iowa as much as it has honored him." Ret Clarkson mourned with Carpenter's friends over the defeat. While praising Carpenter—"He deserved and the State needed his renomination"—Clarkson could not conceal his pleasure at the "adroit move" by which Scott had been "unhorsed." "It was a brilliant maneuver foiling and out witting a very shrewd one, and the best playing of a last card which has yet been in Iowa." Scott had been the "most active and bitterest opponent of Carpenter;" now Carpenter's friends had "paid their debt to the Colonel most handsomely" and given the district a nominee upon whom all could unite with the least hard feelings.[22]

A few days later, Senator Allison visited Carpenter at Fort Dodge, and Carpenter introduced him to "several of the gentlemen about town." That evening George Roberts and Jonathan Dolliver called at the Carpenter home to see the Senator.[23] Very possibly this was the first meeting of Allison and Dolliver, the two men who were to be so important in each other's careers.

Never one to hold a grudge, Carpenter entered into the congressional campaign with vigor, traveling a good deal about the district with Holmes.[24] Adoniram J. Holmes, a native of Ohio, had many of the requisites for a political career. He had served in the Civil War as a member of the 24th and 37th Wisconsin regiments, and had been a prisoner of war in the South; he had studied law at Ann Arbor, Michigan, and had moved to Boone in 1867. Since that time he had served two terms in the Iowa legislature.[25]

The redistricting of Iowa brought to the congressional election many new faces. Moses A. McCoid, in the First, Marsena E. Cutts in the Sixth, John A. Kasson in the Seventh, and William P. Hepburn in the Eighth won re-election, but Cutts died before the new Congress convened and was succeeded by John C. Cook, the Democrat who had contested his 1880 election. Republicans also won in the Third District (David B. Henderson), in the Tenth (Holmes), and in the Eleventh (Isaac S. Struble). In the Second and Ninth Districts, Democrats Jeremiah H. Murphy and William H. M. Pusey won; in the Fourth, Luman H. Weller, a Greenbacker-Democrat, was elected; while in the Fifth James Wilson of Traer, Iowa's famous

The Old Brick Capitol in Des Moines

The Carpenter Home in Ft. Dodge

Cyrus Carpenter

"Tama Jim," a Republican, won but lost in a contest for his seat to Benjamin T. Frederick, a Democrat. Thus Iowa would have only six Republicans in the Forty-eighth Congress, out of a total of eleven Representatives. The Democratic victory that year was nationwide as far as the House was concerned; the Forty-eighth Congress had only 119 Republicans, while the Democrats had won 201 seats, assorted "Independents," five.[26] Carpenter must have been relieved to know that he would not again be a member of the minority in the House, with all that that meant. The Republican prospects for 1884 were not good.

Carpenter served out his term in the Forty-seventh Congress with his usual lack of distinction. When Congress adjourned on March 3, 1883, private citizen Carpenter returned to Fort Dodge and an uncertain future. During the post-election months of 1882 he and several friends had established the Fort Dodge Loan and Trust Company.[27] Doubtless, when his congressional career closed, Carpenter planned to continue this business venture, but the demands of politics soon took him to Des Moines.

The campaign of 1883 was important both to the Republican party and to Senator Allison. The legislature elected that year would either re-elect Allison to his third term in the Senate, or it would replace him. If the Democrats won the legislature, an unlikely but always feared eventuality, Allison's career would be ended. Furthermore, the state was agitated from end to end by the prohibition question in 1883, and Allison feared that this local fight might hurt his chances for re-election, since the division on liquor seemed to follow party lines—the Republicans favoring and the Democrats opposing the prohibitory amendment approved at a special election in June of 1882. In January 1883, the State Supreme Court had declared the amendment unconstitutional on a technicality; a new fight on the issue was inevitable in the fall campaign.[28]

Webster County Republicans wanted to send one of their men to the Iowa House in 1884. The county was never safely Republican with John F. Duncombe leading the Democrats; the only sure thing would be to nominate a man who could not lose, and that man was C. C. Carpenter. Although Carpenter, now busy with his farm and his business ventures, protested to the last moment, he was nominated by the county convention on September 5. This is a "splendid thing," said Clarkson; it "insures a Republican from that county, and one of the strongest of Iowa men for the next House." [29] So, whether he liked it or not, Carpenter was forced back onto the political scene, for one last campaign.

Iowa was treated to a rousing canvass in 1883. A gubernatorial election seldom aroused much outside interest, but this time, with a senatorship to be decided, both sides imported prominent speakers from other states. As in the past, there were three parties in the field. Incumbent Republican

Governor Buren R. Sherman was opposed by Democrat L. G. Kinne and Greenbacker James B. Weaver, and the three engaged in a series of joint debates throughout the state. To add flavor to the contest, the Democrats brought in Congressman John G. Carlisle of Kentucky, the Democratic leader who would be elected Speaker of the Forty-eighth Congress, and Carter H. Harrison, the Democratic mayor of Chicago. The Republicans, not to be outdone, sought help from Senators Benjamin Harrison of Indiana, Joseph R. Hawley of Connecticut, and Eugene Hale of Maine, all of whom were vitally interested in the re-election of their colleague, Allison.[30] Weaver, unable to get outside help, attracted attention to his candidacy by bitter attacks on Allison, attacks which Clarkson parried with his most venomous pen. With the new national House surely Democratic, Republicans were fighting desperately to keep the Senate, at least, in their hands, and on the eve of election Clarkson warned the voters: "The Republican who votes for a Democratic or Fusion candidate for the legislature votes for a Democratic United States Senator, and to give the control of the United States Senate to the Democrats." [31]

On election day the Republicans could rejoice. The Twentieth General Assembly was safely Republican, and Allison's re-election assured. The Iowa Senate would have thirty-nine Republicans and eleven Democrats; the House, fifty-one Republicans, forty-two Democrats, and six Greenbackers.[32] Governor Sherman was re-elected by a comfortable margin over Democrat Kinne, but the combined vote of Kinne and Weaver left Sherman the victor by a mere 1,000 votes, a considerable reduction from his 1882 margin. The Republicans had lost seats to the Democrats in many areas, but they still held control, and among the Republicans who had won handily was Cyrus Clay Carpenter of Fort Dodge, ex-legislator, ex-Governor, ex-Congressman, who now returned to Des Moines as an elder statesman, at the age of fifty-four.

When the legislature convened in January 1884, Carpenter was made chairman of the ways and means committee of the House and also placed on the committees on schools, constitutional amendments, the Agricultural College, and federal relations.[33] It is significant to note that on the roster of the Assembly he listed himself as a "farmer." [34] Although still active in various business enterprises in Fort Dodge, Carpenter no doubt thought the title of "farmer" was still a good one in politics.

The first order of business was the nomination of Allison by the Republican caucus, which met on January 15. Carpenter, as chairman of the caucus, added his words of praise of Allison to those of the many others spoken for the Senator. He had always admired Allison, said Carpenter, but since he had come to know him better while serving in Washington, he had found that he had "never comprehended the full measure of the man." If Allison were not returned to the Senate, where he stood so high, it would be "a shame and a reproach to the intelligence of the people of the State of Iowa. . . ." Allison's nomination was unanimous, and a few days later the Republican majority in the General Assembly elected him to his third term in the Senate.[35]

The legislature had convened. in the small brick capitol that had served Iowa as a statehouse since 1858, when Carpenter had been the green young representative from Webster County. Now a new capitol, built of traditional limestone, and with the equally traditional golden dome, stood in the center of Capitol Square, ready for use. On January 17, at the afternoon session, the members of the House and Senate began a solemn procession from the old to the new capitol. The clerk of the House—Sidney A. Foster of Worth County—whose factual accounts of the proceedings of the Assembly were seldom enlivened by comment, was so moved by the scene that he described the exodus in a rash of mixed metaphors, closing with the words: "These rough old walls, scarred and nicked, seamed and worn by the work of weary years, saw the departing shadow of its former greatness, as at 2:14 P.M. the last line of members left the old House, and silence fell like leaves from memory's journal upon the beach of years, whispering a regret, yet sighed relief, that time had worked such changes." [36]

In the new capitol Governor Sherman took the oath for his second term, and the building itself was dedicated by John A. Kasson, whose work as an Iowa legislator had begun the task of erecting the new structure. The two houses then repaired to their "elegant legislative halls," where resolutions were passed thanking all who had had a hand in the building, including ex-Governor Carpenter, for their work over the years in behalf of the capitol.[37] Then, worn out by emotion and excitement, the Assembly adjourned. Now the real work of legislation could begin.

The Twentieth General Assembly moved forward in some things, stood still on others. The members re-enacted the prohibitory amendment and passed several laws to enforce it; they established a state bureau of labor statistics, certainly a farsighted move for a state still largely agricultural; and they rejected an amendment giving women the vote. Remembering the 1878 October–November election controversy, they also added an amendment to the Constitution, setting all elections on the November date decreed by the federal government. Carpenter, chairman of the ways and means committee, and thereby floor leader for the Republicans, favored the prohibitory amendment, as did all other members of his party, while the Democrats, almost to a man, voted against it. On the woman suffrage amendment, however, Carpenter was among the thirty-nine Republicans, two Democrats, and two Greenbackers who approved the measure; thirty-nine Democrats, eight Republicans, and four Greenbackers combined to vote to postpone "indefinitely" a decision to remove the word "male" from the Iowa constitutional provision on suffrage.[38]

Important as the prohibition issue was in 1884, national politics soon crowded it out of the picture, at least for a time. This was the year when Carpenter's protégé, Jonathan Prentiss Dolliver, sprang from local to national prominence almost overnight. Realizing the young orator's potentialities, Carpenter had urged that Clarkson use Dolliver's oratorical gifts in behalf of the Republican party. As a consequence, Dolliver had stumped the state for Garfield and Arthur in 1880 under the auspices of the state central committee, and Clarkson had then called him "the young man eloquent." [39] In 1882, Dolliver had attracted some attention in a brief nominating speech at a state convention; at the May 1884, state convention, called to name delegates to the national convention, Dolliver had nominated Clarkson as one of the delegates-at-large. That he had been chosen to do this (Clarkson's membership on the delegation was a foregone conclusion) indicates Dolliver's acceptance by the party leaders as a promising young man.[40]

But the greatest moment was yet to come. The Republicans had at last named James G. Blaine as their candidate for the presidency. In spite of the admiration for Blaine of a great number of Republicans, including Clarkson, his nomination was not popular with many of the rank and file. In order to arouse enthusiasm, the state convention held on August 20 to nominate minor state officers was also used to stir up interest in the presidential candidate. And the honor of the temporary chairmanship, which carried with it the giving of the keynote address, went to young Dolliver, still hardly known outside his own state. The speech, carefully rehearsed and memorized, caused a sensation.

Carpenter, a delegate to that convention, must have glowed with pride as he listened to Dolliver and as he watched the enthusiasm grow, heard the cheers echo and re-echo, saw men jump on their chairs, waving hats and handkerchiefs. Clarkson had asked Carpenter's opinion on naming Dolliver as the keynoter, and Carpenter had approved. Now he saw his trust in the young man vindicated: Dolliver's future was assured. Clarkson telegraphed the speech to some of the eastern papers, and before long the Iowa keynoter was in demand everywhere. He spent six weeks of the campaign that year touring the East, sometimes in company with Blaine himself, and when he returned to Fort Dodge to speak at the final rally before election, his reception was tremendous. A Utica paper had called him "the oratorical revelation of 1884," and his home town was proud.[41]

Almost unnoticed, in the excitement of the presidential campaign, Adoniram J. Holmes had been renominated for the customary second term in Congress from the Tenth District without opposition.[42] On election day, Iowa Republicans had cause to mourn; their spirited campaign had carried the state into the Blaine column by 20,000 votes, but the nation had rejected the "Plumed Knight" by a narrow but sufficient margin. For the first time since the war the people had turned against the Republican party. Grover Cleveland, who had been the butt of sarcastic Republican attacks in one of the most unsavory campaigns in American history, had defeated Blaine by some 62,000 votes, and he had carried the House with him. In Iowa, three of the eleven congressional seats went to the Democrats again, and Green-backer James B. Weaver won election in the Sixth District, but seven seats were safely Republican. All this was some slight consolation, but to most Republicans the national picture looked black indeed. Clarkson, after printing the usual crowing roosters in the few days when the election was in doubt, had to admit defeat at last, although he insisted that the Democrats had stolen the election by fraud in New York, where the Cleveland margin had been close. Without New York, Cleveland would have lost; therefore, according to the Clarkson logic, the count was wrong and the election stolen.[43]

To Carpenter, the election—"freighted with crime that touched the very heart of our civilization"—had "reversed the course of history." He was now more than ever determined to retire from politics. However, there were friends whose political ambitions he wanted to see "gratified," and he would not "become a recluse until this is done." "Among them, and first on the list, is Dolliver." [44]

The 1886 campaign for the congressional seat from the Tenth District began privately early in the year, publicly in April. The editor of the newspaper in Dayton, a small town in Webster County, wrote Dolliver to ask if he were willing to be considered as a candidate for Congress. Since Dolliver had been corresponding with numerous Republicans throughout the district for some months, this was what might be called a leading question. Dolliver's reply was that, "accepting the advice of trusted friends, he would ask the republicans of Webster county for their support." [45]

Some Republicans approached Dolliver's candidacy warily, since they would have preferred to put Carpenter up for a return to Congress, but Carpenter steadfastly refused to consider such a thing and urged his friends to support Dolliver. In May, Carpenter wrote a letter to A. D. Bicknell of Humboldt in which he spelled out his position:

> I am not a candidate. And while I am not insensible to the Good-will of such friends as remember with favor my efforts to serve the old ninth District four years ago, still I fully resolved, after the Webster City convention, never again to enter the lists as a candidate for an office. At that time it would have gratified me to have been nominated, as I then thought, that my short experience in Congress and the acquaintance with public affairs which it had afforded me, would enable me to serve the interests of my District and my county. But I was not nominated, and without re-

pining or regret I turned my attention to the farm which for years I had neglected; and am now interested and absorbed in efforts to secure what did not come to me in the public service: viz a competence for old age.[46]

The chief objection to Dolliver seemed to have been his age. Born in 1858, Dolliver was only twenty-eight years old in 1886. To some men of the district, who had been fighting the battles of Republicanism before Dolliver was born, he seemed a mere youngster. Why should they turn from the older men, who deserved recognition, to a young man whose only fame so far lay in a few political speeches? Carpenter met this objection squarely, citing names of several great men who had begun their congressional careers at an early age. "I think," said Carpenter, "I may say without the fear of successful contradiction that no public man in the history of this country, has ever attained great distinction and usefulness who did not enter the public service in early life." Should Dolliver be nominated and elected, he would be thirty years old when he entered the House, "five years beyond the age which the wisdom of the fathers who framed the constitution fixed as the limit of eligibility." [47]

Much newspaper support came to Dolliver during the following months. Papers both in and out of the Tenth District lauded him.[48] But one man, who could have done much to further Dolliver's ambitions in 1886, could not help him then. By June, Congressman Holmes had let it be known that he was a candidate for a third nomination. Dolliver wrote to Senator Allison to sound him out on his position and received this discouraging reply:

> I am your good friend & have rejoiced at your steady growth & popularity, & if I could in any way I would cheerfully promote your plans, but Mr Holmes has always been my friend. He & I were born in the same Tp. in Ohio, & he would have a right to feel hurt if I took any part against him and he has not suggested that I do anything for him, so I feel that I ought not to interfere. I am sure you will appreciate my situation & position respecting the canvass. Should you receive the nomination it will give me pleasure to aid you in any way that I can.[49]

So the powerful voice of Iowa's senior Senator would not be raised in Dolliver's behalf, this time.

Carpenter continued to work and write letters for Dolliver, but the answers were not always encouraging. "He is too young," was the constant tone; let him wait another two years.[50] Meanwhile, other candidates entered the field. In addition to Holmes and Dolliver, there was Carpenter's old opponent in the 1878 contest, John J. Russell of Jefferson. W. L. Culbertson of Carroll, J. M. Comstock of Algona, and a number of other favorite sons also sought the honor.[51]

When the convention met at Algona on August 19, 1886, there was no effort to combine against any one man, as there had been in 1880 against

Carpenter. Perhaps the experience of that convention had taught the politicians the hazards of such a move. There were ninety-six delegates gathered at Algona, making a vote of forty-nine necessary for victory. On the first ballot Dolliver led with thirty-one; Holmes had only fifteen; and Russell had twenty-six. The rest of the votes were scattered. It would have seemed, with Dolliver leading and only eighteen votes short of the required forty-nine, that he could have picked up the necessary ballots by the usual process of courting the second-choice votes. But the delegates remained firm, and ballot followed ballot without any significant changes. After seventy-five ballots, the delegates adjourned for dinner; during the evening session eighty-nine more ballots were taken without a decisive swing. At one time Dolliver reached $45\frac{10}{11}$ votes, his highest, but at the end of the evening he had dropped back to thirty-eight, while Holmes had thirty-four, and Russell twenty-five.

The deadlocked convention finally adjourned until the following morning, when an effort to swing the anti-Dolliver votes to Russell almost succeeded. Russell at one time drew forty-seven ballots, two short of the nomination. At last, on the 188th ballot, the break came, the Russell forces withdrew, and the nomination went to Holmes, while a stubborn thirty-four clung to Dolliver to the end.[52]

Taking a leaf from Carpenter's book, Dolliver appeared before the convention and made a witty and good-natured speech, congratulating the winner and promising his aid in the coming canvass. Privately, he was not so happy about it. His brother wrote that he did not blame him for saying that he would not again try for public office.[53] Carpenter, too, was depressed. Some observers even claimed that there were tears in the Governor's eyes at the end of the balloting. The Holmes men, who had forgotten the two-term argument they had used against Carpenter in 1880, could now send their man back to Congress for a third term. They had played up the age question in regard to Dolliver, fearing that if elected he would "remain in Congress for a long time," and the politicians of the Tenth District—the "thimble-riggers" of conventions, as Dolliver's brother called them—still operated on the theory that public office should be passed around among the faithful, not relegated to one man for a longer period than four years, or possibly six, if by so doing they could hold power in their district.[54]

If 1884 and 1886 had been unhappy years politically for Carpenter and the Iowa Republicans, 1888 brought both triumph and defeat: triumph in that J. P. Dolliver and Benjamin Harrison won nomination and election; defeat in that this same Benjamin Harrison had defeated the presidential hopes of Iowa's William B. Allison. Dolliver, forgetting his post-convention threat to withdraw from politics, was in the thick of the state and national conventions in 1888, served as both temporary and permanent chairman of the state convention and as one of the four delegates-at-large to the national convention. The Iowa delegates did their best for Allison, but their best was far from good enough; Allison was one of the also-rans, although at one time early in the balloting his chances were more than good.[55]

Even before the national convention, congressional politics again drew the attention of the Tenth District. Holmes, now serving his third term, wanted renomination; Dolliver, with two more years of political oratory and prominence behind him, again wanted to replace Major Holmes in the House. And Carpenter, more determined than ever that Dolliver should have his wish, began the endless round of letter-writing, traveling, and influencing necessary for success at a district convention. And still again, the question of Dolliver's age was raised, since few could find anything else to object to in the Fort Dodge lawyer and orator. The Fort Dodge *Messenger* replied to these charges by printing a long list of names of men who had entered Congress at an early age.[56]

Carpenter's 1878 opponent in Fort Dodge, M. D. O'Connell, had tried to get the Webster County delegation away from Dolliver, but without success. Encouragement came from other areas in the district, and as the county conventions met to name delegates, Dolliver was notified of their action. All in all, his prospects were better in 1888 than in 1886, but he went into the convention short of the magic number, which was forty-eight this time.[57]

The convention met at Webster City on August 20. In addition to Dolliver and Holmes, other men had their supporters who hoped to cash in on a deadlock between the leaders. Judge J. P. Conner of Dennison in Crawford County claimed eight votes when the convention opened; Captain Albert Head of Green County had ten; and Captain E. J. Hartshorn of Emmetsburg, one of the 1886 contestants, had some small support. Balloting did not begin until the evening session on opening day, and on the informal ballot Dolliver led with forty; Holmes had eighteen, Head seventeen, Hartshorn twelve, and Conner eight. No change came on the first formal ballot, and the long fight set in in earnest. Voters switched back and forth, booming one candidate, throwing out another, but never combining enough strength to push one man over. At one time Holmes's vote fell to one, later it rose to forty-seven, within one of victory. Dolliver's total fell at one time to thirty-two, Captain Head's backing rose to forty on another ballot. Finally, on the following day and after 109 fruitless ballots, the delegates surrendered to the inevitable and named Jonathan Prentiss Dolliver as their candidate. They had realized, reported the Fort Dodge *Messenger,* that the Dolliver men would deadlock the convention "until frost came" rather than nominate anyone else.[58]

At last Carpenter had won. His man was going to Congress, to the seat Carpenter had lost six years before, and those who had defeated him then were now on the outside. Brother Emmett wrote from South Dakota, where he now lived, of his delight at the "defeat and burial of that combination of malevolence and mediocrity in the 10th district." He had been worried, but now everything was all right, and the "political jugglers" who had defeated Carpenter in 1880 would "sink out of sight forever." [59]

Governor Carpenter could now try to become a political recluse. He had done his best for Dolliver, and that best had been sufficient. Nor would Dolliver ever forget what he owed Carpenter. To the day of the "old Governor's" death, the young Congressman would look to him for encouragement, advice, and friendship.

-SIXTEEN-

A Good Life Closes

———•—•—•———

IF GOVERNOR CARPENTER thought he could ever really leave the political scene, he was mistaken. The genuine affection and respect of the leading men of the state for the quiet little man in Fort Dodge led them to call on him repeatedly for help and advice.

In 1885, when an ugly political tangle developed in Des Moines, which threatened to hurt the Republican party, Jacob Rich and James S. Clarkson had asked Samuel J. Kirkwood, Senator James F. Wilson, and Carpenter to help iron out the difficulties. Governor Sherman, on the slimmest of excuses, had removed State Auditor John L. Brown. Brown had refused to surrender his position, and the Governor had used the state militia to eject him from his office. Law suits were threatened, and the Republicans trembled for the effect of such publicity in an election year. Rich wrote to Carpenter that he wanted him to help Kirkwood and Wilson "make a supreme effort to settle the Brown-Sherman matter." Clarkson thought it important that the three men "take hold of it." Evidently the three succeeded in quieting both sides; a lull occurred in the controversy until after the inauguration of the new Governor, William Larrabee, in January 1886. Brown then asked for impeachment and a trial, at which he was easily exonerated and restored to office.[1]

Aside from helping his party out of trouble, Carpenter continued to work for Republicanism, stumping the state at election time, sending modest contributions to the state chairman, using his influence in behalf of young and deserving aspirants. In early January 1886, he went to Des Moines to help in George E. Roberts's fight for re-election as state printer. A few months later he was off to Washington in the interests of a courthouse for Fort Dodge. Congressman Holmes and Senators Allison and Wilson were working to get the courthouse bill through, and they had called on Carpenter for help in "talking up Ft. Dodge quietly" with the members of the congressional committee. The Fort Dodge postmastership also caused considerable excitement in 1886, and Carpenter's influence was again solicited, but this time his support was not successful. In spite of Republican objections, and in spite of Senator Allison's influence, President Cleveland gave the naming of the postmaster to John F. Duncombe, whose choice of Patrick Cain raised a minor tempest, with accusations of fraud leveled at Democrat Duncombe.[2]

Carpenter's opinions on various issues of the day brought him both honor and attack. Having always been a supporter of that radical idea, woman suffrage, and having supported the amendment in the 1884 legislature, he was made an honorary member of the Iowa Woman Suffrage Association at Des Moines.[3] But his stand on prohibition caused trouble: in August 1885, Carpenter was attacked on the streets of Fort Dodge by a saloon keeper, who objected to the Governor's stand on the question, accusing him of reporting an infraction of the liquor law. The intervention of friends saved Carpenter from bodily harm, and the fracas did the liquor interests little good.[4]

Some Iowans still wanted to send Carpenter to the Senate; whenever there was a senatorial election, someone was bound to bring up the Governor's name. Senator James F. Wilson was up for re-election in 1888, and as early as January of 1887 the *Register* published a letter signed "Blue Coat," suggesting Carpenter for the job. Carpenter constantly scotched such ideas. He wrote to Emmett: "I have not got the Senatorial Bee in my bonnet. I dont think people get into the Senate these days without spending a great deal of money. And candidly I cannot see why Wilson should not be re-elected." [5]

Evidently the Grand Army of the Republic, growing in political influence, did not agree with Carpenter. Wilson asked the Governor to come to Des Moines duing the 1888 session, to help him keep "his line unbroken by the pressure that is trying to be made on the line of the soldier dodge, by Hepburn and some of his friends." Carpenter was glad to use his influence.[6] He had urged his friends to support Wilson's first election in 1882, for he thought him a man who would "take his place among the statesmen of this century," and his high opinion of Wilson had not changed during the Senator's first term in office.[7]

With Wilson safely re-elected, Iowa Republicans turned their attention to the campaign to win the presidential nomination for Allison. As one of the party's influential members, Carpenter received many appeals for aid, both from the Allison backers and from local politicos yearning for the brief glory of a place on the Iowa delegation to the convention. David B. Henderson of Dubuque, Allison's friend and now Representative from the Third District, thought it would be a good idea for Carpenter to go to the convention as one of the delegates-at-large; George W. Hanna of Kossuth County wanted to be on the delegation and solicited Carpenter's support in Webster County, since, as he said, Carpenter and George E. Roberts did the "figuring" there in political affairs. Carpenter was willing to go to Chicago if he could help Allison, but as things turned out, Dolliver rather than Carpenter was chosen.[8]

Friends next wanted Carpenter to be a candidate for railroad commissioner, positions on the board having been made elective that year. Anti-railroad sentiment was rising in the state, and Governor William Larrabee was leading a strong fight against the roads.[9] But Carpenter could not be enticed into running for office again. His home affairs were taking all of his time; as usual, he was in a shaky financial condition. Public office no longer attracted him.

Even national affairs sometimes intruded on Carpenter in retirement. With the election of Harrison in 1888, the House was returned to the Republicans, and a struggle for the speakership at once developed. Henderson of Iowa was among the candidates, while other aspirants were Thomas B. Reed of Maine, Julius C. Burrows of Michigan, and Joseph G. Cannon of Illinois, all of whom Carpenter had known during his four years in the House. Not wanting to overlook any support, both Cannon and Burrows wrote Carpenter, asking for his influence in spite of the fact that the Governor's natural tendency would be to back the Iowa man, David B. Henderson. Burrows realized this when he asked only for *"second choice"* preference from Carpenter. Cannon wrote a long letter setting forth the claims of a western man and asking Carpenter's help with the Iowa delegation, in the event Henderson should withdraw.[10] Whatever influence Carpenter might have had with the delegation was no doubt on the side of Henderson, whose chances were slight anyhow. Reed of Maine won the speakership and started on the path—interrupted by several Democratic Congresses—to the "Czardom" that ended in his resignation in 1899 and the succession then of Iowa's Henderson.[11]

Dolliver's intention, when he entered Congress in 1889, was to appoint Carpenter to the Fort Dodge postmastership, now due for a change with the return of the Republicans to power. It was the "least" he could do, Dolliver explained to a Fort Dodge friend. Carpenter was "unwilling to leave his home and his business to reenter politics in the national field," Dolliver continued, and since the Governor's finances were "somewhat disarranged" by the "fallen market," he needed help.[12] But in spite of his need, Carpenter had urged Dolliver not to appoint him, at least "not for the present." "Now if I take an office it would look as though there was a mercenary element in my friendship for you; and the bare suggestion of a thing of this kind wounds my self-respect," he wrote. Meanwhile, Carpenter was swamped with letters begging him to further this or that cause with Dolliver. He apologized for sending so many of these requests on, instead of "kicking the fellows out-doors," but he could not do that—"shoe-leather wouldn't hold out." Finally, Carpenter agreed to let Dolliver appoint him postmaster of Fort Dodge, but he still did not want to "hurry" the incumbent.[13] At last Dolliver had his way, and Carpenter became post-master at Fort Dodge, the ideal berth for a retired but still influential politician.

Carpenter's last years, like all the years of his life, were filled with politics on the one hand and the constant struggle to make a living on the other. He had never been good at anything except serving the public. His loan office was not successful, and the ups and downs of the farm prices usually caught him in the market on the downward trend, so that his farm, which he grandly called the "Oak Lawn Stock Farm," was usually in the red. In 1890, he had to have a stock sale in order to meet the demands of his creditors. The sale concluded successfully, and his "good name and credit" restored, he sent $40 to Edgar E. Mack, chairman of the Republican state committee for the 1890 campaign, promising also to go out on the stump and make a few speeches, if Mack did not send him "far from home," as he wanted to be able to get home every night.[14] The old campaigner was losing some of his fire.

Meanwhile, the postmastership helped him keep his head above water. When, with the victory of the Democrats in 1892 and the expiration of his appointment in 1894, the office was about to go to a Democrat, Dolliver held up the decision on his successor as long as he possibly could, managing to keep Carpenter in office until June. "Let there be the utmost deliberation," Roberts had urged. "Every month of salary now goes to Gov. Carpenter, and while he is delicate about saying that he wants it, we all know that it is very useful to him. . . ."[15] On the day of his retirement, Carpenter wrote: "So I am foot-loose. And barring the little item of about six $s per day I am not particularly sorry." He thanked Dolliver for his kindness, and again re-tired to private life and the endless struggle to make a little money.[16]

And so the years passed. Carpenter farmed, tried the real estate business for a time, and in his leisure moments wrote a number of articles for the *Annals of Iowa,* now edited by his old and good friend, Charles Aldrich.[17] In February 1896, Carpenter had a serious illness which frightened his friends. Hearing of this, Dolliver wrote a letter which expressed sentiments often only written after a man's death:

> I find it hard to think of you as an invalid because you have always seemed so strong and well. I could not feel a greater anxiety on account of sickness in my own home than I do on hearing that you are called to suffer. I have often talked with you about the many acts of kindness you have done for me, since I came a stranger to Fort Dodge. Your kindly interest in me, beginning the first Sunday after I came to Iowa, when you took R. H. [Dolliver's brother] and me home to dinner, has been one of the chief joys of my whole life. I owe to you not only the ambition to enter public

life, but the opportunity to do so, and I wish you to know that you are the one friend whose friendship has been so far above the motives and interests of politics, that it has inspired not only a sense of gratitude but an affection which is almost filial and which has been always present in my heart. My hope and prayer is that you may speedily regain your health and strength and that you may be spared for many years of usefulness, to enjoy the universal honor which all the people of Iowa give you.[18]

But the time had now grown short. In 1898, Dolliver again had the opportunity to do something for the Governor. The post office was again open, and Dolliver sent in Carpenter's name. But before President William McKinley—another of Carpenter's old colleagues from the Forty-sixth Congress—could act, Carpenter was dead. In April, there had been a recurrence of his old sickness, a kidney disease, and almost before his friends knew that he was ill again, he had sunk into a coma. He died at 9 o'clock on a Sunday evening, May 29, 1898, at the age of sixty-eight.

Dolliver received the news in Washington, too late to make the complicated train connections necessary for him to reach Fort Dodge in time for the funeral. Pacing the floor of his suite at the Hamilton, he talked for a long time to his wife about the Governor, of all he had meant to him, and of his deep affection for the older man. "I have never seen him show so much feeling," Mrs. Dolliver wrote to Mrs. Carpenter. "I wish you might know all he said for it was very beautiful." Later Dolliver tried to put his feelings into words in an extended article on Carpenter, published in the *Midland Monthly* in July 1898. To Mrs. Carpenter, Dolliver expressed his sorrow at the loss "of the man whose life belongs to the history of Iowa and whose memory will be cherished forever by the people of the state which he served so long." [19]

Nor was Dolliver the only one deeply moved by Carpenter's death. Old friends and former political enemies all joined in expressions of sorrow and regret. The public funeral, held on June 1, 1898, was thought to be the largest ever held in Fort Dodge, the funeral cortege being nearly a mile long. State officials paid their respects, Governor Leslie M. Shaw attending in person, accompanied by Carpenter's former secretary, William H. Fleming. Democrats and Republicans alike spoke feelingly of the kind and gentle man they had come to honor. The business houses in Fort Dodge and the government offices in Des Moines closed during the hour of the funeral, and all government buildings flew their flags at half-mast.[20]

Politics, which Carpenter had served all his life, could not even take a holiday for his funeral. The postmastership was again open, and Dolliver was immediately besieged with advice. Even before the funeral, a *"Clique"* had begun laying plans. But their voices were soon stilled by an insistent demand, "from the best of the Republicans and Democrats" that Mrs. Carpenter be appointed in her late husband's stead. By so doing, all other claimants would be silenced, and the "good lady" would be provided for. J. A. O. Yeoman of Fort Dodge, a Democrat, urged Dolliver to appoint Mrs. Carpenter and thus avoid "an ugly post-office fight." "Few communities are fortunate enough to have had within its limits so simple minded, clean and honorable a man as Governor Carpenter," Yeoman wrote. "In his devotion to the public service he has failed to properly care for those whom he leaves behind. I think it is our duty to care for them." No one could have agreed with Yeoman more than Dolliver: on June 9, he wrote that he was asking the President to appoint Mrs. Carpenter. "Personally, I could not have done otherwise." And this decision was popular. Members of the "clique" promptly withdrew their claims.[21]

A good life had ended. Not a great life, not a life that influenced events or changed the course of history; merely a good life, an average life. Carpenter was a politician, a loyal party member, who worked for his party and his community in the light of his beliefs, which were typical of his time. A newspaper friend of Dolliver's characterized Carpenter as well as any man has done:

> I never knew a man in public life who had nobler virtues and nobler faults than Cyrus Carpenter; but I think his faults outshine his virtues, or the world would have known more of him. If the man were not so outrageously diffident he might have been very useful both to himself and to his fellow man, for his ability is greater than most of his friends suspect. That such a man as he should hide himself from public view and spend his time in a cornfield, is worse than a crime.[22]

Carpenter had the character and high standards needed in government, but he lacked the drive to power necessary to rise in public life. Had he possessed this drive, the self-assurance, and perhaps the certain amount of ruthlessness that go to make a successful politician, he might indeed have been more useful to himself and to his fellow men, but during all his life his retiring nature held him back. He was, thus, one of the many minor public officers who make no outstanding mark on their time but are the warp and woof of the political fabric. The self-important, the pushers, the ruthless, the corrupt receive more attention and exert more temporary power; while the quiet ones, the "diffident," give that party its real strength and lasting influence at which is now called the "grass roots." They personalize and epitomize the party in local areas across the country, and eventually they bring honor to themselves by an integrity and honesty that the people respect and trust.

The Olympian Henry Adams has said that "One might search the whole list of Congress, judiciary, and executive during the twenty-five years 1870–1895, and find little but damaged reputations." This was not true of Cyrus Clay Carpenter.

Dolliver once called Carpenter that "great and good man." [23] The adjective "great" might be questioned, in the historical sense, but that he was a "good" man, loved by his friends and respected by his enemies, cannot be questioned.

Notes

ONE—A Young Man Goes West

[1] Carpenter's description of his arrival at Fort Dodge is contained in an undated typescript speech (evidently given late in life) in the *Cyrus Clay Carpenter Papers* (State Historical Society of Iowa, Iowa City), hereafter referred to as "Undated Typescript Speech." Carpenter's personal appearance was described in a letter to the author from his nephew, Judge Clay Carpenter of California, July 26, 1950. For an account of the founding of Fort Dodge, see Major William Williams, "History of Webster County, Iowa," *Annals of Iowa* (1st ser.), 7:286–93 (July 1869).

[2] Genealogical information on the Carpenter family was kindly furnished the author by Clifford K. Shipton, librarian of the American Antiquarian Society, Worcester, Mass. The passenger list of the *Bevis* is given in Charles Edward Banks, *The Planters of the Commonwealth. . .* (Boston: Genealogical Publishing Co., 1930), 198–200.

[3] Amos B. Carpenter, *A Genealogical History of the Rehoboth Branch of the Carpenter Family in America. . .* (Amherst: Carpenter and Morehouse, 1898), 17–20, 38.

[4] *Ibid.*, 38. Richard LeBaron Bowen, *Early Rehoboth: Documented Historical Studies of Families and Events. . .* (4 vols.: Concord, N. H.: Rumford Press, 1945), *passim*, gives much information on the founding of Rehoboth and on the Carpenters. For the various spellings of Seekonk, see *ibid.*, 2:11. An early description of Rehoboth can be found in Samuel Maverick, "A Brief Discription of New England and the Severall Townes therein, together with the Present Government therof" [written about 1660], *Proceedings*, Massachusetts Historical Society (2nd ser.), 1:243–44 (1884–1885). See also, John Warner Barber, *Historical Collections. . . History and Antiquities of Every Town in Massachusetts. . .* (Worcester, Mass.: Door, Howland & Co., 1840), 132–36.

[5] Adam Miller, *Incidents in the Origin and Progress of the Congregational Church and the Settlement of the Township of Harford, Pa. . . .* (pamphlet published at Montrose, Pa., 1844), 3–4. A copy of the pamphlet is in the *Carpenter Papers*.

[6] Miller, *Incidents*, 4.

[7] *Ibid.*

[8] From the manuscript of an undated speech given by Carpenter at Harford, Pa. in *Carpenter Papers*. (Hereafter cited as "Harford Speech.")

[9] "Amanda Thayer . . . was of a family widely known in literature, statesmanship, and military affairs. Among the most distinguished of the family was Gen. Sylvanus Thayer, who is called the 'father of the United States Military Academy,' of which he was among the first graduates, and afterwards for many years its superintendent." From Carpenter biography in *Illustrated Fort Dodge. . .* (Des Moines: Historical Illustrative Co., 1896), 237.

[10] This information was furnished the author by Judge Clay Carpenter, the son of Robert Emmett Carpenter. Further information in letter of G. J. Carpenter (a nephew) to Carpenter, June 25, 1877, *Carpenter Papers*. (Hereafter in these notes, Carpenter will be referred to as "CCC.")

[11] ". . . that worst of all hereditary diseases, whose deadly blight had previously

laid in the grave my father and mother—*I mean that destroying angel called the consumption.*" CCC to Kate Burkholder, Nov. 2, 1858, *Carpenter Papers.* There are very few references to his parents in Carpenter's letters; one written in 1865 to his wife gives a glimpse of a traditional stern upbringing. In discussing the shortcomings of the present generation, Carpenter commented: "My father would have punished me severely if I had set by and seen my mother get wood or bring in water." CCC to his wife, Apr. 4, 1865, *ibid.*

[12] From Harford Speech, *ibid.*

[13] *Ibid.* See also Miller, *Incidents,* 14. There is a hint in the *Carpenter Papers* that Cyrus at one time strayed into the Democratic party. In a letter in 1878 from an old Harford friend, in reminiscing about younger days, the friend wrote: "You were a strong Democrat in those days. Many & hard were the contests we had with Little Lyon Lung & others of the Whig persuasion. And when I heard that you are a Republican I gave Whittiers poems credit for doing much to bring about this result. . . . Something of this kind together with your natural abhorrence of slavery I suppose took you into that party." Wm. Blanding to CCC, Dec. 19, 1878, *Carpenter Papers.*

[14] See biographical sketch in Des Moines *Iowa State Register,* Sept. 21, 1871. (Hereafter cited as Des Moines *Register.*) Other Carpenter biographies are to be found in *Dictionary of American Biography* (20 vols., New York: Charles Scribner's Sons, 1928), 3:508–09; *The United States Biographical Dictionary . . . Iowa Volume* (Chicago: American Biographical Publishing Company, 1878), 781–83; various county histories of Webster County; J. P. Dolliver, "Ex-Governor Cyrus C. Carpenter," *Midland Monthly,* 10:75–81 (July 1898). The Des Moines *Register* account of his early life claims that Carpenter was in his youth "apprenticed to a clothier," but this is the only mention of such a fact in any of his biographies.

[15] Letters of Judd Carpenter to his brothers, from St. Joseph, Mo., June 2, 1850, and from California, Dec. 3, 1850, *Carpenter Papers.* Judd felt responsible for his brothers: "But in the meantime keep cool—leave me to myself and wait for further advises. Till then you must each one of you be a law unto himself—take good care of each others health and happiness—'hope on, hope ever,' and if I find a nest of Eagles (golden), I will Stick some new feathers in your caps. . . . Borrow no trouble about me. I am not a wild venturer. My steps, I assure you, shall all be well guarded and careful." (letter of June 2, 1850). Mention of schools taught are in Harford Speech and in CCC Diary, Oct. 2, 1878, *ibid.*

[16] Information on Harford obtained from an unidentified newspaper clipping [c. 1889] in *Carpenter Papers,* titled "Harford's Centennial History," by James P. Taylor.

[17] *Ibid.,* and Harford Speech, *Carpenter Papers.*

[18] Harford Speech, *ibid.*

[19] Letter of Claude Britell to CCC, Oct. n.d., 1868, *ibid.* "Neither have I forgotten your teaching at Johnstown O. & your 4th of July Orations there."

[20] CCC Diary, miscellaneous entries, May 15 to 30, [1854], *ibid.*

[21] Undated Typescript Speech, *ibid.* See also CCC to Kate Burkholder, Nov. 2, 1858, *ibid.*

[22] Undated Typescript Speech, *ibid.;* J. M. Dixon, *Centennial History of Polk County, Iowa* (Des Moines: State Register, Print, 1876), 320.

[23] Undated Typescript Speech, and CCC Diary, June 27, 1854, *Carpenter Papers.*

TWO—From Surveyor to Politician

[1] For Major Williams' own account of Fort Dodge, see Major Wm. Williams, *The History of Early Fort Dodge and Webster County, Iowa* (Fort Dodge?: n.p., copyright 1950). This book, edited by Edward Breen, is based on a manuscript by Major Williams now in the possession of the Webster County Historical Society. For the founding of Fort Dodge, see pp. 18–35. Other information on the Fort is contained in "Fort Dodge, Iowa," *Annals of Iowa* (3rd ser.), 4:534–38 (Oct. 1900), and an article by C. C. Carpenter, "Major William Williams," *ibid.*, 2:146–59 (July–Oct. 1895).

[2] Williams, *History of Early Fort Dodge*, 47–48; Carpenter, "Major William Williams," 149–50. According to Carpenter, the state land office for the selling of the Des Moines River land grant was located at Ottumwa at this time.

[3] Williams, *History of Early Fort Dodge*, 49.

[4] CCC to E. G. Morgan, March 4, 1874, CCC Letterbook E, 142, *Carpenter Papers*.

[5] Undated Typescript Speech; CCC to Williams, Feb. 19, 1872, CCC Letterbook A, 203–05, *Carpenter Papers*.

[6] This detailed account of Carpenter's first evening in Fort Dodge, and his description of Landlord Miller, is found in the Undated Typescript Speech and in a letter of Carpenter's to L. F. Parker, written Nov. 25, 1872, CCC Letterbook B, 332–35, *ibid.*

[7] Undated Typescript Speech, *ibid.*

[8] *Ibid.*

[9] CCC to G. Dahlem, July 30, 1874, CCC Letterbook F, 109–12, *Carpenter Papers*. Dahlem was a member of George Berry's surveying crew in 1854.

[10] Undated Typescript Speech; CCC to L. F. Parker, Nov. 25, 1872, CCC Letterbook B, 332–35, *ibid.*

[11] Letters to CCC from Emmett, Nov. 2, Dec. 6, 1854, from Judd, Nov. 10, 1854, from his Uncle Henry Tullary of Johnstown, Ohio, Dec. 17, 1854, *ibid.*

[12] C. C. Carpenter, "A Chapter of Pioneer History," *Annals of Iowa* (3rd ser.), 3:300–01 (Jan. 1898).

[13] CCC to Williams, Feb. 19, 1872, CCC Letterbook A, 203–05, *Carpenter Papers*.

[14] Manuscript copy of "Records of the Claim Club of Fort Dodge Iowa" (State Historical Society of Iowa, Iowa City), taken from the original records at the Iowa State Department of History and Archives, Des Moines. Carpenter's claim was located in what is now Jackson Township in northwestern Webster County. See map of Webster County in *A. T. Andreas' Illustrated Historical Atlas of the State of Iowa* (Chicago: Andreas Atlas Co., 1875), 111. For the latest research on Iowa's claim clubs, see Allan G. Bogue, "The Iowa Claim Clubs: Symbol and Substance," *Mississippi Valley Historical Review*, 45:231–53 (Sept. 1958).

[15] U. S. *Statutes at Large*, vol. 10, 714–15.

[16] W. Oakley Ruggles, "Early Recollections of Fort Dodge," originally published in the Fort Dodge *Iowa North West* in 1871, reprinted in *Iowa Journal of History*, 49:168–84 (Apr. 1951). Reference to Carpenter's nickname is on p. 184.

[17] CCC to G. Dahlem, July 30, 1874, CCC Letterbook F, 109–12, *Carpenter Papers*.

[18] "Articles of Agreement" with McMullen and Reed, both dated Nov. 5, 1855, at Fort Dodge, are in *ibid.* See also letter of Alpheus Reed to CCC, Dec. 8, 1855, *ibid.*

[19] Undated Typescript Speech, *ibid.*

[20] Williams, *History of Early Fort Dodge*, 59–60.

[21] Ruggles, "Early Recollections of Fort Dodge," 174.

[22] Undated Typescript Speech, *Carpenter Papers.*

[23] CCC to Emmett, Dec. 15, 1855, *ibid.*

[24] Undated Typescript Speech, *ibid.*

[25] Williams, *History of Early Fort Dodge,* 64–65.

[26] H. M. Pratt, *History of Fort Dodge and Webster County, Iowa* (2 vols., Chicago: The Pioneer Publishing Co., 1913), 1:86; certificate of election, dated Aug. 3, 1855, and signed by Judge William N. Meservey, is in *Carpenter Papers.*

[27] J. M. Davies, Aug. 10, 1855, and Claude Britell, Oct. 12, 1854, to CCC, *ibid.*

[28] Louis Pelzer, "The Origin and Organization of the Republican Party in Iowa," *Iowa Journal of History and Politics,* 4:487–525 (Oct. 1906); David S. Sparks, "The Birth of the Republican Party in Iowa, 1854–1856," *ibid.,* 54:1–34 (Jan. 1956).

[29] Pratt, *History of Fort Dodge,* 1:86; Williams, *History of Early Fort Dodge,* 62–63.

[30] Call signed by Simon B. Keffer, C. H. Pemberton, and James Gilchrist of Homer, Webster County, dated May 27, 1856, in *Carpenter Papers.*

[31] C. C. Carpenter, "Declining a Nomination," *Annals of Iowa* (3rd ser.), 1:408–10 (Apr. 1894).

[32] Iowa City *Daily Evening Reporter,* Sept. 29, 1856; Pratt, *History of Fort Dodge,* 1:86; Williams, *History of Early Fort Dodge,* 67–68.

[33] Ruggles, "Early Recollections of Fort Dodge," 173.

[34] Williams, *History of Early Fort Dodge,* 50–52, 92–135. The accounts of the Spirit Lake Massacre are numerous: Thomas Teakle, *The Spirit Lake Massacre* (Iowa City: H. M. Smyth Printing Company, 1918); Mrs. Abbie Gardner Sharp, *History of the Spirit Lake Massacre and Captivity of Miss Abbie Gardner* (Des Moines: Mills & Co., Printers, 1885); Charles E. Flandrau, *The Ink-pa-du-ta Massacre of 1857 in Minnesota and Iowa* (St. Paul: H. M. Smyth Printing Company, 1895); C. C. Carpenter, "The Spirit Lake Massacre," *Midland Monthly,* 4:17–31 (July 1895).

[35] Williams, *History of Early Fort Dodge,* 95–96.

[36] *Annals of Iowa* (3rd ser.), 3:481–553 (Oct. 1898), contains a series of speeches made by members of the expedition in 1887 at the unveiling of a tablet at Webster City commemorating the Spirit Lake Expedition. The published speeches in the *Annals* were by Carpenter, John F. Duncombe (who was captain of Company B), John N. Maxwell, Frank R. Mason, Michael Sweeney, and W. K. Laughlin. The account of the expedition given here is based upon these speeches.

[37] *Illustrated Fort Dodge,* 277.

[38] The bodies of Johnson and Burkholder were not found until 1868. Fort Dodge *Iowa North West,* June 17, 1868.

THREE—A Legislator in Des Moines

[1] Williams, "History of Webster County, Iowa," 344. This chapter, here somewhat revised, appeared under the title "C. C. Carpenter in the 1858 Iowa Legislature," *Iowa Journal of History,* 52:31–60 (Jan. 1954).

[2] Fort Dodge *Sentinel,* quoted in Dubuque *Daily Times,* Sept. 18, 1857.

[3] Andrew Hood to CCC, May 30, 1857, *Carpenter Papers.*

[4] Webster City *Hamilton Freeman,* July 30, 1857.

[5] Report of Hamilton County convention, held on Aug. 13, 1857, in *Carpenter Papers.*

[6] For a report of the convention, see Mitchell *Mitchell County Republican,* Aug. 27, 1857; for the platform, see Webster City *Hamilton Freeman,* Sept. 3, 1857.

[7] Webster City *Hamilton Freeman,* Aug. 27, 1857.

[8] *Ibid.,* Sept. 17, 1857.

[9] *Ibid.,* Sept. 10, 1857.

[10] *Ibid.,* Sept. 17, 24, Oct. 8, 1857.

[11] Benjamin F. Gue, *History of Iowa. . .* (4 vols., New York: Century History Co., 1903), 4:81; Webster City *Hamilton Freeman,* Sept. 17, 1858; I. J. Croll to CCC, Feb. 2, 1858, *Carpenter Papers.*

[12] J. W. Grimes to CCC, Nov. 11, 1857 in "Letters of James W. Grimes," *Annals of Iowa* (3rd ser.) 22:486 (Oct. 1940); Webster City *Hamilton Freeman,* Oct. 8, 1857.

[13] C. B. Richards to CCC, Oct. 6, 1857, *Carpenter Papers;* Webster City *Hamilton Freeman,* Oct. 8, 1857.

[14] Webster City *Hamilton Freeman,* Oct. 29, 1857.

[15] R. A. Smith, *A History of Dickinson County, Iowa. . .* (Des Moines: The Kenyon Printing & Mfg. Co., 1902), 181–82.

[16] M. M. Trumbull, Oct. 22, 1857, and D. G. Frisbie, Nov. 23, 1857, to CCC, *Carpenter Papers.*

[17] Grimes to CCC, Nov. 11, 1857, "Letters of James W. Grimes," 486. See Mitchell *Mitchell County Republican,* Jan. 14, 1858, for make-up of Iowa House and Senate.

[18] Dubuque *Daily Times,* Nov. 5, 1857.

[19] Webster City *Hamilton Freeman,* Nov. 5, 1857.

[20] *Ibid.,* Nov. 12, 1857.

[21] Dan E. Clark, *History of Senatorial Elections in Iowa* (Iowa City: State Historical Society of Iowa, 1912), 114–15.

[22] Des Moines *Tri-Weekly Citizen,* Jan. 12, 1858; Des Moines *Tri-Weekly Iowa State Journal,* Jan. 15, 18, 20, 1858. These tri-weekly papers were special editions, published during the sessions of the General Assembly.

[23] Grimes to CCC, Nov. 11, 1857, "Letters of James W. Grimes," 485–87; Elijah Sells to CCC, Nov. 17, 1857, *Carpenter Papers.*

[24] Roscoe L. Lokken, *Iowa Public Land Disposal* (Iowa City: State Historical Society of Iowa, 1942), 210–19. Another study of this extremely complicated land problem is Leonard F. Ralston, "Iowa Railroads and the Des Moines River Improvement Land Grant of 1846," *Iowa Journal of History,* 56:97–128 (Apr. 1958).

[25] Grimes to CCC, Nov. 30, 1857, "Letters of James W. Grimes," 488–89.

[26] Webster City *Hamilton Freeman,* Jan. 7, 1858.

[27] James Harlan, Dec. 29, 1857, and Timothy Davis, Dec. 31, 1857, to CCC, *Carpenter Papers.*

[28] B. F. Gue, "The Seventh General Assembly," *Pioneer Lawmakers Association of Iowa. Reunion of 1898* (Des Moines: F. R. Conway, State Printer, 1898), 87. The population of Des Moines was probably closer to 4,000, since the census of 1856 gave the town's population as 3,830. John A. T. Hull (ed.), *Census of Iowa for 1880 and the Same Compared with the Findings of Each of the Other States . . .* (Des Moines: F. M. Mills, State Printer and Geo. E. Roberts, State Printer, 1883), 564.

[29] Hoyt Sherman to CCC, Dec. 2, 1857, *Carpenter Papers.*

[30] Gue, "Seventh General Assembly," 88.

[31] For the membership of the Seventh General Assembly, see *Journal of the House of Representatives of the Seventh General Assembly of the State of Iowa . . .* (Des

Moines: J. Teesdale, State Printer, 1858), 5 (hereafter cited as *House Journal, 1858*); *Journal of the Senate of the Seventh General Assembly of the State of Iowa* (Des Moines: J. Teesdale, State Printer, 1858), 3–4 (hereafter cited as *Senate Journal, 1858*); Mitchell *Mitchell County Republican*, Jan. 14, 1858; Des Moines *Tri-Weekly Citizen*, Jan. 28, 1858.

[32] C. C. Carpenter, "Reminiscences of the Winter of 1858 in Des Moines," *Pioneer Lawmakers Association of Iowa. Reunion of 1892* (Des Moines: G. H. Ragsdale, State Printer, 1893), 59.

[33] For descriptions of the Old Brick Capitol, as it came to be known, see H. B. Turrill, *Historical Reminiscences of the City of Des Moines. . .* (Des Moines: Redhead & Dawson, 1857), 86; H. W. Lathrop, "The Capitals and Capitols of Iowa," *Iowa Historical Record*, 4:111–12 (July 1888); Jacob A. Swisher, "The Capitols at Des Moines," *Iowa Journal of History and Politics*, 39:52–57 (Jan. 1941). For a contemporary description, see Dubuque *Daily Times*, Jan. 7, 1858.

[34] CCC to Kate Burkholder, Jan. 15, 1858, *Carpenter Papers*.

[35] Des Moines *Tri-Weekly Iowa State Journal*, Jan. 18, 1858.

[36] Dubuque *Daily Express and Herald*, Jan. 20, 1858.

[37] Clark, *History of Senatorial Elections in Iowa*, 117–18; Des Moines *Tri-Weekly Iowa State Journal*, Jan. 27, 1858.

[38] Grimes had earlier written Carpenter: "My principle competitor will be Mr. Bissell of Du Buque. He runs on the geography question. I understand him to be a very good man but he is a man I have never even seen." Grimes to CCC, Nov. 11, 1857, "Letters of James W. Grimes," 486.

[39] Grimes to Mrs. Grimes, Jan. 25, 1858, in William Salter, *Life of James W. Grimes. . .* (New York: D. Appleton, 1876), 113.

[40] Clark, *History of Senatorial Elections in Iowa*, 118. For the career of Samuels, see Owen Peterson, "Ben Samuels in the Democratic National Convention of 1860," *Iowa Journal of History*, 50:225–32 (July 1952).

[41] Carpenter, "Reminiscences of the Winter of 1858 in Des Moines," 54–55; CCC to Kate Burkholder, Jan. 15, 1858, *Carpenter Papers*.

[42] Grimes to Mrs. Grimes, Jan. 26, 1858, Salter, *Grimes*, 113–14.

[43] *Senate Journal, 1858*, 81–84, 90, 93, 96, 103, 105, 108–09; *House Journal, 1858*, 104–05, 107–08; Des Moines *Tri-Weekly Iowa State Journal*, Jan. 22, 27, 1858.

[44] *House Journal, 1858*, 108.

[45] *Ibid.*, 311–14.

[46] *Ibid.*, 314–17; Des Moines *Tri-Weekly Iowa State Journal*, Feb. 19, 1858.

[47] *Ibid.*

[48] *House Journal, 1858*, 322–25.

[49] *Ibid.*, 311–13, 322–25.

[50] George Fort Milton, *The Eve of Conflict: Stephen A. Douglas and the Needless War* (New York: Houghton Mifflin, 1934), 273. For the break of the Democrats over Lecompton, see Roy Franklin Nichols, *The Disruption of American Democracy* (New York: MacMillan, 1948), 117–31; John Bach McMaster, *A History of the People of the United States. . .* (8 vols., New York: D. Appleton, 1914), 8:303–16.

[51] Dubuque *Daily Express and Herald*, March 4, 1858.

[52] Constitution of 1846, Article 9, in Benjamin F. Shambaugh (ed.), *Documentary Material Relating to the History of Iowa* (3 vols., Iowa City: State Historical Society of Iowa, 1895–1901), 1:205; Constitution of 1857, Article 8, *ibid.*, 1:244.

[53] Benjamin F. Shambaugh (ed.), *The Messages and Proclamations of the Governors*

of Iowa (7 vols., Iowa City: State Historical Society of Iowa, 1903–1905), 2:45. See also Howard H. Preston, *History of Banking in Iowa* (Iowa City: State Historical Society of Iowa, 1922), 70–82.

[54] *House Journal, 1858,* 587; Preston, *History of Banking in Iowa,* 74–82.

[55] *Ibid.,* 84.

[56] For brief accounts of the various roads, see Mildred Throne, "The Burlington & Missouri River Railroad," *The Palimpsest,* 33:1–32 (Jan. 1952); Dwight L. Agnew, "Iowa's First Railroad," *Iowa Journal of History,* 48:1–26 (Jan. 1950), and "The Mississippi & Missouri Railroad, 1856–1860," *ibid.,* 51:211–32 (July 1953); *History of Clinton County, Iowa. . .* (Chicago: Western Historical Co., 1879), 491–95 (for Iowa Central Air Line RR); and Franklin T. Oldt (ed.), *History of Dubuque County, Iowa. . .* (Chicago: Goodspeed Historical Association, n.d.), 240–50 (for Dubuque & Pacific).

[57] *House Journal, 1858,* 60.

[58] *Ibid.,* 304–05, 310–11.

[59] *Ibid.,* 311; *Senate Journal, 1858,* 246, 250, 254–56.

[60] Kate Burkholder to CCC, Feb. 25, 1858, *Carpenter Papers.* Beal letter in Des Moines *Tri-Weekly Iowa State Journal,* Feb. 27, 1858.

[61] *House Journal, 1858,* 311.

[62] "As it afterwards developed the navigation company was really the Keokuk, Fort Des Moines & Minnesota Railroad Company, and instead of improving the river it had been devoting a portion of its time to the building of the railroad which, at the time of the settlement, was completed from Keokuk to Benton's Port, a distance of about forty miles." N. E. Goldthwait (ed.), *History of Boone County, Iowa* (2 vols., Chicago: Pioneer Publishing Co., 1914), 1:141. This same paragraph appears in a Webster County history published one year earlier, in a chapter credited to C. L. Lucas, see Pratt, *History of Fort Dodge,* 1:236.

[63] *House Journal, 1858,* 304–05.

[64] See C. L. Lucas, "The Des Moines River Land Grants," in Pratt, *History of Fort Dodge,* 1:231–37. See also Jacob A. Swisher, "The Des Moines River Improvement Project," *Iowa Journal of History and Politics,* 35:142–80 (Apr. 1937); Leonard F. Ralston, "Iowa Railroads and the Des Moines River Improvement Land Grant of 1846," *ibid.,* 56:97–128 (Apr. 1958).

[65] Jno. L. Lewis to CCC, Jan. 20, 1858, *Carpenter Papers.*

[66] Carpenter presented a number of petitions to the House during the session. *House Journal, 1858,* 86, 96, 125, 207. He also received many private letters on the subject: Elijah Sells, Dec. 8, 1857, Isaac Whicher, Dec. 4, 1857, S. H. Lunt, Jan. 15, 1858, Asa C. Call, Feb. 17, 1858, to CCC, *Carpenter Papers.*

[67] *Acts and Resolutions Passed at the Regular Session of the Seventh General Assembly of the State of Iowa . . . 1858.* (Des Moines: J. Teesdale, State Printer, 1858) 427–29. (Hereafter *Acts and Resolutions . . .* cited as *Laws of Iowa.*)

[68] Des Moines *Tri-Weekly Citizen,* March 11, 1858; *Senate Journal, 1858,* 430–32,

[69] Des Moines *Iowa Weekly Citizen,* March 17, 24, 1858; *House Journal, 1858,* 692.

[70] A. B. Miller, Register. *Report of the Register of the State Land Office, November 7, 1859* (Des Moines: J. Teesdale, State Printer, 1859), 25–26.

[71] Lokken, *Iowa Public Land Disposal,* 221.

[72] Des Moines *Iowa Weekly Citizen,* March 17, 1858.

[73] Webster City *Hamilton Freeman,* March 18, 1858.

[74] Des Moines *Tri-Weekly Iowa State Journal,* March 19, 1858.

[75] Letters to CCC from A. M. Dawley, March 2, 1858, J. J. Barclay, March 14, 1858, and J. D. Burkholder, March 17, 1858, *Carpenter Papers.* For the boundary dispute, see Frank Harmon Garver, "Boundary History of Iowa Counties," *Iowa Journal of History and Politics,* 7:53–54 (Jan. 1909).

[76] *Senate Journal, 1858,* 275; *House Journal, 1858,* 572–73; Des Moines *Tri-Weekly Iowa State Journal,* March 12, 1858.

[77] Earl D. Ross, *A History of the Iowa State College of Agriculture and Mechanic Arts* (Ames: Iowa State Press, 1942), 16–21.

[78] Clarence Ray Aurner, *History of Education in Iowa* (5 vols., Iowa City: State Historical Society of Iowa, 1914–1920), 1:49–54.

[79] Webster City *Hamilton Freeman,* Oct. 29, 1857.

[80] Elijah Sells to CCC, Apr. 8, 1858, *Carpenter Papers.*

FOUR—Politics and Pike's Peak

[1] CCC to Kate Burkholder, Nov. 2, 1858; Judd Carpenter to CCC, Feb. 1, 1859, and to Emmett Carpenter, July 1, 1860, *Carpenter Papers.*

[2] Thomas F. Withrow to CCC, Apr. 14, 1858, *ibid.*

[3] Webster City *Hamilton Freeman,* May 27, Oct. 8, 1858.

[4] For the whole subject of local aid to railroads, see Earl S. Beard, "Local Aid to Railroads in Iowa," *Iowa Journal of History,* 50:1–34 (Jan. 1952).

[5] Constitution of Iowa, 1857, Article 7, Sec. 1, 5, in Shambaugh (ed.), *Documentary Material,* 1:242–43.

[6] Des Moines *Iowa Citizen,* Dec. 8, 1858; Iowa City *Republican,* Dec. 8, 1858. For call of convention, see Des Moines *Iowa Citizen,* Nov. 3, 1858.

[7] Platt Smith to CCC, Nov. 2, 1858, *Carpenter Papers.*

[8] Hull (ed.), *Census of Iowa for 1880. . . ,* 202.

[9] Withrow to CCC, Nov. 8, 1858, *Carpenter Papers.*

[10] Grimes to Kirkwood, May 29, 1859, "Letters of James W. Grimes," 499–500. In discussing the coming nominations, Grimes wrote: "Our democrats are all for Lowe, of course. They hope [for] his nomination & then they will publish some of his foolish letters in favor of state aid written by him last autumn. In this way they hope to get the question drawn into the canvass, by which they can lose nothing & may gain."

[11] Withrow to CCC, Dec. 23, 1858, *Carpenter Papers.*

[12] Cyrenus Cole, *Iowa Through the Years* (Iowa City: State Historical Society of Iowa, 1940), 268; Thomas Teakle, "The Defalcation of Superintendent James D. Eads," *Iowa Journal of History and Politics,* 12:204–44 (Apr. 1914).

[13] This campaign is covered fully in Edward Younger, *John A. Kasson* (Iowa City: State Historical Society of Iowa, 1955), Chap. VI.

[14] Des Moines *Iowa Citizen,* Apr. 20, May 4, 1859.

[15] John W. Thompson to CCC, Feb. 26, 1859, *Carpenter Papers;* Dan E. Clark, *Samuel Jordan Kirkwood* (Iowa City: State Historical Society of Iowa, 1917), 123; "Letters of James W. Grimes," 496–500.

[16] For the report of the convention, see Des Moines *Iowa Citizen,* June 29, 1859.

[17] A. B. Miller (Register of State Land Office) to CCC, March 31, 1859: ". . . regret your decision announced in your last—hoped to have you with us next winter." See also John H. Charles, Dec. 18, 1858, Sam Lunt, Feb. 13, 20, 1859, E. H. Talbott, Apr. 18, 1859, to CCC, *Carpenter Papers.*

18 S. M. Robbins to CCC, June 24, 1859, *ibid.*

19 Benjamin F. Reed, *History of Kossuth County, Iowa. . .* (2 vols., Chicago: S. J. Clarke Publishing Co., 1913), 1:340; Sioux City *Eagle,* Aug. 6, 1859.

20 E. H. Edwards to CCC, Aug. 20, 1859, *Carpenter Papers.*

21 John H. Charles to CCC, March 28, Aug. 30, 1859, *ibid.*

22 Sioux City *Register,* Sept. 15, 1859.

23 *Ibid.,* Sept. 29, 1859; Carl H. Erbe, "Constitutional Provisions for the Suffrage in Iowa," *Iowa Journal of History and Politics,* 22:206 (Apr. 1924); J. W. Denison to CCC, Dec., n.d., 1859, *Carpenter Papers.*

24 See *Iowa Official Register, 1909–1910* (Des Moines: Emory H. English, State Printer, and E. D. Chassell, State Printer, 1909), 523, for vote on Governor. See also Kenneth F. Millsap, "The Election of 1860 in Iowa," *Iowa Journal of History,* 48:99 (Apr. 1950); Louis Pelzer, "The History of Political Parties in Iowa from 1857 to 1860," *ibid.,* 7:209 (Apr. 1909); Morton M. Rosenberg, "The Election of 1859 in Iowa," *ibid.,* 57:1–22 (Jan. 1959).

25 CCC to Kate Burkholder, Oct. 30, 1859, *Carpenter Papers.*

26 CCC to Kate Burkholder, Oct. 17, Nov. 2, 1858; Kate to CCC, Oct. 29, 1858, *ibid.*

27 CCC to Kate Burkholder, June 5, 1859, *ibid.*

28 Judd Carpenter to CCC, Nov. 17, Dec. 16, 1859, *ibid.*

29 Letter from Carpenter, dated Omaha, Apr. 6, 1860, in Webster City *Hamilton Freeman,* May 19, 1860 (from the Dubuque *Times*).

30 F. W. Palmer to CCC, March 6, 1860, *Carpenter Papers;* Dubuque *Times,* May 19, 1860.

31 Dubuque *Times,* May 19, 1860; CCC to Kate Burkholder, Apr. 13, 1860, *Carpenter Papers.*

32 CCC to Kate Burkholder, May 1, 1860, to Judd Carpenter, May 1, 1860, *Carpenter Papers.*

33 CCC to Kate Burkholder, Sept. 3, 1860, *ibid.*

34 CCC to Kate Burkholder, July 8, Sept. 8, 1860, *ibid.;* Dubuque *Times,* Dec. 27, 1860; Webster City *Hamilton Freeman,* July 28, 1860.

35 CCC to Kate Burkholder, Sept. 8, 1860, *Carpenter Papers.*

36 CCC to Kate Burkholder, Nov. 17, 1860; Judd Carpenter to Emmett, Feb. 3, 1861, *ibid.*

37 CCC to Kate Burkholder, Apr. 11, 1861, *ibid.*

38 Hubert Howe Bancroft, *History of Nevada, Colorado, and Wyoming* (San Francisco: The History Company, 1890), 413–14; CCC to Kate Burkholder, Apr. 11, 1861, Judd Carpenter to Emmett, Oct. 17, 1861, *Carpenter Papers.*

39 CCC to Kate Burkholder, Nov. 17, Dec. 9, 1860, Jan. 12, 1861, *Carpenter Papers.*

40 CCC to Kate Burkholder, May 5, May 26, Sept. 1, 1861, *ibid.*

41 Judd Carpenter to CCC, Oct. 5, 1860; CCC to Kate Burkholder, Nov. 17, 1860, May 5, Sept. 1, 1861, *ibid.*

42 CCC to Kate Burkholder, May 5, 1861, *ibid.*

43 CCC to Kate Burkholder, Sept. 8, 1861, *ibid.*

44 Des Moines *Register,* Nov. 27, 1861.

FIVE—Feeding the Union Soldiers

[1] Mildred Throne (comp.), "Iowans in Congress, 1847–1953," *Iowa Journal of History,* 51:334 (Oct. 1953).

[2] James F. Wilson to CCC, Jan. 18, 1862, *Carpenter Papers.*

[3] James G. Randall, *Lincoln the President; Springfield to Gettysburg* (New York: Dodd, Mead & Company, 1945), 2: 54–62.

[4] CCC to Judd, Apr. 9, 1862, to Emmett, March 3, 20, 1862, *Carpenter Papers.*

[5] CCC to Emmett, Apr. 19, 1862, *ibid.*

[6] Kenneth P. Williams, *Lincoln Finds a General* (4 vols., New York: The Macmillan Company, 1949–1956), 3:102.

[7] *Personal Memoirs of U. S. Grant* (2 vols., New York: Charles L. Webster & Co., 1885), 1:371. (Hereafter cited as Grant, *Memoirs.*)

[8] CCC to Kate Burkholder, Apr. 23, 1862, and to Emmett, Apr. 24, 1862, *Carpenter Papers.* For the letters Carpenter wrote during the war, see Mildred Throne (ed.), "A Commissary in the Union Army: Letters of C. C. Carpenter," *Iowa Journal of History,* 53:59–88 (Jan. 1955).

[9] CCC to Emmett, May 3, 1862, and to Kate Burkholder, May 3, 1862, *Carpenter Papers.*

[10] CCC to Kate Burkholder, June 15, 1862, to Emmett, May 25, 30, 1862, and to Judd, May 11, 1862, *ibid.*

[11] CCC to Emmett, May 25, 1862, *ibid.*

[12] T. Harry Williams, *Lincoln and His Generals* (New York: Alfred A. Knopf, 1952), 120.

[13] CCC to Kate Burkholder, July 4, Aug. 4, 1862, *Carpenter Papers.*

[14] Grant, *Memoirs,* 1:392–93; Williams, *Lincoln Finds a General,* 3:440.

[15] CCC to Judd, June 30, 1862, and to Emmett, July 20, 1862, *Carpenter Papers.*

[16] Special Order No. 189, Rosecrans to CCC, July 24, 1862; CCC to Emmett, Aug. 31, 1862, *ibid.*

[17] CCC to Kate Burkholder, Aug. 4, 1862, *ibid.*

[18] CCC to Kate Burkholder, Sept. 3, 1862, *ibid.*

[19] CCC to Kate Burkholder, Aug. 29, 1862, *ibid.*

[20] CCC to Emmett, Sept. 24, 1862, *ibid.* For the background of the issuing of the Emancipation Proclamation, see Randall, *Lincoln the President,* 2:151–69.

[21] CCC to Emmett, Sept. 4, 1862, *Carpenter Papers.*

[22] Grant, *Memoirs,* 1:405.

[23] CCC to Emmett, Sept. 20, 1862, to Kate Burkholder, Sept. 28, 1862, to Capt. S. Simmons, Chief Commissary of Subsistence, Army of the Mississippi, Sept. 17, 1862, *Carpenter Papers.*

[24] CCC to Emmett, Sept. 20, 1862, *ibid.;* Grant, *Memoirs,* 1:410–13.

[25] CCC to Kate Burkholder, Sept. 28, 1862, and to Emmett, Sept. 28, 1862, *Carpenter Papers.*

[26] CCC to Emmett, Oct. 10, 1862, and to Kate Burkholder, Oct. 13, 1862, *ibid.*

[27] CCC to Kate Burkholder, Nov. 5, 1862, and to Judd, Feb. 24, 1863, *ibid.*

[28] CCC to Kate Burkholder, March 29, 1863, *ibid.*

[29] Clark, *Kirkwood,* 284.

[30] CCC to Emmett, March 21, 1863, and to Kate Burkholder, June 28, 1863, *Carpenter Papers.*

[31] CCC to Kate Burkholder, June 28, 1863, and to Emmett, June 30, Nov. 25, 1863, *ibid.*

[32] CCC to Kate Burkholder, May 3, 1863, and to Emmett, May 24, 1863, *ibid.*

[33] CCC to Judd, May 28, 1863, *ibid.*

[34] CCC to Kate Burkholder, Oct. 18, 28, 1863, *ibid.*

[35] Grant, *Memoirs,* 2:18–40.

[36] *Ibid.,* 2:47–48.

[37] CCC to Judd, Nov. 20, 1863, *Carpenter Papers.*

[38] CCC to Emmett, Dec. 8, 10, 1863, *ibid.*

[39] CCC to Emmett, Jan. 24, 1864, *ibid.*

[40] CCC to Kate Burkholder, Feb. 8, 1864, *ibid.*

[41] Kate Burkholder to CCC, Feb. 5, 1864; CCC to Kate, Feb. 21, 1864, *ibid.*

[42] CCC to Judd, Apr. 22, 1864, *ibid.* Date of wedding from an unidentified newspaper clipping, possibly an army newspaper, in *ibid.*

[43] Mrs. CCC to CCC, Apr. 9, 16, 1864; CCC to wife, Apr. 30, 1864, *ibid.*

[44] Grant, *Memoirs,* 2:114–16; Williams, *Lincoln and His Generals,* 298–99; CCC to wife, March 26, 1864, *Carpenter Papers.*

[45] CCC to wife, Apr. 3, 1864, *Carpenter Papers.*

[46] Lloyd Lewis, *Sherman, Fighting Prophet* (New York: Harcourt, Brace and Company, 1932), 344–45.

[47] *Memoirs of Gen. W. T. Sherman. . .* (2 vols., New York: Charles L. Webster & Co., 1891), 2:8, 10. (Hereafter cited as Sherman, *Memoirs.*)

[48] See Dodge's report on the Atlanta Campaign, *War of the Rebellion . . . Official Records. . .* (128 vols., Washington: Government Printing Office, 1880–1901), Series I, Vol. XXXVIII, Part III, 374–75. (Hereafter cited as *Official Records.*)

[49] Grenville M. Dodge, "Personal Recollections of General William T. Sherman" (pamphlet of speech delivered at 28th annual encampment, Department of Iowa, GAR, May 21, 1902, Des Moines, Iowa), 12–13.

[50] CCC to Emmett, May 5, 1864, and to wife, May 8, 1864, *Carpenter Papers.*

[51] *Official Records,* Series I, Vol. XXXVIII, Part III, 48. The total strength of the Army of the Tennessee was 35,245 at the start of the campaign. For number of wagons Carpenter had, see CCC to Emmett, May 8, 1864, *Carpenter Papers.*

[52] From a printed circular, evidently issued to commissaries, in *ibid.*

[53] Mildred Throne (ed.), "Civil War Diary of C. F. Boyd, Fifteenth Iowa Infantry," *Iowa Journal of History,* 50:168 (Apr. 1952).

[54] From circular in *Carpenter Papers.* See note 52.

[55] Letter dated Sept. 27, 1864, from CCC to Des Moines *Register,* published Nov. 2, 1864.

[56] *Ibid.*

[57] CCC letter dated Sept. 11, 1864, in Des Moines *Register,* Oct. 5, 1864.

[58] Draft of a letter by CCC, evidently intended for some newspaper, in *Carpenter Papers.*

[59] CCC letter in Des Moines *Register,* Oct. 5, 1864.

[60] Lewis, *Sherman, Fighting Prophet,* 573–76; Des Moines *Register,* June 7, 1865.

[61] Draft of CCC letter in *Carpenter Papers.* See note 58.

[62] CCC letter dated Sept. 11, 1864, in Des Moines *Register,* Oct. 5, 1864.

[63] Sherman, *Memoirs,* 2:105.

[64] Dodge, "Personal Recollections of . . . Sherman," 22; J. R. Perkins, *Trails, Rails and War: The Life of General G. M. Dodge* (Indianapolis: The Bobbs-Merrill Company, 1929), 151; Sherman, *Memoirs,* 2:104–05.

[65] CCC to Emmett, Oct. 17, 1864, and to wife, Oct. 27, 1864, *Carpenter Papers.*

[66] CCC to wife, Nov. 8, 1864, *ibid.*

[67] CCC to Emmett, Dec. 25, 1864, *ibid.*

[68] CCC to Emmett, Oct. 2, 1864, *ibid.*

[69] Emmett, Nov. 17, Dec. 19, 1864, and Mrs. CCC, Nov. 24, 1864 to CCC; CCC to Emmett, Jan. 18, 1865, *ibid.*

[70] CCC to wife, Sept. 18, 1864, to Emmett, Jan. 18, 1865, *ibid.*

[71] Sherman, *Memoirs,* 2:324–44.

[72] CCC to wife, Apr. 9, 1865, *Carpenter Papers.*

[73] CCC to wife, Apr. 14, 1865, *ibid.*

[74] Sherman, *Memoirs,* 2:344.

[75] *Ibid.,* 2:347–80.

[76] CCC to wife, Apr. 18, 1865, *Carpenter Papers.*

[77] CCC to Emmett, Apr. 20, 1865, to wife, May 12, 1865, *ibid.*

[78] CCC to wife, May 30, 1865, *ibid.;* Fort Dodge *Iowa North West,* June 27, 1865.

[79] CCC to wife, March 30, Apr. 1, 1865, *Carpenter Papers.*

[80] CCC to Kate Burkholder, Nov. 23, 1862, *ibid.*

[81] Geo. C. Tichenor to CCC, May 10, 1865, *ibid.*

[82] Fort Dodge *Republican,* quoted in Webster City *Hamilton Freeman,* May 10, 1862.

[83] CCC to wife, Apr. 10, 1864, to Emmett, Apr. 11, 1864, to Judd, Apr. 22, 1864; Tichenor to CCC, May 10, 1865, *Carpenter Papers.*

SIX—Carpenter and Iowa Radicalism

[1] Fort Dodge *Iowa North West,* Aug. 29, 1865; CCC to Judd, Jan. 8, 1866, *Carpenter Papers.*

[2] Fort Dodge *Iowa North West,* Oct. 2, 1865.

[3] CCC to Judd, Jan. 8, 1866, *Carpenter Papers.*

[4] Emmett to CCC, June 11, 1865, *ibid.*

[5] Fort Dodge *Iowa North West,* Oct. 10, 17, 1865.

[6] *Ibid.,* Oct. 17, 1865.

[7] CCC to Judd, Jan. 8, 1866, *Carpenter Papers.*

[8] Clark, *History of Senatorial Elections in Iowa,* 134, quoting a letter from Stone to Kirkwood of June 2, 1865. *See also* Leland L. Sage, "William B. Allison and Iowa Senatorial Politics, 1865–1870," *Iowa Journal of History,* 52:97–128 (Apr. 1954).

[9] See Throne, "Iowans in Congress, 1847–1953," 335–36.

[10] Younger, *Kasson,* Chap. XI.

[11] CCC to Judd, Jan. 8, 1866, *Carpenter Papers.*

[12] Younger, *Kasson,* Chap. XI.

[13] CCC to Emmett, Aug. 12, 1862, *Carpenter Papers.*

[14] CCC Diary, March 4, 1879, *ibid.*

[15] CCC to Emmett, March 25, 1865, *ibid.*

[16] Clark, *History of Senatorial Elections in Iowa,* 140–41, 286; Younger, *Kasson,* Chap. XI.

[17] Fort Dodge *Iowa North West,* May 8, 1866.

[18] *Code of Iowa . . . Revision of 1860,* Chap. 9.

[19] CCC to Judd, Nov. 1, 1866, *Carpenter Papers.*

[20] Letters to CCC from Tichenor, May 20, 1866, Dodge, May 26, 1866, Weaver, May 28, 1866, and Palmer, May 27, 1866, *ibid.*

[21] Aldrich to Emmett, June 14, 1866, *ibid.*

[22] Fort Dodge *Iowa North West,* June 27, 1866; Webster City *Hamilton Freeman,* June 30, 1866.

[23] Quoted in Fort Dodge *Iowa North West,* July 4, 1866.

[24] Dodge, Aug. 11, 1866, and Fuller, Aug. 22, 1866, to CCC, *Carpenter Papers;* Fort Dodge *Iowa North West,* Sept. 19, 1866; Webster City *Hamilton Freeman,* Sept. 15, 1866.

[25] The other candidates: Secretary of State, Ed Wright; State Treasurer, Samuel E. Rankin; State Auditor, John A. Elliott; Attorney General, E. E. Bissell; Reporter of the Supreme Court, E. H. Stiles; and Clerk of the Supreme Court, C. L. Linderman. Fort Dodge *Iowa North West,* July 25, 1866.

[26] M. E. Cutts (state chairman) to CCC, Aug. 27, 1866, printed notice with Carpenter's assessment filled in, *Carpenter Papers.*

[27] Quoted in Fort Dodge *Iowa North West,* Sept. 19, 1866; Webster City *Hamilton Freeman,* Oct. 6, 1866.

[28] Fort Dodge *Iowa North West,* Oct. 10, 1866.

[29] Claude G. Bowers, *The Tragic Era: The Revolution After Lincoln* (New York: Blue Ribbon Books, 1929), 4–8.

[30] Fort Dodge *Iowa North West,* Sept. 19, 1866.

[31] *Ibid.,* Oct. 29, 1868.

[32] Marshalltown *Marshall County Times,* Oct. 3, 1868.

[33] Fort Dodge *Iowa North West,* May 30, 1865; Council Bluffs *Nonpareil,* June 17, July 7, 1865.

[34] Iowa City *Republican,* Aug. 9, 16, 1865.

[35] Grimes to E. H. Stiles, Sept. 14, 1865, in *ibid.,* Sept. 27, 1865.

[36] CCC to wife, Apr. 1, 1865, *Carpenter Papers.*

[37] CCC to Judd, Nov. 1, 1866, *ibid.*

[38] CCC Diary, Apr. 18, 1865, *ibid.*

[39] Council Bluffs *Nonpareil,* Apr. 29, 1865; Fort Dodge *Iowa North West,* Apr. 25, 1865.

SEVEN—Radicalism Triumphant

[1] For details of these lands, see *Report of the Register of the State Land Office* for 1867, 1868, 1869, published at Des Moines.

[2] Lokken, *Iowa Public Land Disposal,* 267.

[3] Tichenor, Dec. 11, 1866, Elliott, Nov. 5, 1866, and Palmer, Dec. 12, 1866, to CCC, *Carpenter Papers; Report of the Register of the State Land Office, 1869,* 385.

[4] *Report of the Register of the State Land Office* for 1867 and 1869, and *Supplemental Report* for 1868, published at Des Moines.

[5] See *Report of Register of State Land Office, 1869,* 380, for recapitulation of railroad grants.

[6] Shambaugh (ed.), *Messages and Proclamations,* 3:432.

[7] Gue, *History of Iowa,* 3:234–35. For full accounts of the whole River Land controversy, see *ibid.,* 215–47; Lokken, *Iowa Public Land Disposal,* 210–35; C. H. Gatch, "The Des Moines River Land Grant," *Annals of Iowa* (3rd ser.), 1:354–70, 466–92 (Apr., July 1894); Swisher, "The Des Moines River Improvement Project," 142–80; Lucas, "History of the River-Land Grant," in Pratt, *History of Fort Dodge and Webster County,* 1:231–37; Ralston, "Iowa Railroads and the Des Moines River Improvement Land Grant of 1846," 97–128.

[8] Notices of Settlers' Union meetings in Fort Dodge *Iowa North West*, July 31, 1867, Dec. 9, 1869, Jan. 20, 27, May 12, 26, 1870.

[9] *House Journal, 1868,* 569–77; *Senate Journal, 1868,* 523.

[10] *Laws of Iowa, 1870,* Chap. 104; Joint Resolution XX.

[11] Lokken, *Iowa Public Land Disposal,* 232–35.

[12] CCC to Emmett, Jan. 1, 1867; Emmett to CCC, July 27, 1867, *Carpenter Papers.*

[13] Mrs. Henry Burkholder to Mrs. CCC, March 24, 1867; Arthur Burkholder, May 10, 1868, Mrs. CCC, May 20, 1868, to CCC, *ibid.* Fort Dodge *Iowa North West,* Sept. 23, Dec. 17, 1868, Nov. 25, 1869.

[14] Grinnell, Jan. 16, March 29, 1867, M. C. Woodruff, Nov. 18, 1867, E. W. Rice, Apr. 13, 1868, and Emmett, March 22, 1869, to CCC, *Carpenter Papers.*

[15] Charles E. Payne, *Josiah Bushnell Grinnell* (Iowa City: State Historical Society of Iowa, 1938), 219–31.

[16] Letter by E. W. Rice, in *Lacey Papers,* quoted in *ibid.,* 232. *See also* Iowa City *Press,* July 4, 1866.

[17] Fort Dodge *Iowa North West,* May 29, 1867. See Payne, *Grinnell,* 231: "Grinnell's defeat in the 1866 nominating convention was chiefly due to the fact that he had not resisted the Rousseau assault." Cyrenus C. Cole's two histories of Iowa—*A History of the People of Iowa* (Cedar Rapids: The Torch Press, 1921), 380, and *Iowa Through the Years* (Iowa City: State Historical Society of Iowa, 1940), 315—also repeat this error in the interpretation of Grinnell's defeat. See Leland L. Sage, *William Boyd Allison, A Study in Practical Politics* (Iowa City: State Historical Society of Iowa, 1956), 83, for correction of error.

[18] Grinnell to CCC, Jan. 16, 1867, *Carpenter Papers.*

[19] Aldrich to CCC, Jan. 2, 1867, *ibid.*

[20] Fort Dodge *Iowa North West,* June 12, 1867.

[21] Iowa City *Republican,* June 26, 1867.

[22] Charles Mason Remey (ed.), *Life and Letters of Charles Mason. . . ,* (12 type-script vols., Washington: n.p., 1939), 8:1000.

[23] C. C. Nourse, Aug. 26, 1867, H. H. Griffiths, Sept. 13, 21, 1867, to CCC, *Carpenter Papers.*

[24] Herbert S. Fairall, *Manual of Iowa Politics . . .* (Iowa City: Republican Publishing Company, 1884), Part I, 76, 78.

[25] Iowa City *Republican,* March 4, 1868; *House Journal, 1868,* 247–49.

[26] E. W. Rice to CCC, Apr. 13, 1868, *Carpenter Papers.*

[27] Grimes to Lyman Cook, Dec. 11, 1870, in Salter, *Grimes,* 382.

[28] Fort Dodge *Iowa North West,* May 20, 1868; Cedar Falls *Gazette* quoted in Fort Dodge *Iowa North West,* May 27, 1868; Iowa City *Republican,* May 20, 1868; Marshalltown *Marshall County Times,* May 23, 1868.

[29] CCC Diary, Feb. 8, 1872, *Carpenter Papers.*

[30] CCC to wife, May 9, 1868, *ibid.*

[31] Iowa City *Republican,* May 13, 1868.

[32] CCC to wife, May 9, 1868, *Carpenter Papers.* For a discussion of this pre-convention rally of the Civil War soldiers, see Ellis Paxson Oberholtzer, *A History of the United States Since the Civil War* (5 vols., New York: The Macmillan Company, 1937), 2:154–55. For report of the convention, see Des Moines *Register,* May 27, 1868. For the "Grand Union Rally" see *ibid.,* July 15, 1868.

[33] Fort Dodge *Iowa North West,* Sept. 16, 30, 1868; Sioux City *Journal,* quoted in *ibid.,* Oct. 29, 1868.

[34] From "Skeleton of speech made during the Presidential Canvass of 1868," in notebook in *Carpenter Papers*.

[35] Des Moines *Register*, Oct. 28, 1868.

[36] Fairall, *Manual of Iowa Politics*, Part I, 80; (Iowa) Census Board, *The Census of Iowa as returned in the year 1869 . . .* (Des Moines: F. M. Mills, State Printer, 1869), 262–63.

[37] Des Moines *Register*, Jan. 6, March 10, 1869; Palmer to CCC, March 18, 1869, *Carpenter Papers*. For comments on Grant's Cabinet, see Oberholtzer, *History of U. S.*, 2:214–16; Horace White, *The Life of Lyman Trumbull* (Boston: Houghton Mifflin Company, 1913), 333–38.

[38] Des Moines *Register*, March 17, 1869.

[39] *Ibid.*, May 5, 1869. Wilson gave Horace White substantially the same story, and it was confirmed by Grenville M. Dodge. See White, *Trumbull*, 334.

[40] Iowa City *Republican*, March 17, 24, 1869.

[41] From Kirkwood speech in 1866 campaign in Iowa City *Republican*, Aug. 29, 1866.

[42] Iowa City *Republican*, Jan. 9, Feb. 6, 1867, Apr. 8, 1868. For attacks on the Court in Congress, see Oberholtzer, *History of U. S.*, 1:463–67.

[43] CCC to Grenville M. Dodge, Jan. 18, 1867, *Grenville M. Dodge Papers* (Iowa State Department of History and Archives, Des Moines). I am grateful to Wallace Farnham for calling this letter to my attention.

[44] Quoted from Chicago *Post* in Fort Dodge *Iowa North West*, Jan. 7, 1869.

[45] Robert Rutland, "The Copperheads of Iowa: A Re-Examination," *Iowa Journal of History*, 52:29 (Jan. 1954).

[46] Marshalltown *Marshall County Times*, Sept. 11, 1869; Iowa City *Republican*, Oct. 13, 1869; Des Moines *Register*, Nov. 3, 24, 1869; Salter, *Grimes*, 372.

[47] Wm. Vandever to CCC, Sept. 29, Oct. 18, 23, Nov. 23, 1869, *Carpenter Papers*.

[48] Fort Dodge *Iowa North West*, Dec. 23, 1869. The Clarkson article in the Chicago *Tribune* was republished in the Des Moines *Register*, Dec. 1, 1869.

[49] Vandever to CCC, Oct. 23, 1869, *Carpenter Papers*. *See also* Sage, "Allison and Iowa Senatorial Politics," 126–27.

[50] Fort Dodge *Iowa North West*, Jan. 20, 1870; Marshalltown *Marshall County Times*, Jan. 20, 1870; Des Moines *Register*, Jan. 19, 1870; Vandever to CCC, Dec. 4, 1869, *Carpenter Papers*.

[51] Sage, "Allison and Iowa Senatorial Politics," 126–27.

[52] Des Moines *Register*, Dec. 1, 1869, Jan. 19, 1870; Clark, *History of Senatorial Elections in Iowa*, 148–49; Payne, *Grinnell*, 245, 252.

[53] Younger, *Kasson*, 229–32.

[54] Emmett to CCC, July 10, 1870, *Carpenter Papers;* Fort Dodge *Iowa North West*, July 22, 1868, Aug. 11, 1870.

[55] Fort Dodge *Iowa North West*, July 21, Aug. 11, 1870.

[56] Fairall, *Manual of Iowa Politics*, Part I, 85.

[57] Emmett to CCC, Jan. 23, 1870, *Carpenter Papers;* Fort Dodge *Iowa North West*, June 30, 1870.

[58] For the whole story of this railroad fight, see Mildred Throne, "Fort Dodge and the Des Moines Valley Railroad," *Iowa Journal of History*, 54:263–84 (July 1956).

EIGHT—The 1871 Gubernatorial Campaign

[1] This chapter, in slightly different form, appeared in the *Iowa Journal of History,* 48:335–70 (Oct. 1950), under the title "Electing an Iowa Governor, 1871: Cyrus Clay Carpenter." See also Russell M. Ross, "The Powers of the Governor of Iowa," *ibid.,* 52:129–40 (Apr. 1954).

[2] Dubuque *Herald,* July 5, 1871.

[3] Des Moines *Register,* June 22, 1871.

[4] Allan Nevins, *The Emergence of Modern America, 1865–1878* (New York: The Macmillan Company, 1927), 181–82.

[5] The so-called "Doud Amendment" had been introduced into a railroad bill in the 1868 session of the General Assembly, and had been included in all subsequent railroad bills. It stated: "The company accepting the provisions of this act shall at all times be subject to such rules, regulations, and rates of tariff for transportation of freight and passengers as may from time to time be enacted by the General Assembly of the State of Iowa." See *Laws of Iowa, 1868,* 66–67, 167; also, see Earl S. Beard, "The Background of State Railroad Regulation in Iowa," *Iowa Journal of History,* 51:21–22 (Jan. 1953).

[6] Iowa City *State Press,* March 1, 1871.

[7] Quoted in Fort Dodge *Iowa North West,* Dec. 8, 1870.

[8] Sage, "Allison and Iowa Senatorial Politics," 97–128.

[9] Tichenor, Jan. 7, 25, 1871, Allison, Jan. 14, 1871, to Dodge, *Dodge Papers.* I am grateful to Leland L. Sage for calling these letters to my attention.

[10] CCC to Dodge, Jan. 31, 1871, *ibid.*

[11] Muscatine *Weekly Journal,* Dec. 9, 1870, Feb. 24, Apr. 14, 28, May 5, 12, 26, 1871.

[12] G. L. Godfrey to CCC, Jan. 16, 1871, *Carpenter Papers.*

[13] Des Moines *Register,* Jan. 8, 1871.

[14] Iowa City *Republican,* Jan. 11, Feb. 22, 1871; Marshalltown *Marshall County Times,* Jan. 26, Feb. 9, 1871; Storm Lake *Pilot,* Feb. 15, 1871; Des Moines *Register,* quoted in Osage *Mitchell County Press,* Feb. 16, 1871. For insurance law, see *Laws of Iowa, 1868,* Chap. 138.

[15] John A. Elliott, Feb. 3, 1871, and Isaac Brandt, Feb. 15, 1871, to CCC, *Carpenter Papers.* Elliott's letter of withdrawal, dated Apr. 3, 1871, appeared in Des Moines *Register,* Apr. 4, 1871.

[16] Tichenor to Dodge, Jan. 7, 25, 1871, *Dodge Papers.*

[17] Tichenor to CCC, Apr. 5, 1871, *Carpenter Papers.*

[18] G. L. Godfrey to CCC, Jan. 16, 1871, *ibid.*

[19] CCC to wife, Feb. 3, 1871, *ibid.*

[20] CCC to John McKean, March 27, 1871, *ibid.*

[21] Fort Dodge *Iowa North West,* Jan. 26, 1871; Arthur Burkholder to CCC, Jan. 20, 1871, *Carpenter Papers.*

[22] "Mum" [James S. Clarkson] to CCC, Apr. 22, 1871, *Carpenter Papers.* For the "Des Moines Regency," see Emory H. English, "Evolution of Iowa Voting Practices," *Annals of Iowa* (3rd ser.), 29:249–51 (Apr. 1948).

[23] John F. Duncombe to CCC, Feb. 14, 1871, *Carpenter Papers.*

[24] For Platt Smith, see Thomas C. Cochran, *Railroad Leaders, 1845–1890. The Business Mind in Action* (Cambridge, Mass.: Harvard University Press, 1953), 461–66.

[25] For the complete story of this railroad fight, see Throne, "Fort Dodge and the Des Moines Valley Railroad," 263–84.

[26] Isaac Brandt, Feb. 15, 1871, N. B. Baker, Apr. 16, June 12, 13, 1871, John Russell, March 28, 1871, and Arthur Burkholder, Jan. 27, 1871, to CCC, *Carpenter Papers.*

[27] Joseph Dysart, March 2, 1871, W. P. Hepburn, Apr. 8, 1871, Lafe Young, March 18, 1871, and William Larrabee, March 17, 1871, to CCC, *ibid.*

[28] James B. Weaver to CCC, March 15, 1871, *ibid.* Weaver's refusal to be a candidate appeared in the Des Moines *Register,* March 25, 1871. Kirkwood to CCC, Apr. 3, 1871, *Carpenter Papers.*

[29] Emmett, Feb. 14, 1871, Palmer, March 20, 1871, to CCC, *Carpenter Papers;* Allison to Dodge, Jan. 14, 1871, *Dodge Papers.*

[30] James Harlan to CCC, May 3, 1871, *Carpenter Papers.*

[31] George Mills, "The Des Moines Register," *The Palimpsest,* 30:283 (Sept. 1949).

[32] Arthur Burkholder to CCC, Jan. 20, 1871, *Carpenter Papers.*

[33] Emmett, Feb. 1, 1871, M. M. Trumbull, Feb. 7, 1871, E. A. Teeling, March 21, 1871, James Davidson, Feb. 4, 1871, A. W. Hubbard, undated, but probably written in March 1871, James W. Weart, March 18, 1871, and G. W. Cook, Apr. 20, 1871, to CCC, *ibid.*

[34] John Scott to CCC, March 20, 1871, *ibid.*

[35] A. K. Welles, Feb. 7, 1871, J. M. Parker, Apr. 15, 1871, Aldrich, Apr. 26, 1871, to CCC, *ibid.* See also, for a newspaper account of his "agreement," Dubuque *Daily Times,* Apr. 15, 1871.

[36] John Scott to Aaron Brown, March 22, Apr. 10, 1871, *Aaron Brown Papers* (State Historical Society of Iowa, Iowa City).

[37] "Mum" [Clarkson] Apr. 22, 1871, Aldrich, Apr. 7, 1871, J. B. Powers, Apr. 11, 1871, to CCC, *Carpenter Papers;* Gue, *History of Iowa,* 4:235–36.

[38] Aldrich, March 22, 1871, T. W. Harrison, March 31, 1871, Geo. W. Jones, March 31, 1871, John Russell, March 28, 1871, to CCC, *Carpenter Papers;* Dubuque *Herald,* June 7, 1871.

[39] Aldrich, Apr. 7, 1871, Trumbull, March 20, 1871, Wm. H. Gibbon, Apr. 24, 1871, J. B. Powers, Apr. 11, 1871, and Elijah Sells, Apr. 5, 1871, to CCC, *Carpenter Papers.*

[40] Geo. W. Jones to CCC, Apr. 29, 1871, *ibid.*

[41] Tichenor to CCC, May 2, 1871, *ibid.*

[42] Allison to CCC, June 24, 1871, *ibid.*

[43] New York *Tribune,* Oct. 18, 1871; Marshalltown *Marshall County Times,* quoted in Des Moines *Register,* July 2, 1871; Dubuque *Herald,* July 5, 1871.

[44] Iowa City *State Press,* March 1, 1871.

[45] Des Moines *Register,* Jan. 14, 1871; Fort Dodge *Iowa North West,* Jan. 19, 1871; Aldrich to CCC, Apr. 23, 1871, *Carpenter Papers.*

[46] See letters to CCC from Arthur Burkholder, Jan. 17, March 3, 1871, Emmett, Jan. 25, 1871, C. V. Gardner, Feb. 22, 1871, Wm. Toman, Feb. 20, 1871, M. C. Woodruff, March 5, 1871, Geo. D. Perkins, March 14, 1871, and Andy Felt, March 20, 1871, *Carpenter Papers.* Also Fort Dodge *Iowa North West,* Jan. 26, Feb. 23, March 16, 23, 1871; Des Moines *Register,* May 7, 9, 12, 26, 1871; Storm Lake *Pilot,* Feb. 22, March 15, 29, Apr. 5, 26, May 3, 17, 1871; Sioux City *Daily Journal,* March 3, 1871; Iowa Falls *Sentinel,* March 29, 1871; Marshall County *Times,* Jan. 19, 1871; Iowa City *Republican,* Apr. 26, 1871.

[47] Sam S. Haislet to CCC, Apr. 19, 1871, *Carpenter Papers.*

[48] A. M. Bryson to CCC, Feb. 25, March 16, 1871, *ibid.*

[49] Emmett to CCC, March 3, 1871, *ibid.*

[50] Letters to CCC from Charles Beardsley, Feb. 9, 1871, O. B. Brown, March 17, 1871, Aldrich, [March] 17, [1871], T. V. Shoup, March 25, 1871, Geo. H. Powers, Apr. 8, 1871, H. J. B. Cummings, Apr. 5, 1871, H. M. Belvel, Apr. 21, 1871, and W. S. Moore, May 1, 1871, *ibid.* See also Birmingham *Enterprise,* quoted in Storm Lake *Pilot,* Feb. 22, 1871; Iowa City *Republican,* March 15, 29, 1871; Clarinda *Page County Herald* and Burlington *Hawk-Eye,* quoted in Fort Dodge *Iowa North West,* Feb. 16, March 23, 1871; Indianola *Warren County Leader,* June 15, 1871; and various papers quoted in Des Moines *Register,* May 7, 9, 10, 12, 16, 20, 26, 1871.

[51] Aldrich, March 21, 1871, Charles Dudley, March 22, 1871, A. H. Hamilton, March 13, 1871, N. B. Baker, Apr. 7, 1871, to CCC; D. M. Dimmick to Emmett, March 15, 1871, *Carpenter Papers.*

[52] CCC to wife, June 8, 1871, *ibid.*

[53] Isaac Brandt, June 4, 1871, J. W. Bull, June 7, 1871, Emmett, June 16, 1871, to CCC; CCC to wife, June 11, 1871, *ibid.* See also Geo. W. Jones to CCC, June 5, 1871, and Godfrey to Emmett, June 5, 1871.

[54] Iowa City *State Press,* June 21, 1871; Des Moines *Register,* June 21, 1871.

[55] Godfrey to CCC, Apr. 4, 1871, *Carpenter Papers.*

[56] For a complete account of the convention, see Des Moines *Register,* June 22, 1871. The call for the convention, which listed the number of delegates for each county, appeared in *ibid.,* Apr. 2, 1871.

[57] *Ibid.,* June 22, 1871.

[58] Iowa City *State Press,* May 24, June 14, 28, 1871.

[59] Dubuque *Herald,* May 10, 17, 1871.

[60] Muscatine *Tribune,* quoted in Iowa City *State Press,* Aug. 23, 1871; Dubuque *Herald,* Sept. 6, 1871.

[61] Tichenor to Dodge, Jan. 25, 1871, *Dodge Papers.*

[62] Dodge to CCC, June 28, 1871, *Carpenter Papers.* Edward F. Noyes of Ohio, formerly on Dodge's staff during the Civil War, had just been nominated by the Republican convention in Ohio for Governor.

[63] Iowa City *Republican,* June 28, 1871.

[64] Fort Dodge *Iowa North West,* July 27, 1871; also quoted in Storm Lake *Pilot,* Aug. 2, 1871. For Carpenter's campaign schedule, see Des Moines *Register,* Aug. 9, 10, 11, Sept. 1, 1871.

[65] For Iowa Democratic platform, see Fairall, *Manual of Iowa Politics,* Part I, 85–86.

[66] Ottumwa *Courier,* June 1, 1871. For Carpenter's acceptance speech, see Des Moines *Register,* June 23, 1871. Carpenter's notebook contains a "Skeleton of a Speech made by C. C. Carpenter in the campaign of 1871." This speech was published in the Indianola *Warren County Leader,* Sept. 14, 1871, and received favorable comment in the Centerville *Weekly Citizen,* Sept. 2, 1871, Ottumwa *Courier,* Aug. 24, 1871, and Lyons *Mirror,* Aug. 26, 1871.

[67] Council Bluffs *Nonpareil,* quoted in Fort Dodge *Iowa North West,* Aug. 24, 1871 and Lyons *Mirror,* Aug. 26, 1871; Des Moines *Register,* June 23, 1871.

[68] Fort Dodge *Iowa North West,* June 22, 1871.

[69] Des Moines *Register,* June 23, 1871.

[70] The Springfield *Illinois State Register* article appeared in the Iowa City *State Press,* July 12, 1871. See also Fort Dodge *Iowa North West,* July 13, Aug. 3, 1871 (for quotes from Birmingham *Enterprise*); Dubuque *Daily Times,* July 9, 1871; J. M. Shaffer to CCC, July 8, 1871, *Carpenter Papers.*

[71] Fairall, *Manual of Iowa Politics,* Part I, 88. The official vote, in "Rules of the 14th General Assembly," *Legislative Documents . . . 1872,* 2:28–30, gives slightly different totals.

[72] Baker to CCC, Nov. 13, 20, Dec. 4, 1871, *Carpenter Papers.*

[73] Baker to CCC, Dec. 30, 1871, *ibid.*

[74] Joseph Shields to Edw. Russell, Dec. 6, 1871; Russell to CCC, Dec. 6, 1871, *ibid.;* Centerville *Weekly Citizen,* Jan. 13, 1872.

[75] W. Oakley Ruggles to CCC, Nov. 16, 1871, *Carpenter Papers.*

[76] Merrill, Nov. 17, 27, 1871, to CCC, *ibid.*

NINE—First Year as Governor

[1] CCC Diary, Jan. 1–3, 1872, *Carpenter Papers.*

[2] *Bushnell's Des Moines City Directory . . .* (Des Moines: J. P. Bushnell & Co., Publishers, 1874), 50, 145. Carpenter's address is given as the northwest corner of East Court and Eleventh. The statehouse was on East Walnut, between Eleventh and Twelfth Streets.

[3] CCC Diary, Jan. 7, 1872, *Carpenter Papers.*

[4] This story is told by Mills in "The Des Moines *Register,"* 283, and is attributed to Ora Williams, longtime curator of the Iowa State Department of History and Archives and a friend of the Clarksons. For James S. Clarkson's own account of this incident, see "James S. Clarkson's Letter on Allison's 1872 Election," *Iowa Journal of History,* 57:74–85 (Jan. 1959), a reprint of a letter originally published in the Des Moines *Register,* Jan. 24, 1909. See also Sage, *Allison,* 111–12.

[5] Dubuque *Herald,* Aug. 9, 1871.

[6] Iowa City *Iowa State Press,* July 5, 1871; Dubuque *Herald,* quoted in Fort Dodge *Iowa North West,* July 6, 1871.

[7] Dubuque *Herald,* July 12, 1871, Jan. 24, 1872; Fort Dodge *Iowa North West,* July 20, 1871. For accounts of the Harlan-Allison contest, see Clark, *History of Senatorial Elections in Iowa,* Chap. X; Johnson Brigham, *James Harlan* (Iowa City: State Historical Society of Iowa, 1913), Chap. XIV; Sage, *Allison,* Chap. VIII.

[8] For a complete study of Allison, see Sage, *Allison.*

[9] Dubuque *Herald,* Dec. 20, 1871.

[10] Iowa City *Iowa State Press,* Jan. 10, 17, 1872.

[11] *Ibid.,* Jan. 17, 1872.

[12] CCC Diary, Jan. 10, 18, 19, 1872, *Carpenter Papers.*

[13] CCC to Harlan, Feb. 16, 1872, Letterbook A, 190, *ibid.*

[14] *House Journal, 1872,* 87–88; Iowa City *Iowa State Press,* Jan. 24, 1872.

[15] CCC Diary, Jan. 11, 1872, *Carpenter Papers.*

[16] Shambaugh (ed.), *Messages and Proclamations,* 4:5–30.

[17] See Ross, "Powers of the Governor of Iowa," 129–40.

[18] Johnson Brigham, *Iowa, Its History and Its Foremost Citizens* (3 vols., Chicago: The S. J. Clarke Publishing Company, 1915), 1:432.

[19] Dolliver, "Ex-Governor Cyrus C. Carpenter," 78–79.

[20] Letters to CCC from Aldrich, Jan. 29, 1872, Grinnell, Jan. 13, 1872, Palmer, Jan. 20, 1872, John Kennedy, Jan. 18, 1872, G. W. Chapman, Jan. 22, 1872, Wm. L. Smith, Jan. 23, 1872, D. A. Mahony, Jan. 20, 1872, *Carpenter Papers.*

[21] Mahony to CCC, Jan. 20, 1872; CCC Diary, Jan. 13, 1872, *ibid.;* Iowa City *Iowa State Press,* Jan. 17, 1872; Dubuque *Herald,* Jan. 24, 1872.

[22] Letters to CCC from I. J. Mitchell and C. W. Lowrie, Feb. 3, 1872; CCC to

Mitchell, Feb. 7, 1872, Letterbook A, 168–69, *Carpenter Papers.*

[23] Dodge to CCC, Jan. 23, 1872; CCC to Dodge, Jan. 26, Feb. 1, 1872, Letterbook A, 102–03, 130, and to Baldwin, July 24, 1873, Letterbook D, 158–59, *ibid.*

[24] CCC Diary, Feb. 13, 15, 1872, *ibid.* For biographical sketch of O'Connor, see Gue, *History of Iowa*, 4:203–04.

[25] M. E. Cutts to CCC, Feb. 15, 1872; CCC Diary, Feb. 16, 1872, *Carpenter Papers.*

[26] Letters to CCC from Aldrich, Feb. 27, 1872; Harlan, Feb. 19, 1872; CCC to Wright, Feb. 24, 1872, Letterbook A, 219–20, *ibid.*

[27] CCC to Cutts, Feb. 23, 1872, and to Harlan, Feb. 24, 1872, Letterbook A, 210–12, 227; CCC Diary, Feb. 24, 1872, *ibid.;* Younger, *Kasson,* 234.

[28] J. D. Wright to CCC, March 13[?], 1872; CCC to Wright, March 18, 1872, and to C. C. Cole, March 15, 1872, Letterbook A, 266–70, 285; CCC Diary, March 14, 1872, *Carpenter Papers.* CCC to Kirkwood, Dec. 27, 1871, No. 1556, Box 4, *Samuel J. Kirkwood Papers* (Iowa State Department of History and Archives, Des Moines). I am grateful to Leland Sage for bringing this letter to my attention.

[29] CCC to Henderson, Aug. 9, 1872, Letterbook B, 130–31, *Carpenter Papers.*

[30] B. F. Reno to CCC, Jan. 12, 1872; CCC Diary, Jan. 17, 1872, *ibid.*

[31] Dubuque *Herald,* quoted in Osage *Mitchell County Press,* March 7, 1872.

[32] Marshalltown *Marshall County Times,* March 14, 1872.

[33] Members of the House and Senate are listed in *Laws of Iowa, 1872,* vii–x.

[34] Younger, *Kasson,* 74–249; Edward Younger, "The Education of John A. Kasson," *Iowa Journal of History,* 49:289–310 (Oct. 1951). For committees in the House of the 14th General Assembly, see *House Journal, 1872,* 89–91.

[35] See Mildred Throne, "The Grange in Iowa, 1868–1875," and "The Repeal of the Iowa Granger Law, 1878," *Iowa Journal of History,* 47:289–324 (Oct. 1949); 51:97–130 (Apr. 1953).

[36] Beard, "Background of State Railroad Regulation in Iowa," 2, 5–6.

[37] Constitution of 1857, Article VIII, Sec. 12, in Shambaugh (ed.), *Documentary Material,* 1:245.

[38] Beard, "Background of State Railroad Regulation in Iowa," 22–24.

[39] Iowa City *Iowa State Press,* Feb. 28, 1872.

[40] *Laws of Iowa, 1862,* Chap. 173; *1868,* Chap. 196; *1870,* Chap. 106.

[41] George H. Miller, "Origins of the Iowa Granger Law," *Mississippi Valley Historical Review,* 40:657–80 (March 1954); Throne, "Repeal of the Iowa Granger Law, 1878," 97–130; and Beard, "Background of State Railroad Regulation in Iowa," 1–36.

[42] Ottumwa *Weekly Courier,* March 14, 1872.

[43] *Laws of Iowa, 1872,* Chap. 69.

[44] Shambaugh (ed.), *Messages and Proclamations,* 3:369; 4:24–26.

[45] Iowa City *Iowa State Press,* Jan. 24, 1872. For Republican platform, see Fairall, *Manual of Iowa Politics,* Part I, 87.

[46] Iowa City *Daily Press,* March 14, 1872.

[47] *House Journal, 1872,* 421–26.

[48] Des Moines *Register,* Apr. 14, 1872, *Senate Journal, 1872,* 460–61.

[49] Burlington *Hawk-Eye,* quoted in Des Moines *Register,* March 19, Apr. 10, 1872; Iowa City *Daily Press,* March 14, 1872; Dubuque *Herald,* March 20, 1872.

[50] Marshalltown *Marshall County Times,* March 28, 1872.

[51] A. W. Brownlie to CCC, Jan. 30, 1872; CCC to Brownlie, Feb. 1, 1872, Letterbook A, 133, *Carpenter Papers.*

[52] Ottumwa *Weekly Courier,* Feb. 22, 1872.

[53] *House Journal, 1872,* 433; Iowa City *Daily Press,* March 15, 1872.

[54] Dubuque *Herald,* March 27, Apr. 17, 1872.

[55] *House Journal, 1872,* 485–87; *Senate Journal, 1872,* 413–16; Des Moines *Register,* March 20, 21, 22, 29, Apr. 4, 5, 6, 10, 18, 20, 1872; Iowa City *Daily Press,* March 20, 21, 27, Apr. 8, 10, 1872.

[56] *Iowa Homestead and Western Farm Journal,* 17:161 (May 24, 1872).

[57] Younger, *Kasson,* 245–46, 255–64.

[58] *House Journal, 1872,* 317–18; *Senate Journal, 1872,* 632–34.

[59] CCC Diary, March 9, 21, 22, 25, 28, Apr. 2, 3, 4, 1872, *Carpenter Papers.* For an account of the murder, see W. O. Payne, *History of Story County, Iowa . . .* (2 vols., Chicago: The S. J. Clarke Publishing Co., 1911), 1:328–31.

[60] CCC to Rev. P. M. Delaney, March 22, 1872, Letterbook A, 302–06, *Carpenter Papers.*

[61] *Laws of Iowa, 1872,* Chap. 242. This law was abolished and capital punishment restored in 1880. See *Laws of Iowa, 1880,* Chap. 2. In 1902, Stanley received a full pardon, Payne, *History of Story County,* 1:330–31.

[62] CCC Diary, Apr. 9, 1872, *Carpenter Papers.*

[63] Indianola *Warren County Leader,* Apr. 25, 1872; Des Moines *Register,* Apr. 21, 1872.

[64] CCC Diary, Apr. 23, 1872, *Carpenter Papers.*

[65] *Daily Davenport Democrat,* March 28, 1872.

[66] Salter, *Grimes,* 386–87.

[67] CCC Diary, Feb. 8, 1872, *Carpenter Papers.*

[68] Des Moines *Register,* May 20, 1868, Feb. 9, 1872.

[69] *Ibid.,* Feb. 24, 1872; CCC Diary, Feb. 10, 1872, *Carpenter Papers;* Burlington *Hawk-Eye,* Feb. 13, 1872.

[70] *Senate Journal, 1872,* 331–33; Des Moines *Register,* March 16, 1872.

[71] Iowa City *Iowa State Press,* March 20, 1872.

[72] Grinnell to CCC, Jan. 13, 1872, *Carpenter Papers;* Grinnell letter of Jan. 20, 1872, in Marshalltown *Marshall County Times,* Feb. 8, 1872.

[73] See Mildred Throne, "The Liberal Republican Party in Iowa, 1872," *Iowa Journal of History,* 53:121–52 (Apr. 1955), for the detailed story of this period.

[74] Des Moines *Register,* March 23, 1872.

[75] The call for the convention appeared in the Des Moines *Register,* Feb. 25, 1872. See also Elkader *Journal,* Feb. 28, 1872, for criticism of the call.

[76] CCC Diary, March 22, 1872, *Carpenter Papers.* Grinnell's speech was printed in full in the Ottumwa *Democrat,* Apr. 4, 1872. See also Des Moines *Register,* March 23, 1872; Ottumwa *Democrat,* March 28, 1872. Clarkson took occasion, in his comments on the speech, to point out at least four times that Grinnell read from a manuscript.

[77] Throne, "Liberal Republican Party in Iowa," 130–41.

[78] CCC to Aldrich, May 13, 1872, Letterbook A, 480–82, *Carpenter Papers.*

[79] CCC Diary, June 4, 1872, *ibid.;* Des Moines *Register,* June 5, 1872. For full story of the Wilson boom see Sage, *Allison,* 117–18.

[80] Throne, "Liberal Republican Party in Iowa," 141–43.

[81] CCC Diary, Sept. 9–Nov. 5, 1872, *passim, Carpenter Papers.*

[82] Notebook of Carpenter speeches, *ibid.*

[83] Webster City *Hamilton Freeman,* Oct. 9, 1872.

[84] Throne, "Liberal Republican Party in Iowa," 147–49.

[85] Rich to CCC, Nov. 9, 1872; CCC to Rich, Nov. 16, 1872, Letterbook B, 297–98, *Carpenter Papers.*

[86] Keokuk *Daily Gate City*, Jan. 29, 1873; CCC Diary, Nov. 5–Dec. 30, 1872, *passim, Carpenter Papers.*

TEN—Scandal and Politics in 1873

[1] Merrill testimony before Rankin investigating committee, Elkader *Journal*, Feb. 12, 1873.

[2] Carpenter testimony in Keokuk *Weekly Gate City*, Jan. 29, 1873; Des Moines (Daily) *Register*, Jan. 24, 1873; CCC Diary, Dec. 12, 1872, *Carpenter Papers.*

[3] CCC Diary, Dec. 15, 1872, *Carpenter Papers.*

[4] See Des Moines (Daily) *Register*, Dec. 31, 1872, for first publication of the affair. Thereafter, during January and into February (until publication of the report of committee on Feb. 14), each issue of the paper was full of the Rankin investigation. Other papers gave it more or less space, such as Elkader *Journal*, Indianola *Warren County Leader*, Iowa City *Press*, Keokuk *Gate City*, Davenport *Democrat*, Dubuque *Herald*, etc. Some reports, such as those in the Elkader *Journal*, seem much fuller than those in the *Register*, especially in the case of Gov. Merrill's testimony. That something was being covered up is obvious.

[5] Des Moines (Daily) *Register*, Dec. 31, 1872; Jan. 22, 1873.

[6] *Ibid.*, Feb. 2, 4, 1873.

[7] CCC Diary, Feb. 1, 1873, *Carpenter Papers.*

[8] CCC to M. E. Cutts, Feb. 3, 1873, Letterbook C, 98–9, *ibid.* The letter was published in the Des Moines (Daily) *Register*, Feb. 5, 1873. Notice of discovery of the bond had already appeared in the issue of Feb. 2, 1873.

[9] Des Moines (Daily) *Register*, Feb. 5, 1873.

[10] *Weekly Davenport Democrat*, Feb. 13, 1873.

[11] Des Moines (Daily) *Register*, Dec. 31, 1872; CCC Diary, Dec. 31, 1872; CCC to Seward Smith, July 7, 1875, Letterbook H, 147–50, *Carpenter Papers.*

[12] *Patrons of Husbandry . . . Proceedings . . . for the Year 1872 . . .* (Des Moines: Iowa Homestead Steam Print, 1873), 23–24. See Throne, "The Grange in Iowa, 1868–1875," 289–324.

[13] *Report . . . Iowa State Agricultural Society . . . 1872* (Des Moines: G. W. Edwards, State Printer, 1873), 194–95.

[14] Norman V. Strand, "Prices of Farm Products in Iowa, 1851–1940," *Agricultural Experiment Station Research Bulletin 303* (Vol. 25, Agricultural Research Bulletins, Ames, Iowa, May 1942), 959–61.

[15] *Report . . . Iowa State Agricultural Society . . . 1872*, 194–216, *passim.*

[16] CCC Diary, Dec. 22, 24, 1872; Jan. 2, 5, 6, 7, 8, 1873, *Carpenter Papers.*

[17] Clarkson to CCC, Jan. 10, 1873, *ibid.*

[18] *Ibid.;* CCC Diary, Jan. 9, 1873, *Carpenter Papers;* Des Moines (Daily) *Register*, Jan. 9, 10, 1873.

[19] CCC Diary, Sept. 15, 1873, *Carpenter Papers.*

[20] *Senate Journal, 1873*, 125; *Patrons of Husbandry . . . Proceedings . . . for the Year 1872. . .* , 23–24.

[21] Des Moines (Daily) *Register*, Feb. 11, 1873; Iowa City *Press*, Feb. 14, 1873; Webster City *Hamilton Freeman*, Feb. 19, 1873. For progress of bill through the General Assembly, see Senate File 9 in *House* and *Senate Journals* for 1873.

[22] Letter quoted in *Senate Journal, 1873,* 241, and in Burlington (Daily) *Hawk-Eye,* Feb. 19, 1873.

[23] Biographical sketch of B. F. Allen in L. F. Andrews, *Pioneers of Polk County, Iowa* . . . (2 vols., Des Moines: Baker-Trisler Company, 1908), 1:55–65.

[24] Burlington (Daily) *Hawk-Eye,* Feb. 19, 1873.

[25] *Senate Journal, 1873,* 256–57; CCC Diary, Feb. 14, 1873, *Carpenter Papers.*

[26] Des Moines (Daily) *Register,* Feb. 16, 18, 21; Council Bluffs *Daily Nonpareil,* Feb. 16, 1873.

[27] CCC Diary, Feb. 15, 1873, *Carpenter Papers.*

[28] Burlington (Daily) *Hawk-Eye,* Feb. 16, 1873.

[29] Des Moines (Daily) *Register,* Feb. 18, 1873. For a biographical sketch of Graves, see *History of Dubuque County, Iowa* . . . (Chicago: Western Historical Company, 1880), 795–96.

[30] Des Moines *Register,* Feb. 21, 1873; Council Bluffs *Daily Nonpareil,* Feb. 18, 1873.

[31] CCC Diary, Feb. 17, 1873, *Carpenter Papers.*

[32] Des Moines (Daily) *Register,* Feb. 6, 1873.

[33] Belle Plaine *Union,* Jan. 30, 1873; Wayne County *Republican* quoted in Centerville *Weekly Citizen,* March 8, 1873.

[34] CCC Diary, Jan. 27, 1873, *Carpenter Papers.*

[35] William Duane Wilson to CCC, Apr. 3, 1873; CCC Diary, Apr. 9, 11, 1873, *ibid.*

[36] CCC to Emmett, June 14, 1873, Letterbook D, 50–53, *ibid.*

[37] Letter from D. W. Adams to President of Waterloo Association of Granges, dated Waukon, Apr. 16, 1873, published in Waukon *Standard,* Apr. 24, 1873. Waterloo meeting reported in *The Iowa Homestead and Western Farm Journal,* Apr. 11, 1873, 117.

[38] Aldrich to CCC, Apr. 1, 9, 1873; CCC to Aldrich, Apr. 11, 1873, Letterbook C, 406, *Carpenter Papers.*

[39] CCC to Jacob Rich, Apr. 12, 1873, Letterbook C, 405, *ibid.*

[40] CCC to Arthur T. Reeve, Apr. 15, 1873, and to Elijah Sells, March 20, 1873, Letterbook C, 419, 296, *ibid.*

[41] CCC Diary, March 15, 17, 1873, *ibid.*

[42] Rich to CCC, Apr. 9, 1873; CCC to Rich, Apr. 12, 1873, Letterbook C, 405, *ibid.*

[43] Des Moines (Daily) *Register,* May 7, 1873. For Anti-Monopoly party, see Mildred Throne, "Anti-Monopoly Party in Iowa, 1873–1874," *Iowa Journal of History,* 52:289–326 (Oct. 1954).

[44] Des Moines (Daily) *Register,* June 8, 1873; Belle Plaine *Union,* July 17, 1873; Newton *Free Press,* June 18, 1873.

[45] Des Moines (Daily) *Register,* Aug. 14, 1873.

[46] CCC Diary, Aug. 13, 1873; CCC to Emmett, Aug. 8, 1873, Letterbook D, 200, *Carpenter Papers.*

[47] Des Moines (Daily) *Register,* June 26, 1873; Centerville *Weekly Citizen,* June 27, 1873; CCC Diary, June 25, 1873, *Carpenter Papers.*

[48] CCC to Rich, Apr. 24, 1873, Letterbook C, 443–44, *Carpenter Papers.* Account of Republican convention in Centerville *Weekly Citizen,* June 27, 1873.

[49] Throne, "Anti-Monopoly Party in Iowa," 289–326, *passim.* See also Horace Merrill, *Bourbon Democracy of the Middle West, 1865–1896* (Baton Rouge, La.: Louisiana State University Press, 1953), *passim.*

[50] CCC Diary, Aug. 28, 1873, *Carpenter Papers.*

[51] R. H. Dutton to CCC, Aug. 8, 1873, *ibid.*

[52] A. H. Neidig to CCC, Aug. 1, 9, 1873, *ibid.*

[53] CCC Diary, 1873; Dutton to CCC, Oct. 17, 1873, *ibid.* Fairall, *Manual of Iowa Politics,* 88, 93. For official vote for Governor in 1873, see *Rules of Fifteenth General Assembly of . . . Iowa* (Des Moines: R. P. Clarkson, State Printer, 1874), 30–32. Carpenter received 105,132 votes; Vale, 81,035. Des Moines (Daily) *Register,* Oct. 24, 1873 has a breakdown by county of Carpenter's majorities.

[54] Throne, "Anti-Monopoly Party in Iowa," 312–13.

[55] Voting totals for 1872 in *Census of Iowa . . . 1873* (Des Moines: R. P. Clarkson, State Printer, 1874), 74–80; for 1873, *Rules of Fifteenth General Assembly,* 30–32.

[56] Throne, "Anti-Monopoly Party in Iowa," 314–15.

[57] CCC to Emmett, Oct. 18, 1873, Letterbook D, 312–15, *Carpenter Papers.*

[58] CCC to Atlantic Publishing Co., Oct. 31, 1973, Letterbook D, 353, *ibid.*

[59] Council Bluffs *Daily Nonpareil,* Nov. 16, 18, 1873.

[60] *Ibid.,* Nov. 20, 1873; *Report of . . . Adjutant General . . . of the State of Iowa . . . January 1, 1873, to January 1, 1874* (Des Moines: R. P. Clarkson, State Printer, 1874), 23–29, hereafter cited as *Adjutant General's Report, 1873–74;* Carpenter's 1874 message in Shambaugh (ed.), *Messages and Proclamations,* 4:44–46.

[61] Council Bluffs *Nonpareil,* Nov. 19, 1873.

[62] *Adjutant General's Report, 1874,* 27.

[63] CCC Diary, Nov. 18, 1873, *Carpenter Papers;* Shambaugh (ed.), *Messages and Proclamations,* 4:45–46.

[64] Council Bluffs *Daily Nonpareil,* Nov. 19, 1873.

[65] Shambaugh (ed.), *Messages and Proclamations,* 4:46; *House Journal, 1874,* 233, 368. A law making prize fighting illegal in Iowa was passed by the 25th General Assembly in 1894 and is still a part of the Iowa Code, *Laws of Iowa, 1894,* Chap. 97.

[66] Cedar Rapids *Republican,* quoted in Indianola *Warren County Leader,* Dec. 4, 1873; Council Bluffs *Daily Nonpareil,* Nov. 20, 21, 1873.

[67] Strand, "Prices of Farm Products in Iowa, 1851–1940," 955–75.

[68] CCC Diary, Dec. 31, 1873, *Carpenter Papers.*

ELEVEN—The Iowa Granger Law of 1874

[1] Estherville *Vindicator,* Jan. 31, 1874; Iowa City *Daily Press,* Jan. 13, 1874.

[2] *House Journal, 1874,* 9; Iowa City *Daily Press,* Jan. 14, 1874.

[3] *House Journal, 1874,* 9–48.

[4] Keokuk *Weekly Gate City,* Jan. 28, 1874; Iowa City *Press,* Jan. 14, 1874.

[5] CCC Diary, Jan. 21, 23, 1874, *Carpenter Papers.*

[6] Compilation of editorial comment in Iowa City *Daily Press,* Jan. 30, 1874.

[7] Throne, "Anti-Monopoly Party in Iowa," 322–26.

[8] CCC Diary, Jan. 27, 1874, *Carpenter Papers;* Des Moines *Register,* Jan. 30, 1874; Iowa City *Daily Press,* Jan. 28, 1874.

[9] CCC Diary, Jan. 28, 1874, *Carpenter Papers.*

[10] Shambaugh (ed.), *Messages and Proclamations,* 4:104–23.

[11] Des Moines *Register,* Jan. 30, 1874.

[12] CCC Diary, Jan. 27, 1874, *Carpenter Papers;* Des Moines *Register,* Jan. 30, 1874; Keokuk *Weekly Gate City,* Feb. 4, 1874; Webster City *Hamilton Freeman,* Jan. 28, 1874.

[13] CCC Diary, Jan. 17, 1874, *Carpenter Papers.*

[14] Shambaugh (ed.), *Messages and Proclamations*, 4:90–91.

[15] From compilation of information on members in the *Rules* of the 1872, 1874, and 1876 General Assemblies.

[16] CCC Diary, Feb. 5, 1874, *Carpenter Papers;* Shambaugh (ed.), *Messages and Proclamations*, 4:231–43.

[17] Burlington *Weekly Hawk-Eye*, Feb. 5, 1874; *Rules of the Fifteenth General Assembly, 1874*, 23–24.

[18] *Rules of the Fifteenth General Assembly, 1874.*

[19] Iowa City *Press*, Feb. 6, 10, 1874; Throne, "Repeal of the Iowa Granger Law, 1878," 98.

[20] *Senate Journal, 1874*, 138, 198–219.

[21] *House Journal, 1874*, 328, 333–34, 344–51, 388–404; Keokuk *Weekly Gate City*, Feb. 18, 1874.

[22] CCC to Milo Smith, March 11, 1874, Letterbook E, 153, *Carpenter Papers.*

[23] Keokuk *Weekly Gate City*, March 4, 1874.

[24] CCC Diary, March 23, 1874, *Carpenter Papers.*

[25] Iowa City *Press*, Feb. 28, 1874; Burlington *Weekly Hawk-Eye*, March 12, 1874; Waukon *Standard*, March 19, 1874; Estherville *Vindicator*, Apr. 4, 1874.

[26] Des Moines *Register*, March 27, 1874.

[27] See Beard, "Background of State Railroad Regulation in Iowa," 1–36; Throne, "Grange in Iowa, 1868–1875," 289–324, and "Repeal of the Iowa Granger Law, 1878," 97–130; Miller, "Origins of the Iowa Granger Law," 657–80.

[28] Estherville *Vindicator*, March 28, 1874.

[29] In the House, the four who voted against the bill were: Samuel B. Gilliland (representing Woodbury, Plymouth, Sioux, and Lyon counties); Eldin J. Hartshorn (Pocahontas, Buena Vista, Palo Alto, Emmet); James N. Miller (Greene, Carroll, Calhoun, Sac); and Henry B. Wood (Clay, Dickinson, Osceola, O'Brien). All four were Republicans. Coming as they did from sparsely populated western Iowa, their districts covered a wider geographical area than their numbers would indicate. *House Journal, 1874*, 404. In the Senate, the nine voting against the bill were: George W. Bemis (Buchanan); William H. Fitch (Dickinson, Emmet, Clay, Palo Alto, Buena Vista, Pocahontas, Ida, Sac, Calhoun, Webster); William Larrabee (Fayette); Joseph H. Merrill (Wapello); George D. Perkins (Lyon, Osceola, O'Brien, Sioux, Plymouth, Cherokee, Woodbury, Monona, Harrison); John J. Russell (Greene, Carroll, Crawford, Shelby, Audubon, Guthrie); John Y. Stone (Pottawattamie, Mills); Horatio A. Wonn (Davis); and James A. Young (Mahaska). All but Wonn were Republicans. *Senate Journal, 1874*, 219.

[30] For a biographical sketch of Larrabee, see Gue, *History of Iowa*, 4:163. Waukon *Standard*, March 19, 1874; Des Moines *Register*, March 6, 1874.

[31] *Laws of Iowa, 1874*, Chap. 68, Sec. 7.

[32] Dubuque *Times*, quoted in Des Moines *Register*, Apr. 17, 1874.

[33] Des Moines *Register*, May 8, 1874.

[34] *Ibid.*, May 15, 1874.

[35] CCC Diary, June 3, 1874, *Carpenter Papers.*

[36] Clarkson to CCC, June 9, 1874, *ibid.*

[37] New York *Bulletin*, quoted in Waukon *Standard*, June 18, 1874.

[38] Des Moines *Register*, June 19, 1874.

[39] Riddle to CCC, June 29, 1874, quoted in *ibid.*, July 3, 1874.

[40] Albert Keep (telegram), July 5, 1874, John Given (telegram), July 3, 1874, to CCC; CCC to James Grant, July 7, 1874, Letterbook F, 35–37, *Carpenter Papers.* See

also Keokuk *Weekly Gate City,* July 8, 15, 1874; Des Moines *Register,* July 10, 1874.

[41] Des Moines *Register,* July 24, 1874.

[42] See George H. Miller, "Chicago, Burlington and Quincy Railroad Company *v.* Iowa," *Iowa Journal of History,* 54:289–312 (Oct. 1956), for a discussion of this lawsuit and a new interpretation of the "Granger" cases.

[43] Chicago *Tribune,* July 7, 1874, quoted in Muscatine *Journal,* July 10, 1874; Keokuk *Weekly Gate City,* July 15, 1874. See also Throne, "Repeal of the Iowa Granger Law, 1878," 104.

[44] CCC to John Teesdale, Nov. 28, 1874, Letterbook G, 67, *Carpenter Papers; Laws of Iowa, 1874,* Chap. 68, Sec. 8.

[45] Des Moines *Register,* Nov. 13, 1874.

[46] Miller, "Chicago, Burlington and Quincy Railroad Company *v.* Iowa," 301–03.

[47] *Ibid.,* 303–04; Des Moines *Register,* May 21, 1875.

[48] CCC to John Porter, May 21, 1875, Letterbook H, 67–68, *Carpenter Papers.*

[49] Miller, "Chicago, Burlington and Quincy Railroad Company *v.* Iowa," 304.

[50] Des Moines *Register,* March 9, 1877. For the case of CB&Q *v.* Iowa, see 94 *U. S. Reports,* 155–64.

[51] See Throne, "Repeal of the Iowa Granger Law, 1878," 97–130.

[52] For a brilliant discussion of this interpretation of the "Granger" cases, see Miller, "Chicago, Burlington and Quincy Railroad Company *v.* Iowa," 289–312.

TWELVE—Last Years as Governor

[1] Seward Smith, July 5, 1875, and J. E. Williams, July 16, 1875, to CCC; CCC to Smith, July 7, 1875, and to Williams, July 16, 1875, Letterbook H, 147–50, 169–70; CCC Diary, Mar. 26, 1874, July 7, 16, 17, 1875, *Carpenter Papers.* Des Moines *Register,* July 23, Aug. 20, 1875.

[2] CCC Diary, March 28, 1874, *Carpenter Papers.*

[3] CCC Diary, Apr. 2, 1874; Cutts to CCC, Apr. 3, 1874, *ibid.*

[4] Iowa City *Daily Press,* Apr. 3, 1874; Des Moines *Register,* Apr. 10, 1874; Fort Dodge *Messenger,* Apr. 9, 1874; CCC Diary, Apr. 7, 8, June 2, 1874, *Carpenter Papers.*

[5] Des Moines *Journal,* quoted in Dubuque *Times,* Apr. 15, 1874.

[6] CCC Diary, June 20, 1874, *Carpenter Papers.*

[7] Des Moines *Register,* Apr. 10, Nov. 27, 1874.

[8] Dubuque *Weekly Times,* Apr. 28, 1875; Des Moines *Register,* May 7, 1875; CCC Diary, Apr. 8, 1874, *Carpenter Papers.*

[9] Iowa City *Daily Press,* Sept. 8, 1875; Des Moines *Register,* Sept. 10, 1875; Dubuque *Weekly Times,* Sept. 15, 22, 1875; State *v.* Brandt, 41, *Iowa Reports,* 593–632; CCC Diary, Apr. 9, 1874, *Carpenter Papers.*

[10] Cutts to CCC, Oct. 16, 1875; CCC to Cutts, Oct. 14, 1875, Letterbook H, 336–37, *Carpenter Papers;* State *v.* Brandt, 632–49; Iowa City *Daily Press,* May 8, 1875; Des Moines *Register,* Sept. 17, 24, Dec. 17, 1875.

[11] Des Moines *Register,* May 7, 14, 1875; CCC to Emmett, Apr. 28, 1875, Letterbook H, 25–26, *Carpenter Papers.*

[12] Ottumwa *Democrat,* Jan. 1, 1874; Clinton *Age,* Jan. 9, 1874.

[13] Iowa City *Iowa Anti-Monopolist,* Jan. 17, 1874. For a biographical sketch of Sehorn, see *History of Iowa County, Iowa* . . . (Des Moines: Union Historical Company, Birdsall, Williams & Co., 1881), 536.

[14] Des Moines *Register*, Feb. 27, 1874; manuscript of "Campaign Speech, 1874," in *Carpenter Papers*.

[15] CCC to Aldrich, March 20, 1874, to Neidig, Apr. 24, 1874, to M. D. O'Connell, May 12, 1874, to R. G. Orwig, May 18, 1874, to M. A. Knight, May 24, 1874, Letterbook E, 165, 214, 249–52, 261, 271–72, *Carpenter Papers*.

[16] Gear to CCC, May 1, 1874; CCC to Gear, May 4, 1874, Letterbook E, 234, *ibid.*

[17] CCC Diary, July 26, Aug. 5, 1874, *ibid.;* Des Moines *Register*, Aug. 7, 14, 28, 1874. For the Clarkson feud with Kasson and the libel suit, see Younger, *Kasson*, 256–64, 267–69.

[18] CCC Diary, Sept. 7, 1874, *Carpenter Papers*.

[19] CCC Diary, Sept. 14–Oct. 13, 1874. See also manuscript of "Campaign Speech, 1874," *ibid.*

[20] Des Moines *Register*, Nov. 20, 1874. For biographical sketches of Ainsworth, Donnan, and Granger, see Gue, *History of Iowa*, 4:3, 79, 107.

[21] Ottumwa *Democrat*, Oct. 15, 1874; Clinton *Age*, Oct. 23, 1874.

[22] Iowa City *Daily Press*, Oct. 25, 1874; Iowa City *Iowa Anti-Monopolist*, Oct. 22, 1874.

[23] Ottumwa *Democrat*, Apr. 8, 1875.

[24] Call for convention in Iowa City *Press*, May 12, 13, 1875; report of convention, Ottumwa *Democrat*, July 1, 1875.

[25] For platform, see Iowa City *Press*, July 2, 1875; Fairall, *Manual of Iowa Politics*, Part I, 97–98. For a biographical sketch of Leffler, see Gue, *History of Iowa*, 4:167.

[26] For the complete story of this nomination see Leland L. Sage, "Weaver in Allison's Way," *Annals of Iowa* (3rd ser.), 31:485–507 (Jan. 1953).

[27] *Ibid.*, 493–94; Des Moines *Register*, July 2, 1875; for call of the convention see Dubuque *Weekly Times*, May 9, 1875.

[28] CCC Diary, June 30, 1875, *Carpenter Papers*.

[29] CCC to Judd, Feb. 10, 1874, Letterbook E, 101, *ibid.*

[30] Letters to CCC from Al Swalm, March 9, 1875, H. C. Van Leuven, March 6, 1875, M. D. O'Connell, March 13, 1875, and Emmett, March 9, 1875, *ibid.*

[31] CCC to Van Leuven, March 9, 1875, and to O'Connell, March 22, 1875, Letterbook G, 204, 220–21; CCC Diary, March 15, 1875, *ibid.*

[32] CCC Diary, March 20, 1875; CCC to W. T. Clark, Sept. 9, 1875, Letterbook H, 275, *ibid.*

[33] Des Moines *Register*, Aug. 27, 1875; CCC Diary, Aug. 18, 1875, *Carpenter Papers*.

[34] CCC Diary, Dec. 14, 1875; Harlan to CCC, Dec. 13, 1875, *Carpenter Papers*.

[35] CCC to Harlan, Dec. 15, 1875, Letterbook I, 23–24, *ibid.*

[36] Harlan to CCC, Dec. 25, 1875; CCC to Harlan, Dec. 28, 1875, Letterbook I, 43–44; CCC Diary, Dec. 27, 1875, *ibid.*

[37] CCC Diary, Dec. 30, 31, 1875; Allison, Dec. 30, 31, 1875, Emmett, Dec. 31, 1875, to CCC; CCC to Allison (2 telegrams), Dec. 31, 1875, and to Emmett, Dec. 31, 1875, Letterbook I, 49, 54, *ibid.*

[38] Belknap, Jan. 2, 1876, Lowe, Jan. 2, 1876, and Aldrich, Dec. 31, 1875, to CCC, *ibid.*

[39] CCC Diary, Dec. 31, 1875, *ibid.*

[40] Dubuque *Weekly Times*, Jan. 5, 1876; Burlington *Gazette*, quoted in *ibid.*, Jan. 12, 1876; letter from "15th Army Corps" in Des Moines (Daily) *Register*, Jan. 12, 1876; Missouri Valley *Times*, quoted in Des Moines (Weekly) *Register*, Jan. 14, 1876.

[41] Des Moines *Register*, Jan. 14, 1876.

[42] Wright to CCC, Jan. 5, 1876, *Carpenter Papers.*

[43] Allison to CCC, Jan. 3, 7, 1876 (telegrams), *ibid.*

[44] Shambaugh (ed.), *Messages and Proclamations,* 4:174.

[45] Des Moines *Register,* Jan. 14, 1876; Iowa City *Daily Press,* Jan. 13, 1876; CCC Diary, Jan. 4, 7, 8, 1876, *Carpenter Papers;* Sage, *Allison,* 140–41.

[46] Des Moines *Register,* Jan. 21 (weekly), 22 (daily), 1876; Arthur Burkholder to CCC, Jan. 25, 1876, *Carpenter Papers.*

THIRTEEN—Election to Congress

[1] CCC Diary, March 15, May 1, 1876, *Carpenter Papers.*

[2] CCC Diary, Feb. 16, 1876, *ibid.*

[3] CCC Diary, Jan. 24, 25, 1876, *ibid.*

[4] *Congressional Directory,* 44 Cong., 2 sess. (Washington: Government Printing Office, 1877), 112.

[5] CCC Diary, March 2, 1876, *Carpenter Papers.*

[6] For the Belknap scandal, see Philip D. Jordan, "The Domestic Finances of Secretary of War W. W. Belknap," *Iowa Journal of History,* 52:193–202 (July 1954); Robert C. Prickett, "The Malfeasance of William Worth Belknap," *North Dakota History,* 17:5–51, 97–134 (Jan., Apr. 1950). For a biographical sketch of Belknap, see *DAB,* 2:147–48.

[7] The Committee consisted of Democrats Hiester Clymer of Pennsylvania (chairman), William McK. Robbins of North Carolina, and Joseph C. S. Blackburn of Kentucky; and Republicans Lyman K. Bass of New York and Lorenzo Danford of Ohio. *Congressional Record,* 44 Cong., 1 sess., 251.

[8] For details of the Belknap impeachment and trial, see "Trial of William W. Belknap," *Congressional Record,* 44 Cong., 1 sess., Vol. 4, Part 7.

[9] CCC Diary, March 5, 7, 1876, *Carpenter Papers.*

[10] Allan Nevins, *Hamilton Fish, The Inner History of the Grant Administration* (New York: Dodd, Mead & Company, 1936), 811.

[11] CCC Diary, Apr. 19, May 22, 1876, *Carpenter Papers;* Nevins, *Fish,* 831–33.

[12] CCC Diary, June 2, 1876, *Carpenter Papers.*

[13] CCC Diary, June 3, 6, 1876, *ibid.* For Blaine and the 1876 nomination, see Charles Edward Russell, *Blaine of Maine, His Life and Times* (New York: Cosmopolitan Book Corporation, 1931), 287–91; Edward Stanwood, *James Gillespie Blaine* (Boston: Houghton Mifflin Company, 1905), 145–76.

[14] CCC Diary, June 16, 1876, *Carpenter Papers.*

[15] CCC Diary, Jan. 24, June 19, 21, 1876, *ibid.*

[16] Des Moines *Register,* May 5, 19, June 2, 1876; CCC Diary, May 29, June 6, 1876, *Carpenter Papers.*

[17] CCC Diary, June 19, 1876, *Carpenter Papers.*

[18] Henry Jenkins, July 16, 1876, Aldrich, July 31, 1876, Henry C. McCoy, Aug. 3, 1876, E. E. Carpenter, Aug. 30, 1876, Martin Olsen, Sept. 8, 1876, to CCC, *ibid.*

[19] Al Swalm, Sept. 14, 1876, Emmett, Sept. 18, Oct. 2, 1876, to CCC, *ibid.*

[20] CCC Diary, Oct. 23–Nov. 15, 1876, *ibid.*

[21] CCC Diary, Jan. 23–Feb. 21, 1877, *ibid.* See also C. Vann Woodward, *Reunion and Reaction: The Compromise of 1877 and the End of Reconstruction* (Boston: Little, Brown and Company, 1951).

[22] CCC Diary, Oct. 9, 1876, *Carpenter Papers.*

23 CCC Diary, Apr. 16, 17, 1877, *ibid.*

24 CCC Diary, March 16, 22, 23, 25, 26, Apr. 6, 1877; Emmet, Feb. 3, 5, 15, March 16, Apr. 3, 4, 24, 1877, Al Swalm, Feb. 4, 15, March 3, Apr. 3, 1877, W. N. Meservey, Apr. 2, 1877, to CCC, *ibid.*

25 CCC Diary, May 16, 17, 1877, *ibid.;* Des Moines *Register,* May 25, 1877.

26 CCC to Clarkson, May 22, 1877, *James C. Clarkson Collection* (Library of Congress). A photostat of this letter was obtained for me through the kindness of Leland L. Sage.

27 *Ibid.*

28 Des Moines *Register,* May 25, Nov. 9, 1877.

29 N. W. Page, March 16, 1877, and Emmett, Apr. 4, 1877, to CCC, *Carpenter Papers.*

30 Oliver to CCC, Nov. 21, 1877, *ibid.*

31 CCC Diary, Nov. 8, Dec. 12, 15, 1877; Jan. 25, 1878; letters of support from W. J. Covill, Jan. 26, 1878, W. W. Boak, Jan. 30, 1878, James N. Miller, Jan. 31, 1878, T. W. Harrison, Feb. 6, 1878, T. J. Ross, Feb. 23, 1878, Elijah Peake, Feb. 22, 1878, to CCC, *ibid.*

32 Aldrich's remark quoted by Arthur Burkholder in letter to CCC, March 4, 1878, *ibid.* Letters to CCC from other candidates were Geo. D. Perkins, Feb. 13, 1878, Wm. R. Smith, Feb. 12, 1878, I. N. Kidder, Feb. 7, 1878, *ibid.*

33 Fleming to CCC, June 15, 1877, *ibid.*

34 *Laws of Iowa, 1878,* Chap. 77. For an account of the repeal, see Throne, "Repeal of the Iowa Granger Law, 1878," 97–130.

35 CCC Diary, March 21, 22, 23, 25, 26, 1878; Fleming to CCC, March 21, 1878, *Carpenter Papers.*

36 Des Moines (Daily) *Register,* March 26, 1878.

37 CCC to Prentiss Carpenter, May 11, 1878, *Carpenter Papers.* The salary of a Congressman in 1878 was $5,000; the pay of the railroad commissioners was set at $3,000. Carpenter evidently felt that the expense of living in Washington would more than offset the $2,000 difference in salary.

38 Throne, "Repeal of the Iowa Granger Law, 1878," 128–30.

39 I. N. Kidder, Apr. 13, 24, 1878, Fred H. Taft, March 27, 1878, Geo. D. Perkins, March 27, 1878, to CCC, *Carpenter Papers;* Pomeroy *Journal,* quoted in Des Moines (Daily) *Register,* Apr. 2, 1878.

40 S. Addison Oliver, Apr. 24, 1878, M. D. O'Connell, Apr. 30, 1878, T. J. Ross, May 2, 1878, C. W. Lowrie, May 15, 1878, Chas. McAllister, June 14, 1878, to CCC, *Carpenter Papers;* Nevada *Representative,* May 22, 1878.

41 C. W. Lowrie, May 15, 1878, O. J. Jolley, Apr. 1, 8, 1878, I. N. Kidder, Apr. 29, 1878, J. D. Ainsworth, Apr. 30, 1878, Emmett, May 1, 1878, M. R. McCrary, May 2, 1878, John A. Hull, May 11, 1878, petition from voters of Sumner Township, Webster County, May 13, 1878, petition from Boone County voters (enclosed with Kidder letter of Apr. 29, 1878), to CCC, *Carpenter Papers.* Petition from Fort Dodge, published in Fort Dodge *Gazette* and *Messenger,* May 17, 1878, and reprinted in Des Moines (Daily) *Register,* May 18, 1878.

42 CCC letter of May 13, 1878, to several citizens of Fort Dodge, in answer to their petition, published in Fort Dodge *Gazette* and *Messenger,* May 17, 1878, and in Des Moines (Daily) *Register,* May 18, 1878.

43 Carpenter to Perkins, May 21, 1878, *George D. Perkins Papers* (Iowa State Department of History and Archives, Des Moines). This letter was called to my attention by Wallace Farnham.

[44] Des Moines (Daily) *Register,* June 14, July 16, 1878.

[45] Emmett to CCC, July 30, 1878; CCC Diary, Aug. 6, 1878, *Carpenter Papers.*

[46] CCC Diary, Aug. 7, 1878, *ibid.;* Des Moines (Daily) *Register,* Aug. 9, 1878.

[47] Iowa City *Iowa State Press,* Aug. 21, 1878. For a biographical sketch of Hoggatt, see *Annals of Iowa* (3rd ser.), 2:408 (Apr. 1896).

[48] John A. Hull to CCC, Aug. 23, 1878, *Carpenter Papers;* Des Moines (Daily) *Register,* Sept. 1, 1878. For the Greenback movement in Iowa, see Fred E. Haynes, *Third Party Movements Since the Civil War . . .* (Iowa City: State Historical Society of Iowa, 1916), Chaps. 12, 13.

[49] Des Moines (Daily) *Register,* Sept. 4, 7, 1878, and Sioux City *Journal,* quoted in *ibid.,* Oct. 15, 1878.

[50] CCC Diary, Apr. 7, 25, 1878, *Carpenter Papers.* See Thomas R. Ross, *Jonathan Prentiss Dolliver . . .* (Iowa City: State Historical Society of Iowa, 1958), 28–29, 32.

[51] Des Moines (Daily) *Register,* Oct. 10, Nov. 10, 1878; Fairall, *Manual of Iowa Politics,* Part II, 48.

[52] Fairall, *Manual of Iowa Politics,* 103, 114; *Iowa Official Register, 1909–1910,* 523. Gear's opposition in 1877 had been John P. Irish, Democrat; Daniel P. Stubbs, Greenbacker; and Elias Jessup, Prohibitionist.

[53] Iowa Constitution, Article XII, Sec. 6; *Iowa Code, Revision of 1860* (Des Moines: 1860), Chap. 31, Sec. 1.

[54] U. S., *Statutes at Large,* vol. 17, Chap. 11, Sec. 2, 28; 18 *ibid.,* Part 3, Chap. 130, 400–01.

[55] Des Moines (Daily) *Register,* Aug. 30, 31, 1878; Fairfield *Tribune,* quoted in Iowa City *Iowa State Press,* Sept. 4, 1878; Dubuque *Weekly Times,* Sept. 4, 1878.

[56] Des Moines (Daily) *Register,* Sept. 5, 6, 1878; Clinton *Herald,* quoted in *ibid.,* Sept. 10, 1878.

[57] Fairall, *Manual of Iowa Politics,* Part II, 46–48.

[58] Iowa City *Press,* Oct. 16, 23, 1878; Des Moines (Daily) *Register,* Oct. 16, 24, 1878; CCC Diary, Oct. 15, 1878, *Carpenter Papers.*

[59] CCC Diary, Oct. 29, Nov. 4, 1878, *Carpenter Papers;* Des Moines (Daily) *Register,* Nov. 12, 1878.

[60] Iowa City *Iowa State Press,* Nov. 27, 1878. October elections continued in Iowa, except in presidential years, until 1884, when the state constitution was amended to provide for holding all general elections in November.

FOURTEEN—Congressman Carpenter

[1] CCC to wife, March 16, 1879, *Carpenter Papers.*

[2] For members of the 46th Congress, and biographical sketches, see *Biographical Directory of the American Congress, 1774–1949* (Washington: Government Printing Office, 1950), 358–67.

[3] See Nathaniel Wright Stephenson, *Nelson W. Aldrich, A Leader in American Politics* (New York: Charles Scribner's Sons, 1930).

[4] See Donald Barr Chidsey, *The Gentleman from New York: A Life of Roscoe Conkling* (New Haven: Yale University Press, 1935); Russell, *Blaine of Maine;* Stanwood, *Blaine.*

[5] Woodward, *Reunion and Reaction, passim.*

[6] Des Moines *Register,* Apr. 27, 1877. Issue of May 4 carries a column of quotations from other Iowa newspapers, attacking the President.

[7] CCC Diary, Apr. 2, 1877, *Carpenter Papers.*

[8] For the Hayes-Conkling struggle over the New York custom house appointments, see Chidsey, *Conkling,* 244–54; H. J. Eckenrode, *Rutherford B. Hayes, Statesman of Reunion* (New York: Dodd, Mead & Company, 1930), 270–78; Charles Richard Williams (ed.), *Diary and Letters of Rutherford Birchard Hayes . . .* (5 vols., Columbus, Ohio: Ohio State Archaeological and Historical Society, 1924), 3:453–64, *passim.* (Hereafter cited as Hayes, *Diary and Letters.*)

[9] CCC Diary, March 20, 1879, *Carpenter Papers.*

[10] Chidsey, *Conkling,* 374.

[11] Carpenter, *Genealogical History of the . . . Carpenter Family,* 499, 558. For a biography of Matthew Carpenter see E. Bruce Thompson, *Matthew Hale Carpenter: Webster of the West* (Madison, Wisconsin: State Historical Society of Wisconsin, 1954).

[12] *Biographical Directory of the American Congress, 1774–1949,* 357–67, *passim.*

[13] Edwin Erle Sparks, *National Development, 1877–1885* (New York: Harper & Brothers, Publishers, 1907), 120–26.

[14] CCC Diary, March 4, 1879; Duncombe to CCC, July 1, 1879, *Carpenter Papers.*

[15] Des Moines (Daily) *Register,* Apr. 27, 1879.

[16] Chidsey, *Conkling,* 116–18.

[17] Des Moines (Daily) *Register,* Apr. 27, 1879.

[18] New York *Weekly Sun,* Apr. 30, 1879.

[19] CCC Diary, Apr. 24, 1879, *Carpenter Papers.*

[20] J. P. Dolliver to CCC, June 3, 1879, *ibid.*

[21] Cedar Rapids *Times,* June 26, 1879.

[22] CCC Diary, Apr. 17, 1879, *Carpenter Papers.*

[23] For progress of Army Bill, see *Congressional Record,* 46 Cong., 1 sess., 82–270, *passim,* 355–913, *passim,* 993–9, 1014–15.

[24] *Ibid.,* 1932–42, 2199–243, 2289; CCC Diary, June 11, 1879, *Carpenter Papers.*

[25] *Congressional Record,* 46 Cong., 1 sess., 1092–95, 1177–89, 1267–68; CCC Diary, May 12, 1879, *Carpenter Papers.*

[26] Hayes, *Diary and Letters,* 3:564.

[27] Eckenrode, *Hayes,* 238–41.

[28] Hayes, *Diary and Letters,* 3:564.

[29] CCC Diary, Apr. 11, 1879, *Carpenter Papers; Congressional Record,* 46 Cong., 1 sess., 397.

[30] *Congressional Record,* 46 Cong., 1 sess., 93–96.

[31] Chicago *Tribune,* New York *Times,* and Dubuque *Herald,* quoted in Des Moines (Daily) *Register,* March 29, Apr. 1, 2, 3, 1879.

[32] *Congressional Record,* 46 Cong., 1 sess., 397.

[33] Des Moines (Daily) *Register,* Apr. 12, 23, 1879; St. Louis *Globe-Democrat,* quoted in *ibid.,* Apr. 20, 1879; Cincinnati *Gazette,* quoted in *ibid.,* Apr. 25, 1879; Dubuque *Weekly Times,* May 21, 28, June 11, 1879; CCC Diary, May 13, 20, 22, 27, 28, June 2, 1879; Jan. 31, 1881, *Carpenter Papers.* For report of committee, see *House Report No. 19,* 46 Cong., 3 sess.

[34] CCC Diary, Sept. 17, Oct. 13, 1879, *Carpenter Papers.*

[35] CCC Diary, Oct. 15, March 4, 1880, *ibid.*

[36] CCC Diary, March 4, 1880, *ibid.*

[37] CCC Diary, Jan. 31, May 5, 10, 13, 1880, *ibid.*

[38] CCC Diary, June 7, 1880, *ibid.*

[39] Cedar Rapids *Weekly Times,* Feb. 26, 1880; Iowa City (Weekly) *Republican,* March 3, 1880.

[40] Des Moines *Register,* June 11, 1880; Sage, *Allison,* 162–63.

[41] CCC Diary, June 8, 1880, *Carpenter Papers.*

[42] E. J. Hartshorn, June 23, 1880, John Gabrielson, June 23, 1880, Henry C. Laub, June 30, 1880, to Dolliver, *Jonathan P. Dolliver Papers* (State Historical Society of Iowa, Iowa City); CCC Diary, July 8, 1880, *Carpenter Papers.*

[43] Des Moines *Register,* Sept. 14, 1880, quoting letter from Buchanan to CCC, Aug. 6, 1879; original of letter in *Carpenter Papers.*

[44] CCC Diary, Aug. 19, 1880, *Carpenter Papers;* Des Moines *Register,* Aug. 27, 1880; Younger, *Kasson,* 299–303.

[45] For Hepburn, see John E. Briggs, *William Peters Hepburn* (Iowa City: State Historical Society of Iowa, 1919).

[46] Des Moines *Register, passim,* during 1880 campaign.

[47] *Ibid.,* Nov. 6, 19, 1880.

[48] *Biographical Directory of the American Congress, 1774–1949,* 370, 1014.

[49] *Congressional Record,* 47 Cong., special session of the Senate, 32–34.

[50] Des Moines *Register,* Dec. 15, 1880.

[51] CCC Diary, Jan. 16, 17, 1881, *Carpenter Papers. Congressional Record,* 46 Cong., 3 sess., 693–707.

[52] CCC Diary, March 4, 1881, *Carpenter Papers.*

[53] Sage, *Allison,* 165–76.

[54] CCC Diary, March 14, 1881, *Carpenter Papers.*

[55] CCC Diary, May 17, 1881, *ibid.*

[56] *Congressional Record,* 47 Cong., special session of the Senate, 459.

[57] Chidsey, *Conkling,* 329–41.

[58] CCC Diary, March–Nov., 1881, *passim, Carpenter Papers.*

[59] Russell, *Blaine of Maine,* 387–88.

[60] CCC Diary, Dec. 3, 1881, *Carpenter Papers;* Younger, *Kasson,* 307–09.

[61] CCC Diary, Feb. 15, March 18, 1882, *Carpenter Papers; Congressional Record,* 47 Cong., 1 sess., 2037–38.

[62] CCC Diary, May 8, 1882, *Carpenter Papers; Congressional Record,* 47 Cong., 1 sess., 3719–25, 3795–96, 2 sess., 1154–59, 1176–79.

[63] CCC Diary, Dec. 12, 13, 1881, *Carpenter Papers;* Sage, *Allison,* 105, 129, 183–84; *Congressional Record,* 47 Cong., 1 sess., 99, 957, 3476–80, 4772–73, 6024; 22 *U. S. Statutes at Large,* Chap. 312, 172–73.

[64] CCC to Dolliver, July 25, 1882, *Carpenter Papers.*

[65] CCC to Judd, June 25, 1882, *ibid.*

[66] CCC Diary, Aug. 11, 1882, *ibid.*

FIFTEEN—Defeats and Victories

[1] Paul S. Peirce, "Congressional Districting in Iowa," *Iowa Journal of History and Politics,* 1:347–51 (July 1903). Compare maps for 1872 and 1882 at end of article.

[2] Geo. F. Wattson to CCC, June 30, 1882, *Carpenter Papers.*

[3] CCC to Dolliver, July 25, 1882, *Carpenter Papers.*

[4] Des Moines *Register,* Aug. 18, 30, 1882; Iowa City *Republican,* Aug. 16, 1882.

[5] Webster City *Freeman,* quoted in Des Moines *Register,* Aug. 19, 1882.

[6] For a biographical sketch of Roberts, see *Annals of Iowa* (3rd ser.), 29:484–85 (Oct. 1948).

[7] CCC Diary, Aug. 11–29, 1882, *passim, Carpenter Papers.*

[8] L. B. Raymond, "How Colonel Scott Missed a Nomination," Des Moines *Register and Leader,* Oct. 4, 1903.

[9] *Ibid.;* Des Moines *Register,* Sept. 1, 3, 1882.

[10] Council Bluffs *Nonpareil,* Sept. 2, 1882; Des Moines *Register,* Aug. 31, 1882.

[11] Story of convention compiled from various accounts in the Des Moines *Register,* Aug. 31, Sept. 1, 3, 1882; Sioux City *Journal* and Fort Dodge *Messenger,* quoted in *ibid.,* Sept. 5, 8, 1882; Raymond, "How Colonel Scott Missed a Nomination;" Reed, *History of Kossuth County, Iowa,* 1:350–52.

[12] Reed, *History of Kossuth County,* 1:351–52.

[13] Webster City *Argus,* quoted in Des Moines *Register,* Sept. 5, 1882.

[14] Des Moines *Register,* Sept. 1, 2, 1882.

[15] CCC Diary, Aug. 30, 1882, *Carpenter Papers.*

[16] CCC Diary, Sept. 10, 1881, *ibid.* Unfortunately for a more factual interpretation of this period in Carpenter's life, most of his letters for the years 1880 through 1885 are not included in the collection of papers he left; they were probably lost.

[17] From July 16 to 26, 1879, there are some 14 letters in the *Carpenter Papers* from various residents of Algona, asking the appointment of one or the other of the two men.

[18] Reed, *History of Kossuth County,* 1:351.

[19] Geo. E. Roberts to Benj. F. Shambaugh, Aug. 29, 1936, in the files of the State Historical Society of Iowa, Iowa City. It was through the encouragement of Roberts that Carpenter's nephew, Judge Clay Carpenter, deposited his uncle's papers with the State Historical Society of Iowa at Iowa City.

[20] See Throne (comp.), "Iowans in Congress, 1847–1953," 331–44, *passim.*

[21] CCC to Clarkson, Jan. 26, 1885, *Clarkson Collection.* A copy of this letter was loaned to me by Leland L. Sage.

[22] Des Moines *Register,* Sept. 1, 1882; Keokuk *Gate City,* quoted in *ibid.,* Sept. 5, 1882.

[23] CCC Diary, Sept. 8, 1882, *Carpenter Papers.*

[24] CCC Diary, Oct. 1882, *passim, ibid.*

[25] See obituary of Holmes in *Annals of Iowa* (3rd ser.), 5:397–98 (Apr. 1902).

[26] Sparks, *National Development,* 120. For Iowans, see Throne (comp.), "Iowans in Congress, 1847–1953," 342–44.

[27] CCC Diary, Oct.–Nov., 1882, *passim, Carpenter Papers.*

[28] Sage, *Allison,* 187–88.

[29] Des Moines *Register,* Sept. 14, 1883.

[30] Iowa City *Iowa State Press,* Sept. 12, Oct. 3, 1883; Des Moines *Register,* Sept. 28, 1883.

[31] Des Moines *Register,* Sept. 21, 1883; Sage, *Allison,* 193.

[32] *Rules of the Twentieth General Assembly of the State of Iowa . . .* (Des Moines: Geo. E. Roberts, State Printer, 1884), 29–34.

[33] *Ibid.,* 22–25.

[34] *Ibid.,* 32.

[35] Des Moines *Register,* Jan. 18, 1884; *House Journal, 1884,* 45. Vote for Senator, on Jan. 23, 1884, was Allison, 90; Benton J. Hall, 48; D. M. Clark, 10; L. G. Kinne, 1.

[36] *House Journal, 1884,* 28.

[37] *Ibid.,* 29.

[38] *Ibid.,* 278, 523–24; Cole, *History of the People of Iowa,* 456–57.

[39] Gordon F. Hostettler, "The Oratorical Career of Jonathan Prentiss Dolliver"

(Ph.D. dissertation, State University of Iowa, 1947), 75. See also, Hostettler, "Jonathan Prentiss Dolliver: The Formative Years," *Iowa Journal of History*, 49:23–50 (Jan. 1951); Ross, *Dolliver*, 43–44.

[40] Cyrenus Cole, *I Remember, I Remember: A Book of Recollections* (Iowa City: State Historical Society of Iowa, 1936), 113–15; Cole, *History of the People of Iowa*, 458–59; Des Moines *Register*, May 2, 1884; Ross, *Dolliver*, 49, 52–53.

[41] Hostettler, "Jonathan Prentiss Dolliver: The Formative Years," 47–50; Cole, *I Remember*, 114–15; Ross, *Dolliver*, 55–59.

[42] Des Moines *Register*, Aug. 22, 1884.

[43] *Ibid.*, Nov. 7, 14, 21, 1884. For Cleveland, see Allan Nevins, *Grover Cleveland, A Study in Courage* (New York: Dodd, Mead & Company, 1932), Chap. XI.

[44] CCC to Clarkson, Jan. 26, 1885, *Clarkson Collection.*

[45] Fort Dodge *Messenger*, Apr. 22, 1886.

[46] CCC to A. D. Bicknell, May 4, 1886, *Dolliver Papers.* This is a rough copy of a letter, evidently sent to Dolliver for his approval, and which Dolliver preserved. The letter was also published in the Fort Dodge *Messenger*, May 13, 1886.

[47] *Ibid.*

[48] Fort Dodge *Messenger*, May 6, 13, 1886, quoting from many other papers.

[49] Allison to Dolliver, June 20, 1886, *Dolliver Papers.*

[50] H. Ross, July 7, 1886, to CCC, *Carpenter Papers.*

[51] Fort Dodge *Messenger*, Aug. 12, 1886.

[52] *Ibid.*, Aug. 26, 1886; Jacob Van Ek, "Two District Conventions," *The Palimpsest*, 5:47–52 (Feb. 1924); Ross, *Dolliver*, 67–71.

[53] Van Ek, "Two District Conventions," 52–54; R. H. Dolliver to J. P. Dolliver, Aug. 23, 1886, *Dolliver Papers.*

[54] R. H. Dolliver to J. P. Dolliver, Aug. 23, 1886, *Dolliver Papers;* Marshalltown *Times-Republican*, quoted in Fort Dodge *Messenger*, May 17, 1886; letter from Geo. E. Roberts to Hostettler, quoted in "The Oratorical Career of Jonathan Prentiss Dolliver," 90n; Van Ek, "Two District Conventions," 54.

[55] For the complete story of this convention, see Sage, *Allison*, Chap. XIV. For Dolliver in state convention, see Fort Dodge *Messenger*, March 15, 22, 1888; Ross, *Dolliver*, 75–76.

[56] J. G. Durrell to CCC, March 31, 1888, *Carpenter Papers;* Fort Dodge *Messenger*, Aug. 9, 1888.

[57] Clarkson, Apr. 19, 1888, A. J. Barkley, June 5, 1888, W. E. Bradford, May 5, 1888, Aldrich, May 23, 1888, Geo L. Tremain, Aug. 1, 1888, S. C. Highbee, Aug. 13, 1888, to Dolliver, *Dolliver Papers;* Oscar O. Jay, Aug. 5, 1888, H. C. Laub, Aug. 15, 1888, S. C. Highbee, Aug. 16, 1888, Howard Beadle, July 22, 1888, to CCC, *Carpenter Papers.*

[58] Van Ek, "Two District Conventions," 55–59; Fort Dodge *Messenger*, Aug. 16, 23, 1888; Ross, *Dolliver*, 79–81.

[59] Emmett to CCC, Aug. 26, 1888, *Carpenter Papers.*

SIXTEEN—A Good Life Closes

[1] Jacob Rich to CCC, July 23, 25, 27, 1885, *Carpenter Papers; Autobiography of Charles Clinton Nourse . . .* (privately printed, 1911), Chap. XIV. Nourse, an attorney, defended Brown in the impeachment trial.

[2] Roberts, Jan. 1, 1886, Holmes, Jan. 22, Feb. 5, 8, 1886, Allison, Feb. 8, 1886,

Wilson, Apr. 16, 1886, plus numerous letters during Feb. and March 1886, regarding the postmastership, to CCC, *Carpenter Papers;* Fort Dodge *Messenger,* Apr. 29, May 6, 1886.

[3] Martha C. Callanan to CCC, Dec. 18, 1885, *Carpenter Papers.*

[4] Iowa City (Daily) *Republican,* Aug. 7, 1885.

[5] A. J. Barkley to CCC, Jan. 12, 1887 (quoting *Register* article); CCC to Emmett, Feb. 8, 1887, *Carpenters Papers.*

[6] Wilson to CCC, Jan. 5, 8, 1888, *ibid.* For Wilson's re-election, see Clark, *History of Senatorial Elections,* Chap. XV.

[7] CCC to Dolliver, Jan. 12, 1882, *Dolliver Papers.*

[8] D. B. Henderson, Feb. 4, 1888, Geo. W. Hanna, Feb. 20, 1888, G. L. Tremain, March 2, 1888, to CCC, *Carpenter Papers;* CCC to Allison, March 3, 1888, *William B. Allison Papers* (Iowa State Department of History and Archives, Des Moines). A copy of this letter was furnished me by Leland L. Sage.

[9] Peter A. Dey, March 31, Apr. 13, 1888, James W. McDill, Apr. 3, 1888, Ed Wright, Apr. 7, 1888, to CCC, *Carpenter Papers.*

[10] Julius C. Burrows, Jan. 29, 1889, Joseph G. Cannon, Dec. 27, 1888, to CCC, *ibid.*

[11] For Henderson's career as Speaker, see Willard L. Hoing, "David B. Henderson: Speaker of the House," *Iowa Journal of History,* 55:1–34 (Jan. 1957).

[12] Dolliver to F. E. Bean, March 30, 1889, *Carpenter Papers.*

[13] CCC to Dolliver, Feb. 19, March 23, 1889, *Dolliver Papers.*

[14] CCC to E. E. Mack, Oct. 18, 1890, *Edgar E. Mack Papers* (State Historical Society of Iowa, Iowa City).

[15] Geo. E. Roberts to Dolliver, Apr. 22, 1894, *Dolliver Papers.*

[16] CCC to Dolliver, June 11, 1894, *ibid.*

[17] Among the articles that Carpenter contributed to the *Annals of Iowa* (3rd ser.), are: "The Charge on Battery Robinet," 1:99–106, 214–21 (Apr., Oct. 1893); "Major-General G. M. Dodge," 1:161–80, 302–328 (Oct. 1893, Jan. 1894); "James W. Grimes, Governor and Senator," 1:505–25 (Oct. 1894); "Major William Williams," 2:146–60 (July–Oct. 1895); "A Chapter of Pioneer History," 3:297–301 (Jan. 1898); "The Spirit Lake Expedition," 3:481–91 (Oct. 1898). The Spirit Lake article was a speech given by Carpenter in Aug. 1887, at the dedication of a plaque at Webster City, honoring the members of the expedition.

[18] Dolliver to CCC, Feb. 7, 1896, *Carpenter Papers.*

[19] Mrs. Dolliver to Mrs. Carpenter, May 21, 1898; Dolliver to Mrs. Carpenter, May 30, 1898, *ibid; Midland Monthly,* 10:75–81 (July 1898).

[20] Fort Dodge *Times,* June 2, 1898; Governor's proclamation of mourning, in Fort Dodge *Messenger,* June 1, 1898.

[21] J. A. O. Yeoman to Dolliver, June 2, 1898; J. H. Pearsons [Mrs. Dolliver's brother] to Mrs. Dolliver, May 31, 1898; S. T. Meservey to Dolliver, June 12, 1898, *Dolliver Papers,* Dolliver to J. A. O. Yeoman, June 9, 1898, *Carpenter Papers.*

[22] William E. Curtis, of Washington Bureau of the Chicago *Daily News,* to Dolliver, Jan. 12, 1889, *Dolliver Papers.*

[23] Dolliver to J. A. O. Yeoman, June 9, 1898, *Carpenter Papers.*

Index

Abolitionism, 7, 52, 61–62.
Adams, Dudley W., 164, 166, 167.
Adams, Henry, 253–54.
Agriculture: discontent in, 105, 126, 211; power of in Fourteenth Assembly, 177; and the railroads, 142, 146, 179.
Ainsworth, Lucien L., 191.
Albee, E. H., 16.
Alcorn, Robert, 78.
Aldrich, Charles, 26, 51, 82, 117, 119, 164, 197; advises CCC, 137; as critic of Andrew Johnson, 93; on CCC's First Inaugural Address, 135; on O'Connell, 207; supports CCC, 44, 109–10, 115, 118.
Aldrich, Nelson W., 216.
Algona, 27.
Algona *Upper Des Moines,* 117.
Allamakee County, 124.
Allen, B. F., 111, 161–63, 187–88.
Allen, Byron, 214.
Allison, William B., 111, 128–30, 136, 149, 194, 195, 201, 236, 248; and the Army Appropriation Bill, 221; and CCC's Treasury job, 196–98; and the Crédit Mobilier scandal, 160; declines Garfield Cabinet post, 226; and the "Des Moines Regency," 134; and Dodge, 101, 102, 106, 107; and Dolliver, 244; as a Presidential hopeful, 245–46, 249; reelected to third term in Senate, 239, 240; and the 1872 Senate race, 106, 107, 113, 114, 116, 128–30; seeks first Senate seat, 100–01; supports CCC for Governor, 113, 115, 116; as U. S. Representative, 80.
American party, *see* Know-Nothing party.
Ames, 45.
Annals of Iowa, 251.

Anti-Monopoly party, 157, 173, 174, 186, 190–91, 211; and the Democratic party, 167, 168–69, 189, 191–92; and the farmer, 167; in the General Assembly, 173, 174; and the Granger movement, 164; the 1878 state convention of, 166.
Anti-Slavery Society, 7.
Appomattox, 74.
Arthur, Chester A., 216, 224, 227.
Athens (Ala.), 68, 69.
Atlanta (Ga.), 69, 71.
Atlantic, 175.
Atlantic *Telegraph,* 112.
Attleboro (Mass.), 4, 5.
Audubon County, 124.
Avoca, 117.
Ayers, Squire, 40.

Babcock, Orville E., 203.
Baker, Gen. N. B., 111–12, 119, 124, 170, 171.
Baldwin, Judge Caleb, 101, 107, 136, 171.
Ballard, Dr. S. M., 193.
Banshott, Thomas, 3–4.
Barclay, J. J., 44–45.
Barker, Winslow, 135.
Bates, Ellsworth N., 43.
Beal, Cornelius, 40, 41.
Beardsley, Charles, 118, 144.
Beck, Joseph M., 188.
Belgium, 159.
Belknap, William W., 33, 40, 196, 197, 199, 201.
Belvel, H. M., 118.
Bennet, Hiram P., 56.
Bennett, G. G., 121.
Benson, Rufus S., 230.
Bentonsport, 40.
Berry, George, 12, 13, 14.
Bevis, 4.